Emerging Market Economies and European Economic Integration

Emerging Market Economies and European Economic Integration

Edited by

R. Scott Hacker

Associate Professor of Economics, Jönköping International Business School, Jönköping University, Sweden

Börje Johansson

Professor of Economics, Jönköping International Business School, Jönköping University, Sweden

Charlie Karlsson

Professor of the Economics of Technological Change, Jönköping International Business School, Jönköping University, Sweden

Edward Elgar

Cheltenham, UK • Northampton, MA, USA

Published by
Edward Elgar Publishing Limited
Glensanda House
Montpellier Parade
Cheltenham
Glos GL50 1UA
UK

Edward Elgar Publishing, Inc.
136 West Street
Suite 202
Northampton
Massachusetts 01060
USA

A catalogue record for this book
is available from the British Library

ISBN 1 84376 679 5

Printed and bound in Great Britain by MPG Books Ltd, Bodmin, Cornwall

Contents

Figures

Tables

Contributors

Johannes Bröcker	Christian-Albrechts-University, Kiel, Germany
Herbert Brücker	DIW Berlin, Berlin, Germany
R. Scott Hacker	Jönköping International Business School, Jönköping University, Jönköping, Sweden
Mikolaj Herbst	Warsaw University, Warsaw, Poland
Ákos Jakobi	Eötvös Loránd University, Budapest, Hungary
Börje Johansson	Jönköping International Business School, Jönköping University, Jönköping, Sweden
Andreas Johnson	Jönköping International Business School, Jönköping University, Jönköping, Sweden
Charlie Karlsson	Jönköping International Business School, Jönköping University, Jönköping, Sweden
Viesturs Pauls Karnups	University of Latvia, Riga, Latvia
Urmas Kase	University of Tartu, Tartu, Estonia
Tiit Kask	University of Tartu, Tartu, Estonia
Tatiane de Menezes	Cidade University, São Paulo, Brazil
Heli Müristaja	University of Tartu, Tartu, Estonia
Karol Olejniczak	Warsaw University, Warsaw, Poland
Maria Plotnikova	University of Illinois, Urbana-Champaign, USA
Garri Raagmaa	University of Tartu, Tartu, Estonia
Doina Maria Radulescu	IFO Institute for Economic Research, Munich, Germany
Piet Rietveld	Free University, Amsterdam, The Netherlands
Uwe Schubert	University of Economics Vienna, Vienna, Austria
Bernd Schuh	University of Economics Vienna, Vienna, Austria
Boriss Siliverstovs	German Institute for Economic Research, Berlin, Germany
Iulia Traistaru	University of Bonn, Bonn, Germany
Parvati Trübswetter	Ludwig-Maximilians University, Munich, Germany
Jos van Ommeren	Free University, Amsterdam, The Netherlands
Guntram B. Wolff	University of Bonn, Bonn, Germany
Stefan Woudenberg	Free University, Amsterdam, The Netherlands

Preface

The present volume contains revised lectures and papers presented at the fifteenth European Advanced Studies Institute in Regional Science – Summer Institute 2002 – of the European Regional Science Association (ERSA) held in Eksjö, Sweden, from 10 to 16 June 2002, and hosted by Jönköping International Business School (JIBS).

Our special thanks go to Ms Kerstin Ferrouhki for handling all practical arrangements for the Summer Institute 2002 and for the refereeing process, and to Ms Ulla Forslund for undertaking the demanding task of finalising the editorial work, and revising and formatting the contributions.

We thank the municipality of Eksjö for financial support and for generous help with the practical arrangements, and the University of Jönköping for financial support.

We are also grateful for scientific assistance from the Regional Science Association International (RSAI), the European Regional Science Association (ERSA), and the Nordic Section of the Regional Science Association (NS-RSA). Support also came from the Centre for Regional Science in Umeå (CERUM), the Regional Planning Division at the Royal Institute of Technology and the Swedish Institute for Growth Policy Studies (ITPS).

Finally, we thank the publisher, Edward Elgar, for excellent support in the editing process.

Jönköping, February 2004

R. Scott Hacker
Börje Johansson
Charlie Karlsson

1. Emerging Market Economies in an Integrating Europe – An Introduction

R. Scott Hacker, Börje Johansson and Charlie Karlsson

1 TRANSITION AND INTEGRATION

At the beginning of the 1990s market mechanisms were introduced in the former planned economies of Europe. At the same time these previously closed economies opened channels for international trade. Many of the relevant countries also started negotiations with the European Union about trade agreements and other forms of economic cooperation. For a majority of the countries the goal was to become EU members in the future. This book provides a picture of economic change processes in Europe, in which EU harmonisation policies and transition policies form an integrated part.

1.1 The European Union, 1980–2000

The European Union (EU) has a history of more than 50 years of successive enlargements. It started as the Coal and Steel Community in 1951, with three member countries. In 1981 there were ten members and a few years later 12, and the union was soon named the EU12. The accession of another three members at the beginning of the 1990s led to the formation of the EU15. The contributions in this book focus on a union with much larger scope: from 2004 the union will comprise 25 countries, the EU25. This means that non-EU countries in Europe will be in a clear minority.

The stepwise enlargement of the European Community has brought about a gradually increased heterogeneity among the member countries and their regions in terms of population size, GDP per capita, economic structure, and legal and institutional frameworks. Because of this, political ambitions in the period 1980–2000 were centred on issues of integration, harmonisation, cohesion and convergence. At the beginning of the 2000s the three EU15 countries with the lowest GDP per capita were at a considerably lower economic level than the average for the EU15. The inclusion of former planned economies in 2004 will mean that several new member states will have an income level that amounts to 20–30 per cent of the average GDP per capita in the EU15. In other words, the union will consist of both rich countries and developing countries. The management and governance of such a diverse economy is indeed a challenge. This book presents selected aspects of these challenges.

What were the achievements during the integration period 1980–2000? One aspect of the EU's development is the establishment of EU institutions such as the Council, the Commission, the Court of Justice, the European Parliament and the Court of Auditors. There is also the Committee of the Regions, the European Investment Bank and the European Bank for Reconstruction and Development. The last was established in 1991 to foster the evolution of open market economies in the transition countries of Europe.

Building institutions for an economic union that continues to incorporate new member countries is a process that involves so many complexities that it is difficult to assess how successful it has been and may be. In any case the process has remained politically and economically sustainable in a remarkable way. The most prominent successful element of the EU's development is intra-union trade, which has continued to grow over the decades. The share of imports from member states has continued to increase, and the same holds true for the export share. Such an increase of trade among members in a union is indeed what economic integration policies strive to achieve. Outlined policies for the future also rely on trade as a major vehicle for integration, whereas factor mobility is assumed to play a more moderate role.

1.2 Former Planned Economies, 1980–2000

In the 1980s a large share of Europe's territory consisted of socialist countries with planned economies or, more precisely, centrally planned economies. During the second half of the decade small and gradual changes away from the established patterns of these countries were identified. But there were few – if any – predictions indicating that 1989 would be a turning point. This year had two major jubilees, one referring to the French Revolution 200 years earlier and a second related to the fact that the GDR (East Germany) had existed for 40 years.

By 1990 the map of Europe had changed and the CMEA (Council for Mutual Economic Assistance) was dissolved. For a whole set of countries this meant that they were no longer centrally planned economies, nor were they market economies. Instead they were referred to as transition economies, and around 1993 the new economies started to integrate with the market economies of Europe through trade and flows of direct investments. The transition economies include the Baltic States (Estonia, Latvia and

Lithuania), the Czech Republic, Hungary, Malta, Poland, Slovakia, Slovenia and Cyprus. These countries form the set of accession countries for the year 2004. Other European transition economies are Belarus, Bulgaria, Romania, Russia, Turkey and Ukraine.

In general the accession countries differ from the other transition countries in having a higher GDP per capita (Hitris, 2003). One has to bear in mind that existing estimates of the GDP of transition countries are uncertain and include a series of possible mistakes. In spite of this we present such estimates in Table 1.1. The information allows us to at least order countries in terms of the size of their economic activity. Each country's GDP per capita is related to the average level in the EU15, which reveals that the accession countries tend to be more developed than the other transition countries in the table. In this context we can observe that Malta and Cyprus should not be identified as transition countries, and they are also the most prosperous of the accession economies.

Table 1.1 Estimated GDP per capita of transition countries as a percentage of the average GDP per capita of the EU15, 1999

	Less than 25%	25–35%	35–60%	60–110%
Accession countries		Estonia Lithuania Latvia	Poland Hungary Slovakia	Malta Cyprus Slovenia Czech Rep.
Non-accession countries	Ukraine Russia Bulgaria	Belarus Romania	Turkey	

Sources: Eurostat (2001), EBRD (1998–2000).

1.3 Transition and Integration

Integration and transition processes have become related. Transition means that a country transforms its economy from central-plan allocation mechanisms to market mechanisms. Integration on the other hand means that several market economies harmonise their economies in such a way that they are integrated into one single market, sharing the same allocation mechanisms. For accession countries that are also transition countries, these two processes are intermingled.

European economic integration has traditionally been described as a process of removing trade barriers in four different categories of markets – the goods market, the services market, the labour market and the capital market. Two integrated economies should then not only satisfy free trade or free movement of goods and services but also share the same tariff levels with regard to the rest of the world. The expected effects are increased competition, exploitation of scale economies, improved factor allocation and increased growth.

According to another interpretation, integration is about reducing friction in the exchange of goods and services and in the mobility of production factors. By necessity, transaction costs are reduced. Reducing the friction of various forms of interaction comprises a series of changes in areas such as transportation and communication, education systems, knowledge production and transmission, intellectual and other property rights, technical regulations and standards, capital market regulations, regulation of services and the overall legal framework for business. Such integrative changes may be described as a harmonisation policy, which needs to be supervised, especially as regards the establishment of and obedience to common competition rules. The latter area of supervision relates to ambitions of prohibiting collusive behaviour and preventing individual firms from building up a dominant market position. The supervision includes anti-trust and cartel formation, and control of mergers. An associated area is the control of state aids and subsidies to firms and to regions.

For transition countries that are also entering the EU as member states or that are negotiating agreements with the EU, the formation of a country-wide market economy is a natural element of the integration process. In this way the formation of a single European market defines a 'common playing field' for all transition economies in Europe.

2 CREATION OF A MARKET ECONOMY

Once upon a time, a millennium ago, Europe was an extremely fragmented economic area. Although there were examples of long-distance trade in the Mediterranean, the North Sea and the Baltic Sea basins, each territory was divided into separate local economies, each with its own weight and volume systems, its own currency, its own custom duties and its own local commercial regulation and taxation. Around the sixteenth century certain territories such as France, England, Denmark and Sweden – among others – became centralised kingdoms. This was the start of a process in which each country removed internal trade barriers and became integrated with a single currency, a unified measurement system and a country-wide legal commercial framework. This formation process was embedded in what is labelled mercantilism, and represents an integration process of the same kind as today's EU policies.

2.1 What is a Market?

A market economy consists of a large set of different markets that are more or less interlinked. The establishment of a market is an event by which sellers and buyers enter a marketplace. The market is operated according to market rules, and these have to be supported by written law, self-organised behaviour and political governance. In a perfect market, which is a theoretical construct, the operation of the market is costless. This also means that the market actors are fully informed about available transaction options and associated prices.

All markets are in various degrees imperfect. Both buyers and sellers have to search for information, and such activities incur transaction costs on both the buyer's and the seller's side. Transactions also require that the traded items are privatised, and the safeguarding of such property rights also causes transaction costs. When transaction costs are prohibitively high, the pertinent market will just not be opened. Hence reduction of transaction friction means that new markets can be established and those existing are extended or integrated.

The labour market provides a special example of transaction friction. The labour market is separated into local labour markets, and the costs of searching for a job and of commuting from the place of residence to the job are much lower in a local market than between such markets. During the past 50 years one can observe among the EU15 countries a process that has extended the geographical size of local labour markets – due to changes in the built environment in the form of new location patterns and improved transport systems.

Local labour markets interact via migration. For the new EU25 union such migration may also occur between regions far away from each other. The old member states may consider free labour movements as a threat, because the ten accession members have considerably lower wage levels than the old members. On the other hand there are complaints about severe friction phenomena on the European labour market due to differences with regard to language, cultural norms and educational criteria. These friction phenomena are also included in ongoing harmonisation efforts of the EU Commission.

Markets that are considered to be less difficult to integrate are the service markets, e.g. in the form of tourist services, the financial markets and the knowledge provision markets. However, in these cases also obstacles are often much more frequent than for ordinary trade in goods.

2.2 Formation of a Transaction System

A marketplace is a platform for transactions. A transaction system is an arena (or an infrastructure) for exchange activities, for transfers of property rights and for establishment of contracts. A transaction system usually requires a lot of organisation, where middlemen and brokers are essential actors who help to aggregate information and keep transactions costs low. In particular, we may refer to financial markets as examples, because they cover large geographic areas (are global), they generate global price information and they adjust at great speed. At the same time one must recognise that the value of financial assets is highly uncertain, since it is continuously adjusted and may fluctuate in an unpredictable way. Moreover, financial markets are characterised by many participants. Most of these are small but some are very big. Because of this, information is in general unevenly distributed among transacting agents.

The majority of markets are local and are embedded in functional regions that basically correspond to what geographers call daily commuting regions. For instance, property markets are associated with individual functional regions that can be conceived of as 'housing regions' or 'local labour market regions'. For such regions local information is essential and as a consequence dealers tend to be local.

In the transition countries market dealers need to be educated and trained. Such a process may take several decades. It can be shortened if market operators can be imported from the mature market economies of Europe. Lack of human resources for brokerage and middlemen operations will imply that transaction costs will be high and prohibit the development of many markets. As a consequence, their introduction will be delayed.

The transformation of the transition economies into market economies must be founded on two processes, legislation and development of institutionalised norms. Legislation is a time-consuming process and the evolution of norms, rules of conduct, transaction procedures and trust is a very slow process. Failures in this context materialise in corruption and other forms of extra-market operations (transactions outside the market) that will pervert the market allocation principles.

Economic legislation in the transition economies includes establishment of property rights, commercial law, company law, tax law and similar legal instruments that in some sense will change the whole social fabric of the countries. For the accession countries the principles of new legislation will be constrained by the legal framework required by the EU's legal system. For these countries we may also foresee a process in which individual countries adopt existing laws from selected EU countries. Such imitative behaviour will most probably also influence other transition countries.

2.3 Institutions of a Market Economy

In the expression 'market economy' the notion of a market partly represents what might be termed a 'market institution'. On this interpretation we may want to ask: what are the constituencies of the institution, and how is it created, maintained and developed? This view relates to the contributions by North (1990) and has been called Neo-Institutional Economics. In early contributions to institutional theory, especially in the work by Polanyi et al., markets of an economy are conceived as embedded in socialised reciprocal interdependencies, including trust and legitimacy (Polanyi, Arensberg and Pearson, 1957).

More recent contributions that follow the perspective outlined by North and others formulate models that are compatible with orthodox economic theory as a science of individual choice. In this realm, institutions take the form of constraints that individuals impose on themselves. In this way institutions can function as constraints on the choice sets of economic actors. The benefits to actors are that institutions reduce uncertainty about such actions that require various forms of cooperation from others. This may indeed lead to a reduction in transaction costs. However, one has to recognise that institutions have the potential of serving the interests of those groups in a society that have the power to design and enforce formal as well as informal institutional constraints.

What do the considerations above imply for the emerging market economies of Europe that are in a transition process? There are three basic elements in the transition process. The first is the social and economic culture inherited from the past in each transition country. The second is the rise of new political formations in each country and their incentives. The third factor is influence from the European Union. First, the old member countries of the EU provide examples and standards that can be 'imported', and this can facilitate the development of feasible institutions. A partly similar effect may obtain when firms from the established market economies decide to locate subsidiaries in the transition countries, and this means that foreign direct investments (FDI) may have a particular role to play in the development of institutions that support the development of markets. Second, those countries that will join the union in the near future are forced to adjust themselves to EU law and associated rules and regulations, and this process is likely to have a direct impact on the design of formal institutions. Informal institutions are influenced only indirectly, and presumably at a much slower pace.

The expected influence from the European Union is supported by a set of conditions imposed on the new member states. Three such conditions are basic. First, political stability is required in the realms of a democracy where the rule of law applies, where human rights are respected and where minorities are protected. Second, a functioning market economy must be in place with a capacity to adjust to competition and pressure from market forces. Third, the new countries are expected to accept the aims of a political, economic and monetary union and make sure that they are able to implement the EU legislation effectively.

2.4 Transaction Costs of Different Types of Markets

The development of modern market economies can be described in many different ways. Among several development characteristics, one seems especially prevalent. Heterogeneity of products and diversity of consumers and consumer demand have continued to grow steadily. In this process diversity of supply has increased more in large urban agglomerations than elsewhere in the economic geographical areas. This reflects the difference in geographic transaction costs for different products. Products (goods and services) for which transaction costs are distance-sensitive cannot be supplied by profit-maximising firms in regions (functional urban regions) where the demand is too small to allow firms to cover fixed costs.

The theoretical background is as follows. Diversity and variety in consumer goods or in producer inputs can yield external scale economies, even though all individual competitors and firms earn normal profits. The size of an urban region will determine the number of specialised local consumer goods and the number of specialised producer inputs, given the degree of substitutability among the specialised local goods in consumption and among specialised inputs in production.

> A larger city will have a greater variety of consumer products and producer inputs. Since the greater variety adds to consumer well being, it follows that larger cities are more productive, and the well being of those living in cities increases with their size. This is true even when all firms in these cities earn a normal rate of profit. (Johansson and Quigley, 2004, p. 170)

There are two principal models. The first is the core of urbanisation economies and emphasises (i) diversity and consumers' taste for variety and (ii) the productivity of specialised inputs in production. The second model is derived from quite another perspective, where the focus is on firms or producers, and how their efficiency is enhanced by proximity and linkages achieved through agglomeration. At the firm level, the perspective is shifted from input diversity to forward and backward linkages among agents. These linkages may be of a pure-market type or may involve transaction links. These models, inspired by Marshall, are indeed models of agglomeration, but emphasise localisation economies, where linkages among firms may also provide gains to smaller regions (Krugman, 1990; Fujita, 1988; Johansson and Quigley, 2004).

The two models addressed above imply that there is an incentive for transition economies to restructure their urban economies. Such efforts include the introduction of land and real-estate markets, but also efforts to redesign urban regions to reflect well-established principles that date back to von Thünen (1826). In such a development programme there is also a need to invest in new urban transport systems.

In view of the above presentation, modern markets have changed in the direction of product diversity, which favours location of activities in large urban regions. However, this is only one side of the story. Another equally apparent development path is the seemingly unlimited extension of markets to become global. This development is based on two network phenomena. The first has to do with development of economic links that allow transactions to be carried out over long distances at reduced costs. The second associated change is the development of networks for transport of information, services, goods and people. The evolution of such networks reflects ambitions of making transaction less distance-sensitive (Andersson, 1986). In EU policies this long-distance network formation is recognised in ambitions to develop a trans-European transport system that in the future should include all the new accession countries. Another associated ambition is to integrate financial markets in the European Union.

3 GROWTH AND TRADE

Integration of Europe's economies was recognised as a core element of EU policies as early as the 1950s. The reason for establishing a common market is of course to facilitate trade, stressed in the formulation 'one single market'. Trade is also seen as a prime instrument to stimulate the new accession countries to catch up with the established market economies of the EU. We must then ask: what is the theoretical foundation for such a development programme? Moreover, what are the crucial complementary elements in such a growth-enhancing policy?

3.1 Endogenous Growth

Macro analyses of endogenous growth are based on aggregate models that depict investments in production capital, infrastructure, education (human capital) and R&D as the outcome of endogenous processes. A major feature is that these resource-enhancing processes are characterised by increasing returns. It may be claimed that endogenous growth mechanisms have played an important role from the very start of the industrial revolution in the eighteenth century. For the transition economies of Europe, endogenous growth mechanisms are vital, as they stress two things: (i) the economy must be capable of setting aside resources for investments in various forms of knowledge and other collective, infrastructure-like resources, and (ii) it matters how these investments are combined.

The start of the transition process has been quite similar for almost all the new market economies. At the end of the 1980s these economies experienced a period of falling GDP levels. Obsolete firms and techniques had to be removed when competitive pressures increased. At the same time the demand for investment increased, since infrastructure, human capital and technology had to be almost completely renewed in order to match market conditions and demand patterns in the EU.

The growth problem of the transition economies may be illustrated by the following observations. In the Ukraine growth remained negative through the 1990s; in Belarus and Russia positive growth was reported only during the second half of the decade. In Poland, on the other hand, GDP was growing 4–5 per cent annually from 1992 (EBRD, 1999).

Blanchard (1997) has carried out an assessment of the transition process for the first half of the 1990s. According to his study, there is an initial drop in production down to a level with 15–25 per cent lower output than in the years 1989 and 1990. Thereafter production starts to increase again. Blanchard calls this a U-shaped development. A similar U-shape is found for aggregate labour productivity. The productivity improvements have in several of the economies implied that employment has not started to grow in the same way as output, and in some countries employment has remained stagnant or continued to fall during the growth segment of the U-shaped development.

The above observations can be interpreted as a process of fast reallocation of resources, implying the discontinuation of inefficient production with obsolete products. In the short term this form of changed allocation can have a strong impact on growth. In the longer term, the development has to rely on mechanisms of endogenous growth, where firms have to imitate and develop products that can penetrate the markets of the more prosperous countries of the EU and find ways to import the necessary production and commercial techniques. The following processes are vital in this context:

- Organisation and funding of public and private R&D efforts.
- Establishing arrangements that facilitate the privatisation of intellectual capital.
- Renewing education to adjust human capital in order to develop a reliable basis for product and process innovations.
- Investment in infrastructure to facilitate economic interaction with EU countries and the rest of the world.

Recent empirical observations strongly indicate that successful R&D is based on knowledge exchange and spillovers in a firm's interaction with customers and input suppliers, including pure knowledge providers. Another aspect to be mentioned is that university research in the former planned economies was to a large extent disconnected from industrial R&D. Hence university research must also be transformed in order to play a role as knowledge provider for industrial and other economic activities.

The discussion of growth opportunities of the transition economies can also be based on classical findings in growth-accounting studies as reported by Denison (1962). According to these studies, the following change processes stimulate economic growth:

- Increase of labour inputs
- Increase of human capital
- Increase of production capital
- Expansion of the market potential or, in other words, increased accessibility to customers
- Improved allocation of resources that enhance economic efficiency
- Technological development.

These early findings from 40 years ago were at that time thought of as challenges to the existing exogenous growth models. However, the results are indeed consistent with the conclusions from endogenous growth models. These models emphasise that productivity grows as a consequence of investments in capacities that are characterised by increasing returns. As an example, infrastructure investment can facilitate the expansion of firms' market size, which augments the options to exploit scale economies. As a general comment, we observe that policy matters in this process, and includes education, infrastructure and innovation policies.

Growth is a major focus for the European transition economies, implying that capital formation is of great concern. Investments are warranted in many areas, for example huge investments in transport infrastructure and investments in renewed institutions. In this context the development of modern capital markets has a particular role both to stimulate domestic savings and to make foreign direct investments possible. An overall goal is to form an institutional setting in which efficient mechanisms for resource allocation can evolve. Obviously, this is a long-term process that does not allow short cuts.

On the other hand, there are several areas in which the starting point is more mixed. In many of the transition economies there is a long tradition of ambitious education policies, although the profile of human-capital formation may have to change. As indicated in Table 1.2, states in the former Soviet Union (Ukraine and in particular Russia) display a high share of R&D staff with university education, whereas the share of R&D technicians tends to be low. The major issue for countries such as Russia and Ukraine is the areas in which the R&D investments are made. When the patent applications are compared for transition economies and the developed market economies, one can observe one fundamental difference. The number of foreign patent applications is much lower for the transition economies. This shows that the latter are not yet integrated in the global R&D system, most probably because they still represent immature markets in which protection of patents is not a basic problem.

Table 1.2 Research and development in selected countries

	Scientists and engineers in R&D per million inhabitants*	Technicians in R&D per million inhabitants*	Patent applications of residents 1997	Patent applications of non-residents 1997
Russia	3 587	600	15 277 (104)	32 943
Ukraine	2 171	575	4 692 (93)	28 036
Hungary	1 099	510	774 (72)	29 331
Poland	1 358	1 377	2 401 (62)	30 137
USA	3 676	–	125 808 (503)	110 884
Germany	2 831	1 472	62 052 (806)	113 543
UK	2 448	1 017	26 591 (475)	121 618
Sweden	3 826	3 166	7 893 (917)	107 107
Austria	1 627	812	2 681 (352)	108 543
Switzerland	3 006	1 374	5 814 (923)	107 038

Notes:
* denotes the average for the period 1987–97.
Patent applications per million inhabitants are reported in parentheses.

Sources: The World Bank (2000) and von Westernhagen (2002).

3.2 Functional Regions, Agglomerations and Specialisation

Development of economic theory during the past two decades contains several new elements. One of these is known as 'the new economic geography' and another is 'the new trade theory'. The first of these two emphasises that regions – functional urban regions – are looked upon as primarily independent marketplaces that are connected via interregional and international trade (Karlsson and Stough, 2002). According to this view, trade and growth have to be analysed as processes that are initiated and unfolded in interacting regions rather than as country-specific processes. Markets of the functional regions and rational firms create comparative advantages that take the form of localised increasing returns to scale and formation of industrial clusters with positive externalities. The new trade theory has similar messages, but models these phenomena on a more aggregate scale, as illustrated in section 3.3.

The new economic geography literature has a related message. When human capital and other capital resources, including R&D competence, are located together in the same region, self-reinforcing processes can obtain; such concentrations have the power to further stimulate economic growth in these regions. A vital phenomenon in this type of development is the very integration of each specific region. It is exactly here that many regions in the transition countries fail. Having a history of planned economic development, a typical region is not at all integrated, as in most of the EU15 countries. In the setting of a planned economy, suppliers to an industry were frequently located elsewhere than the industry, often far away. Hence local intraregional externalities did not have any opportunities to develop. In a transition country, a region specialising in a certain production will then lack the stimuli from close interaction with alert suppliers and alert customers. This means that promotion of market formation is not just a country-wide problem for the transition economies. The evolution must also bring about the formation of integrated local markets.

The above observations imply that the new market economies have a particular development agenda. Urban regions have to be reshaped so as to encompass agglomeration economies. Moreover, this implies that interregional transport infrastructure is only one component in the transition process. Another component is the development of urban infrastructure. In this context there is also a need to facilitate the development of a land market, and land use policies have to be adjusted accordingly.

3.3 Trade and Growth

The former planned economies in Europe were closed economies with limited international trade – both inside the CMEA and with the rest of the world. In a sense, opening up the countries for trade was one of the first steps taken in the transition process. This step is indeed in line with the widespread idea that openness to international exchange of goods and services is a fundamental ingredient in stimulating growth of GDP. One empirical argument that plays a role in this context is the rapid growth that a set of East Asian countries managed to attain from 1970 and onwards. Another such supporting early observation can be found in the studies of

Denison (1962), in which market accessibility is observed to be growth-enhancing. A more recent contribution is Thirlwall (1999), analysing this phenomenon for developing countries. We may also observe that in gravity-model estimations, such as Holzmann and Zukowska-Gagelman (1998), the importance of market size and market proximity gets strong support.

Established theory suggests, in line with Denison's observations, that growth can be export-led, in a process where participation in world markets influences resource allocation positively and allows scale economies to be exploited. This latter observation is an important element of the new trade theory. In more recent models, trade is also seen as a vehicle for knowledge diffusion and transfer of technology. Although the association between trade and growth has many supporters, the empirical evidence is far from mature, partly because econometric formulations include severe endogeneity problems (e.g. Frankel and Romer, 1999). The association between trade and knowledge diffusion is also present in models of catching up and technology-gap diffusion, where countries that lag behind have the opportunity to adopt recent technology and imitate new products and techniques. Suggestions along these lines can be found in Krugman (1990), Barro and Sala-í-Martin (1995) and Gries and Jungblut (1997). This form of diffusion represents a hope for the accession countries. However, the conditions for catching-up processes to develop are not well understood, and the interaction between leading and lagging regions and countries may also result in divergence of GDP per capita.

What do observations of growth rates during the 1990s tell us? An initial observation is that there is some evidence of a U-shaped growth performance among the transition countries (Blanchard, 1997). According to such observations, the transition process starts with negative growth rates, which reflect reallocation and restructuring efforts in each particular country. This period of negative growth is then followed by a period of positive growth, during which the fruits of the restructuring are harvested. The following sample may illustrate the described phenomenon:

- Hungary experienced negative growth in 1990–93, whereas growth was positive during the rest of the decade.
- The growth rate in Poland was negative in 1990–91. In the following eight years growth was positive and fast.
- For Russia the major part of the 1990s was characterised by negative growth.
- In Belarus negative growth rates were replaced by positive ones from 1996.

What other experiences can shed light on the possible effects of introducing market mechanisms and of joining the common market of the EU? Going back in history we can identify four countries (Ireland, Greece, Portugal and Spain) that were relatively poor at the time of accession. Ireland joined the European Union in 1973, Greece in 1981, and Spain and Portugal in 1986. In Ireland, Portugal and Spain, several important factors accompanied entry into the EU. Market mechanisms were strengthened, the supply of investment capital was attracted to the countries, and the stock markets were vitalised. In addition, trade with other EU countries expanded fast. For each of these three countries – and especially for Ireland – the growth of GDP was high in the period after accession. Many of these ingredients were not present in the case of Greece, and the impacts of accession in the Greek economy have remained less favourable (Baldwin and Wyplosz, 2004).

The above description of economic growth in Ireland, Portugal and Spain can be interpreted as both investment-led and trade-led growth. The most important factor may still be the modernisation aspect, pointing to the role of new institutions and the introduction of better-functioning market mechanisms.

3.4 Capital Formation and FDI

Foreign direct investment (FDI) can be assumed to play a major role in the transformation of the European transition economies. The importance of FDI is two-pronged. First, direct investments by foreign firms augment the supply of capital in the host country, since they represent an inflow of capital. Second, the establishment of management from abroad and links to a foreign firm in a developed country open the way for various kinds of information flows and knowledge transmission from the investing country to the host country. Both these phenomena have the capacity to enhance growth. The role of trade as a catalytic element in knowledge diffusion, imitation and innovation processes is suggested in, e.g., Grossman and Helpman (1994) and Krugman (1990). There are strong reasons to assume that FDI flows are even more important in this regard.

Compared with trade, foreign direct investments have a more distinct influence on technological progress and catching-up processes of the less developed countries, because FDI represents a special type of investment decision. As a general feature an FDI investor has firm-specific assets in the form of a brand, product attributes, production techniques and other knowledge-like resources. Some of these advantages are transferred to the establishment in the country that hosts the direct investment. As a consequence, novel technology is transferred to this country.

For a given firm a direct investment in a foreign country can have two basic reasons. The location of the foreign establishment (including acquisition of existing firms) can be motivated by sales (output-market) opportunities and by input-market opportunities in the foreign country.

Attraction of investments based on output-market advantages usually is based on some form of ownership advantages. Such decisions may be termed 'market-seeking'. The firm-specific assets give rise to economic rents when locating in a foreign place with accessibility to local customers there. A reason for an FDI decision instead of selling, licensing, or leasing the asset would be that these latter alternatives are too costly (or impossible) to contract, i.e. there are internalisation advantages. A motivation for an FDI decision instead of just exporting may be that proximity to the market reduces transport and other transaction costs sufficiently to compensate for the investment costs. This is a form of location advantage; another form is noted in the following paragraph. The necessity of having ownership, location and internalisation advantages to induce FDI was proposed by Dunning (1977, 1980, 1988), who built on earlier work by Hymer (1976) on the determinants of FDI.

Foreign direct investments can also be attracted by resource properties in the host country. Such decisions can be thought of as 'resource-seeking' and 'efficiency-seeking'. In the latter case the place of investment may also have particular localisation advantages. It seems reasonable to assume that efficiency-seeking investments will dominate in the transition economies, where for example low labour costs may be one particular efficiency factor.

Assembly-like production has special features in the context of FDI. Components may then be produced in a transition country, and the country of the investing firm may import these components. In addition, the final products may be exported to the transition country. In this way FDI decisions can stimulate trade in two directions between the countries involved. More generally, for firms that produce in transnational networks, trade and foreign direct investments cannot be considered as substitutes.

4 INSTITUTIONS AND INTEGRATION IN THE EU

4.1 Transportation

Market integration strives to bring supply into contact with manifest demand. In this perspective transport systems have an essential role in making this happen by opening up national markets and introducing Trans-European Networks (TENs). For the EU15 countries such a network remains fairly incomplete at the beginning of the twenty-first century, with national railway systems that are incompatible with each other from both technical and organisational points of view, with a fragmented air transport system and with severe bottleneck problems in the long-distance road networks, including missing links.

For the transition countries transport problems have two dimensions. First, the internal transport systems in each country must be modernised to facilitate specialisation and trade inside the country. Second, the emerging market economies lack good transport links that can connect them with the markets of other countries in the union.

The transport policy of the EU has two principal components. The first relates to regulation and intervention and aims at improving efficiency and taking care of externalities in transport. The ambition is to harmonise the transport markets of the EU. The second component is to coordinate infrastructure development and to liberalise transport markets. Both these components combine into a common transport policy (CTP).

The creation of the Single European Market in 1992 brought important changes to the CTP. Already in the 1980s one can identify an orchestrated effort to remove institutional barriers to free trade in transport services, and initiatives were taken to integrate European transport infrastructure. However, the ambitions that are reflected in the TENs imply large investments and these have to be financed by both individual countries and the EU in concert. The difficulties in finding the resources for the huge investments that relate to the enlargement programme remain unresolved.

4.2 A Common Currency

In 1999 the euro was introduced as a currency in its own right. Partly in the same way as improved transport systems, a common currency has the feature of reducing friction of transactions and trade between the different areas of the EU. A common currency creates price transparency across borders, it eliminates transaction costs of changing one currency into another, it reduces the need for each country to hold international reserves, it removes uncertainty in trade between members of the European monetary union (EMU), and it provides a less volatile market for investors.

In 2004 there are 12 members of the EMU. Denmark, Sweden and the UK remain outside the union. Arguments to stay outside related to the idea that an optimal currency area should be much smaller and more homogeneous in its economic structure than is represented by the EMU. A specific argument against joining the EMU is the fear of asymmetric shocks that may create inconsistent demands for monetary and fiscal policies in different countries of the currency area. Individual countries may also use 'seigniorage policies' as a source of budgetary revenue, and this may affect inflation both in the country with too quickly expanding government expenditure and in neighbouring countries.

The EMU is included in the European System of Central Banks (ESCB), which consists of the European Central Bank (ECB) and the national central banks of all EU member states. However, not all member states have yet joined the monetary union. As a consequence, the term Eurosystem has been introduced as a label for ECB and the national banks.

The new accession countries have committed themselves to joining the EMU. Before this can happen they must satisfy the so-called convergence criteria. These include requirements with regard to inflation, the long-term nominal interest rate, EMS membership and participation in the ERM, budget deficit and public debt. Inflation is not allowed to exceed the average of the three lowest inflation rates achieved by EMU states by more than 1.5 percentage points. Budget deficits should not exceed 3 per cent of GDP. The maximum level of public debt is set at 60 per cent. Moreover, before a country can enter the monetary union, its exchange rate should have been fixed against the euro.

The commitment to join the EMU puts severe constraints on the fiscal and monetary policy of the new accession countries. These constraints may be in conflict with ambitions to foster economic growth and increased employment.

4.3 Equity and Cohesion

In the preamble to the Treaty of Rome, 1958, concerns were expressed with regard to the harmonious development of member states. A goal is to reduce differences between regions and to remedy the backwardness of less favoured regions. This is the area of cohesion and regional policies. What are the arguments of supporters of regional policy?

Armstrong (2001) discusses four arguments in favour of regional policy. The first is equity and fairness, ensuring that all parts of society can share the benefits of a growing economy. The second argument is about 'underutilised' resources, which should be drawn into productive use with the help of regional policy. The third argument is related to 'overutilised' resources. In this case the concentration of production in a few and already prosperous regions can bring about overheated, inflationary growth. The fourth argument addresses urban problems and suggests that large metropolitan areas are associated with crime and lower quality of life. Regional policy is then presented as a way of easing the pressure on the big cities.

As stressed earlier in this chapter, income per capita varies across the EU countries. Around 2000 about one-third of the countries in the EU25 had less than 75 per cent and about one-third had more than 125 per cent of the EU25 average. The distribution is even more skewed if one compares regions, e.g. NUTS-3 regions (Baldwin and Wyplosz, 2004). Economic integration in Europe could potentially bring about convergence in GDP per capita both across countries and across functional regions. Focusing on country differentials for the EU15, one can observe that the differences in income level continued to decrease during the period 1983–2000, although at a gradually decelerating rate (Baldwin and Wyplosz, 2004).

From another perspective one may collect a set of arguments for why further integration might set loose divergence forces that could help to magnify differences. Following Armstrong (2001), the following divergence forces can be identified:

- Internal economies of scale: integration in Europe may be motivated by options to exploit scale economies better. However, exploiting scale economies implies regional concentration, and this may increase regional differences.
- Agglomeration economies (urbanisation and localisation economies): localisation economies arise when firms in the same industry locate close to each other in the same region. Urbanisation economies provide advantages when firms in different industries co-locate and generate mutual variety. Agglomeration economies imply cumulative dynamics that will generate growth differences among regions.
- Intra-industry trade: when two countries export products in the same product group, intra-industry trade applies. Such trade has continued to grow in the EU. Intra-industry trade in similar products is especially frequent and has continued to grow in the prosperous core regions of the EU.
- Selective labour migration: it is the young, skilled and economically active persons who migrate inside the EU. In this process the disadvantaged regions experience labour-force drainage.
- Lack of competitiveness: research commissioned by the EU provides ample evidence that groups of peripheral regions are characterised by a combination of negative factors outside the control of the individual firms.

The last observation above in particular has inspired the regional policy areas of the EU. Objective 1 is development support to the most disadvantaged regions. Objective 2 is to have measures with the aim to remedy structural problems. Objective 3 comprises education and human resource development programmes for disadvantaged regions. There are also areas of community initiative and innovation programmes. In essence, all regional policy areas are formulated as development issues and not as a redistribution system. The same characterisation can be made of the EU's transport policy, but not of the common agricultural policy. It is obvious that the enlargement of the EU will stimulate rethinking and reconsideration of the regional policy structure.

4.4 Europe-wide Environmental Policy Issues

Energy policies are strongly related to environmental issues. The common energy policy of the EU was formulated in a treaty of 1992. This treaty puts forward the idea of trans-European infrastructure networks to establish a single energy market. Objectives for this policy are security of supply, competitiveness, protection of the environment and common research.

Environmental concerns became manifest in the early 1970s and were then recognised by the European Council. The concerns are present in the Single European Act from 1986 and the following four specific objectives can be identified: preserving, protecting and improving the quality of the environment; protecting human health; rational and prudent utilisation of natural resources; and promotion of measures on the international level with regard to global problems, such as the 'greenhouse effect'.

The environmental policy can be structured into the preventive principle, the polluter pays principle, the source principle (rectified at the source), the precautionary principle, and the coordination principle, giving the Community the task of coordinating the policy of the member states. Since the 1970s the Community has organised its efforts in Energy Action Programmes (EAPs). In the fifth EAP (1993–97) the focus is sustainable development, and this is strengthened in the sixth EAP, with priority areas such as climate change, nature and biodiversity, environment and health, and natural resources and waste. For many of the new accession countries, the ambitious programmes of the EU do bring about a great deal of tension by demanding very strong structural change of their industrial system, as well as energy and transport systems.

5 OUTLINE OF THE BOOK

The book is divided into three parts. The first part contains chapters analysing interregional and international trade. There is also a special analysis of border-region economic interaction. The second part deals with regional and migration issues from an EU perspective and with special focus on transition economies. The third part comprises fiscal, financial and environmental policy issues.

5.1 Interregional and International Trade

Part One considers one of the most important elements of European economic integration, that involving the exchange of goods and services through interregional and international trade. Part One's first chapter, a contribution by Johannes Bröcker, provides an overview of recent advances in modelling of trade, interregional or international. The model presented in this chapter has a special relevance, because it has been applied to analyse and forecast intra-European trade as a tool for policy analysis. As such it provides decision support for both transport and environmental policies.

Bröcker indicates how more recent approaches incorporating imperfect competition, product heterogeneity and transfer costs complement the classic Heckscher–Ohlin–Samuelson model. He argues that the more recent approaches have a good fit with the Heckscher–Ohlin–Samuelson model in a general equilibrium framework. The newer trade models are shown in this chapter to be also useful in connecting traditional regional science with mainstream economics by providing a theoretical foundation for the gravity equation, a long-used empirical equation in regional science. This theoretical basis is important, as it helps those doing empirical work using the gravity model to understand how to apply the gravity model appropriately with respect to comparative static analysis, welfare evaluation, and estimation of trade impediments.

Mikolaj Herbst and Karol Olejniczak wrote the second chapter. This chapter is an exceptionally relevant one given the book's focus on emerging market economies and European economic integration since it deals with case studies of towns on the border between the future European Union and Eastern Europe. These towns are Terespol, on the Polish–Belarussian border, and Przemyśl on the Polish–Ukrainian border. A third case study in the chapter deals with Sejny, on the Polish–Lithuanian border and close to the Belarussian border. The chapter reviews theories that examine how a border affects regional development and considers how these theories can explain some phenomena observed in the case studies. There is a discussion in this chapter on how local development in eastern Poland border areas is affected by border physical infrastructure, local government, local society, and asymmetry of local development between areas on opposite sides of the border.

The last chapter in Part One is written by Viesturs Pauls Karnups. This chapter delves deeply into explaining Latvia's patterns of trade with Scandinavia in an earlier period when Latvia was, as today, facing new opportunities to expand its economic relations with its neighbours to the west after cutting a previous strong relationship with Russia. This earlier period starts in 1920, the year in which Latvia signed with Soviet Russia a peace treaty that finalised Latvia's independence, and ends in 1940 with Russia's occupation of the country. There is an extensive discussion in this chapter about various sectors that became important in trade between Latvia and the Scandinavian countries, including why they became important and how and why their importance varied over the time period. The author argues that the lack of regional or European trade structures led to domination of Latvian and Scandinavian foreign trade by the large industrial countries of Europe, which significantly dampened trade between Latvia and Scandinavia.

5.2 Regional and Migration Issues

As stressed in section 3 of this chapter, functional urban regions have a primary role as marketplaces in a market economy. Therefore, the goal to introduce and improve market mechanisms in the transition countries will require renewal and reshaping of existing urban regions. Part Two of the book deals with regional issues of this kind, focusing on urban infrastructure, industrial specialisation and cluster formation, labour markets and migration.

The first chapter of Part Two presents an equilibrium model of a multiregional labour market. The model is formulated with the ambition to show in a precise way that infrastructure investments can make the functioning of labour markets more efficient so that both unemployment and vacancies are reduced in individual labour-market regions. The authors, Jos van Ommeren, Piet Rietveld and Stefan Woudenberg, have formulated their model as a job search model, describing how unemployed job seekers and firms with vacancies have to search for each other. The model makes it possible to examine the effects of improvements in intraregional and interregional infrastructure. In the model, wages, vacancies and unemployment are endogenously determined. Infrastructure improvements in this model reduce local and national unemployment. However, adjacent regions may experience adverse effects. The relevance of the model and its results is obvious for the transition economies, as most of them are characterised by higher than average unemployment rates. In addition, the same countries are confronted with growing regional disparities.

Herbert Brücker, Boriss Siliverstovs and Parvati Trübswetter provide an analysis of migration to Germany in the second chapter in Part Two. The focus on Germany is not arbitrary. This country has for many decades been one of the major destinations for international migration into Europe. Germany's past history of immigration can also provide insights into the potential migration from the ten accession countries that are becoming EU members in 2004. The analysis in the chapter examines the migration to

Germany from five founding members of the EU plus three additional member countries: Belgium, Denmark, France, Italy, Ireland, Luxembourg, the Netherlands and the United Kingdom. The model formulation is based on an assumption of a long-run equilibrium, in which benefits and costs of migration are equalised for the marginal migrant. The observation period is 1967–2000. The results from the model estimations and statistical tests are challenging. In one model formulation the dependent variable is migration stocks. In this basic case there is evidence of a long-run equilibrium relation between GDP per capita differences and migration stocks, such that a positive difference in per capita income between host and home country augments the long-run stock of migrants. When a flow formulation of the model (with migration rates) is applied, the results point in a different direction and contradict earlier findings in the literature. In this latter case differences in GDP per capita and employment rates cannot form a long-run dynamic equilibrium relationship.

The third chapter in Part Two is a contribution by Iulia Traistaru and Guntram B. Wolff. The chapter analyses regional specialisation and traces the associated employment dynamics for three transition countries: Bulgaria, Hungary and Romania. Like many other transition countries, these three have experienced trade reorientation, industrial restructuring and labour redistribution across industries and regions. A shift-share analysis is applied to assess the role of industry mix, region-specific factors and regional competitiveness to decompose and explain regional differentials in employment growth. The result of the analysis is that the change process is primarily determined by region-specific advantages and disadvantages. This implies that regional disparities have a tendency to increase. This pattern of increasing employment differences has been obvious in both Hungary and Bulgaria, but not in Romania.

Hungary is often considered to be one of the more advanced transition economies. In the fourth chapter of Part Two Ákos Jakobi discusses regional inequalities in Hungary and relates these inequalities to the transition process. Several indicators suggest that inequalities have increased during the past 10 to 12 years. The author argues that the gap between rich and poor is due to differences in pace in the process of adopting the new rules of the market economy and to vanishing subsidies of the socialist state. In a structural change process like this, the indicators of regional differences may have to change over time in order to reflect the adjustment process properly. While discussing this issue the author is able to present an intriguing picture of regional development in Hungary. When measuring personal income inequalities, there is ample evidence that these inequalities have increased more or less steadily. And this result holds true at different levels of spatial resolution, covering the difference between Budapest and the rest of the country as well as the differences between settlements (NUTS-5 level). Unemployment inequalities have taken a different path. Initially this inequality measure increased sharply, and it has remained at the same high level.

The fifth chapter in Part Two provides a picture of cluster formation in Pärnu, a town in Estonia. The four authors, Urmas Kase, Tiit Kask, Heli Müristaja and Garri Raagmaa, focus on one potential export industry in the country, namely tourism. In their analyses they apply a product cycle model to the development of the tourism industry. In addition they investigate cluster phenomena in the tourism supply. To some extent this industry really reflects the importance of regionally trapped resource endowments that can cause comparative advantages. The reason for this is obvious: tourist visitors respond to regional attractiveness in terms of amenities, historical landmarks, climate etc. However, such advantages can be developed and transformed into packages of visitor experiences and excitements that can be marketed, and this motivates the employment of product cycle analysis. For Pärnu in particular the presentation also shows how cluster formation has helped the industry to development and how clusters can be strengthened by policy interventions.

The last chapter in Part Two provides an analysis of income disparity in four transition countries: Hungary, Bulgaria, Estonia and Latvia. A successful modernisation of the relevant economies requires that the restructuring efforts have positive effects on income growth. If such income effects are unevenly distributed, support to the change process may be weakened. In this perspective income disparities may be an important policy characteristic. The authors, Maria Plotnikova and Tatiane de Menezes, make use of household survey data in combination with regional characteristics. The ambition is to reveal patterns of regional income distribution in the selected transition countries. Several transition issues are related to regional differentials, e.g. core–periphery aspects, regions' capacities to attract foreign direct investments, and the capability of actors in regions to establish interaction links with firms and other actors in the mature market economies of Europe. Regression results confirm that regional factors have a clear influence on income differences. These findings indicate that regional inequalities in the accession countries can develop to become a basic policy area of the European Union.

5.3 Fiscal, Financial and Environmental Policy Issues

Part Three brings together three chapters that share a macroeconomic perspective, in some respects, but otherwise the chapters deal with a wide range of subjects, specifically fiscal, financial, and environmental policy issues. The first chapter, written by Doina Radulescu, examines the sustainability of Romania's fiscal situation. Considering Romania's hopes of future membership in the EU, its fiscal situation is an important issue for its status within Europe. That is because the matter of when Romania will be allowed to be integrated into the EU could depend heavily on its ability to control its fiscal deficits. The author reviews Romania's general economic development during the transition era and follows that with a discussion on fiscal policy during the 1990s, focusing on the problems of quasi-fiscal subsidies and payment arrears, and the resulting large quasi-fiscal deficits. The chapter has a presentation of a macroeconomic model that uses the inter-temporal budget constraint and provides a means for assessing the degree of fiscal sustainability. The author presents data on Romania's deficit situation and argues on the basis of those data that Romania's fiscal policy has been unsustainable in the transition era, particularly up to 1996. She notes an improved situation in the late 1990s, but problems for sustainability were still present, with high interest rates (higher than Romania's growth rate) being one such problem.

Andreas Johnson provides us with the next chapter on flows of foreign direct investments into the transition economies of Eastern Europe. He first presents and comments on data about these FDI flows during the transition period. He then proceeds to discuss the possible determinants of FDI and presents evidence on the relationship between some of these determinants and FDI in the context of these transitional economies. The chapter indicates that there has been a persistence of large differences in these countries' FDI inflows that showed up early in the transition period. Quality of market demand, privatisation and transition performance are argued to be important in providing explanations for these differences.

The last chapter, by Uwe Schubert and Bernd Schuh, pursues an important topic in environmental economics, that of sustainable development. Greater importance has been attached to this issue in the European Union over the years since its discussion in the Brundtland Commission report in 1987, making its way into the Amsterdam Treaty of the EU and into the constitutional law of all EU countries. With the planned inclusion of many new member states in the EU, the issue of environmental policy goals such as sustainable development takes on additional importance. That arises because many of the planned accession countries have considerably lower levels of economic development than the current EU average, which naturally affects how much weight these countries will place on implementing environmental policies relative to implementing others. Also, many authorities in these countries are likely to be unaccustomed to sustainable development policy issues discussed in the EU. The authors of this chapter review various concepts of sustainable development and focus on the evaluation of policies, programmes and projects with sustainable development as a goal. In their coverage, the authors illuminate concepts and approaches that currently prevail in the EU.

REFERENCES

Andersson, Å.E. (1986), 'The Four Logistical Revolutions', *Papers of the Regional Science Association*, **59**, 1–12.

Armstrong, H.W. (2001), 'Regional Policy', in A. El-Agraa (ed.), *The European Union – Economics and Policies*, Harlow: Prentice-Hall, Pearson Education.

Baldwin, R. and C. Wyplosz (2004), *The Economics of European Integration*, Maidenhead: McGraw-Hill.

Barro, R.J. and X. Sala-í-Martin (1995), 'Technological Diffusion, Convergence, and Growth', NBER Working Paper No. 5151, Cambridge.

Blanchard, O. (1997), *The Economics of Post-Communist Transition*, Oxford: Oxford University Press.

Denison, E. (1962), 'The Sources of Economic Growth in the United States and the Alternatives Before Us', Committee for Economic Development, New York.

Dunning, J.H. (1977), 'Trade, Location of Economic Activity and the MNE: A Search for an Eclectic Approach', in B. Ohlin, P.O. Hesselborn and P.M. Wijkman (eds), *The International Allocation of Economic Activity*, London: Macmillan.

Dunning, J.H. (1980), 'Toward an Eclectic Theory of International Production: Some Empirical Tests', *Journal of International Business Studies*, **11**, 9–31.

Dunning, J.H. (1988), 'The Eclectic Paradigm of International Production: A Restatement and Some Possible Extensions', *Journal of International Business Studies*, **19**, 1–31.

EBRD (1998), *Transition Report 1998*, London.

EBRD (1999), *Transition Report 1999*, London.

EBRD (2000), *Transition Report 2000*, London.

Eurostat (2001), *Yearbook 2001*, Luxembourg: Office for Official Publications.

Frankel, J. and D. Romer (1999), 'Does Trade Cause Growth?', *American Economic Review*, **89** (3), 379–99.

Fujita, M. (1988), 'A Monopolistic Competition Model of Spatial Agglomeration: A Differentiated Product Approach', *Regional Science and Urban Economics*, **18**, 87–124.

Gries, T. and S. Jungblut (1997), 'Catching Up of Economies in Transition', in P.J.J. Welfens and H.C. Wolf (eds), *Banking, International Capital Flows and Growth in Europe*, Heidelberg: Springer-Verlag.

Grossman, G.M. and E. Helpman (1994), 'Endogenous Innovation in the Theory of Growth', *European Economic Review*, **35**, 43–61.

Hitris, T. (2003), *European Union Economics*, Harlow: Prentice-Hall, Pearson Education.

Holzmann, R. and K. Zukowska-Gagelmann (1998), 'Trade Adjustment in Eastern Europe During Transition: the Determined Sophisticated and Proximate', *Journal of Public Policy*, **18**, 29–52.

Hymer, S.H. (1976), *The International Operations of National Firms: A Study of Direct Foreign Investment*, Cambridge, MA: MIT Press.

Johansson, B. and J. Quigley (2004), 'Agglomeration and Networks in Spatial

Economies', *Papers in Regional Science*, **83**, 165–76.

Karlsson, C. and R. Stough (2002), 'Introduction: Regional Policy Evaluation in the New Economic Geography', in B. Johansson, C. Karlsson and R. Stough (eds), *Regional Policies and Comparative Advantage*, Cheltenham, UK, and Northampton, MA, USA: Edward Elgar.

Krugman, P. (1990), *Rethinking International Trade*, Cambridge, MA: MIT Press.

North, D. (1990), *Institutions, Institutional Change, and Economic Performance*, Cambridge: Cambridge University Press.

Polanyi, P.A., C.M. Arensberg and H.W. Pearson (1957), *Trade and Market in the Early Empires*, Glencoe, IL: The Free Press.

Thirlwall, A.P. (1999), *Growth and Development with Special Reference to Developing Economies*, Basingstoke: Macmillan.

von Thünen, J.H. (1826), *Der isolierte Staat in Beziehung auf Landwirtschaft und Nationalökonomie*, Hamburg: Perthes.

von Westernhagen, N. (2002), *Systemic Transformation, Trade and Economic Growth – Developments, Theoretical Analysis and Empirical Results*, Heidelberg: Physica-Verlag.

World Bank (2000), *World Bank Indicators 2000*, http://www.worldbank.org.

PART ONE

Interregional and International Trade Issues

2. Modelling Interregional and International Trade

Johannes Bröcker

1 INTRODUCTION

Why do regions trade among themselves? What do they typically deliver, and what do they receive? Who chooses whom as a trade partner? What are the ultimate explanatory variables helping us to understand patterns of specialisation and spatial patterns of interregional trade? These are the questions that any positive theory of trade must answer. As we go from positive to normative economics, we ask for information on gains or losses from trade. If trade is affected by removing artificial barriers such as tariffs or quotas or by improving the transportation system, will there be gains or possibly losses? What are their respective magnitudes, and – most important for us as regional scientists – where are the gains and where are the possible losses located?

The first comprehensive answer within a modern theoretical framework to these positive and normative questions was given by Bertil Ohlin in his pioneering monograph *Interregional and International Trade* (Ohlin, 1933, 1968). I take this as the leitmotiv of this chapter. Not only the subject, but also the place and the time of the Summer Institute in Eksjö, Sweden, give good reasons to remember this monumental work. Bertil Ohlin was born less than 200 kilometres south of Eksjö, in a village called Klippan, a little more than a century ago. As a child, he was keen on calculating the money worth of certain cakes his mother was baking. As the 1977 Nobel laureate said in his autobiography, this was the reason why, besides maths and statistics, he studied economics at the University of Lund. It is almost exactly 80 years ago that he submitted his master thesis to Knut Wicksell, after he had heard about Eli Heckscher and become his scholar at the Stockholm Business School.

In this thesis Ohlin discovered that the classical issues of trade theory, at that time entirely based on the labour theory of value, could be reconstructed 'in harmony with the mutual interdependence theory of pricing' (Ohlin, 1933, 1968). Mutual interdependence theory of pricing was what we today call general equilibrium theory. This discovery paved the way for elaborating a full theory of trade, which in 1933 was published as *Interregional and International Trade*.

How are the two aspects of this chapter, interregional and international trade, related? Most economists believe that the modern theory of international trade was established first, with the well-known assumptions of costless tradable goods, with factors completely immobile between nations and perfectly mobile between sectors within nations. They believe that only later did regional economists, residing more at the margin of mainstream economics, borrow that theory and apply it to the spatial world in order to study the regional division of labour and interregional trade.

To do Ohlin justice, one must stress that he developed the logic of his argument just the other way round, from interregional to international trade. Part One of his book is about interregional trade and 'Part Two applies the theory of interregional trade to a special case, one in which regions are different countries' (Ohlin, 1933, 1968, p. 49). In his 'Reflections on Contemporary International Trade Theories', added as an appendix to the 1968 edition of the book, Ohlin re-emphasised that this is the only logical way to go: 'Location theory is more extensive than international trade theory. A large part of trade theory can be regarded as a small part of location theory, wherein certain aspects are emphasised more than others' (Ohlin, 1933, 1968, p. 308). There is no international trade theory that is distinct from location theory. The theory of location of economic activity is the basis, interregional trade is its integral component, and international trade is a special case.

Section 2 of this chapter reviews the main discrepancies between the predictions of the Heckscher–Ohlin–Samuelson (HOS) theory and empirical evidence, relying on results from the literature. Section 3 then focuses on bilateral trade, which the HOS model either is silent about (in the case of zero costs for goods transfer), or predicts in a way sharply contradicting the evidence (in the case of positive transfer cost). Section 4 advocates the gravity model as the right tool for modelling bilateral trade flows. I underline Deardorff's (1998) argument that it is a complement of rather than a substitute for the HOS model. The theoretical underpinning of the gravity model discussed in section 4 is not just a value in itself; it also helps us to understand better how to apply it to comparative statics, welfare evaluation, accessibility measurement and econometric specification. Explaining why is the main focus of this chapter (subsections 4.3 to 4.6). Section 5 briefly concludes.

2 HOS THEORY OF TRADE

The main messages of the Heckscher–Ohlin–Samuelson model of trade are well known:

1. Regions specialise partly or fully in those goods that make relatively intensive use (in comparison to other goods) of those factors that are relatively abundant (in comparison to other regions) in the respective region.
2. Even with differing factor proportions, factor prices tend to be equalised between regions through trade. They are completely equalised if factor intensities differ sufficiently between sectors and if factor proportions do not differ too much between regions.
3. As to trade policy on the national scale, the most important conclusion of the theory is the support of the free trade doctrine: free trade is superior to protection for each participating country. And for a country sufficiently small to have no significant influence on world prices, free trade is still superior to any form of protection, even if other countries stick to protectionism.

How does the theory perform empirically (see Helpman, 1998)? As to prediction 1: if specialisation is incomplete, if there are no transport costs, and if the number of factors does not exceed the number of industries, then price equality of goods implies price equality of factors, which implies equality of input–output coefficients, which in turn implies a linear restriction on observations about factor stocks and trade balances:

$$F_{kr} = \sum_i a_{ki}\left(T_{ir} + s_r D_i\right).$$

F_{kr} is the stock of factor k in region r. a_{ki} is the (direct plus indirect) input of factor k per unit of final demand for goods from industry i; it is everywhere the same, because technologies and prices are everywhere the same. T_{ir} is the net export of industry i in region r, s_r is region r's share in world income. D_i is worldwide final demand for goods from industry i. Stacking these equations for all factors, this becomes in matrix notation:

$$\mathbf{F}_r = \mathbf{AT}_r + s_r\mathbf{AD}.$$

$\mathbf{F}_r$, $\mathbf{T}_r$ and $\mathbf{D}$ are column vectors with entries F_{kr}, T_{ir} and D_i, respectively. $\mathbf{A}$ is a matrix with entry a_{ki} in row k and column i. After rearrangement we obtain:

$$\mathbf{AT}_r = \mathbf{F}_r - s_r\mathbf{AD}$$

factor content of trade = factor abundance

For international trade data such defined factor abundance correlates significantly positively with trade factor content – good news for the theory. But the correlation is small, and the slope of the regression line, which should be close to one, is closer to zero – bad news for the theory. Trefler (1995) shows that the factor content measure on the left-hand side tends to be much smaller in absolute value than the abundance measure on the right-hand side, even if the signs of both sides coincide, as they should. That means countries trade much less in factors than they should, given their respective factor abundance. This is the so-called missing trade puzzle.

As to prediction 2: this prediction is dramatically at odds with the data.

One common cause for partial failure of prediction 1 and total failure of prediction 2 is quality differentials in factors, the neglect of which leads to biased factor stock estimates. As always, if a theory fails, you may modify assumptions until you reproduce the data well, but at the cost of losing the predictive power of the theory. The extreme case in point is to regard factor price differentials as indicators of factor qualities. If Swedish wages are five times Polish wages, say, then one Swede's hour of labour is counted as equivalent to five hours of a Polish worker's labour. Then factor price equalisation holds true again, in this case, however, not as a theoretical conclusion, but as a definition.

Similarly, prediction 1 can be reconciled with the data by allowing technologies as well as final demand compositions to vary over regions. But eventually, if you take regional accounts to infer on region specific A_r and D_s, then the prediction mutates to an accounting identity that is of course always true, and the predictive power of the theory is completely lost.

Finding deeper reasons without stepping into the tautology trap means seeking explanations under the assumption that, a priori, the set of potential technologies as well as the wants of human beings are everywhere the same. Different lines of thought have emerged in the last two decades, seeking a deeper explanation for the missing trade phenomenon. One is to allow for imperfect competition and economies of scale; this is a very wide field of research, and I only touch upon it later in this chapter in a different context. Another, and – surprisingly enough – one that has only very recently been pursued in mainstream trade economics, is to go back to Ohlin. He reminds us that interregional trade with zero transfer costs is just a very special, though pedagogically helpful, case of his theory of interregional trade.

Obstfeld and Rogoff in a recent paper (2000) itemise six puzzles in international economics, of which the missing trade puzzle is number 2. They point to the fact that transfer costs are an obvious explanation of this, and what is more remarkable, at the same time an explanation of the other puzzles as well. Of course this is already crystal clear in chapter eight of Ohlin's book, showing that 'costs of transfer thus reduce trade and weaken its tendency to equalize commodity and factor prices' (Ohlin, 1933, 1968, p. 100). It is still open to question in empirical trade research whether the missing trade phenomenon is completely explained by transfer costs. Transfer costs also help in explaining worldwide factor price differentials (Obstfeld and Rogoff, 2000).

To what extent lack of fit of the two mentioned predictions with the data can be reconciled by introducing transfer costs is still a matter of current research. This research requires incorporating transfer costs into trade models, and I will explain shortly how this is accomplished. Before I do so, however, I want to mention another contradiction between Ohlin's trade model and the data.

3 BILATERAL TRADE

Up to now, I have only mentioned net trade balances of regions, not gross bilateral flows. Without transfer costs, bilateral trade flows are indeterminate in Ohlin's model, and with transfer costs, their pattern is strange: there would be no cross-hauling, and almost the entire trade matrix would be filled with zero entries.

In an equilibrium, the complementarity

$$x_{rs} \geq 0, p_s \leq p_r + \tau_{rs}, x_{rs}(p_s - p_r - \tau_{rs}) = 0$$

must hold, with x_{rs} and τ_{rs} denoting trade from r to s and its transfer cost per unit, respectively, and p_r and p_s denoting prices in r and s, respectively. This complementarity implies that x_{rs} solves the linear programming transportation problem

$$x_{rs} = \text{argmin}\left\{ \sum_{rs} x_{rs}\tau_{rs} \middle| \sum_{r} x_{rs} = D_s, \sum_{s} x_{rs} = S_r, x_{rs} \geq 0 \right\}$$

with total supply S_r in region r and total demand D_s in region s. This, in turn, implies that – except for non-generic degenerate cases – there are only $2R-1$ (or fewer) positive entries in the trade matrix, if there are R regions (Dorfman, Samuelson and Solow, 1958). The complementarity has further implications, bringing the theory in sharp contradiction with the data. It says in particular that there should be little or no trade between regions that are similar or alike. Hence, in world trade, we should observe the bulk of trade flows between developed and less developed countries, and little or no trade within the developed world. Just the opposite is true. Another implication is that there should be no intra-industry trade. But, in particular within the developed world, even small regions export and import goods belonging to one and the same industry.

Regional scientists doing applied research, for example in transportation, were often not so much interested in net regional exports as in gross bilateral flows. For them, a model with such a strange implication as Ohlin's was of little help. Hence, for purely empirical reasons, they relied on a different approach, the gravity equation, already known as a tool for describing interregional flows in the nineteenth century. Mainstream economists remained critical of this atheoretical description, even though its ability to describe the data was obvious and well documented again and again. Estimates of the gravity model have produced, as Leamer and Levinsohn (1995, p. 1384) put it, 'some of the clearest and most robust empirical findings in economics'.

But during the last two decades international trade theory has started seriously to take account of product heterogeneity, which is both an undeniable fact of life and an obvious reason for intra-industry trade. What happened was that a gravity formula was the natural outcome of applying standard instruments of microeconomic analysis such as monopolistic competition equilibrium and CES functional forms. The ground was laid by Dixit and Stiglitz (1977); Ethier (1982), Helpman and Krugman (1985) and others applied their formalism to trade modelling. This is a nice event in the development of science: here is the gravity law as an excellent description of stylised facts; there is a theory. In the beginning there is no connection between them. Proponents of one approach even disapprove of the other approach, respectively. But in the end the one approach, the gravity equation, turns out to be a reduced form of the other, the microeconomic equilibrium theory of trade with heterogeneous goods.

4 THE NEW THEORY OF TRADE GRAVITY

Let us concentrate now on bilateral gross flows, taking output S_r and demand D_s in the origin and destination as given. (Note, however, that taking them as given does not mean regarding them as constant. We shall come back to that.) Then the theory of trade with heterogeneous goods is nothing but equating demand and supply, with choice between varieties of goods governed by a CES function (for derivations see, e.g., Bröcker, 1995 or 2000):

$$\tilde{x}_{rs} = \frac{n_r (p_r t_{rs})^{1-\sigma}}{\sum_{r'} n_{r'} (p_{r'} t_{r's})^{1-\sigma}} \tilde{D}_s,$$

$$\tilde{S}_r = \sum_s \tilde{x}_{rs}.$$

$\tilde{x}_{rs}$ is trade in value rather than in quantity terms (similarly for total supply and demand). p_r is the producer price in the region of origin. n_r denotes the number of symmetrical varieties available in r. The parameter $\sigma > 1$ is the elasticity of substitution among varieties. Transfer cost is assumed to have the 'iceberg form' going back to von Thünen (1826) (though not under this name), meaning that transferred goods are partly melting on their way, such that of one unit sent off from r only $1/t_{rs}$, $t_{rs} > 1$, units arrive in the destination s.[1] The consumer price for one unit of a single variety in the destination region s is $p_r t_{rs}$.

One can define a composite price for the destination, measuring the minimal cost per unit of a composite good:

$$q_s = \left(\sum_r n_r (p_r t_{rs})^{1-\sigma} \right)^{1/(1-\sigma)}.$$

Using this, the trade model shows up in a form very familiar to regional scientists:

$$\tilde{x}_{rs} = n_r p_r^{1-\sigma} t_{rs}^{1-\sigma} q_s^{\sigma-1} \tilde{D}_s,$$

$$\tilde{S}_r = \sum_s \tilde{x}_{rs},$$

$$\tilde{D}_s = \sum_r \tilde{x}_{rs}.$$

Even more familiar is the case where n_r, the number of brands, is proportional to real output S_r, defined as $S_r = \tilde{S}_r / p_r$. This is the special case of Dixit–Stiglitz (1977) competition. Output variation comes in the form of variation in the number of brands, while output per brand is constant. The system then reads:

$$\tilde{x}_{rs} = \tilde{S}_r p_r^{-\sigma} t_{rs}^{1-\sigma} q_s^{\sigma-1} \tilde{D}_s, \tag{2.1}$$

$$\tilde{S}_r = \sum_s \tilde{x}_{rs}, \tag{2.2}$$

$$\tilde{D}_s = \sum_r \tilde{x}_{rs}. \tag{2.3}$$

This is, in Wilson's (1970) terminology, a doubly constrained gravity model with distance term $t_{rs}^{1-\sigma}$, masses $\tilde{S}_r$ and $\tilde{D}_s$, and with prices playing the role of balancing factors. Note, however, that the masses are themselves endogenous in a mutual interdependence theory, depending *inter alia* on prices.

What is gained with this theoretical derivation of the gravity equation? It helps in completing the theory as well as in applying it to empirical research, as we show in the following sections.

4.1 Filling the Bilateral Trade Gap in Ohlin's Theory

The gravity model closes the gap left by Ohlin's theory that left bilateral gross flows unexplained. Comparative advantage theory of specialisation and gravity theory of bilateral trade are not competitors; they are complements (see Deardorff, 1998). In a combined approach there is a gravity equation for each sector within a general equilibrium model. The endogenous prices link the trade equation with regional production and consumption, which themselves appear in the trade equation. In regional science terminology, the trade equation is a doubly elastically constrained gravity model. In value terms, trade flows consistently add up to supply and demand. Supply and demand, though, are not fixed, but react to prices.

We said before that, in Ohlin's model, trade flows are undetermined when transfer costs are zero. Even this gap can be closed now. The world with homogeneous goods and vanishing transfer costs can be understood as an extreme limiting case, where σ goes to infinity and – at the same time – t_{rs}, the mark-up factor for trade costs, goes to one.

Look at the limiting behaviour exhibited by the solution of Equations 2.1 to 2.3, if σ goes to infinity, while S_r, D_s, and $f_{rs} := t_{rs}^{-\sigma}$ are held constant. We may rewrite these equations as:

$$\tilde{x}_{rs} = a_r b_s f_{rs},$$
$$\tilde{S}_r = \sum_s \tilde{x}_{rs},$$
$$\tilde{D}_s = \sum_r \tilde{x}_{rs}.$$

For f_{rs}, $\tilde{S}_r$ and $\tilde{D}_s$ all strictly positive, and $\sum_r \tilde{S}_r = \sum_s \tilde{D}_s$, a solution is well known to exist and to be unique with respect to $\tilde{x}_{rs}$ (McGill, 1977). Obviously, this solution does not depend on σ, given our assumptions. Hence there are constants $c_{rs} := \log(a_r b_s)$ for all pairs $\{r, s\}$, such that

$$-\sigma \log p_r + (\sigma - 1)\log q_s = c_{rs}.$$

Dividing by σ and letting σ go to infinity yields $\log p_r = \log q_s$ for all pairs $\{r,s\}$. This implies that all prices tend to be equal if σ becomes large, though with a common limit undetermined by the equation system. Hence, in the limiting case we return to Ohlin's model for determining production and consumption in each region, and embed into it a doubly constrained gravity model for determining gross bilateral trade flows.

A different limit is obtained if the rate with which $\log t_{rs}$ goes to zero is faster than that with which σ goes to infinity. Then $t_{rs}^{1-\sigma}$ tends to one, and $\tilde{x}_{rs}$ tends to

$$\tilde{x}_{rs} = \frac{\tilde{S}_r \tilde{D}_s}{\Sigma_r \tilde{S}_r},$$

a familiar expression as well.

4.2 Using the Gravity Equation for Estimating Trade Barriers

It is widely recognised now that the gravity model is an extremely powerful tool for estimating factors impeding or enhancing trade. One estimates the equation in its value form, with $\log t_{rs}$ typically assumed to depend linearly on distance and other metric or nominal variables g_{rs}^i, measuring for example tariffs, exchange rate volatilities, the belonging or not belonging to a common market or to a common currency union, speaking or not speaking a common language, having or not having historical ties and, most importantly, belonging or not belonging to the same country:

$$t_{rs}^{1-\sigma} = \exp\left[(1-\sigma\left(\sum_i \alpha^i g_{rs}^i\right)\right]$$

$$= \exp\left[\sum_i \beta^i g_{rs}^i\right]$$

with $\beta^i := (1-\sigma)\alpha^i$. A positive α^i indicates a trade-impeding effect.

Since Tinbergen's (1962) and Linnemann's (1966) pioneering work, an endless series of estimates has been published on effects of all kinds of trade-impeding or trade-promoting factors. It is time for a meta-study on gravity estimates, showing means and medians, ranges and standard deviations of all these effects, listing references and so forth. This is beyond the scope of this chapter, however. Just as an illustration I pick from my own work and that of a few others some rough subjective point estimates for a couple of qualitative variables, shown in Table 2.1. The effect given in the table is the trade multiplier, defined as

$$M^i := \exp(\beta^i)$$

for effect i and $g_{rs}^i \in \{0,1\}$. The multiplier says by which factor trade is higher or lower if the effect is there, compared to if it was absent, other things equal. I give a warning, however, about what 'other things equal' means here, and come back to that later.

Table 2.1 Gravity estimates of effects on trade

Effect	Reference	Multiplier M^i
Common EU membership	Bergstrand (1985), Bröcker and Rohweder (1990), Helliwell (1998)	3/2
Adjacency	Bergstrand (1985), Bröcker and Rohweder (1990)	2
Common language	Bröcker (2001a, b), Helliwell (1998)	2
Former iron curtain	Bröcker (2001a, b)	1/2
Currency union	Rose (2002)	2
National border within EU	Bröcker (1984), Helliwell (1998)	1/6

To be sure, the gravity equation has been used widely for estimating trade impediments and factors enhancing trade long before its revival in mainstream economics. However, we now understand some problems related to the gravity equation better than before, namely:

1. the use of the gravity equation in comparative statics,
2. the use of the gravity equation in welfare evaluation,
3. the relation between prices and accessibility measurement, and
4. possible misspecification biases resulting from neglecting price terms in the equation.

I briefly touch upon these points in turn.

4.3 Comparative Statics

As to 1: we have just defined the trade multiplier M^i using the *ceteris paribus* clause. The point we now understand better than before is that the other terms in the equation cannot remain constant, in general, if trade impediments change. To see this, just notice that prices depend on trade costs, and remember that – in a mutual interdependence theory of prices, as Ohlin called it – supply and demand are not constant either but react to prices. How prices are related to trade costs is seen better if the equilibrium condition is solved for the supply price. That gives the system (in real terms) in the following form:

$$x_{rs} = S_r p_r^{-\sigma} t_{rs}^{1-\sigma} q_s^{\sigma} D_s, \qquad (2.4)$$

$$q_s = \left(\sum_r S_r (p_r t_{rs})^{1-\sigma} \right)^{1/(1-\sigma)}, \qquad (2.5)$$

$$p_r = \left(\sum_s D_s q_s^{\sigma} t_{rs}^{1-\sigma} \right)^{1/\sigma}. \qquad (2.6)$$

The question is: if the endogeneity of the other terms in the equation is taken into account, will the multiplier then be larger than, equal to, or smaller than the true effect of the respective factor on trade? Formally, which relation will hold in

$$M^i \begin{Bmatrix} < \\ = \\ > \end{Bmatrix} x_{rs}^1 \,/\, x_{rs}^0,$$

with x_{rs}^1 and x_{rs}^0 denoting trade with effect i being in place or absent, respectively?

There is one special case where equality holds, that is, where one can accept the 'other things equal' assumption. Suppose the respective trade flows x_{rs} directly affected by the change of the impediments are small, both in relation to supply in the respective regions of origin r and in relation to demand in the respective regions of destination s. Then there is hardly any price change, because the respective t_{rs} has only a small weight in the price equations.

But what about the general case? No conclusive answer can be given, but in practice the multiplier is likely to be an overestimate more often than the opposite, and sometimes even a large overestimate. For understanding the general case, assume constant price elasticities of supply and demand,

$$S_r = \zeta_r p_r^{\varepsilon},$$
$$D_s = \delta_s q_s^{-\mu},$$

and insert this into the real trade equation:

$$x_{rs} = \zeta_r p_r^{\varepsilon-\sigma} t_{rs}^{1-\sigma} q_s^{\sigma-\mu} \delta_s,$$

$$q_s = \left(\sum_r \zeta_r p_r^{\varepsilon+1-\sigma} t_{rs}^{1-\sigma} \right)^{1/(1-\sigma)},$$

$$p_r = \left(\sum_s \delta_s q_s^{\sigma-\mu} t_{rs}^{1-\sigma} \right)^{1/\sigma}.$$

Now another case shows up, where the multiplier is just the correct prediction, namely when $\varepsilon = \sigma = \mu$. Then the price terms cancel, and trade changes exactly as predicted by the multiplier.

The realistic case is that the price elasticities of supply and demand are smaller than the elasticity of substitution. If this is the case, the multiplier always exaggerates the two effects. Why? Assume for example that we remove transfer costs between r and s by establishing a currency union that both r and s now belong to. Then t_{rs} shrinks, hence $t_{rs}^{1-\sigma}$ increases by the multiplier (by the factor 2, according to the estimate in Table 2.1). But that is not the end. Region r gets closer to the market, making p_r rise (see Equation 2.6). Region s also gets closer to the market, making q_s decline (see Equation 2.5). Both effects compensate for a part of the primary effect (see Equation 2.4), and trade increases by less than the factor 2. This is the more important, the larger the share of flows affected by the cost reductions is in the deliveries from region r and in the deliveries to region s.

4.4 Trade Impediments and Welfare

As to 2: the second thing we have learned is that the theoretical underpinning of the gravity equation also helps in understanding the welfare implications of trade impediment reductions (or increases). If, for example, a currency union halves the impediment factor in the equation, what does that mean in terms of welfare for currency union members and non-members? Look at the respective multiplier

$$M_{rs}^i = \exp\left[(1-\sigma)\alpha^i g_{rs}^i\right],$$

$$g_{rs}^i = \begin{cases} 1 \text{ if } r \text{ and } s \text{ have a common currency,} \\ 0 \qquad\qquad \text{else.} \end{cases}$$

The gravity estimate shows the impact on trade, but not the impact on welfare, because the cost term and the elasticity term are not estimated separately. If σ is large, a tiny cost change generates large trade effects. But the welfare effects would still be tiny, because small cost changes lead to small price changes (see Equations 2.5 and 2.6). If σ is small, even large cost changes leave trade almost unaffected, while price changes and, hence, welfare effects would also be large. Separating out the two effects is therefore – though immaterial for description and prediction – essential for evaluation.

Once we have reliable estimates on σ, the evaluation of welfare effects of changing impediments to trade is straightforward: in a partial equilibrium with price-dependent supply and demand we calculate the new equilibrium after removing some impediment, and then obtain welfare changes in each region by the areas left of the supply and demand curves, between old and new prices. In particular, assuming constant elasticity supply and demand as above,

$$S_r = \zeta_r p_r^{\varepsilon},$$

$$D_s = \delta_s q_s^{-\mu},$$

we obtain welfare measures for each location as

$$\text{producer} - \text{surplus}_r = \frac{1}{1+\varepsilon}\tilde{S}_r^0\left[\left(\frac{p_r^1}{p_r^0}\right)^{1+\varepsilon} - 1\right],$$

$$\text{consumer} - \text{surplus}_s = \begin{cases} \dfrac{1}{1-\mu}\tilde{D}_s^0\left[1 - \left(\dfrac{q_s^1}{q_s^0}\right)^{1-\mu}\right] & \text{for } \mu \neq 1 \\ \tilde{D}_S^0 \log\left(\dfrac{q_s^0}{q_s^1}\right) & \text{for } \mu = 1. \end{cases}$$

Superscripts 0 and 1 denote pre-change and post-change, respectively.

If we embed the gravity model into a general equilibrium, then we evaluate welfare effects by households' utility functions and translate them into monetary terms by Hicks's measures of variation – as usual in applied general equilibrium analysis.

4.5 Gravity and Potential

As to 3: a nice observation is that with new trade theory we have not only a theory of gravity, but also one of potential. To see why, let us repeat the price equations:

$$q_s = \left(\sum_r S_r (p_r t_{rs})^{1-\sigma} \right)^{1/(1-\sigma)},$$

$$p_r = \left(\sum_s D_s q_s^{\sigma} t_{rs}^{1-\sigma} \right)^{1/\sigma}.$$

The supply price p_r obtained in the origin r is an increasing function of the demand potential in the traditional sense, though with a slight, but important, modification: demand is not only discounted by a transfer cost factor; it is also weighted by the price in the destination. This price measures the degree of competition a supplier is facing in the destination. A high price q_s means bad access of the consumers in the destination to other suppliers and, hence, low competition (and vice versa).

Similarly, the demand price q_s to be paid per unit of a composite good in the destination is a decreasing function of the supply potential in the traditional sense, though with a slight, but important, modification: supply is not only discounted by a transfer cost factor; it is also weighted by the inverse price in the origin. Higher supply prices reduce the supply potential and, hence, increase the demand price.

4.6 Improving the Estimates

As to 4: a final point is that we know now that market sizes as well as prices have to appear in the trade equation. If we omit the latter, as in the traditional estimates of gravity equations, than we get an omitted variable bias, because prices and other explaining variables are not orthogonal. In the context of estimating border effects this bias has recently been shown to be considerable (Anderson and van Wincoop, 2001), and reliability of the estimates is improved now, since we better understand the theory behind the equation.

5 SUMMARY AND CONCLUSION

Summing up, we can say that, regarding the development of theory, we are in a comfortable position now, having at hand a toolbox of theories that are attractive in several respects:

1. They fit the data well, at least as far as trade itself is concerned. With regard to further implications for spatial factor prices and income distribution, additional factors explaining productivity differentials have to be added.
2. The different brands of theory, traditional Ohlin theory and the more

recent heterogeneous markets theory, are not contradictory, and they turn out not to be separated from one another, but they deal with different aspects and fit well together in modern general equilibrium theory, including product heterogeneity and monopolistic competition.

3. The toolbox is operational in the sense that, on the basis of the theory, we can set up parametric models that can be estimated or calibrated and used for quantitative simulation studies on effects of policies affecting trade, such as deepening integration, enlarging the EU, improving transportation, taxing externalities in transport and so forth.

We have seen much progress in the eight decades after Ohlin's first contribution to modern trade theory. It has brought us from abstract models to operational tools for analysing real trade data that are deeply rooted in modern microeconomics. Only a small subset of these developments, those related to the gravity equation, has been discussed in this chapter. Many other interesting developments such as trade and endogenous agglomeration (the subject of New Economic Geography), trade and strategic interaction in oligopolistic markets, and trade and location in a dynamic setting could not be dealt with in this brief chapter. None of these developments would have been possible without Ohlin teaching us the power of 'mutual interdependence theory' for understanding trade.

NOTE

1 Icebergs have been strongly attacked by Isard et al. (1998); one can do without the somewhat strange iceberg assumption in trade modelling (see Bröcker, 2001a), but at the cost of some equation aesthetics.

REFERENCES

Anderson, J.E. and E. van Wincoop (2001), 'Gravity with Gravitas: A Solution to the Border Puzzle', NBER Working Paper No. 8079.

Bergstrand, J.H. (1985), 'The Gravity Equation in International Trade: Some Microeconomic Foundations and Empirical Evidence', *Review of Economics and Statistics*, **67**, 474–81.

Bröcker, J. (1984), 'How do International Trade Barriers Affect Interregional Trade?' in W. Isard and T. Puu (eds), *Regional and Industrial Development Theories: Models and Empirical Evidence*, Amsterdam: North-Holland, pp. 219–39.

Bröcker, J. (1995), 'Chamberlinian Spatial CGE Modelling: A Theoretical Framework', *Economic Systems Research*, **7**, 137–49.

Bröcker, J. (2000), 'How Would an EU-membership of the Visegrád Countries Affect Europe's Economic Geography?', *Annals of Regional Science*, **32**, 91–114, 1998. 'Erratum', **34**, 469–71.

Bröcker, J. (2001a), 'Spatial Effects of Transport Infrastructure: The Role of Market

Structure', in J.R. Roy and W. Schulz (eds), *Theory of Regional Competition*, Baden-Baden: Nomos, pp. 181–93.

Bröcker, J. (2001b), 'Trans-European Effects of "Trans-European Networks"', in F. Bolle and M. Carlberg (eds), *Advances in Behavioral Economics, Essays in Honor of Horst Todt*, Heidelberg: Physica-Verlag, pp. 141–57.

Bröcker, J. and H.C. Rohweder (1990), 'Barriers to International Trade: Methods of Measurement and Empirical Evidence', *Annals of Regional Science*, **24**, 289–305.

Deardorff, A.V. (1998), 'Determinants of Bilateral Trade: Does Gravity Work in a Neoclassical World?', in J.A. Frankel (ed.), *The Regionalization of the World Economy*, Chicago: University of Chicago Press.

Dixit, A. and J. Stiglitz (1977), 'Monopolistic Competition and Optimal Product Diversity', *American Economic Review*, **67**, 297–308.

Dorfman, R., P.A. Samuelson and R.M. Solow (1958), *Linear Programming and Economic Analysis*, New York: McGraw-Hill.

Ethier, W.J. (1982), 'National and International Returns to Scale in the Modern Theory of International Trade', *American Economic Review*, **72**, 389–405.

Helliwell, J.F. (1998), *How Much Do National Borders Matter?*, Washington, DC: Brookings Institution Press.

Helpman, E. and P.R. Krugman (1985), *Market Structure and Foreign Trade: Increasing Returns, Imperfect Competition, and the International Economy*, Cambridge, MA: MIT Press.

Helpman, Elhanan (1998), 'The Structure of Foreign Trade', *NBER working paper No. 6752*.

Isard, W., I.J. Azis, M.P. Drennan, R.E. Miller, S. Saltzman and E. Thorbecke (1998), *Methods of Interregional and Regional Analysis*, Regional Science Studies Series, Aldershot: Ashgate.

Leamer, E.E. and J. Levinsohn (1995), 'International Trade Theory: The Evidence', in G. Grossman and K. Rogoff (eds), *Handbook of International Economics, Vol. 3*, Amsterdam: North-Holland, pp. 1339–94.

Linnemann, H. (1966), *An Econometric Study of International Trade Flows*, Amsterdam: North-Holland.

McGill, S.M. (1977), 'Theoretical Properties of Biproportional Matrix Adjustments', *Environment and Planning A*, **9**, 687–701.

Obstfeld, M. and K. Rogoff (2000), 'The Six Major Puzzles in International Macroeconomics: Is There a Common Cause?' *NBER Macroeconomics Annual*, **15**, 339–90.

Ohlin, B. (1933), *Interregional and International Trade*, 2nd rev. edition (1968), Cambridge: Cambridge University Press.

Rose, A. (2002), The Effect of Common Currencies on International Trade: A Meta-analysis, Draft, 8. April, http://faculty.haas.berkeley.edu/arose/meta.pdf.

Tinbergen, J. (1962), *Shaping the World Economy: Suggestions for an International Economic Policy*, New York: The Twentieth Century Fund.

Trefler, D. (1995), 'The Case of Missing Trade and Other Mysteries', *American Economic Review*, **85**, 1029–46.

Wilson, A.G. (1970), *Entropy in Urban and Regional Modelling*, London: Pion.

von Thünen, J.H. (1826), *Der isolierte Staat in Beziehung auf Landwirtschaft und Nationalökonomie*, Hamburg: Friedrich Perthes.

3. Cross-Border Cooperation and Local Development: Evidence from Eastern Poland Border Regions

Mikolaj Herbst and Karol Olejniczak

1 INTRODUCTION

Transformation of Central and Eastern Europe in the decade of the 1990s opened the borders between countries of the region and enabled cross-border cooperation. This had a tremendous impact on the development of the border areas.

This chapter is devoted to the role of the state border in the economic and social development of regions in transition. Observations and findings presented below are the result of three case studies of towns located on Poland's eastern border, namely: Sejny, at the Polish–Lithuanian border, Terespol, at the Polish–Belarussian border and Przemyśl, at the Polish–Ukrainian border (see Figure 3.1). The project was conducted by the Centre for European Regional and Local Studies, Warsaw University, within a wider research programme in the summer of 2001.

Sejny is a small town (6000 inhabitants), situated in the north part of Podlaskie region. It is the capital of the Sejnenski county. Despite the proximity of the crossing point (situated 6 km from the town), its location must be considered as peripheral and its position as continuously declining. In 1994 a new, modern border-crossing point was established in Budzisko (the corridor of Via Baltica), taking much of the international traffic out of Sejny. Second, as a result of the new administrative division of the country imposed in 1998, the distance to Bialystok (the new capital of Podlaskie region) is 140 km in comparison to 30 km between Sejny and Suwalki, the former capital of Suwalskie region.

Terespol is also a small town of 6000 inhabitants. It is located in the north-east part of Lubelskie region. The border location of the municipality is favourable owing to the main road connecting Berlin (via Warsaw and Minsk) and Moscow. Furthermore, the municipality is situated in a corridor of the planned A-2 highway, which runs quite close to a large Belarussian town – Brzesc (200 000 inhabitants).

Przemyśl is a medium-size city of 68 000 inhabitants, situated in the south-east part of Podkarpackie region, 12 km from the border-crossing point in Medyka and 100 km from Lviv (1 000 000 inhabitants). Before the new administrative division of the country was imposed, the city was the capital of Przemyskie region.

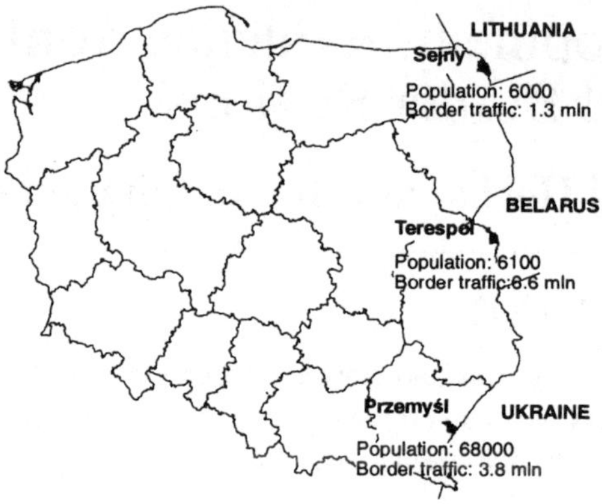

Figure 3.1 Location of case study municipalities in Poland

The chapter consists of three further sections. Section 2 provides a brief overview of selected theoretical concepts on the role of the border as a regional or local development factor.

Sections 3 and 4 are devoted to local development in eastern Poland's border areas. The following factors influencing development processes are discussed:

- The role of border physical infrastructure in local development.
- The asymmetry of local development across the border (with special reference to differences in GDP, price level and access to commodities).
- The role of local government and local society.

2 SELECTED THEORETICAL CONCEPTS

Traditional theories assign the national frontiers, the role of the separation factor – the demarcation lines between two political–institutional systems. Borders have three functions (Guichonnet and Raffestin, 1974):

- A legal function delimiting the territories under the jurisdiction of a particular state.
- A control function where each crossing is controlled by the state.

- A fiscal function where the tariffs, tax law and norms of the entered state are applied.

These functions depend on the central government and in practice they limit the power of the regions to govern their internal and external relations (House, 1980; Ratti, 1993). This perspective, dominated by the national order and international politics, justifies the peripheral character of the border region.

Following this approach and looking from the perspective of local development, the borders are barriers (of very limited permeability) regulating, controlling and limiting the flow of people, goods and services. Thus the borders are definitely considered as a negative factor of local development. Consequently, the border regions are described as backward and handicapped areas. We can say that the disadvantages of the border regions come from three factors:

- Peripheral location to the central regions of the nation states (and marginal for the national market).
- Limited – or 'truncated' as Scott et al. (1996) put it – economic spheres.
- High trans-boundary transaction costs (coming from trade barriers, disjoined and nationally oriented infrastructures, different value systems).

The historic, political changes in Europe (the fall of communism), together with the processes of globalisation and the new post-Fordist economy (transnational flows, technology and transport innovation, global market strategies, global division of work, spaceless economy), forced the revision of the traditional perception of the role of borders and position of border areas.

The new theories pointed out that, due to the processes of internationalisation of economic and political life, border regions have certain advantages, overcoming traditional barriers (Hansen, 1981). These are such positive effects as:

- easier access to the cheaper resources on the opposite side of the border (labour, capital),
- easier access to the new, international markets,
- diversification of the sources of supply and directions of sale,
- a richer cultural environment (which results in a wider tourist offer as well as cross-cultural learning processes).

In this perspective the border can be seen as a contact line and can become a functional space – an intermediate element between different societies, collectivities and economic spaces (Ratti, 1993). Therefore, the border itself can be a positive factor of local development. However, the new theories do not totally oppose the old ones and they recognise the dual function of the frontier (as the dividing line and contact zone) (Ratti, 1993). They state that not every border region can develop from political and economic periphery into a zone of international cooperation and synergy.

The positive effects of synergy can take place only under the following conditions:

1. high permeability (openness) and low cost of crossing the border, and
2. asymmetry (in costs, prices, level of development, specialisation, etc.) between two sides of the border.

Where the border has high permeability but the asymmetry between areas is low, the border itself is simply a neutral factor of growth.

The interrelations and contacts between two border areas can have a different level of intensity, character and form of complexity. The different categorisations are summarised in Table 3.1, which illustrates the evolution of the border region from the divided area to a functional, integrated space with a highly developed cooperation network.

For the assessment of the border regions' development perspective we should consider theories on endogenous growth (Gorzelak, 2000). In fact, such endogenous elements as strong leadership, existence of a local elite, attitudes and mobilisation of the local community (innovation, openness, trust) and well-established local institutions (economic: agencies, incubators, etc.; and social: societies, clubs, etc.) can strengthen or multiply the positive effects of synergy coming from the border. Moreover, they can transform impulses into durable relations. They provide sustainability and stability for growth impulses that, as we shall see from the case studies, are highly unstable and temporary. Therefore, the high endogenous potential is a crucial facilitator of the transformation to higher stages of cross-border interrelations.

This chapter explores to what extent the conditions for synergy of the border areas are fulfilled in the three researched locations. It also ponders the role of 'soft factors' – endogenous potential as an additional factor of border integration. Finally, it assesses the character of the particular border areas as well as the stage of cross-border interactions (following the types presented in Table 3.1).

Table 3.1 Changes in cross-border interactions

	Social interactions	Economic interactions	Political interactions
Phase I	Alienation and hostility	No contacts, no interrelations	Informal contacts of the representatives of the legal authorities
Phase II	More or less peaceful coexistence	Spontaneous trade	Joint actions aimed at quick profits (e.g. opening of new border checkpoints)
Phase III	Inter-dependence and cooperation	Regular trade	Formalisation of contacts (e.g. Euroregions – twin associations of municipalities and districts established on both sides of the border on the basis of their national legal systems)
Phase IV	Trans-border integration	Productive cooperation Phase IV A: limited logistic cooperation Phase IV B: coordination and cooperation of the commerce associations, promotional institutions Phase IV C: close cooperation and integration – integrated productive complex	Joint actions aimed at long-term benefits (joint investments, spatial planning, etc.) Local associations merge and establish, on the basis of cross-border agreement, the cross-border region (CBR)

Sources: Based on Szul and Mync (1999), Scott et al. (1996), Krätke (1995), Perkmann (2003), Ratti (1993).

3 STATE BORDER IMPACT ON LOCAL DEVELOPMENT IN EASTERN POLAND

3.1 Local Development and the Permeability (Openness) of the Border

It is commonly recognised that economic development in border areas is dominated by factors related to the border. This involves:

1. The important role of specific physical infrastructure[1] for the local economy. The custom offices, checking points and cargo stores provide additional revenues from taxes and fees for the local budget as well as new job opportunities for the citizens.
2. The border-related services sector (hotels and restaurants, specific financial services).
3. Small-scale retail trade between individuals crossing the border and carrying small amounts of commodities.
4. Exports and imports by local manufacturing and wholesale companies.

For the last three factors on the list, the relationship between permeability (openness) of the border and local development seems self-explanatory. The greater the turnover of travellers and commodities moving from one country to another, the more revenues and indirect development opportunities the community has. One could thus put the gains related to points 2, 3 and 4 under the common name of turnover benefits. Turnover benefits rise along with increasing openness of the border, but it seems rational to assume that the relationship is characterised by diminishing returns to border permeability. While the barriers to the international flow of people and commodities are reduced, there are fewer reasons for travellers to stay in the border area, eat there or sleep there. Furthermore, increased permeability of the border will also lower the asymmetry of prices on both sides, reducing the profitability of small cross-border trade.

Let B represent turnover benefits of the local economy coming from the presence of the border. If t is a measure of border permeability, then:

$$\begin{aligned} B &= b(t) \\ b'(t) &> 0 \\ b''(t) &< 0. \end{aligned}$$

Distinct from turnover benefits, physical border infrastructure (number 1 on the list above) constitutes a development factor that is almost perfectly exogenous to the local economy. The location of the crossing points is decided by the central government in the light of international agreements, macroeconomic interests, road networks and geographic conditions. The performance and will of the local government may result in efficient or inefficient exploitation of the 'heaven-sent' opportunity (see the subsection on local government), but its appearance seems to be independent of local efforts.

The relationship between infrastructure benefits and openness of the border is less obvious than in the case of turnover benefits. Let's imagine that the border between two countries is highly impermeable, with lots of formalities required from travellers in order to go abroad and high duties imposed on international trade. The gradual lowering of barriers will initially cause increased investment in border infrastructure in response to rising turnover of travellers and commodities. This will provide new employment opportunities to the local population and additional revenues to the local government budget (due to local taxes). However, after reaching some threshold value of openness $t = T$, the border infrastructure will turn out to be unnecessarily extended. Reducing barriers in the border crossing will cause a decline in demand for border-related labour in the area. There will be fewer guards, office employees, policemen and duty officers needed to ensure proper functioning of the crossing point. As some of the offices and cargo stores are finally closed down, the municipality will lose part of its budget revenues. Municipal direct benefits from 'hosting' border-related infrastructure will then drop to zero as the border becomes completely open, as it is between most EU countries now.

Let A denote direct municipal surplus coming from border infrastructure (employment + taxes). Then:

$$\begin{aligned} A &= a(t) \\ a'(t) &> 0 \ \forall t < T \\ a'(T) &= 0 \\ a'(t) &< 0 \ \forall t > T \\ a''(t) &< 0. \end{aligned}$$

As shown in Figure 3.2, the B curve is asymptotic to some constant value representing the 'turnover benefit' of a municipality in a situation where there are no barriers to crossing the border for people or for commodities. In turn, the A curve has an inverted U-shape and drops to zero as the border is abolished. The curve A+B represents total benefits generated by the border in favour of the border area.

Let us note that the importance of A-type and B-type benefits for the municipality or region depends on endogenous potential and the scale of the local economy relative to the size of turnover for the crossing point. In particular, the smaller and/or weaker the local/regional economy is, the less it will be able to generate and exploit turnover benefits of the border (B) and the more it will be dependent on direct benefits of border infrastructure (A). The small local economy is shown in Figure 3.2 as achieving turnover benefits B_{small} and total benefits of ($A+B_{small}$) as opposed to B_{big} and ($A+B_{big}$). Note that the threshold value of openness is higher for big economies (t_b) than it is for the small one (t_s).

In small municipal economies located near the crossing points (such as Terespol and Sejny) one would expect physical border infrastructure to be dominant in determining local development.

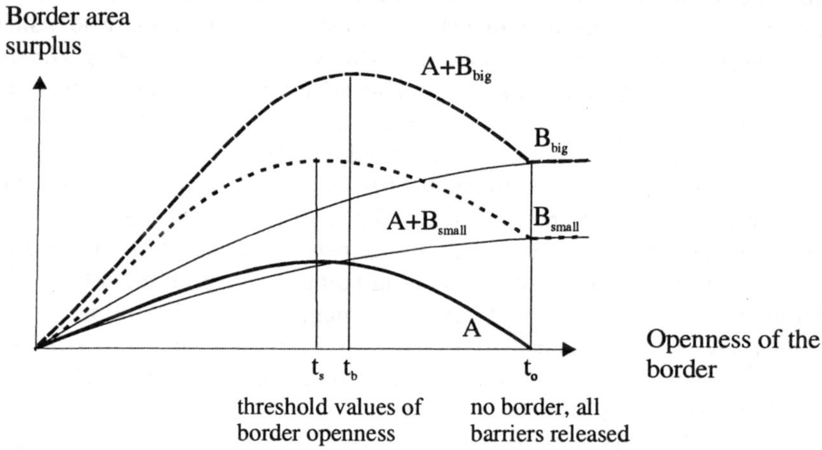

Figure 3.2 Permeability of the border and border-related benefits for the municipality

As we can see in Table 3.2, in all three municipalities the border should be regarded as a strong determinant of local economic development, but in Terespol the average number of travellers per day even exceeds the town's population. Not surprisingly, the local authority estimates the share of local population performing jobs related to border infrastructure as at least one third. Both Terespol and Sejny have to be considered as B_{small} type of local economy.

Which type of border benefits contributes more to long-term local development? Economic relationships between Polish towns and their counterparts in Ukraine and Belarus are very specific. They rely mostly on shopping and small market trade (in large part unregistered) done by local inhabitants on both sides of the crossing points. In Terespol, this very basic form of cooperation is the most important source of revenue for 20–30 per cent of the population and completely dominates other forms of B-type benefits. Although such cross-border trade involves the significant mobility of goods and travellers (some of them crossing the border 10 to 15 times a day), it does not contribute to any sustainable development of the municipality. The only factor related to the border that seems to be of strategic importance for the local communities is the physical infrastructure built by the state. Most job opportunities and tax revenues for the municipalities lying in the border area are closely related to formalities and barriers in cross-border traffic. It is the need to pay custom fees that creates jobs in stores and offices for local inhabitants. Similarly, the visa requirements (non-existent between Poland and its eastern neighbours, but to be imposed after EU accession) increase the local demand for labour in the checking points and guard units. Reducing the border-crossing restrictions makes some of the infrastructure useless, which may worsen the economic situation of the municipality.

Table 3.2 Population and the number of travellers in the municipalities located at the border in 2000

Crossing point in	Average number of travellers per day	Municipality population
Przemyśl (Polish-Ukrainian)	10 500	68 000
Sejny (Polish-Lithuanian)	3 500	10 500
Terespol (Polish-Belarussian)	18 000	13 500*

Note: * Both urban and rural municipality of Terespol included.

Source: Central Statistical Office (CSO).

When thinking of long-term development, the main weakness of municipalities located on the Polish eastern border is that although many individuals' incomes depend heavily on the openness of the border (small trade and services), it seems that only the barriers and sustaining asymmetry between two neighbouring countries constitute a serious (but only a short-term) basis for the growth of municipal economies. In fact those municipalities are more A-type than B-type beneficiaries of the border, and moreover, even those activities within the B-type that are well developed (such as small trade) do not contribute to the long-term accumulation of income.

3.2 Asymmetry as a Local Development Factor in Border Areas

Up to now, the analysis has been conducted under the strong assumption that opening the border will have no effect on asymmetries between neighbouring countries. This assumption, although helpful, does not seem very realistic. We are going to relax it and see how the change in asymmetry level affects the mechanisms described in the preceding paragraph.

Observations made in eastern Poland border regions revealed three types of asymmetry inducing cross-border cooperation:

- asymmetry in income,
- asymmetry in prices,
- asymmetry in access to commodities.

Asymmetry may be perceived as a 'catalyst' for cross-border cooperation. As suggested by international trade theory, uneven availability of production factors (and related asymmetry in prices and income) should lead to specialisation of production on both sides of the border. A physical proximity of local economies on each side of the border also allows a direct import of foreign production factors. The higher the asymmetry, the more profitable is cross-border business cooperation. Equalising the level of development between countries inevitably contributes to lowering border location rent by reducing benefits from cross-border trade of goods and services.

Considering again Figure 3.2, one should note that a decrease in asymmetry (of any type) between countries will depress only B-type (turnover) benefits of a local economy, leaving the A-type (direct infrastructure) benefits unchanged. Turnover benefits consist in large part of profits from international trade of goods, services and production factors, while direct gains from border infrastructure depend mostly on political decisions of central government and are insensitive to the performance of the local economy or the intensity of cross-border relationships. As a consequence, a decrease in asymmetry between countries will (*ceteris paribus*) cause a downward and leftward shift in total benefits generated by the border (A+B). As shown in Figure 3.3, the optimal (threshold) value of border openness is expected to be lower in the case of low asymmetry between countries than it would be between highly differentiated neighbours.

Differences in the level of income between Poland and its eastern neighbouring countries are not as significant as between Germany and Poland; however, they are noticeable. The greatest asymmetry is observed between Poland and Ukraine. In 1996 Ukrainian GDP per capita was only 23 per cent of Polish GDP per capita. The gap between these two countries is still widening. In 2000 the value of this indicator was only 16 per cent. According to official World Bank data, GDPs per capita in Lithuania and Belarus were similar, at about 75 per cent of Polish GDP in 2000, with the gap showing a tendency to decrease. Such disparities should provide a strong incentive for economic cooperation between the neighbouring countries, and should induce firms to establish closer supply linkages.

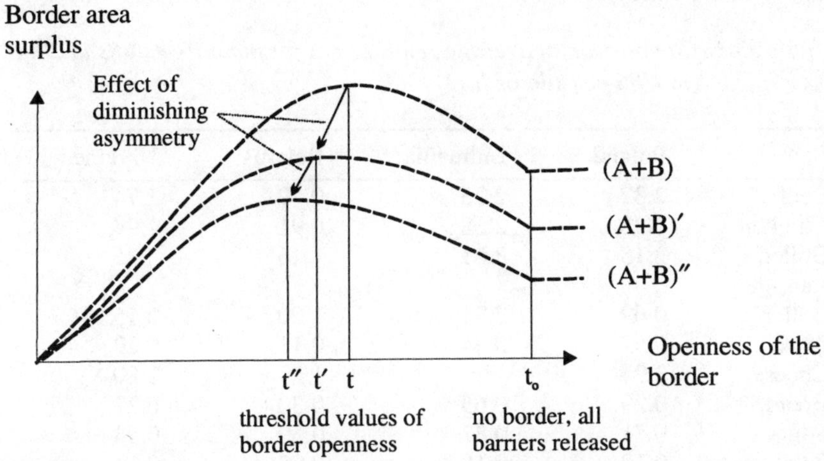

Figure 3.3 *The role of asymmetry in development of border areas*

Table 3.3 *Four countries' GDP per capita (US$); Poland = 100%*

Country	1996	1998 (US$)	2000	1996	1998 (%)	2000
Belarus	2124	2562	2993	57	63	73
Lithuania	2128	2902	3062	57	71	75
Ukraine	872	833	642	23	20	16
Poland	3724	4098	4081	100	100	100

Source: World Development Indicators, database of the World Bank.

Besides the asymmetry in income, an important role in the development of cross-border economic cooperation is played by the differences in prices of commodities. Eastern neighbours of Poland are its most important partners in international trade. In 1997 (shortly before the financial crisis in Russia), trade with ex-Soviet Union countries amounted to 17.3 per cent of total Polish exports.

Asymmetry in prices induces both large-scale wholesale trade and small-scale trade, carried on in marketplaces located along the border. In municipalities located at the Ukrainian or Belarussian borders, the marketplaces are a very important part of local economies and frequently the principal employer on the local labour market. As shown in Table 3.4, the differences in prices of main foodstuffs between those countries and Poland are still substantial, while Lithuanian prices have already become equal to or higher than Polish ones.

Table 3.4 Comparison of average retail prices for main foodstuffs in 2000 (in US$ per kilo or litre)

Item	Poland	Lithuania	Belarus	Ukraine
Beef	2.37	2.26	0.79	1.74
Chicken	1.38	2.58	0.91	1.94
Boiled sausage	2.15	3.81	1.46	2.35
Butter	0.69	2.71	1.00	2.15
Milk	0.52	0.44	0.11	0.29
Cheese	3.95	–	1.29	2.80
Bread	0.29	0.63	0.30	0.27
Sugar	0.71	0.87	0.30	0.53
Potatoes	0.18	0.18	0.05	0.14
Eggs (10)	0.79	0.81	0.35	0.74
Beer	0.63	–	0.24	0.53
Vodka	5.90	7.27	1.52	2.51

Sources: *Statistical Yearbooks* for Poland (2001), Lithuania (2001), Belarus (2001), Ukraine (2000).

In general, the evolution of marketplace trade in the three towns covered by this research reflects gradual change in development asymmetry between Poland and its neighbours. After the initial explosion of border marketplaces, as a result of the opening of borders at the beginning of the 1990s, one can observe a gradual decline of this form of trade. The most spectacular example of this process is Sejny, where the marketplace is now open only twice a week and has only local (domestic) significance, while at the beginning of 1990s it was a very important centre of Polish–Lithuanian cross-border small trade. Also the largest among the examined marketplaces (and one of the largest in Poland), located in Przemyśl, has gradually lost its importance. In the period 1997–2001 the number of stalls decreased by a half (from 1500 to 700) and the marketplace lost its international character. Most of the sellers and buyers are Polish. The dawn of small trade caused a significant cut in city revenues from trade fees – from 4.1 million PLN in 1997 (7.3 per cent of total revenues) to 1.6 million PLN in 1999 (1.2 per cent of total revenues).

Terespol in turn provides an example of an international market place that remains a crucial element of the local economy. However, its significance is expected to drop as visa requirements are introduced in the border traffic after Poland's accession to the EU.

3.3 Results of the Surveys on Travellers and the Enterprise Sector in Border Areas

The analysis of statistical data from the surveys carried out at the Polish eastern border showed that the majority of the travellers are foreigners – mainly citizens of neighbouring countries (95 per cent in Terespol, 85 per cent in Przemyśl, 71 per cent in Sejny). The most common destinations of their visit to Poland were the border regions (55 per cent in Terespol, 50 per cent in Przemyśl). In Sejny (Polish–Lithuanian border) local travel was of marginal importance. In Terespol and Przemyśl the border traffic is dominated by so-called 'ants' – people who carry small amounts of commodities (as personal luggage) across the border, to be traded in the marketplaces, mostly on the Polish side. The revenues from this small trade are in turn spent on other commodities that can be sold at a profit after returning to the home country. Although 'ants' constitute almost 50 per cent of the travellers at the Ukrainian and Belarussian borders, they no longer appear in Sejny, since with the equalisation of prices and access to commodities between Poland and Lithuania small trade has turned out to be unprofitable.

Most foreigners trading in Polish marketplaces offer alcohol and cigarettes, which are much more expensive in Poland than in their home countries. In turn they buy food, clothes and furniture.

In all three locations where the survey was conducted, it showed that for people travelling to destinations located further into Poland, border areas were not attractive as a place for shopping, resting or eating, which indicates the underdevelopment of the local services sector in Sejny, Terespol and Przemyśl.

The research carried out in the three border municipalities quite unambiguously proved that, at the current stage of cross-border economic cooperation, it is difficult to detect significant supply linkages across the border. The production sector is underdeveloped, as local enterprises prefer to engage in trade activities. The number of firms in the manufacturing and construction sector in eastern border areas is small compared to other locations in Poland. Local businessmen prefer to engage in low-risk activities aimed at short-term profits. Since they consider business relations with foreign partners unstable, they are not interested in long-term investment and planning. It is worth mentioning that of 700 loans to entrepreneurs made in 2000 by the local bank in Terespol (Polish–Belarussian border), there was not even one long-term investment credit.

The dominance of the trade sector is also visible in Przemyśl at the Polish–Ukrainian border. Table 3.5 shows the number of firms per 10 000 inhabitants in selected industries (NACE sections) in Przemyśl and a few other cities located in central, western and southern Poland.

Table 3.5 The number of firms in selected industries in Przemyśl and cities of similar size in 1999

City	Nowy Sacz	Ostrowiec Swietokrzyski	Ostrow Wielkopolski	Pila	Przemyśl
Population	83 911	79 047	74 635	76 810	68 345
Manufacturing	96.89	55.41	107.05	87.75	58.67
Construction	78.06	74.26	85.88	88.53	55.01
Wholesale and retail trade	321.17	333.60	360.55	380.42	471.29
Hotels and restaurants	23.36	18.85	17.69	27.99	34.82
Transport, storage and communication	77.94	59.33	56.14	89.44	97.30

Source: CSO (Polish Central Statistical Office).

When it comes to existing manufacturing businesses, the territorial scope of their cross-border cooperation very rarely goes beyond the border area in the neighbouring country. Interestingly enough, entrepreneurs from eastern Poland more frequently seek long-term business partners in Western Europe than in the East. Sometimes, as in Terespol, the links take the form of ownership – some of the firms located at the Polish eastern border are controlled by shareholders from Italy or Belgium. This results in re-orientation of exports towards destinations in Western, rather than Eastern, Europe.

The situation seems different in the export-oriented trade enterprises. The wholesalers from Przemyśl act as intermediaries between the producers of clothing, footwear, furniture and building materials from central and western Poland and the buyers of these commodities in Ukraine. Once again it should be underlined that local merchants are not interested in establishing their own production plants. Their strategy relies on keeping their own costs at a low level and being able to adjust quickly to the changing structure of Ukrainian demand. In the case of Terespol, on the Polish–Belarussian border, the wholesale trade is of smaller importance – the majority of goods are transported in small quantities by individuals crossing the border.

In theory the proximity of the border should promote the development of specific services: restaurants, hotels, petrol stations, exchange offices, transport etc. Clearly, this is not the case for the three examined border towns. In Sejny services for travellers have marginal importance in the local economy – the contribution of Lithuanians to the annual turnover of shops and restaurants did not exceed 10 per cent. Most hotel facilities are targeted at Polish holiday-makers and weekend tourists.

The services for travellers are more developed in Przemyśl, although the contribution of foreigners to the turnover of shops and restaurants usually does not exceed 5 per cent (the neighbourhood of the marketplace is an exception – 50 per cent share). Also the hotels are relatively well developed. The average share of Ukrainians in the total number of guests is 25 per cent.

When it comes to passenger transport services, Polish businesses lost the competition with Ukrainian operators. The number of cross-border destinations offered by Polish transport firms decreased from 34 in 1997 to 3 in 2001. Nevertheless, there is an association of about 20 private mini-bus drivers, who provide transport from the border-crossing point to the city.

As shown by the survey, services for travellers had much more impact on the economy of Terespol, which might partly be explained by the small population of the town. According to local authorities, the revenues of 20–30 per cent of inhabitants are closely related to the border (trade, services). In more than half of the local shops and bars Belarussians generate over 30 per cent of turnover. They also comprise 30 to 60 per cent of hotel and motel guests.

The research revealed that, although eastern Polish border regions are slightly differentiated in terms of economic cooperation with neighbouring countries, they have much in common (low GDP, dominance of agriculture in the local economy, low inflow of foreign direct investment). The common features of the Polish eastern border are as follows:

1. Despite the decline of local market places, small trade remains the most common form of cooperation.
2. The production sector and cross-border supply linkages are underdeveloped.
3. The sector of services related to border traffic is weak.
4. There is a considerable lack of sustainability and long-term economic cooperation.
5. Speculative and short-term-oriented attitudes dominate economic activities.

3.4 High- versus Low-level Asymmetry

Development processes that take place in eastern regions of Poland may be compared to those at the Polish–German border in the early 1990s. In the West the decreasing volume of Polish–German small cross-border trade (due to equalisation of prices and access to commodities) is successfully offset by the production links established between companies, employment opportunities for the citizens of the neighbouring country and cooperation of local governments (e.g. joint investments). Numerous Polish companies were able to switch from price- to quality-based competitiveness. As a result, despite the fact that asymmetry between Poland and Germany no longer constitutes a strong incentive for cooperation, the cross-border links are now stronger and more sustainable than they were in the past. Comparing the eastern and western borders of Poland, one can speak of asymmetry at a high level (between two partners being relatively well off) versus asymmetry at a low level (when there is asymmetry between two poor neighbours – one is even more underdeveloped than the other). Local communities living on both sides of the Polish–German border are more developed in terms of income, infrastructure and organisational skills than their counterparts in the East. This makes the effects of international cooperation long-lasting and not necessarily related to physical border infrastructure, nowadays losing its importance. Obviously, the differences in economic and organisational potential refer not only to Germany versus the eastern neighbours of Poland, but also to huge regional disparities inside Poland.

Table 3.6 The role of the border in local development – interactions between asymmetry and initial development potential

		Cross-border asymmetry	
		Low	High
Income and development level of neighbouring areas	Low	No economic surplus from the existence of the border for local communities (Polish–Lithuanian case)	Short-term gains due to spontaneous trade, no sustainable development. Limited capability to exploit the opportunities offered by the border (Polish–Belarusian case)
	High	Border as neutral development factor (borders between EU countries)	Sustainable cooperation and development. Both sides consciously exploiting their comparative advantages (Polish–German case)

The basic conclusion coming from the research conducted at the eastern border of Poland is that the impact of cross-border asymmetries on local development, as well as the sustainability of the border-related benefits, depends strongly on the initial performance of the cooperating areas. As shown in Table 3.6, the weaker the development potential of the neighbours, the lower their ability to exploit the opportunities created by the border, even in the presence of significant asymmetry.

4 THE ROLE OF 'SOFT FACTORS' – LEADERSHIP AND CITIZENS' PARTICIPATION

4.1 Local Government and Development of Border Areas

As stated in many publications (e.g. see Gorzelak, 2000), leadership is one of the most important factors of local development. The leader's creativeness and strategic vision allow the municipality to take advantage of existing development opportunities or overcome adverse external conditions. However, if the location of border infrastructure – which creates revenues for the government and jobs for people living in the area – depends only in small part on local efforts, the question arises as to what is the role of local leaders in the municipalities lying near the border. Are they able to influence significantly the development of their communities or should they restrict their activities to administrative functions and watching 'the harvest' brought by the state border? The experience of municipalities located at the Polish eastern border seems to prove that the role of the leader in border areas is as important as everywhere else.

One can speak of two types of strategic approach to local development in this region. The first approach – let's call it a passive one – is well represented by the authorities of Sejny at the Polish–Lithuanian border and the town of Terespol at the border with Belarus. The second approach – 'long-term active planning' – can be observed in the rural municipality of Terespol.

The crossing point in Sejny was established in 1988 and until 1994 was the only one at the Polish–Lithuanian border. The maximum intensity of international traffic was observed in the first half of 1993, when the border was crossed by 1.5 million travellers and almost 380 000 vehicles. Traffic problems, oppressive noise and the degradation of the environment were seen as unbearable by local society. According to the local authorities, the impact of those negative phenomena exceeded the value of development opportunities generated by the border. Following their requests and suggestions, in 1994 the Polish Ministry of Transport decided to move all the cargo traffic out of Sejny to the newly established crossing point in

Budzisko–Kalwaryja.

At the time, the economy of Sejny was dominated by small cross-border trade with the Lithuanians, which was the main source of revenue for the local population. It seems that the authorities assumed that such a situation would last forever, and did not make any attempt to use the border as a basis for more sustainable development. But after 1998 the small trade ceased (mostly because of equalising income and access to commodities on both sides of the border). The unemployment rate in Sejny reached 20 per cent in 2001. Now the 1993 lobbying for taking international cargo traffic out of Sejny is perceived by the local government and some citizens as a mistake. There is a belief that restoring the admissible tonnage level of vehicles crossing the border at Sejny will contribute to solving the problems of the local labour market.

Still, in the strategic plan of local development, the cross-border cooperation or the border itself is not mentioned at the level of strategic or operational goals. Moreover, some border-related infrastructure investments proposed in that document are no longer feasible because of unsuccessful past investment policy of the local government, resulting in an overwhelming debt on the town's account.

The case of Sejny is indeed a good example of how the local authorities' performance influences the development of the municipality even in the presence of such strong development factors as the state border.

The case of Terespol at the Polish–Belarussian border provides even more striking arguments. Until 1992 there existed one municipality of Terespol consisting of the town and surrounding rural area. Since the rebirth of local democracy in Poland in 1990, Terespol has had only one true leader – mayor Krzysztof Iwaniuk. His view of local development involved the strategic approach to exploiting the border infrastructure in order to ensure a sustainable surplus for the local population. In particular, the mayor intended to:

- cooperate with the border institutions to improve the technical infrastructure and the quality of life in the municipality (water distribution, sewage system, telephones);
- solve the problems related to small cross-border trade (safety, illegal transactions, smuggling) by establishing a new market, fulfilling all necessary requirements and standards;
- attract new investors, taking into account future EU integration (the Polish eastern border will become the external border of the community) and future development of road infrastructure in the proximity of the border.

The implementation of these plans appeared infeasible within the existing municipality, mostly because of the resistance of other local authority representatives (the council, municipal board). Most of them preferred to continue with the day-to-day survival strategy for the underdeveloped town, relying mainly on citizens' revenues from small cross-border trade and related basic services. Any long-term planning or investment activity was, in their opinion, too risky.

Therefore in 1992 the mayor, in order to implement his vision of local development, forced the split of Terespol into two separate units – the town and the rural municipality – and was instantly elected as mayor (wojt) of the latter. After this he was re-elected three times (1994, 1998 and 2002), becoming one of the most experienced mayors in Poland.

Not surprisingly, there is a striking difference between the development policies of the urban and the rural municipalities of Terespol in the 1992–2002 period. Since most of the border infrastructure facilities are located in the rural area, by separating from the town, rural Terespol took from it all the revenues coming from international cargo traffic.[2] Still, knowing that, most of the town leaders voted for the separation in 1992, which has to be seen as a successful attempt at economic suicide by the urban part of Terespol.

In the 1992–2002 period, the town leaders did not implement any significant investment and, even more important, they did not work out any strategic vision of further development. The town appears as a huge marketplace with citizens buying vodka and cigarettes from the Belarussian guests and selling them food, clothes and furniture. Even some town councillors are engaged in small cross-border trade, owning boutiques or shops. The leaders are conscious that, after Poland's accession to the EU, visa requirements will be imposed on Belarussian citizens and the volume of small trade will fall dramatically, possibly to zero. However, this consciousness does not lead to any creativity in planning the town's future. On the contrary, the town council assumes that after accession (probably in 2004), the fate of Terespol will depend exclusively on state aid. European integration is regarded as a catastrophe that ought to be compensated by the Polish government.

At the same time, the rural area of Terespol is exploiting the border infrastructure opportunities and adjusting its long-term development plan to the expected repercussions of European integration. Table 3.7 shows the results of municipal investments in technical and network infrastructure between 1992 and 1998.

Since all border infrastructure is located in the rural municipality of Terespol, all tax and fee revenue goes to the rural budget. We can thus evaluate the impact of border infrastructure on local development potential opportunities by comparing the budgets of the two municipalities (Table 3.8).

Table 3.7 Investment in technical infrastructure in the rural municipality of Terespol, 1992–98

Indicators	1992	1998
Number of telephone lines	60	1500
Number of households connected to the water distribution system	90	1365
Number of street lights	138	700
Number of households connected to the sewage system	0	427
Length of municipal high-quality roads (km)	4	22
Length of municipal pavements (km)	0.6	7

Source: Central Statistical Office (CSO).

Table 3.8 The impact of border infrastructure on local budgets

Municipality	Total budget revenues per capita in PLN (2000)	Share of own revenues[a] in total revenues	Share of real-estate tax in own revenues (%)	Share of investments in total expenditures (%)
Terespol (town)	1185	52	11	7
Terespol (rural)	1208	61	29	25

Note: [a] own revenues are revenues excluding state subsidies and grants.

Source: Central Statistical Office (CSO).

The rural municipality of Terespol has higher budget revenues than the neighbouring town, which is a rare phenomenon in Poland, since urban areas usually have many more sources of revenue than the countryside. Further indicators are even more striking, showing that rural Terespol is much less dependent on state subsidies and grants than the town, and has made a much bigger investment effort. The location of border infrastructure outside the town has resulted in 25 per cent of employed inhabitants of the urban municipality working in the rural area, which is an inversion of the usual job migration pattern.

The lack of activity of the town authorities and the future construction (planned by the central government) of a highway connecting the western and eastern Polish border, as a part of the Berlin–Moscow road system, has led rural leaders to create a brave long-term strategic plan, involving the location of a new town centre and, in 50–100 years, incorporating the 'old Terespol' as part of a new city.

The case of Terespol shows that the surplus generated by the border may easily be wasted if the local society lacks leaders able to take advantage of the opportunities. Local success depends on the performance of local government even if the municipality is strongly influenced by exogenous factors such as location at the state border.

4.2 The Border and Local Society

As it was stated in the introduction to this chapter, the attitude and engagement of local citizens is another crucial factor of endogenous development. On the one hand, local society may benefit from the impulses generated by border location. On the other hand, people are also affected by the specific socio-economic climate of the border area, reshaping their attitude toward legal and illegal work, foreigners, law etc. During our research we explored how the local communities are influenced by the proximity of the border. Additionally, we tried to discern what kind of attitudes the communities developed in the situation of permanent contact with 'the others' from the opposite side of the border. We were also interested in whether the border and close contact with another culture enriched some essential elements of civil society – the ability to organise, curiosity about other cultures, bottom-up initiatives.

Sejny has a time of spontaneous, dynamic (not always legal) trade already behind it. The smuggling *Eldorado* ended here in the middle of the 1990s, but it left its mark on the local community. First, there is still a feeling of longing for the past, vivid border (at the same time there is a consciousness that intensive, illegal trade on the border was only a temporary solution and bothersome for local people). Second, the opportunities created by the border changed people's attitudes towards regular, legal work. As local entrepreneurs pointed out, the quick profit from smuggling made legal work unattractive. Despite the end of small trade prosperity, this perception remained, and the official labour market is still weak and unstable.[3] Finally, once heavy traffic at the crossing point disappeared, the feeling of peripherality returned. The local community fell into apathy and passiveness. 'Nothing will change; we are not able to change anything' is the mantra repeated by most of the people questioned. This attitude is even strengthened by the failure of the municipality's largest investment venture – the construction of a sewage treatment plant.

In Sejny the attitude towards Lithuanians is neutral. In fact Polish and

Lithuanian people coexisted in these areas for years without any major conflicts. Both sides are equally poor, so there is no jealousy, but on the other hand there is no interest in cooperation or exchange. The learning of peaceful coexistence and arousal of interest in the 'other' culture is concentrated in three centres of local life, which are the most vivid and positive examples of local initiative and potential driven by the individuals devoted to the life of the local community. The first is the primary school, where student exchanges, trips and cultural days are organised. The second is the Pogranicze (Borderland) Foundation, which is the cultural centre of an international range (promoting the specificity and cultural richness of all borderlands in Europe). Last, but not least, is the Development of Sejny and Sejny Region Foundation, which promotes agrotourism on both sides of the border. The activities of these three institutions confirm the important role of leadership, animators and visionaries in local development. In the first case, it is the local teacher who animates the initiatives; in the second, it is an artist who came to Sejny from Poznan in search of a magical, poetic location; and in the last case it is an elderly beekeeper devoted to the local life and community. In comparison with the organisations mentioned above, the local chamber of commerce is very passive. The local entrepreneurs definitely prefer independent action, and see small benefit in cooperating.

In contrast to Sejny, Terespol and Przemyśl are still at the stage of spontaneous, buzzing trade driven by existing asymmetries between the neighbouring communities. In Terespol the border-related pathologies are especially vivid. The attitude towards illegal work is similar to that in Sejny. However, while in Sejny illegal work is slowly fading out, in Terespol it is still common and is even strengthening. Shady business or even crime has become a norm for the local community. When asked at school, some pupils perceive smuggling and robbery as a 'job at the border', as normal as the work in a custom office or city hall. The consciousness of what is legal and illegal, right and wrong, has been blurred.

A second alarming tendency is the perception of and attitude towards Belarussian people. In many cases they are victims of crime (robberies, extortion, offers of 'unrefusable' protection, etc.). They are seen as easy targets, and at the same time as the worst category of people. There is little contact with their culture and traditions – the Belarussians are known only through the prism of the 'little smugglers pulling their big bags'. This stereotype is transferred to schools. The children do not perceive harm to Belarussians as a bad thing. Also, they do not see any value in the people from 'the other side'. Very dangerous relativism takes place. What is even more alarming is that the local community does not activate any repair mechanism. During the research we did not find any local associations or bottom-up initiatives to deal with this problem. In local schools children usually do not learn Russian; English is much more common.

The third case, the Przemyśl case, is different from the first two. The border does not influence the attitudes and work of the inhabitants in any special way. The community is ten times larger than in the two other towns; thus it was impossible to cover the area with the same type of analysis as in the other two cases. The official local statistics do not say anything about a higher level of crime related to the border. The city has its own cultural life, being the local centre of arts and culture. It is dynamic, but organises mainly local events. None of them has any relation with cultural cooperation or exchange with the Ukrainian side. The local chamber of commerce does not relate its activities in any special way to the border location either.

To summarise, the cases of Sejny and Terespol show that the existence of the border and spontaneous (also illegal) trade markedly changes the life of the communities. It promotes a certain type of activity and entrepreneurship (usually aimed at gaining short-term profits) but at the same time strengthens alienation and negative stereotyping towards foreigners. These changes are deep and the process of reversing them is a long-term one. At the same time, individuals play a crucial role in activating people and overcoming the stereotypes. Strong leadership, citizens' engagement and institutional infrastructure are also necessary conditions for the community to take long-term advantage of the economic opportunities generated by the border.

The performance of local government and local society may be jointly considered as endogenous development potential. In what way does it affect the relationship between border openness and total border area surplus described earlier in this chapter? In contrast to the shift in asymmetry, a change in endogenous potential has an influence on both turnover benefits (B-type) and direct gains from infrastructure (A-type) at any given level of permeability.

The positive shift in endogenous potential of the community (e.g. due to the appearance of a new leader or the establishment of a new high school or non-governmental organisation) changes the shape of the A+B curve, representing the relationship between openness of the border and the gains for the local community. At the given level of permeability, the increase in endogenous potential raises the ability of the community to generate turnover benefits, but also (as shown by the cases of Sejny and Terespol) to exploit the opportunity offered by border infrastructure. The A+B curve will therefore move upward. If both types of benefits are equally elastic to the endogenous potential of the community, the optimal (threshold) value of openness will remain the same, but the local benefits for any level of permeability will be higher than they were before (see Figure 3.4).

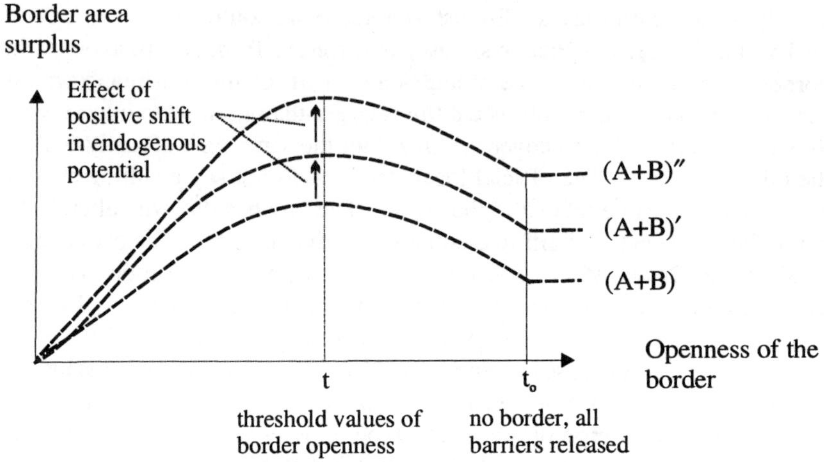

Figure 3.4 Endogenous potential (human capital, leadership, institutions) and the development of border areas

4.3 Conclusions

To summarise our observations of the three localities on the Polish border (Sejny, Terespol, Przemyśl), we can conclude that the functional character of the border is still traditional – as a separation factor. To relate this to Table 3.1 presented in the theoretical part of this chapter, we can state that the cross-border interactions in the field of social and economic interactions are predominantly in Phase II (more or less peaceful coexistence with spontaneous trade). The day-to-day political interactions are limited to informal contacts (Phase I), although officially the contacts are formalised in the form of Euroregions (in practice these are very passive structures having little influence on the intermunicipal relationships between small towns such as Sejny). Of course, some slight variations appear. In the case of social interactions in Terespol there are some alarming tendencies in growth of alienation and hostility. Economic interactions in Przemyśl are slowly transforming towards Phase III (regular trade), while in Sejny they are moving backwards (freezing of spontaneous trade). The conducted research has shown that in all locations there is an absence of networks for cooperation.

The prepared integration with the EU, with the resulting changes in the organisation on the border with Ukraine and Belarus (introduction of visas), could further strengthen the negative, traditional role of the border – as a filter and dividing line.

The three cases show that favourable external impulses from the border (usually temporary ones) are able to improve the cross-border interactions no further than to the level of Phase II. From there, further development is possible only in the presence of strong endogenous potential. The local society and leaders must exploit the opportunity in a creative and dynamic way.

NOTES

1 We define this specific infrastructure in the narrow sense of the term as the basic facilities such as roads, power supplies, communications and – most of all – buildings that enable the border crossing to function.

2 The most important elements of the border infrastructure located in the rural area are the cargo terminal in Koroszczyn and the cargo rail loading facility.

3 Unregistered work is a common phenomenon. Many of the officially unemployed work on a regular basis in the local firms (both sides are 'better off' – the entrepreneurs avoid paying high taxes and insurance; employees obtain higher wages).

REFERENCES

Gorzelak, G. (2000), 'Zewnetrzna Interwencja Jako Czynnik Rozwoju Lokalnego (na Przykladzie PIL*)*' (External Intervention as a Factor of Local Growth – Case Study of Programme of Local Initiatives), *Studia Regionalne i Lokalne* **3**, EUROREG, Warsaw University.

Guichonnet, P. and C. Raffestin (1974), *Géographie des Frontiers* (Geography of Frontiers), Paris: Presses Universitaires de France.

Hansen, N. (1981), *The Border Economy: Regional Development in the Southwest,* Austin: University of Texas Press.

House, J.W. (1980), 'The Frontier Zone: A Conceptual Problem for Policy Makers', *International Regional Science* Review, **1** (4).

Krätke, S. (1995), 'Where East meets West: Prospects of the German–Polish Border Region', European Urban and Regional Studies Conference.

Perkmann, M. (2003), 'Cross-Border Regions in Europe: Significance and Drivers of Regional Cross-border Co-operation', *European Urban and Regional Studies*, **2** (10), 153–71.

Ratti, R. (1993), 'How can Existing Barriers and Border Effects be Overcome? A Theoretical Approach', in R. Cappellin and P.W. Batey (eds), *Regional Networks, Border Regions and European Integration*, London: Pion Limited, pp. 60–69.

Scott, J., A. Sweedler, P. Ganster and W.-D. Eberwein (eds) (1996), 'Border Regions in Functional Transition', *Regio series of IRS,* no. 9, Institute for Regional Development and Structural Planning, Berlin.

Statistics – Belarus (2001), *Republic of Belarus Statistical Yearbook 2001*, Ministry of Statistics and Analyses of Republic of Belarus, Minsk.

Statistics – Lithuania (2001), *Statistical Yearbook of Lithuania for 2001*, Statistics Lithuania, Vilnius.

Statistics – Poland (2002), *Prices in the National Economy in 2001,* Central Statistical Office, Warsaw.

Statistics – Ukraine (2000), *Statistical Yearbook of Ukraine for 2000*, State Statistics Committee of Ukraine, Kiev.

Szul, R. and A. Mync (eds) (1999), *Rola Granicy i Wspolpracy Transgranicznej w Rozwoju Regionalnym i Lokalnym* (The Role of Border and Cross-border Cooperation in Regional and Local Development), EUROREG, Warsaw University.

4. Latvian Foreign Trade with the Scandinavian Countries, 1920–40[1]

Viesturs Pauls Karnups

1 INTRODUCTION

Trade, whether international or within a nation, will take place if both parties believe that it is mutually beneficial, that is, if it is believed that it will increase the welfare of both parties. From a theoretical perspective, national trade and international trade are explained in parallel fashion. Economic theory explains national trade in terms of the advantage of the division of labour among companies and individuals in a given society. The ability to trade internationally allows for the international division of labour; that is, it allows countries to specialise in the production of particular goods and services. Throughout history international trade has played a critical role in the ability of countries to grow, develop and be economically strong.

International trade of course is not a new phenomenon in the Baltic countries or in Scandinavia, or between the Baltic countries and Scandinavia.[2] What was new in the period between 1920 and 1940 was that trade and economic relations occurred between three independent Baltic States and three independent Scandinavian countries, one of which, Norway, only became independent as late as 1905.

In the broader context, since its regaining of independence in 1991 there have been a number of studies of Latvia's reintegration into the Baltic Sea Region and European trade as a whole, utilising the analytical framework known as the 'gravity model' to evaluate the current trade patterns of the Baltic States including Latvia.[3] The gravity model attempts to explain trade between two market economies in terms of the distance between them, their population and their income levels. In the context of this chapter the work by Eichengreen and Irwin (1996) and, in particular, Lasser and Schrader (2002) is of relevance. Eichengreen and Irwin made the point that history plays a role in shaping the direction of international trade, or put another way, 'past trade patterns influence current trade flows in a way that a passing historical event causes lasting cost reductions' (Eichengreen and Irwin, 1996, p. 5). Within the gravity model framework, Eichengreen and Irwin found that historical factors which are associated with the sunk costs of market entry and exit exercise an important influence on trade flows. Thus, history matters. Moreover, in their recent paper, Lasser and Schrader have provided some historical data within a gravity model framework on Baltic regional trade patterns and have attempted to integrate the ideas of Eichengreen and Irwin into the analysis (Lasser and Schrader, 2002). They suggest that 'history may play a special role for current Baltic trade relations', and that 'the changes in regional trade patterns following [the regaining of] independence show parallels to the development of Baltic trade after World War I' (Lasser and Schrader, 2002, pp. 12–13). Indeed, the results of their analysis showed that the process of EU association was not reflected in the regression analysis, but that in fact 'the process of European integration mainly runs [for the Baltic States] via their Baltic Rim neighbours' and thus, 'in this respect EU integration means reintegration into regional markets to which a historical affinity exists' (Lasser and Schrader, 2002, pp. 44–5). This chapter is an attempt to provide an empirical examination of the basis of that historical affinity, at least in respect of Latvia's foreign trade with the Scandinavian countries.

In terms of general economic theories of international trade, Latvia's foreign trade with the Scandinavian countries would seem to reflect in a broad sense the classic Heckscher–Ohlin theory of relative factor endowments. Latvia in the interwar period was relatively well endowed with labour, but was relatively poor in capital stock. Its main export commodities to the Scandinavian countries were labour-intensive agricultural and forestry goods, while imports from the Scandinavian countries were mainly capital-intensive manufactured goods and minerals. Thus, in general terms, Latvia exported to Scandinavia those goods that had a high content of Latvia's abundant production factor (labour) and imported from Scandinavia those goods that had a high content of the Latvia's scarce production factor (capital). This is true for that part of Latvia's foreign trade that comprised Latvia's exchange of agricultural (forestry) products for manufactured goods from the Scandinavian countries. However, Latvia also exported capital-intensive manufactured goods to the Scandinavian countries, as well as importing raw materials, processing them and exporting final goods back to Scandinavia. In this sense, features of intra-industry trade can also be seen in Latvian foreign trade. On the other hand, the distortions of tariffs and other protectionist measures, the onset of the Great Depression and its consequences, the return to and later abandonment of the gold standard, the establishment of the Oslo Group and the general dominance of state control over foreign trade from 1930, all reflected the general instability in foreign trade in Europe during the interwar period, as well as between Latvia and the

Scandinavian countries. In turn this limits the usefulness of general trade theories in analysing actual trade relations in the interwar period.

Even though the Latvian market was on the periphery of Scandinavian foreign trade it was still sufficiently important for some sectors, especially the agricultural machinery sector. Latvia was also a stable market for raw materials from the Scandinavian countries that were not in competition with those of the larger industrial countries, such as chalk, cellulose, cork tree bark, stones, saltpetre, cast iron, zinc, etc. Latvia, on the other hand, provided the Scandinavian countries with a stable source of raw materials, both specialised products, such as gypsum and flax, and incidental (according to need) products, such as pulpwood, raw hides, food and agricultural products, etc.

2 LATVIAN FOREIGN TRADE, 1920–40, IN GENERAL

Latvia between the wars was a small open economy on the periphery of Europe. As there did not exist at this time such supranational trading organisations as the EU, EFTA etc., each country had to do the best it could on its own by concluding bilateral trade agreements with other states. Latvia had to contend not only with the necessity of rebuilding an economy shattered by war, but also with the loss of the former Russian market and hence a need to completely reorient its economy toward Europe and the rest of the world. Despite Rīga being one of the largest industrial centres of tsarist Russia before the First World War, Latvia had to restructure its economy into one based on agriculture and forestry and was throughout the interwar years highly dependent upon agricultural and forestry product exports as the mainstay of its foreign trade. Latvia's main exports during this period were timber, plywood, paper and paper products, butter, flax, bacon, hides and linseed. For example, in 1937 timber, plywood and butter made up 71 per cent of total exports and 73 per cent of these exports went to two countries – Britain and Germany (Aizsilnieks, 1968, pp. 795–9). Britain and Germany dominated Latvia's foreign trade throughout the interwar period. Other important export partners were Belgium and the Netherlands (timber, plywood and flax), and the USA (butter, canned fish, cellulose). Latvia's exports to its near neighbours of the Baltic Rim (except for Germany) were small, and relative to Britain and Germany, negligible – total exports in 1937 to Estonia, Lithuania, Denmark, Sweden, Norway, Finland, Poland and Russia (USSR) were only 8.6 per cent of all exports (*Latvijas ārējā tirdzniecība un transits 1937* (1938), pp. x–xi).

Latvia's main imports during this period were agricultural and industrial machinery, coal and coke, wool and cotton, fertiliser, oil and oil products, vehicles, metals and metal products. In 1937, some 48 per cent of all imports came from Britain and Germany, while imports from the countries of the Baltic Rim (except for Germany) made up 14.3 per cent of all imports (*Latvijas ārējā tirdzniecība un transits 1937* (1938), pp. x–xi). Thus Latvia's imports from its near neighbours were significantly higher than exports in percentage terms and, relative to Britain and Germany, of greater importance than exports. Other important countries for imports were Belgium and the Netherlands (fertiliser, metal products and radios).

3 LATVIAN FOREIGN TRADE WITH THE SCANDINAVIAN COUNTRIES, 1920

Until 1920 relations in general between Latvia and the Scandinavian countries were minimal, partly because up until 1917 Latvia was part of tsarist Russia and partly because it was only at the end of 1919 that the National government had stabilised following the fall of the German-backed putschist Niedra government and the defeat of the German-supported Russian adventurer Bermont-Avalov (Spekke, 1951, pp. 350–55). On 30 January 1920, an armistice between Latvia and Soviet Russia was signed with effect from 1 February. The final Peace Treaty was signed on 11 August 1920. The Latvian Republic was still not recognised *de jure* by any European state with the exception of Soviet Russia, which itself was not recognised by any other state.[4]

Latvia's economic situation at the end of 1919 and the beginning of 1920 was unenviable. Industry had collapsed, with buildings empty of machinery and other assets that had been evacuated to Russia in 1915 (*The Latvian Economist*, 1923, p. 159). The land was ruined and the population scattered. 'Independence was proclaimed . . . with ruined industries, empty coffers and plundered rural economies' (Hiden and Salmon, 1991, p. 77). The main source of government income was the 'money printing press' (Aizsilnieks, 1968, p. 117), in order to cover the costs of the War of Independence, the maintenance of the civil service and the minimal requirements of the economy. Of the state revenues for the period between 18 November 1918[5] and 1 April 1920 paper money to the value of 37.9 million lats was printed (58.5 per cent of the total revenue) (Aizsilnieks, 1968, p. 111).

In 1919, some Scandinavian trading houses established branches in Rīga, Liepāja and Ventspils, and a lively trade was maintained through the establishment of steamship lines between Scandinavia and Latvia (*Economists*, 1920, No. 1, p. 13). In the last six months of 1919, Latvia's total trade (exports plus imports) with the Scandinavian countries amounted to 50.2 million Latvian roubles (37.1 per cent of Latvia's total trade) – 4.9

per cent of exports (19.6 million Latvian roubles) and 31.9 per cent of imports (30.6 million Latvian roubles) (*Economists*, 1920, No. 4, p. 106).

In 1920, the total value of Latvia's foreign trade was 3136.6 million Latvian roubles – imports being 2061.1 million Latvian roubles and exports 1075.5 million Latvian roubles (*Latvijas statistikā gada grāmata 1920* (1921), p. 119). Of this, total imports from Scandinavia amounted to 801.9 million Latvian roubles and exports to Scandinavia amounted to 60.1 million roubles, as indicated in Table 4.1. This was to be the high-water mark of Latvia's foreign trade with Scandinavia. In 1920, the total volume of trade between Latvia and the Scandinavian countries reached 27.5 per cent of Latvia's total trade (imports plus exports). Of Latvia's total trade in 1920, 15.1 per cent was with Denmark, 3.8 per cent was with Norway and 8.6 per cent was with Sweden (*Latvijas statistikā gada grāmata 1920* (1921), p. 119).

Table 4.1 Latvian exports to and imports from Scandinavia, 1920

State	Imports (million roubles)	Per cent of total imports	Exports (million roubles)	Per cent of total exports	Total trade (million roubles)	Per cent of total trade
Denmark	442.17	21.5	31.06	2.9	473.23	15.1
Sweden	239.37	11.6	28.81	2.7	268.18	8.6
Norway	120.33	5.8	0.21	0.02	120.54	3.8
Total	801.87	38.9	60.08	5.62	861.95	27.5

Source: *Latvijas statistikā gada grāmata 1920* (1921), p. 119.

In this year (1920) Norway was the first country to offer long-term credits to the infant Latvian state at a time when it had not been recognised *de jure*, and when its financial resources were particularly low.

The gesture of goodwill by the Norwegian government was of course also based on sound economic reasons. The Norwegian government was under pressure to clear its stocks of herrings purchased during and immediately after the First World War. Without large sales in the near future, Statens Fiskecentral, in order to save on further upkeep and storage costs, would be forced to liquidate its old herring stocks by using them as feedstuffs or handing them over to oil and fertiliser manufacturers (Norway in 1920 (1921), p. 19). This was why Norway so willingly embraced the international relief credit programme – as a means of clearing government stocks.

The risk of a complete breakdown of the economies of East European countries prompted a number of countries, led by the United States and

Great Britain, to set up a relief credit programme. The idea was to grant long-term credits in the form of commodities, that is, until 1 January 1925, with an interest rate of 6 per cent per annum (Norway in 1920 (1921), p. 18). The credits were also subject to further regulations from the International Committee for Relief Credit sitting in Paris, which had overall responsibility for the relief programme. Norway participated in the programme by offering to supply herring and other fish products, as well as technical whale oil from government stocks, to a total amount of 17 million kroner (Norway in 1920 (1921), p. 18). Sweden and Denmark participated mainly by extending export credits to their exporters.[6]

From the Latvian government's point of view the commodity credits were a godsend, especially when they were long-term and could be secured with Treasury Bills instead of hard currency, which was in short supply. However, the lure of quick profits turned an essentially bona fide commercial transaction into an object of a parliamentary inquiry and harsh criticism of the government. An expectation of selling excess barrels of herrings to Soviet Russia for a profit led to over-ordering, haste and waste for which, in the end, Latvia paid dearly. Only the continuing needs of Soviet Russia allowed the Ministry of Supply to limit its losses and barter the herrings to Soviet Russia through the trade and exchange concessions on the Latvian–Soviet Russian border. Nevertheless, despite the internal storm raised by the purchase, it did not affect Latvian–Norwegian relations. By 1921, Latvia had already opened negotiations for a Commercial Treaty with Norway (LVVA (Latvian State Historical Archives), f. 2570, apr. 13, p. 131).

4 LATVIAN FOREIGN TRADE WITH THE SCANDINAVIAN COUNTRIES, 1921–33

Latvia's foreign trade in the 1920s was based in large measure on a system of commercial and trade treaties. Up to 1929, Latvia had concluded commercial treaties with all important European states, including Norway (14 August 1924), Denmark (3 December 1924) and Sweden (22 December 1924). All of Latvia's commercial treaties were similar in content and the trade policies included in the treaties were the same for all of them. This included the acceptance of the most-favoured-nation principle and the inclusion of the Baltic Clause.[7] These treaties set the trade regime by which Latvia conducted its trade with the Scandinavian countries. They provided the regulatory framework within which were stated the obligations undertaken by Latvia in its foreign trade relations with the Scandinavian countries.

However, notwithstanding the important role trade agreements played in the foreign trade policy of Latvia during the interwar years, the trade agreements with the Scandinavian countries were rarely able to change significantly the volume of foreign trade to the advantage of Latvia. Although in 1923, Latvian exports to Scandinavian countries reached 5.1 per cent of total Latvian exports, by 1924 (when trade agreements were signed with all three Scandinavian countries) it had decreased to 3.4 per cent of total exports and remained at this level until 1928, when it fell to 2.8 per cent. On the other hand, imports from Scandinavian countries in 1923 were 5.9 per cent of total Latvian imports, in 1924 they were 7.5 per cent and in 1927 already 11 per cent of total imports. Thus the trade agreements appear to have been more advantageous to the Scandinavian exporters than to Latvian ones, at least up to 1929.

By 1929, Latvia enjoyed increasing economic development and an upsurge in foreign trade.[8] However, most of this upsurge was directed towards Germany and Britain rather than to the Scandinavian countries.

From Table 4.2 we can see that in the period 1921–29 the average percentages of total imports from each Scandinavian country individually are low, with Denmark and Sweden having the highest averages, aided by an upsurge in imports from 1924 to 1927. This could have been partly due to the commercial treaties signed with the Scandinavian countries in 1924, and partly to the general recovery in Europe after the recession of 1921–22 and, in the case of Denmark, to large imports of cereals.[9] The fall in imports from Denmark and Sweden after 1927 is probably partly due to the increase in customs tariffs on agricultural machinery and other manufactures (Aizsilnieks, 1968, pp. 404–5), particularly in respect of Sweden, and the beginning of import substitution in relation to cereal imports, as well as the general higher cost of Danish exports as the Danes returned to the gold standard at full prewar parities during this period.[10] The increase in imports from Norway is due to the expansion and intensification of agriculture production to combat falling prices and the consequent increased need for fertiliser. Moreover, imports from Scandinavia as a whole only averaged 8.2 per cent of total Latvian imports in this first period when the prevailing economic trend was a free trade orientation – in comparison, British imports averaged 13.1 per cent of total Latvian imports at this time, while German imports averaged a massive 41.3 per cent.[11]

In this first period the main imports from Denmark were: motor vehicles, various vegetable oils, chalk, wheat, barley, rye, oats, tobacco and tobacco products, and edible animal fats. Despite the 1920s being a substantial growth period for Danish manufacturing, Danish exports to Latvia consisted mainly of agricultural products and re-exports (e.g. automobiles).[12] The main imports from Sweden were: cement, coal and wood tars, tanning agents, rubber products, fireproof bricks, cork bark, agricultural and industrial machinery, herrings, various types of tin, and superphosphate. In terms of value, the most important import from Sweden was agricultural and industrial machinery – each year between 1925 and 1929 Latvia imported over 2 million lats worth of machinery, making up some 22 per cent of the value of all imports from Sweden at this time (*Economists*, 1929, No. 24, p. 987). From Norway, the main imports were: herrings, animal fats and fish oils, fertiliser, cotton cloth, and agricultural and industrial machinery. The most important import from Norway during this period was herrings.

During the Great Depression Denmark lost the most ground *vis-à-vis* exports to Latvia, as Latvia's import-substitution efforts centred in large measure on the replacement of cereal imports from Denmark.[13] Likewise, imports from Sweden were reduced by about 39 per cent in money terms during the Great Depression, but the percentage of total Latvian imports from Sweden remained in the same position as previously.[14] On the other hand, Norway's exports to Latvia substantially increased in 1933 (particularly of saltpetre and zinc). Overall, imports from Scandinavia only averaged 4.7 per cent of total Latvian imports between 1930 and 1933, which was nearly half the average for the first period.

The percentage of Latvian exports to Scandinavia in 1922–29 showed a downward trend and, as with imports, they were never a substantial part of total Latvian exports.

From Table 4.3 we can see that Latvian exports to Scandinavia were only a minor percentage of total Latvian exports, some 3.2 per cent on average during the period 1921–29. In comparison, Latvian exports to Britain averaged ten times more, at 35.6 per cent of total exports for the period.

Latvia's main exports to Denmark during this first period were: plywood, clover and timothy seeds, butter, logs, boards and planks, animal fodder, linoleum and vetch. It is interesting that Latvia exported butter to Denmark – some 1706 tons between 1924 and 1929 – when Denmark itself was Europe's main exporter of butter.[15] Latvia exported to Sweden mainly lubricants, gypsum, plywood, logs and boards, linoleum, seeds, animal hair, fish, vetch, eggs and flax. Latvia's main export to Sweden during this time was linoleum (*Economists*, 1929, No. 24, p. 989), which interestingly enough was produced at the Liepāja branch factory of a Swedish company, Wicander.[16] Latvian exports to Norway were mainly butter, meat, plywood, pit-props and boards, thread, linoleum and paper. Exports to Norway played only a very minor role in Latvia's total exports, although from 1924 to 1929 they had been slowly increasing in quantity and value.[17]

Table 4.2 Latvian imports from Scandinavian countries, 1921–33

Year	Denmark (million Ls)	Per cent of all imports	Norway (million Ls)	Per cent of all imports	Sweden (million Ls)	Per cent of all imports	Total Scand. (million Ls)	Per cent of all imports
1921	5.51	7.8	0.69	1.0	2.22	3.1	8.42	11.9
1922	4.96	4.6	0.84	0.8	2.19	2.0	7.99	7.4
1923	6.57	3.1	0.74	0.4	5.05	2.4	12.36	5.9
1924	11.75	4.6	0.44	0.2	6.87	2.7	19.06	7.5
1925	14.92	5.3	0.51	0.2	9.27	3.3	24.70	8.8
1926	15.47	5.9	0.64	0.3	9.87	3.8	25.98	10.0
1927	16.71	6.7	0.33	0.1	10.48	4.2	27.52	11.0
1928	9.97	3.2	0.57	0.2	9.55	3.1	20.09	6.5
1929	7.91	2.2	0.58	0.2	9.70	2.7	18.19	5.1
Average 1921–29	10.42	4.8	0.59	0.4	7.24	3.0	18.26	8.2
1930	5.63	1.9	0.59	0.2	8.82	3.0	15.04	5.1
1931	2.93	1.7	0.30	0.2	4.84	2.7	8.07	4.6
1932	1.05	1.2	0.43	0.5	1.72	2.1	3.20	3.8
1933	0.80	0.9	1.51	1.7	2.25	2.5	4.56	5.1
Average 1930–33	2.60	1.4	0.71	0.7	4.41	2.6	7.72	4.7

Source: *Latvijas statistikā gada grāmata 1921–33.*[18]

Table 4.3 *Latvian exports to Scandinavian countries, 1921–33*

Year	Denmark (1000 Ls)	Per cent of all exports	Norway (1000 Ls)	Per cent of all exports	Sweden (1000 Ls)	Per cent of all exports	Total Scand. (1000 Ls)	Per cent of all exports
1921	551	1.9	84	0.3	319	1.1	954	3.3
1922	2135	2.1	364	0.4	2361	2.3	4860	4.8
1923	5233	3.2	842	0.5	2235	1.4	8310	5.1
1924	3782	2.2	372	0.1	1905	1.1	6059	3.4
1925	3819	2.1	621	0.4	1570	0.9	6010	3.4
1926	3520	1.9	763	0.4	1616	0.9	5899	3.2
1927	4277	1.9	977	0.4	3061	1.4	8315	3.7
1928	2245	0.9	1354	0.5	3627	1.4	7226	2.8
1929	3135	1.1	1827	0.7	2739	1.0	7701	2.8
Average 1921–29	3189	1.9	800	0.4	2159	1.3	6148	3.2
1930	4144	1.7	566	0.2	2754	1.1	7464	3.0
1931	2297	1.4	274	0.2	1219	0.7	3790	2.3
1932	1144	1.2	151	0.2	852	0.9	2147	2.3
1933	795	1.0	141	0.2	776	1.0	1712	2.2
Average 1930–33	2095	1.3	283	0.2	1400	0.9	3778	2.5

Source: *Latvijas statistikā gada grāmata 1921–33*.[19]

Latvia's share of the total imports and exports of the Scandinavian countries during this period was very minor. For example, in the period from 1921 to 1929 Latvia's share of the Swedish and Danish export trade was on average only 0.3 per cent per year (Nordlund, 1994, p. 248). Thus Sweden and Denmark were more than ten times more important to Latvian exports than Latvia was to Swedish and Danish exports. By 1934, Latvia's share of Swedish and Danish exports had been reduced to an average of 0.1 per cent per year (Nordlund, 1994, p. 248). The main reason why Latvia's trade relations with Scandinavia were not very significant was that Latvia was basically an agricultural country and its exports were mainly agricultural products (butter, meat, flax) and timber products (plywood, timber, paper) and the Scandinavian countries exported the same or similar products. Denmark was a significant exporter of butter and meat, while Norway and Sweden were significant exporters of timber products.[20] Thus, despite geographical proximity and the advantage of shorter sea routes than to Britain or Germany, the fact of similar export products made significant interregional trade between Latvia and the Scandinavian countries unprofitable. Even in industrial goods, Sweden did not compete very well with the cheaper industrial goods from Germany (*Economists*, 1929, No. 24, p. 989).

As with imports, Scandinavia's share of Latvian exports was reduced during the Great Depression. Exports to Norway were most affected (exports to Norway in 1933 were only some 8 per cent of the level in 1929), those to Sweden and Denmark markedly less so (to Sweden 28 per cent and to Denmark some 25 per cent of the level in 1929). Apart from the obvious effect of the Depression on the export of agricultural products, the decision of the government to maintain the gold standard when the Scandinavian countries (following Britain) had abandoned it probably contributed to the decline in Latvian exports by making them more expensive on the Scandinavian markets.

In 1929, at the beginning of the Great Depression, Latvia's foreign trade with Scandinavia was hardly affected. This is because in Latvia (and in fact also in the Scandinavian countries) the crisis only really began in 1930. Latvia, following the lead of the rest of Europe, did all it could to reduce imports and halt the outflow of foreign currency, including the establishment of a currency commission and import credit restrictions, the establishment of a contingent (quota) system for imports, increases in import duties and the promotion of import substitution. The most successful import substitution was in the area of cereals and animal fodder imports, which by 1933 had almost disappeared as an import item. In 1931, the customs tariff was amended six times, in 1932 also six times, but in 1933 ten times (*Ekonomists*, 1934, No. 13/14, p. 474). Looking at Latvia's total foreign trade (exports plus imports) with the Scandinavian countries, these measures radically reduced total trade with Scandinavia in money terms – in 1930 by 17 per cent compared to 1929, but by 56 per cent in 1931, by 82 per cent in 1932 and by 75 per cent in 1933 compared to 1929, as not only were imports affected by the Latvian measures, but so too were exports.

A more complete picture regarding Latvia's trade with Scandinavia can be seen in Table 4.4, which analyses the total volume of trade between Latvia and the Scandinavian countries.

Table 4.4 Total volume of trade between Latvia and the Scandinavian countries (% of total Latvian foreign trade – imports plus exports), 1921–33

Year	Denmark	Norway	Sweden	Total Scandinavia
1921	6.1	0.8	2.5	9.4
1922	3.4	0.6	2.2	6.2
1923	3.2	0.4	2.0	5.6
1924	3.6	0.1	2.1	5.8
1925	4.1	0.3	2.4	6.8
1926	4.2	0.3	2.6	7.1
1927	4.5	0.3	2.9	7.7
1928	2.1	0.3	2.3	4.7
1929	1.7	0.4	2.0	4.1
Average 1921–29	3.7	0.4	2.3	6.4
1930	1.8	0.2	2.1	4.1
1931	1.5	0.2	1.8	3.5
1932	1.2	0.3	1.4	2.9
1933	0.9	0.1	1.8	2.8
Average 1930–33	1.4	0.2	1.8	3.3

Source: *Latvijas statistikā gada grāmata 1921–33*.[21]

Table 4.4 shows the devastating effect of the Great Depression on trade between Latvia and the Scandinavian countries. The percentage of Latvia's average total trade for the period 1930–33 was practically half that for the period 1921–29. This percentage had already begun to decline in 1928, probably due to falling world prices for agricultural products and early moves to import substitution in agricultural products (the most affected was cereal imports from Denmark), import credit restrictions (to reduce the amount of imported intermediate and final goods), higher customs tariffs for agricultural machinery and other manufactures, as well as the return of Denmark and Norway to full gold parity, held at approximately the 1928 level until 1931 when the full force of the Depression struck. Thus the percentage of Latvia's total trade with the Scandinavian countries was reduced by 39 per cent in 1928 compared to 1927, and further reduced by 40 per cent in 1933 compared to 1928.

5 EFFECT OF SCANDINAVIAN INVESTMENT ON LATVIAN FOREIGN TRADE, 1920–33

Scandinavian capital investment in Latvia in the period 1920–33 was relatively small and practically confined to Danish and Swedish entrepreneurs. Although complete figures are difficult to obtain, Table 4.5 gives some indication of the level of Scandinavian investment in Latvian joint-stock companies during the interwar period.

Table 4.5 Scandinavian investments in Latvian joint-stock companies (% of total foreign investment and amount in million lats – cumulative base), 1925–33

	Swedish capital		Danish capital		Norwegian capital	
	%	Ls	%	Ls	%	Ls
1925	3.5	1.98	8.7	4.86	0.1	0.35
1926	4.7	3.47	6.7	4.88	..	0.21
1927	4.7	3.99	5.8	4.97	..	0.32
1928	5.1	4.83	5.2	4.97	..	0.26
1929	6.7	6.35	5.5	5.19	..	0.26
1930	9.4	9.71	1.6	1.68	..	0.26
1931	11.3	11.83	1.4	1.48	..	0.21
1932	12.4	12.15	1.4	1.40	..	0.03
1933	12.8	12.16	1.5	1.44	..	0.01

Source: *Latvijas statistikā gada grāmatas 1930* and *1937–38*.

From Table 4.5 we see that while Swedish capital investments grew up to 1932 (especially after the syndicate agreement with the Swedish Match Company in 1928) and then remained practically at the 1932 level, Danish capital investment remained practically unchanged up to 1929, but there was a dramatic flight of Danish capital with the onset of the Great Depression. Similarly, from a very low base, Norwegian capital took flight in 1932 and had disappeared altogether by 1936. In the period 1920 to 1933 Swedish and Danish capital was mainly invested in the chemicals industry (linoleum, vegetable oil, match-heads), and there was a major investment of Swedish capital in the wood-working industry (matchsticks). There were also minor investments of Swedish and Danish capital in the metals industry (nails and sheet metal) and banking. Norwegian capital was mainly in the wood-working industry.

The types of manufactured goods which Latvia could offer for export were significantly affected during this period by international cartels and syndicates. These cartels and syndicates, which unified production on a European or world scale, bought up existing Latvian undertakings and, after a time, for the purposes of centralising production, either closed them down or left just sufficient to service the small domestic market. For example, in the period from 1925 to 1928, the Swedish match syndicate Svenska Tändsticks Aktiebolaget had bought up four of the five match factories in Latvia (*Ekonomists*, 1928, No. 10, p. 473). In 1928, Latvia signed an agreement with the Swedish match syndicate, which provided for the syndication of the Latvian match industry and the granting of an external loan to Latvia of US$ 6 million. The agreement was in fact the legalisation of the existing situation (*Ekonomists*, 1928, No. 12, p. 556). Matches as serious export goods disappeared from the foreign trade of Latvia, and in 1936 the export of matches ceased altogether.

A similar fate befell the Liepāja branch of the Swedish entrepreneurial family firm of Wicander (Linoleum Aktiebolaget Forshaga), the 'Liepāja Cork and Linoleum Factory', which before the First World War had produced linoleum for the Russian market. After the war the factory renewed production, but in 1922 it was already subject to the control of an international linoleum cartel based in Britain (Johansson, 1988, p. 260). However, in 1927, the Wicander firm sold its Liepāja branch to another cartel which was based in Germany, while retaining central management functions. The 'continued ownership control of assets in Baltic cork and linoleum manufacture, exercised by the Wicander company in Sweden, is manifested in Wicander's claims for Soviet compensation, supported by the Swedish Foreign Office' (Johansson, 1988, p. 262). The factory completely ceased production in 1930 and linoleum disappeared from the foreign trade of Latvia (Johansson, 1988, p. 261; Aizsilnieks, 1968, p. 537).

6 LATVIAN FOREIGN TRADE WITH THE SCANDINAVIAN COUNTRIES, 1934–39

The political changes in Latvia as a result of the *coup d'état* on 15 May 1934 and the introduction of a dictatorial regime led by the former Prime Minister Kārlis Ulmanis had little effect upon Latvia's imports from Scandinavia, which remained at about the same average percentage level as for the period 1930–33; however, the average percentage level of exports increased by some 63 per cent over the period 1934–39 in comparison to 1930–33. In 1932, Latvia had already signed the so-called bilateral 'clearing' agreements with Germany and France. The bilateral clearing system was an arrangement between the central banking institutions of two countries for carrying out trade transactions between them, including the balancing of credits and debits on a national level. For example, Latvian importers paid lats into the Bank of Latvia account of the trading partner, where the funds were held until they could be used to pay Latvian exporters for goods sold to the other country. If the accounts held insufficient funds, the exporters had to wait for imports to increase, and if there were excess funds, importers had to wait for increased exports. The central bank (or other designated financial institution) of the trading partner held similar clearing accounts for its importers and exporters. The basic idea behind bilateral clearing agreements was to even out or 'balance' trade between two countries, while at the same time conserving scarce foreign currency and gold reserves. In 1935, Latvia also signed a clearing agreement with Sweden. Norway and Denmark remained 'hard currency' trading partners.

As can be seen from Table 4.6, Latvia's imports from the Scandinavian countries in the period 1934–39 were on average the same as the averages during the Great Depression – 4.8 per cent per year of the total Latvian imports for this period (4.7 per cent for 1930–33). The highest level in both money terms and as a percentage of total Latvian imports was achieved in 1937. This was after Latvia had, on 28 September 1936, devalued the lat and abandoned the gold standard. This step, which was simultaneously a rejection of autarkic economic policies, especially in the sphere of industry, freed up foreign currency reserves for the purchase of imports (*The Latvian Economist*, 1938, p. 14). In addition, there were large imports of cereals and flour (from Denmark and Sweden) due to a particularly dry summer in 1937 (Aizsilnieks, 1968, p. 794).

The somewhat large increase in imports from Sweden in the last years of the decade can be ascribed in large measure to the needs of the Ķegums hydroelectric power station, in whose construction Sweden was the major investment partner. On 1 August 1936, the Latvian government signed an agreement with the Swedish companies Svenska Entreprenad Aktiebolaget (SENTAB) and Aktiebolaget Elektro-Invest for the joint construction of the first large-scale Baltic hydroelectric power station on the River Daugava. In accordance with the agreement, the Swedish side provided Latvia with a grant of credit worth 11 million lats to be redeemed in ten years and the Latvian contribution to the project was to be some 30 million lats raised by the issue of public bonds (Johansson, 1994, p. 368). The first stage of the

Ķegums HES became operational on 15 October 1939.

The main goods that were imported from Denmark in this period were: cereals, animal fodder, seed, vegetable oils, animal products, chalk, wood products, agricultural and industrial machinery, motor cars, paints and paint products. From Sweden the main imports were: cereals, animal fodder, various types of metals and metal products, cellulose, stones, seed, cement, agricultural and industrial machinery, paints and paint products, motor cars and superphosphate; while from Norway the main imports were: treated hides, various types of metals and metal products, animal fats and fish oils, drive-belts, stones and wire.

Table 4.7 shows the effects of the 1936 devaluation on exports in 1937, when Latvian exports became cheaper. Total Latvian exports to Scandinavia for the period 1934–39 had on average exceeded even the pre-depression average of 3.2 per cent of all exports for the period 1921–29.

It should be noted, however, that all three Scandinavian countries belonged to the so-called 'Oslo Group', which also included Finland, the Netherlands and Belgium. On 22 December 1930, the Oslo Group had signed an agreement undertaking not to raise tariffs without giving notice to other members. During the 1930s, the Oslo Group concluded a number of mutual agreements aimed at increasing trade between members and reducing trade barriers. For example, in June 1932 the members agreed on a mutual reduction of tariffs of 10 per cent per annum for five years. After the dissolution of the gold bloc (the Netherlands and Belgium retained the gold standard until 1936 after the Scandinavian countries had abandoned it in 1931), the members agreed to impose no new tariffs and to eliminate quotas applied to each other's trade on a mutual basis. As Kindleberger has commented, 'It was a brave example without much impact' (Kindleberger, 1990, p. 135).

At the Oslo Group conference in Copenhagen on 5–6 April 1936, the issue of mutual economic assistance in the event of a possible international crisis or war blockade was discussed. The Latvian Foreign Minister Munters was informed of national committees being established in the Scandinavian countries to coordinate issues of mutual supply at a time of crisis during his visits to Finland and Sweden in 1938. Latvia wanted very much to join the Oslo Group and on 30 August 1938 the Latvian Cabinet took a decision to begin negotiations with the Group. However, nothing came of it and another strategy that Latvia could have adopted from the Scandinavian experience – timely economic preparations for war – was not heeded (LVVA, f. 2575, apr. 8, p. 164). Clearly, however, Latvian export goods were of value for adding to prudent stockpiles, which would probably explain the sudden rise in exports to the three Scandinavian countries in 1939 (exports to Norway and Denmark nearly tripled and to Sweden they doubled).

Table 4.6 *Latvian imports from Scandinavian countries, 1934–39*

Year	Denmark (million Ls)	Per cent of all imports	Norway (million Ls)	Per cent of all imports	Sweden (million Ls)	Per cent of all imports	Total Scand. (million Ls)	Per cent of all imports
1934	0.88	0.9	1.14	1.2	1.50	1.6	3.52	3.7
1935	1.00	1.0	1.16	1.2	2.10	2.1	4.26	4.3
1936	1.74	1.4	0.80	0.7	4.02	3.3	6.56	5.4
1937	5.10	2.2	1.81	0.8	8.40	3.6	15.31	6.6
1938	1.60	0.7	1.41	0.6	6.92	3.0	9.93	4.3
1939	1.92	0.9	0.74	0.3	7.09	3.2	9.75	4.4
Average 1934–39	2.04	1.2	1.18	0.8	5.01	2.8	8.22	4.8

Sources: *Latvijas statistikā gada grāmata*, 1934–39; *Strukturbericht über das Ostland. Teil I: Ostland in Zahlen*, Rīga: Reichskommissar für das Ostland, 1942, pp. 57–8; *Historisk Statistikk 1968*, Oslo: Statistisk Sentralbyrå, 1969, p. 325.

Table 4.7 Latvian exports to Scandinavian countries, 1934–39

Year	Denmark (million Ls)	Per cent of all imports	Norway (million Ls)	Per cent of all imports	Sweden (million Ls)	Per cent of all imports	Total Scand. (million Ls)	Per cent of all imports
1934	1.82	2.1	0.66	0.8	1.36	1.6	3.84	4.5
1935	1.93	2.0	0.30	0.3	1.62	1.6	3.85	3.9
1936	0.82	0.6	0.27	0.2	3.03	2.2	4.12	3.0
1937	1.32	0.5	4.10	1.6	3.10	1.2	8.52	3.3
1938	0.95	0.7	0.73	0.3	4.52	2.0	6.20	3.0
1939	2.76	1.2	1.99	0.9	9.14	4.0	13.89	6.1
Average 1934–39	1.60	1.2	1.08	0.5	3.80	2.1	6.74	4.0

Sources: As for Table 4.6.

The main goods exported to Denmark during the whole of this period were cereals, butter, spirits and liqueurs, round timber and sleepers, plywood, seeds and gypsum. To Sweden Latvia exported potatoes, sprats, cheese, all types of meat, chocolates, flax, pulpwood, gypsum, raw hides, threads, plywood, glues, paints and paint products, and to Norway threads, pulpwood, gypsum, paints and paint products, and radios.

Table 4.8 Total volume of trade between Latvia and the Scandinavian countries (% of total Latvian foreign trade – imports plus exports), 1934–39

Year	Denmark	Norway	Sweden	Total Scandinavia
1934	1.5	1.0	1.6	4.1
1935	1.4	0.7	1.8	3.9
1936	1.0	0.4	2.7	4.1
1937	1.3	1.2	2.3	4.8
1938	0.6	0.5	2.5	3.6
1939	1.0	0.6	3.6	5.2
Average 1934–39	1.1	0.7	2.4	4.3

Sources: As for Table 4.6.

In Table 4.8 it can be seen that total Latvian trade with the Scandinavian countries as a percentage of all Latvian trade never regained its 1921–29 levels, although average total trade for 1934–39 was 30 per cent higher than the average for 1930–33. Trade with Denmark continued to decline during this period, but this was compensated for by an increase in trade with Norway (which increased by 250 per cent over the percentage of average total trade for the 1930–33 period) and Sweden (increased by 33 per cent over the 1930–33 period). In fact, the percentage of average total trade with Norway and Sweden in the period 1934–39 also exceeded the percentage average trade for the 1921–29 (by 75 per cent and 4.4 per cent respectively). This increased trade with Norway and Sweden can partly be explained by the needs of Latvia's growing industry for raw materials, partly by the building of the Ķegums hydroelectric power station with Swedish assistance, and partly by the Oslo Group's purposeful policy of acquiring stockpiles of goods in case of war.

7 SCANDINAVIAN FOREIGN INVESTMENT IN LATVIA, 1934–39

Norwegian foreign investment in Latvian joint-stock companies as noted in Table 4.5 had already started to decline during the Great Depression and had ceased altogether by 1936. Danish capital, after an initial flight during the Great Depression, started to increase in 1937, but then declined slightly for the rest of the decade, as can be seen in Table 4.9. The authoritarian regime made special efforts to reduce the amount of foreign capital in Latvia joint-stock companies during the period 1934–39. The percentage share of foreign capital in Latvian joint-stock companies was halved from 50.4 per cent in 1934 to 25.4 per cent in 1939 (*Finanču un kredita statistika 1939*, (1939), p. 172).

Table 4.9 Scandinavian investments in Latvian joint-stock companies (% of total foreign investment and amount in million lats – cumulative base), 1934–39

		1934	1935	1936	1937	1938	1939
Swedish capital	%	13.5	13.8	17.6	18.9	18.1	15.4
	Ls	12.07	12.03	12.67	12.14	11.13	9.23
Danish capital	%	1.6	1.6	2.0	2.6	2.6	2.6
	Ls	1.44	1.42	1.4	1.69	1.57	1.58
Norwegian capital	%	..	..	–	–	–	–
	Ls	0.01	0.01	–	–	–	–

Source: *Latvijas statistikā gada grāmata 1937–38* and *Finanču un kredita statistika 1939*, pp. 173–4.

This decline was particularly noticeable in those industries in which with state support the government tried to eliminate foreign capital (such as the metal industry, banks etc.). This 'Latvianisation' of the capital market reduced the overall amount of foreign capital in Latvian joint-stock companies and thus proportionally increased the percentage share of those that were left. The percentage share of Swedish capital rises dramatically in this period although the actual amount remains more or less the same.

In relation to Swedish investment, in May 1941 the Swedish and Soviet governments signed a treaty in relation to mutual economic claims regarding the Baltic States including Latvia.[22] The final official calculation of Swedish economic assets in Latvia as presented by the Swedish Foreign Office to the USSR for the payment of compensation is shown in Table 4.10.[23]

Of the companies named by the Swedish Foreign Office, Swedish Match was involved in the chemicals industry (match-heads) and wood industry (matchsticks), Svenska Entreprenad AB in the electricity industry (Ķegums HES), Wingårdh in the chemicals industry (superphosphate), Skånska Cement in the construction industry (cement), Wicander in the chemicals industry (linoleum) and AGA in the chemicals industry (gas and gas equipment).

Table 4.10 Total Latvian assets of Swedish main creditors (million SEK), 1941

Swedish Match	10.9
Svenska Entreprenad AB	12.4
Wingårdh (& associates)	9.9
Wicander	3.6
Skånska Cement	1.1
AGA	0.2
Total	38.1

The Danes also presented a claim for compensation of former Danish assets in the Baltic States, some 16.5 million DKK in relation to nationalisations and 2.5 million DKK in commercial claims. The official calculation of Danish economic assets in Latvia as presented to the USSR (based on large claims) is shown in Table 4.11.[24]

Table 4.11 Total Latvian assets of Danish main creditors (million DKK), 1941

Aarhus Oliemølle Ltd	1.3
Mr G. Haagensen	1.2
Mr O. Klingengberg	1.0
Total	3.5

In addition, there was a claim from Vacuum Oil Co. Ltd, for branches in Rīga and Tallinn (0.7 million DKK). The company Aarhus Oliemølle Ltd partly owned an oil factory in Liepāja, Mr Haagensen had a business and property in Latvia and Mr Klingenberg had a factory in Rīga.

Compensation claims from Sweden in respect of nationalised assets in the Baltic States were basically settled by the USSR in 1946, but commercial claims only in 1964. Sweden received only some 11 million SEK from the USSR for the nationalised assets and 60 000 SEK for commercial claims (Kangeris, 1998, pp. 208–9). Denmark received 2.6 million DKK from the USSR in 1964 as settlement of all claims, and even Norway received in

1959 0.5 million NOK from the USSR in compensation for lost assets in the Baltic States (Kyn, 1998, pp. 233–4).

8 LATVIAN FOREIGN TRADE WITH THE SCANDINAVIAN COUNTRIES, 1939–40

After September 1939, foreign trade became Latvia's weakest point. A great deal of what happened in foreign trade was beyond the control of Latvia and was a consequence of the war.[25] Nevertheless, Latvia could have been better prepared in case of the collapse of foreign trade. At the outbreak of the Second World War, Latvia's foreign trade with the Scandinavian countries and the rest of the world became complicated despite the fact that Latvia, the other Baltic States and the Scandinavian countries had all declared their full neutrality. With Great Britain as Latvia's most important export customer and in the absence of British naval protection in the Baltic Sea, to maintain trade with the Baltic States British authorities suggested alternative routes for Latvian exports to Great Britain. The Germans had effectively blocked Baltic Sea outlets to the North Sea and hence to Britain. Two alternatives were suggested. One was the shipment of exports to Sweden via Finnish or Swedish territorial waters and further through Swedish/Danish/Norwegian territorial waters to Britain. This was extremely difficult due to the increased German naval activity in the region. The alternative route was to ship exports to a Swedish port, transport them across Sweden by rail to a Norwegian port, and reship to Britain. This proved to be the only viable way despite the fact that it was the most expensive, adding some 22 per cent to overall costs in 1939 (LVVA, f. 2574, apr. 4, pp. 64–5).

The presence of German warships in the Baltic Sea interrupted the general free movement of ships. The German navy stopped ships of neutral countries, allegedly looking for contraband. For example, on 21 December the Germans seized the Latvian ship *Atis Kronvalds* (1423 BRT), which was taking 870 tons of Latvian and Lithuanian bacon and butter, as well as 202 tons of plywood, to Sweden for further shipment to Britain (LVVA, f. 2574, apr. 4, p. 46). In the same month, the Germans also seized the *Aija* (575 BRT) en route from Rīga to Stockholm (Bernsone et al. (eds), 1998, p. 152). The Latvian Chamber of Commerce and Industry reported that: 'The number of Latvian vessels detained in Germany has grown from 8 ships on November 18, 1939, to 24 in the middle of December, which represented nearly one-third of the Latvian merchant fleet' (*Latvian Economic Review*, 1940, p. 28).

In Table 4.12, we can see that in the first four months of the war foreign trade with Norway practically ceased. In addition, trade with Denmark was minimal. The best result was for trade with Sweden, which can be partly explained by the fact that it was easier to get to Swedish ports by utilising the neutral territorial waters of Finland and Estonia and thus evading the German naval patrols in the Baltic Sea. With exports twice the size of imports it is clear that the Scandinavians were stockpiling Latvian goods, while at the same time releasing only a bare minimum to Latvia.[26] In April 1940, Germany occupied Denmark and Norway, and in June of the same year, the USSR occupied Latvia. With that ended Latvia's foreign trade with the Scandinavian countries. A 50-year-long interregnum had begun.

Table 4.12 Latvian and Scandinavian imports and exports, 1 September – 31 December 1939

State	Imports		Exports	
	Mill. Ls	Per cent of total imports for the period	Mill. Ls	Per cent of total exports for the period
Denmark	0.65	1.1	1.14	1.8
Sweden	1.84	3.0	3.37	5.4
Norway	–	–	0.01	–
Total	2.49	4.1	4.52	7.2

Sources: Calculation based on *Strukturbericht über das Ostland. Teil I: Ostland in Zahlen*, Rīga: Reichskommissar für das Ostland, 1942, pp. 57–8; *Mēneša Biļetens Nr. 10*, Rīga: Valsts Statistiskā Pārvalde, 1939, October, pp. 1058–59 and 1083–87; and *Historisk Statistikk 1968*, Oslo: Statistisk Sentralbyrå, 1969, p. 325.

9 CONCLUSION

After Latvia's declaration of independence in 1918, it still had another two years of war ahead of it and it was not until 1920 that some semblance of normal economic activity could be contemplated. In a sense, the history of Latvia's foreign trade started with the Scandinavian countries. They were the first to place branch offices of trading houses in the ports of Latvia in 1919, and Norway was the first country in the world to provide Latvia with long-term credits at a time when the main allied nations were not even sure whether Latvia had a right to exist at all.

While the decade of the 1920s was not a very auspicious one for Europe as a whole, for both Latvia and the Scandinavian countries, despite a few hiccups along the way, it was, in the main, a time of expanding trade both in Europe and between Latvia and the Scandinavian countries. In the area of foreign trade, wartime protectionism retreated a little after the recession of 1920–21, and Latvia's foreign trade with the Scandinavian countries, despite the fact that they had in many ways a parallel range of export products, showed an upward trend in both exports and imports. The volume of Latvian trade (exports plus imports) with the Scandinavian countries reached its highest levels in the 1920s (for example, 7.7 per cent of total Latvian foreign trade in 1927; in comparison, total Latvian foreign trade in 1927 with its two main trading partners – the United Kingdom and Germany – was respectively 21.6 per cent and 34 per cent). Early in the decade, both Latvian and Scandinavian entrepreneurs hoped that Latvia was indeed a bridge between West and East and would open the way to the huge market of Russia. By the middle of the decade, these hopes had been dashed and trade between Latvia and the Scandinavian countries waned to a fairly low level (5–6 per cent), where it remained for the rest of the interwar years.

Both Latvia and the Scandinavian countries were heavily dependent upon German and British markets, where they competed with the same agricultural and forestry products. This parallelism in exports meant that Latvia had little to offer the Scandinavian countries in terms of its mainly agricultural and forestry exports. On the other hand, industrial goods produced by the Scandinavian countries were up against the trade advantages of Germany and Britain, which, by virtue of their importance to Latvian exports, also dominated Latvia's mainly industrial and manufactured goods and raw materials import trade. Foreign investment by the Scandinavian countries was also low and throughout the 1920s never exceeded some 12 per cent of total foreign investments in Latvia.

Nevertheless, the Latvian market was important to certain sectors of the Scandinavian economy and, similarly, the Scandinavian market was important to certain sectors of the Latvian economy. For Latvia, the important Scandinavian markets were for foodstuffs, flax, timber products, plywood, paper, gypsum, paint and paint products, and linoleum. For Scandinavia, the important Latvian markets were for cereals, herrings, fodder, metals, stone, seeds, fertiliser, agricultural machinery (particularly separators), industrial machinery, vehicles and metal products.

With the Great Depression protectionism returned to Europe with a vengeance and the percentage of Latvia's foreign trade volume with the Scandinavian countries declined catastrophically (for example, to 2.9 per cent of the total volume of Latvian foreign trade in 1932), and even in the somewhat more stable period of the late 1930s, Latvia's trade with the Scandinavian countries never reached its pre-Depression volumes. However, Swedish investment in the huge Ķegums hydroelectric power station in the late 1930s was a powerful indicator of renewed interest in Latvia by the Scandinavian countries.

The history of Latvia's foreign trade ended as it began – with the Scandinavian countries, and Norway in particular. In attempting to maintain trade contacts not only with the Scandinavian countries but also with its most important export customer, Great Britain, Latvia utilised the ports and railways of Sweden and Norway to get Latvian goods to the British market in 1939/40. With the occupation of Norway and Denmark by the Germans in 1940 and of Latvia by the Russians in the same year, the first era of Latvian trade with the Scandinavian countries came to an abrupt end.

In a broader context, the pattern and structure of Latvia's trade with the Scandinavian countries was a reflection of European economic development during the interwar years. Despite geographical propinquity, the lack of effective regional or European trade structures meant that the large industrial countries of Europe dominated Latvian and Scandinavian foreign trade flows, leaving little room for interregional trade between the Baltic States and the Scandinavian countries. Latvia's exclusion from the Oslo Group in the 1930s meant that even this limited opportunity of coordinating trade within a restricted regional grouping could not be utilised to increase Latvia's trade with the Scandinavian countries.

NOTES

1 This chapter is based upon my PhD dissertation regarding the interwar trade relations between Latvia and the three Scandinavian countries – Norway, Sweden and Denmark – within a theoretical framework of international trade theory and utilising the methodologies of modern economic history. A version of this chapter was presented at the 15th European Advanced Studies Institute in Regional Science: 'Emerging Market Economies and European Economic Integration' held in Eksjö, Sweden, 10–16 June 2002. I would like to thank my fellow participants for their comments and suggestions and especially to session chairperson Assoc. Prof. Andreas Cornett from University of Southern Denmark, as well as discussant Scott Hacker from Jönköping International Business School. In addition, I would like to thank the three anonymous referees for extremely useful and critical comments and suggestions. All remaining errors are my own.

2 A Scandinavian colony was located at a place called Grobiņa not far from Liepāja in Latvia from the seventh to ninth century, which in turn was a large international trading centre. See Buša (2002).

3 See, for example, Byers et al. (2000); Cornett and Iversen (1998); Lasser and Schrader (2002).

4 Latvia was recognised *de jure* by Western Europe on 26 January 1921.

5 The date of the declaration of independence of the Republic of Latvia.

6 For a discussion of Sweden and Denmark and the International Relief Credit Programme, see Nordlund (1994), pp. 219–20.

7 The Baltic Clause stipulates that the priority rights and privileges allowed to the Baltic States may not be made applicable to other contracting states by virtue of the most-favoured-nation principle.

8 For a detailed examination of Latvia's economic development in the first ten years after the establishment of independence see Karnups (2001).

9 During the period 1924–27 Latvia obtained on average 32.5 per cent of its total wheat imports from Denmark (59 562 tons); see *Latvijas ārējā tirdzniecība un transits 1929* (1930), p. xxix.

10 Denmark returned to 75 per cent parity in 1925, 99 per cent in 1926 and full parity on 1 January 1927 (Johansen, 1987, pp. 29–31). Norway returned officially to full parity in May 1928 (Hodne, 1975, p. 386). For Sweden parity had been re-established *de facto* by the end of 1922 and officially in 1924 (Heckscher, 1954, p. 273).

11 Latvijas ārējā tirdzniecība (1929), pp. 2–3. This was of course due to the operation of the 'triangle of trade', where Latvia sold more to Britain than it purchased and used the surplus to purchase manufactured goods from Germany (Hiden and Salmon, 1991, p. 86).

12 Ford in 1919 and General Motors in 1923 established assembly plants in Copenhagen to cover the Baltic markets; see Johansen (1987), p. 40.

13 By 1932, the importation of wheat from Denmark was reduced to zero, see *Latvijas ārējā tirdzniecība un transits 1932* (1933), p. xxii.

14 The value of total Latvian imports in 1933 was only 25.2 per cent of the value in 1929.

15 *Latvijas ārējā tirdzniecība un transits 1929* (1930), p. liii. This was some 4 per cent of all butter exported during the period, see *Economists* (1931), No. 16, p. 554.

16 For detailed account of this Swedish transnational enterprise in Latvia, see Johansson (1988).

17 The volume of exports to Norway increased from 1011 to 21 767 tons from 1924 to 1929.

18 Latvian roubles in 1921 have been converted to Latvian lats in accordance with the recalculations of the Director of the Ministry of Finance Credit Department, A. Kārkliņš. For 1921, 66 267 Latvian roubles = 1 lats (imports) and 66 914 Latvian roubles = 1 lats (exports), but Latvian roubles in 1922 have been converted to Latvian lats in accordance with the rate set by the State Statistical Administration: 50 Latvian roubles = 1 lats (imports and exports); see *Ekonomists* (1925), No. 10, p. 498.

19 See also note 18.

20 Butter was also an important export for Sweden. By 1929 Swedish butter held 8 per cent of the German butter market, which was almost the same as the Latvian share; see Jörgensen (1999), p.120.

21 See also note 18

22 Sweden had recognised the incorporation of the Baltic States into the USSR *de facto* in August 1940 and *de jure* on 30 May 1941. See Balodis (1991) pp. 288–90, 344–5 and 407.

23 Based upon Johansson (1988), pp. 256–8.

24 Based upon Kyn (1998), p. 230.

25 For a comprehensive historian's overview of Latvian foreign trade as a whole for 1939–40, see Stranga (1993).

26 See *Ekonomists* (1939), No. 18, p. 1309, regarding stockpiling in Scandinavia in general. Both Sweden and Norway had already prohibited the export of most goods in August 1939.

REFERENCES

Aizsilnieks, A. (1968), *Latvijas saimniecības vēsture, 1914–1945* (*An Economic History of Latvia, 1914–1945*), Stockholm: Daugava.

Balodis, A. (1991), *Latvijas un latviešu tautas vēsture* (*History of Latvia and the Latvian People*), Rīga: Neatkarīgā teātra 'Kabata' grāmata apgāds.

Bernsone, I. et al. (eds) (1998), *Latvijas jūrniecības vēsture, 1850–1950* (*Maritime History of Latvia, 1850–1950*), Rīga: Rīgas vēstures un kuģniecības muzejs.

Buša, I. (2002), 'Priekšstatu maiņa 20.gadsimtā par Grobiņas archeoloģisko kompleksu' (Changes of Concept in the 20th Century regarding the Grobiņa Archaeological Complex), *Latvijas Vēsture/Jaunie un jaunākie laiki*, **2** (46), 78–89.

Byers, D.A. et al. (2000), 'New Borders and Trade Flows: A Gravity Model Analysis of the Baltic States', *Open Economies Review*, **11** (1), 73–91.

Cornett, A.P. and S.P. Iversen (1998), 'The Baltic States in a European and Baltic Perspective: Trade and Transition in the Baltic Rim', paper presented at the 5th Nordic Baltic Conference in Regional Science, 1998, http://www.geo.ut.ee/nbc/paper/cornett_iversem.htm.

Economists (1920), No. 1, Latvijas Finanču Ministrija (Latvian Ministry of Finance).

Economists (1920), No. 4, Latvijas Finanču Ministrija (Latvian Ministry of Finance).

Economists (1929), No. 24, Latvijas Finanču Ministrija (Latvian Ministry of Finance).

Economists (1931), No. 16, Latvijas Finanču Ministrija (Latvian Ministry of Finance).

Eichengreen, B. and D.A. Irwin (1996), 'The Role of History in Bilateral Trade Flows', NBER Working Paper 5565, National Bureau of Economic Research.

Ekonomists (1925), No. 10, Latvijas Finanču Ministrija (Latvian Ministry of Finance).

Ekonomists (1928), No. 10, Latvijas Finanču Ministrija (Latvian Ministry of Finance).

Ekonomists (1928) No. 12, Latvijas Finanču Ministrija (Latvian Ministry of Finance).

Ekonomists (1934), No. 13/14, Latvijas Finanču Ministrija (Latvian Ministry of Finance).

Ekonomists (1939), No. 18, Latvijas Finanču Ministrija (Latvian Ministry of Finance)

Finanču un kredita statistika 1939 (Finance and Credit Statistics 1939) (1939), Rīga: State Statistics Administration.

Heckscher, E.F. (1954), *An Economic History of Sweden*, Cambridge, MA: Harvard University Press.

Hiden, J. and P. Salmon (1991), *The Baltic Nations and Europe*, London: Longman.

Hodne, F. (1975), *An Economic History of Norway 1815–1970*, Bergen: Tapir.

Johansen, H.C. (1987), *The Danish Economy in the Twentieth Century*, New York: St Martin's Press.

Johansson, A. (1988), 'Swedish Transnational Enterprise in the Baltic Countries: Aspects of Continuity of the Pre-revolutionary Process of Direct Investment in the Russian Market', in J. Hiden and A. Loit (eds), *The Baltic in International Relations between the Two World Wars*, Stockholm: Centre for Baltic Studies, pp. 253–79.

Johansson, A. (1994), 'Towards the Creation of the Kegums Power Station: How Swedish Enterprise Responded to Latvian Plans for Expanded Electricity Production', in A. Johansson et al. (eds), *Emancipation and Interdependence*, Stockholm: Centre for Baltic Studies, pp. 367–85.

Jörgensen, H. (1999), 'Competition and Market: Swedish Views on Estonia's Agricultural Development and Butter Export 1918–39', *Acta Historica Tallinnensia*, **3**, 109–29.

Kangeris, K. (1998), 'Sweden, the Soviet Union and the Baltic Question 1940–1964 – a Survey', in K. Hovi (ed.) *Relations between the Nordic Countries and the Baltic States in the XX Century*, Turku: University of Turku.

Karnups, V.P. (2001), 'Latvijas ekonomiskā attīstība un ārējā tirdzniecība 1918–1928' (Latvia's economic development and foreign trade 1918–1928), in Ļ. Zīle (ed.), *Latvija divos laikposmos: 1918–1928 un 1991–2001* (*Latvia in Two Time*

Periods: 1918–1928 and 1991–2001), Rīga: LU žurnāla 'Latvijas Vēsture' fonds, pp. 365–83.
Kindleberger, C.P. (1990), *Historical Economics: Art or Science?*, Berkeley: University of California Press.
Kyn, P. (1998), 'Aspects of Recognition: Denmark's Relations to the Baltic States and Non-Recognition 1940–1991', in K. Hovi (ed.) *Relations between the Nordic Countries and the Baltic States in the XX Century*, Turku: University of Turku.
Lasser, C.-F. and K. Schrader (2002), 'European Integration and Changing Trade Patterns: The Case of the Baltic States', Kiel Working Paper No. 1088, Kiel Institute of World Economics.
Latvian Economic Review (1940), **1** (17).
The Latvian Economist (1923), Rīga: Latvijas Finanču Ministrija (Latvian Ministry of Finance).
The Latvian Economist (1938), Rīga: Latvijas Finanču Ministrija (Latvian Ministry of Finance).
Latvijas ārējā tirdzniecība (1929) (*Latvian Foreign Trade*), Rīga: Izdevniecība 'Ārējā Tirdzniecība'.
Latvijas ārējā tirdzniecība un transits 1929 (1930) (*Latvian Foreign Trade and Transit 1929*), Rīga: Valsts Statistiskā Pārvalde (State Statistics Administration).
Latvijas ārējā tirdzniecība un transits 1932 (1933) (*Latvian Foreign Trade and Transit 1932*), Rīga: Valsts Statistiskā Pārvalde (State Statistics Administration).
Latvijas ārējā tirdzniecība un transits 1937 (1938) (*Latvian Foreign Trade and Transit 1937*), Rīga: Valsts Statistiskā Pārvalde (State Statistics Administration).
Latvijas statistikā gada grāmata 1920 (1921) *(Latvian Statistical Yearbook 1920)*, Rīga: Valsts Statistiskā Pārvalde (State Statistics Administration).
Latvijas statistikā gada grāmata 1930 (1931) *(Latvian Statistical Yearbook 1930),* Rīga: Valsts Statistiskā Pārvalde (State Statistics Administration).
Latvijas statistikā gada grāmata 1934 (1935) *(Latvian Statistical Yearbook 1934),* Rīga: Valsts Statistiskā Pārvalde (State Statistics Administration).
Latvijas statistikā gada grāmata 1935 (1936) *(Latvian Statistical Yearbook 1935),* Rīga: Valsts Statistiskā Pārvalde (State Statistics Administration).
Latvijas statistikā gada grāmata 1936 (1937) *(Latvian Statistical Yearbook 1936),* Rīga: Valsts Statistiskā Pārvalde (State Statistics Administration).
Latvijas statistikā gada grāmata 1937/38 (1938) *(Latvian Statistical Yearbook 1937/38),* Rīga: Valsts Statistiskā Pārvalde (State Statistics Administration).
Latvijas statistikā gada grāmata 1939 (1939) *(Latvian Statistical Yearbook 1939),* Rīga: Valsts Statistiskā Pārvalde (State Statistics Administration).
LVVA (Latvian State Historical Archives).
Nordlund, S. (1994), 'Temporary Partners or Permanent Connections? Scandinavian Responses to the Baltic States Markets, 1918–1940', in A. Johansson et al. (eds), *Emancipation and Interdependence*, Stockholm: Centre for Baltic Studies, pp. 213–60.
Norway in 1920 (1921), *Norwegian Trade Review*, No. 2, Trade Intelligence Bureau of Norway.
Spekke, A. (1951), *History of Latvia: An Outline*, Stockholm: M. Goppers.
Stranga, A. (1993), 'Latvijas ārējā tirdzniecība 30. gadu nogale' (Latvian Foreign Trade at the End of the 1930s), in *Latvijas Vēsture* Nos 1993/4, 1994/1, 1994/3, 1995/1, 1995/2 and 1995/3.

PART TWO

Regional Issues and Migration Issues

5. The Effect of Infrastructure Improvements on Regional Labour Markets: A Multiregional Equilibrium Job Search Model

Jos van Ommeren,[1] Piet Rietveld and Stefan Woudenberg

1 INTRODUCTION

Most transition countries are confronted with higher than average unemployment rates (see e.g. Hazans et al., 2002; OECD, 2002). At the same time, these countries are confronted with growing regional disparities (Newell, 2001). A standard 'treatment' of these economies is to improve the efficiency of the economies by investing in infrastructure (partially financed by donor countries). This has a number of advantages: it increases the effective demand for goods, which increases income in the short run; further it improves the productivity of firms; and finally, infrastructure improvements are thought to be beneficial to the efficiency of the labour market (Lakshmanan et al., 2001). In the current chapter, we will analyse the effects of local infrastructure improvements on the labour market using a multiregional equilibrium labour model. The improved efficiency argument relies on two underlying ideas. More workers can be recruited within reasonable commuting distances (Lakshmanan et al., 2001). Workers can be recruited at lower costs, because they need less commuting costs compensation (van Ommeren and Rietveld, 2002). Both ideas imply that local unemployment will fall, but the effect on the local vacancy rate is intuitively ambiguous. The vacancy rate may fall because of the increased probability of finding employees, or it may increase because the region has become more competitive and will attract more firms with vacancies. The current chapter indicates that the positive effect dominates the negative effect (in the medium run). The effect on local wages seems also to be ambiguous: wages may increase due to the reduction in unemployment (relative to vacancies), or may decrease due to the reduction in commuting costs compensation. The current chapter indicates that the negative effect dominates the positive effect, but the reduction in wages appears to be small. The effects on the local labour market can be determined in an unambiguous way according to the model. The effect on adjacent regions is ambiguous. Suppose that infrastructure improvements increase the local vacancy rate; this improves the labour market opportunities of unemployed job seekers in adjacent regions. As a result, the unemployed in adjacent regions are more likely to find a suitable vacancy, but, at the same time, they will ask for higher wages, because their labour market position has improved.

It is common to distinguish between different time horizons to analyse the effect of infrastructure. We distinguish here between the short (typically less than one year), medium (typically five to ten years) and long run (typically more than 30 years); see, similarly, Blanchard (2000). We will shortly describe the expected results in the short and long run. The focus of the current chapter is on the medium run. In the short run, infrastructure improvements reduce the cost associated with commuting and may therefore induce unemployed job seekers to accept job offers they otherwise would have rejected. As a result, the local unemployment rate, and the local vacancy rate, will fall (Lakshmanan et al., 2001). In the short run, labour supply (via migration) and wages will react to changes in the labour market. Whether employers immediately adjust the number of new job openings due to improved labour market conditions is not so clear. Presumably, all the labour market effects are local. In the long run, the effects of infrastructure improvements are completely different. Plausibly, house prices, wages, productivity levels and regional levels of labour supply (because of migration) adjust to the infrastructure improvements and, most likely, the effects of the infrastructure improvements on the local and national equilibrium unemployment rate are absent. In the long run, employees are better off when the increase in wages exceeds the additional tax to pay for infrastructure.

In the medium run, the economy will move to its new equilibrium unemployment rate. It is plausible, that during the adjustment process, wages will react to infrastructure improvements and changes in labour market tightness. For example, wages may fall, because employees will receive less compensation for commuting costs. The main difference from the short-run effects is that the fall in wages induces firms to create more job openings and that the labour markets in adjacent regions will be affected. The main difference from the long-run effects is that the effects of changes in productivity levels and in labour supply due to migration can still be ignored (the cumulative effect of interregional migration is quite small in the medium run).

In the current chapter we introduce a multiregional equilibrium job search model. The essential idea is that regional labour supply is fixed (so the labour force is given), and that the number of vacancies, the number of unemployed and wage levels are endogenously determined given the productivity levels. Due to search frictions, in each region, unemployment and a positive number of vacancies exist at the same time. Job seekers search for jobs in their own region but also in other regions. The number of matches between vacancies and unemployed job seekers in a region depends on the regional levels of vacancies and unemployment. Regional labour markets are in equilibrium when the number of individuals who become unemployed in a region is equal to the number of individuals who find employment in this region. Wage levels are endogenously determined. Job seekers and employers bargain about the wage conditional on the commuting costs. Employers decide to create a vacancy when the expected profit of a filled job exceeds the hiring costs.

The outline of the chapter is as follows: in section 2, we will introduce a multiregional job search model for the medium run. Section 3 gives the results of the simulations. Section 4 draws conclusions.

2 THE MODEL

2.1 The Matching Model

We presume that individuals are all identical. Firms are identical but for the level of productivity, which is regionally specific and exogenously determined.[2] Individuals are either unemployed or employed. The unemployed search for jobs, the employed do not search.[3] A firm consists of only one job, which is either filled or unfilled. Firms do not relocate filled jobs to other regions (due to prohibitively high relocation costs), but may relocate unfilled jobs freely at no cost (so employers are free to choose the location of the vacancy). In order to fill a job, firms post a vacancy. We presume that individuals do not move residence either within or between regions.[4]

We presume that there exist n regions.[5] The labour force of each region contains L_i individuals. We let u_i denote the unemployment rate – the number of unemployed as a fraction of the labour force in region i – and v_j the vacancy rate – the number of vacant jobs, as a fraction of the labour force in region j ($i,j = 1, \ldots n$). The unemployed contact vacancies for which they perceive a positive probability of a match.[6]

The unemployed persons are matched to vacancies by a matching function. The matching function M_j gives the number of matches at any one time as a function of the number of unemployed looking for jobs and the number of firms looking for workers in region j (i.e. all firms with vacancies). This function is assumed to be increasing with the number of unemployed and vacancies and has constant returns to scale (Pissarides, 2000).

The matching function M_j is usually assumed to be a Cobb–Douglas function in the empirical literature (see e.g. Pilegaard, 2003). This implies that:

$$M_j = \prod_i (u_i L_i)^{k_{ij}} (v_j L_j)^{1-k_{ij}}, \tag{5.1}$$

where $\Sigma_i k_{ij} < 1$.[7] So, k_{ij} is the elasticity of the number of new filled jobs in region j with respect to the number of unemployed in region i.

The probability that an unemployed person from region i is hired in region j is denoted as s_{ij}. Let q_{ij} denote the rate at which unemployed people located in region i are hired in region j, and q_j denote the match rate in region j. Let θ_{ij} denote *(regional) labour market tightness*, the number of vacancies in region j relative to unemployment in region i. It follows that:

$$q_{ij} = s_{ij} q_j, \tag{5.2}$$

where

$$q_j = \frac{M_j}{L_j v_j} = \prod_i \theta_{ij}^{-k_{ij}} \text{ and } \theta_{ij} = \frac{L_j v_j}{L_i u_i} \tag{5.3}$$

The share of unemployed job seekers from region i who find employment in region j depends on the probability that an unemployed job seeker is matched to a vacancy in region j, denoted as K_{ij}.[8] The share of unemployed job seekers from region i who become employed in region j, denoted as s_{ij}, can be written as:

$$s_{ij} = \frac{K_{ij} u_i L_i}{\sum_{i'} K_{i'} u_{i'} L_{i'}}, \tag{5.4}$$

so $\sum_i s_{ij} = 1$.

The unemployment–employment transition rate

Given q_{ij}, one can write f_{ij}, the rate at which unemployed job seekers in region i find employment in region j, as:[9]

$$f_{ij} = \theta_{ij} q_{ij}. \tag{5.5}$$

So, the rate at which unemployed job seekers in region i find employment, f_i, can be written as:

$$f_i = \sum_j \theta_{ij} q_{ij}. \tag{5.6}$$

2.2 Job Destruction

It is presumed that jobs are destroyed at rate λ. The destruction rate does not vary among regions.

2.3 Equilibrium Employment and Unemployment

In equilibrium, the number of individuals in region i who become unemployed ($\lambda(1-u_i)$) must be equal to the number of individuals in region i who become employed ($u_i f_i$). The *equilibrium regional unemployment rate* u_i can then be written as follows:

$$u_i = \frac{\lambda}{\lambda + f_i}. \tag{5.7}$$

Similarly, it can be shown that the *commuting share*, e_{ij}, defined as the number of jobs filled by residents from region j in region i, divided by the labour force in region i, can be written as:

$$e_{ij} = \frac{f_{ij}}{\lambda + f_i}. \tag{5.8}$$

2.4 Job Creation

Suppose that a firm opens a vacancy. The value of the vacancy depends on the search costs and the expected income stream of finding a suitable worker. More formally, the value of a vacancy in region j, V_j, can be written as:

$$rV_j = -p_j c + \sum_i q_{ij}(J_{ij} - V_j), \tag{5.9}$$

where $p_j c$ denotes the firm's search costs, which are presumed to be proportional to regional productivity p_j, r denotes the discount rate, and J_{ij} denotes the value of a job filled by a worker living in region i. This expression can also be rewritten more conveniently as:

$$rV_j = -p_j c + q_j(J_j^e - V_j), \tag{5.10}$$

where the expected value of a filled job, J_j^e, is defined as $J_j^e = \sum_i J_{ij} s_{ij}$.

The value of a job in region j occupied by a worker living in region i depends on the discounted income stream and can be written as:

$$rJ_{ij} = p_j - w_{ij} - \lambda J_{ij} \text{ or, similarly, } J_{ij} = \frac{p_j - w_{ij}}{r + \lambda}, \quad (5.11)$$

where w_{ij} is the (bargained) wage paid by a firm in region j to a worker in region i. The expected value of a filled job can then be calculated as:

$$rJ_j^e = p_j - w_j^e - \lambda J_j^e, \quad (5.12)$$

where w_j^e denotes the expected wage level in region j, defined as $w_j^e = \sum_{i'} w_{i'j} s_{i'j}$.

In equilibrium, it is assumed that all profit opportunities from new jobs are exploited, driving rents from vacant jobs to zero. So, essentially we presume free entry (and exit) of firms. Therefore, the equilibrium condition for the supply of vacant jobs implies that $V_j = 0$. Consequently:

$$(r + \lambda)J^e = p_j - w_j^e = \frac{(r + \lambda)p_j c}{q_j}. \quad (5.13)$$

This condition states that in equilibrium, regional labour market tightness is such that the expected value from a (new) job in region j is equal to the expected recruitment cost. So, the difference between the regional productivity and expected wage level is equal to the expected capitalised recruitment costs.

2.5 Workers

Here, we determine the lifetime utility of the unemployed and employed workers who anticipate (future) changes in their labour market status. For unemployed workers, lifetime utility U_i can be written as:

$$rU_i = z + \sum_j f_{ij}(W_{ij} - U_i), \quad (5.14)$$

where z denotes the utility of not working (mainly, the unemployment benefit), which is presumed to be the same in each region, and W_{ij} denotes the lifetime utility of a worker in region i who is employed in region j. For employed workers, lifetime utility can be written as:

$$rW_{ij} = w_{ij} - t_{ij} + \lambda(U_i - W_{ij}), \quad (5.15)$$

where t_{ij} denotes the generalised commuting costs (monetary and time costs) between i and j.

2.6 The Spatial Wage Equation

The wage rate is determined by a bargaining process between firms and preselected job applicants. The wage derived from the Nash bargaining solution is the wage that maximises the weighted product of the worker's and firm's net return from the job match (Pissarides, 2000). In order to form the job match, the worker gives up U_i for W_{ij}, and the firm gives up V_j for J_{ij}. Therefore the wage rate satisfies:

$$w_{ij} = \arg\max(W_{ij} - U_i)^{\beta}(J_{ij} - V_j)^{1-\beta}, \qquad (5.16)$$

where $0 \leq \beta \leq 1$. The parameter β may be interpreted as a relative measure of labour's bargaining strength, other than the one implied by the threat points U_i and V_j. For convenience, we will treat β as a parameter strictly between 0 and 1. Maximising the above equation with respect to the wage renders the following first-order condition:

$$W_{ij} - U_i = \beta(J_{ij} - V_j + W_{ij} - U_i). \qquad (5.17)$$

So β can be interpreted as the worker's share of the total surplus. By imposing the equilibrium condition $V_j = 0$, we obtain the following equation:

$$W_{ij} - U_i = \frac{\beta}{1-\beta} J_{ij}. \qquad (5.18)$$

So, the larger the firm's value of employing a worker from region i, J_{ij}, the larger the net value of employment for a worker from region i, $W_{ij} - U_i$. Using the above equations, it can be demonstrated that:

$$w_{ij} = (1-\beta)(t_{ij} + z) + \beta \sum_{j'} \theta_{ij'} s_{ij'} q_{j'} J_{ij} + \beta p_j. \qquad (5.19)$$

So, the wage is an increasing function of the commuting costs t_{ij} and the value of being unemployed, z. Since $1 - \beta < 1$, this implies that the *net wage* (the wage minus the commuting costs) is a decreasing function of the commuting costs. Further, the wage is an increasing function of the productivity level in region j. The penultimate term can be interpreted as the average search/hiring costs per unemployed person. Workers are rewarded for the saving of (future) hiring costs that the firm enjoys when a job is formed.[10] Given the wage rate, it is straightforward to calculate the expected wage level:

$$w_j^e = (1-\beta)(t_j^e + z) + \beta \sum_{i'} s_{i'j} \sum_{j'} \theta_{i'j'} s_{i'j'} q_{j'} J_{i'j'} + \beta p_j, \qquad (5.20)$$

where $t_j^e = \sum_{i'} t_{i'j} s_{i'j}$ denotes the expected commuting costs. Equation 5.20 implies that the regional productivity level has a positive effect on the wage level for three reasons. The first reason is that a higher productivity level increases the surplus (the last term). The second reason is that the expected commuting costs are an increasing function of the regional productivity level. In other words, workers are recruited from a larger area, which increases the commuting costs. The third reason is that the average wage costs are higher, since the ratio of vacancies to unemployment is less favourable, increasing the labour market bargaining position of the unemployed.

2.7 The Reservation Commuting Costs

We have seen above that the wage is an increasing and the net wage a decreasing function of the commuting costs. It will be convenient to make this relationship explicit and we will write the wage rate as $w_{ij}(t_{ij})$. This implies that job seekers and firms will only form a match when the commuting costs are less than a certain maximum, which we will label the reservation commuting costs T_{ij}.

When J_{ij} is less than 0, $W_{ij} - U_i$ is also less than 0, so firms and job seekers agree not to form a match. In contrast, when J_{ij} is more than 0, $W_{ij} - U_i$ is also more than 0, so firms and job seekers agree to form a match. So, the reservation commuting costs T_{ij} are defined by the condition that J_{ij} is equal to 0. This condition implies that:

$$p_j - w_{ij}(T_{ij}) = 0, \tag{5.21}$$

and using the wage equation, the reservation commuting costs can be written as:

$$T_{ij} = p_j - z - \frac{\beta}{1-\beta} \sum_{j'} \theta_{ij'} s_{ij'} q_{j'} J_{ij'}. \tag{5.22}$$

So, the reservation commuting costs are equal to the productivity level minus the unemployment benefits and minus the average search/hiring costs. Clearly, if the commuting costs exceed T_{ij}, workers from i will reject all matches in region j. In the sequel, we will presume that the commuting costs are less than T_{ij}, so firms and job seekers always form a match.[11]

3 SIMULATIONS

3.1 Assumptions

We have assumed an economy consisting of three adjacent regions which contain a workforce of equal size. These regions have different levels of productivity (high, medium and low) and are therefore labelled HP, MP and LP. The unit of time is years. To facilitate interpretation of the results, we presume that the annual average productivity level is equal to 1. The level of unemployment benefits, z, is equal to 0.5. The firms' search costs relative to the productivity level per unit of time is equal to 0.6. In line with the labour market literature, we presume that the workers' bargaining strength, β, is equal to 0.5 (Pissarides, 2000). The annual discount rate equals 0.15 and the annual rate at which jobs are destroyed equals 0.08 (so the expected job duration is 12 years). For convenience of notation, we assume that k_{ij}, the elasticity of the number of filled jobs in j with respect to the number of unemployed in i, equals K_{ij}, the probability that an unemployed job seeker is matched to a vacancy in j. We presume that unemployed people are more likely to be matched in the region of residence than in other regions ($k_{ii} = 0.25$, $k_{ij} = 0.125$). This assumption captures that job seekers do not search at random, but are more likely to search in their own neighbourhood. The commuting costs within the regions are equal to 0.05. Furthermore, the level of commuting costs between regions does not depend on the direction of the commute. The three regions are different only with respect to two characteristics: the productivity level and the commuting costs between regions (see Tables 5.1 and 5.2 and Figure 5.1).

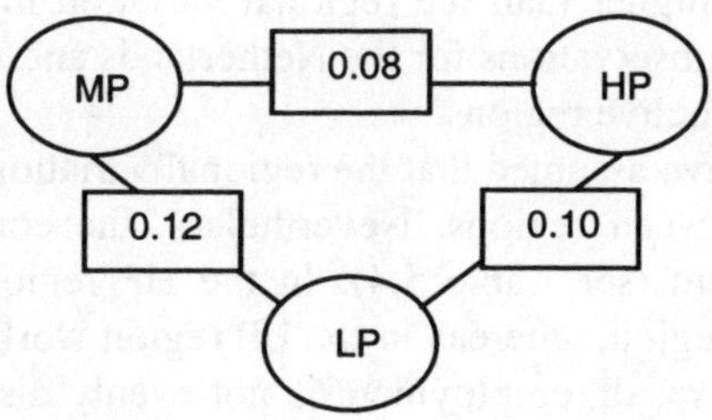

Note: The numbers indicate the commuting costs between regions. Commuting costs within the regions are equal to 0.05.

Figure 5.1 Map of a regional economy

As can be seen from Table 5.1, in the HP region, productivity is 5 per cent higher than MP; in the LP region, productivity is 5 per cent lower than MP. In the MP region, productivity is equal to 1. The commuting costs between regions are the lowest for the HP region, and the highest for the LP region (see Table 5.2). Finally, we emphasise that the parameters have been chosen such that a contact between an unemployed job seeker and an employer with a vacancy always results in a job match. So, for each contact, the commuting costs are less than the reservation commuting costs.

Table 5.1 Productivity parameters

	LP	MP	HP
Productivity	0.95	1.00	1.05

Table 5.2 Commuting costs

	LP	MP	HP
LP	0.05	0.12	0.10
MP	0.12	0.05	0.08
HP	0.10	0.08	0.05

3.2 Base Run

The main results for the base run can be found in Tables 5.3, 5.4 and 5.5. The outcomes of other endogenous variables can be supplied upon request from the authors. In more productive regions, the unemployment rate is lower, and the vacancy rate is higher (see Table 5.3). The main explanation for this result is that a high productivity level induces more firms to open vacancies, which reduces local unemployment levels. The regional variation in the vacancies is higher than the regional variation in unemployment (in line with empirical observations for the Netherlands and the UK). Wages are higher in more productive regions.

Recall that we have assumed that the regional variation in search intensity does not differ between regions. Nevertheless, the commuting flows are dramatically different (see Table 5.4). In the HP regions workers tend to work in their own region, whereas in the LP region workers tend to work in other regions. As a result, employment is not evenly distributed over space (see Table 5.5). Nevertheless, in contrast to models which exclude search imperfections, the results clearly imply simultaneous in- and out-commuting. For example, 29 per cent of the LP labour force commute to the HP region, whereas 16 per cent commute the other way round. These results imply that the expected commuting costs are substantially less in the HP region (see Table 5.3).

Table 5.3 Effects of alternatives on labour-market variables

	I	II	III	IV
Unemployment %				
LP	11.89	–0.18	+0.02	–0.26
MP	11.26	–0.04	+0.02	–0.26
HP	10.72	–0.04	–0.08	+0.07
Vacancies %				
LP	2.65	+0.27	–0.08	+0.23
MP	4.52	–0.11	–0.12	+0.34
HP	6.72	–0.14	+0.30	–0.40
Expected wage				
LP	0.887	–0.003	+0.001	–0.003
MP	0.913	0	+0.001	–0.004
HP	0.937	+0.001	–0.002	+0.003
Expected commuting costs				
LP	0.079	–0.010	0	–0.013
MP	0.076	–0.001	0	–0.016
HP	0.071	0	–0.010	0

Notes:
I = base run, II = infrastructure improvements within LP, III = infrastructure improvements within HP, IV = interregional infrastructure improvements between LP and MP; II, III and IV report changes with respect to the base run.

Table 5.4 Commuting flows (share of labour force: employed and unemployed)

	LP	MP	HP
I			
LP	0.358	0.235	0.288
MP	0.169	0.445	0.273
HP	0.162	0.212	0.520
II			
LP	+0.013	–0.005	–0.006
MP	+0.009	–0.005	–0.003
HP	+0.008	–0.003	–0.006
III			
LP	–0.005	–0.002	+0.008
MP	–0.002	–0.005	+0.007
HP	–0.004	–0.004	+0.008
IV			
LP	+0.010	+0.006	–0.012
MP	+0.005	+0.010	–0.012
HP	+0.007	+0.08	–0.015

Notes: As for Table 5.3.

Table 5.5 Employment distribution (share of national employment)

	LP	MP	HP
I	0.260	0.335	0.405
II	+0.030	–0.013	–0.015
III	–0.011	–0.011	+0.023
IV	+0.022	+0.024	–0.049

Notes: As for Table 5.3.

3.3 Intraregional Infrastructure Improvements

In the first simulation (alternative II) in the LP region, the local commuting costs are assumed to drop from 0.05 to 0.03 (–40 per cent) (e.g., due to infrastructure improvements). For simplicity, we presume that the changes in the commuting costs are exogenous and, if necessary, are financed from outside. For the LP region, this implies a direct drop in the expected wage of 0.004 (because $\beta = 0.5$ and 41 per cent from the LP region work locally; $0.02 * 0.5 * 0.41 = 0.004$, ignoring changes in labour market tightness). This drop in the expected wage increases profitability in the LP region, so more firms create vacancies in the LP region, and local unemployment drops. The 'national' unemployment rate drops 0.08 percentage points; the 'national' vacancy increases 0.04 percentage points. Due to improved workers' labour conditions, the expected wage does not fall by 0.004 but merely by 0.003 (see Table 5.3, alternative II). In the other two regions, unemployment also falls, mainly because the unemployed in these regions are more likely to find employment in the LP region. As becomes clear from Tables 5.3, 5.4 and 5.5, the changes in local unemployment rates are minor compared to the changes in commuting flows and distribution of employment. Finally, note that the vacancy rates in the other regions drop because the number of applicants falls. One of the (surprising) consequences is that the expected wage in the HP region increases, mainly because job seekers from the LP region ask for higher wages in the HP region.

In the second simulation (alternative III), in the HP region the local commuting costs drop from 0.5 to 0.3 (–40 per cent) (see Table 5.3, alternative III). The results are comparable to the results of alternative II. One of the main differences is that the decrease in local unemployment is less pronounced whereas the increase in the local vacancy rate is more pronounced. Another relevant difference is that, in this case, in the adjacent regions unemployment increases. The main reason for the adverse unemployment effects on the adjacent regions is that the wages in these regions increase due to increased labour market power. As a consequence, the decrease in the 'national' unemployment rate is negligible (–0.01 percentage points), and the increase in the 'national' vacancy rate is small (0.04 percentage points). In conclusion, local infrastructure improvements in more productive regions appear to have small adverse effects on adjacent regions, and the 'national' effects tend to be smaller than for less productive regions. Nevertheless, infrastructure improvements increase the expected wages in all regions.

As one expects, the commuting frequency is a declining function of the commuting costs. Furthermore, the results indicate (see Table 5.5) that the average productivity level (productivity divided by the labour force) increases most by investing new infrastructure in the most productive regions, since in these regions the most productive jobs will be created. Investing in less productive regions is less advisable since it lowers the average commuting costs.

3.4 Interregional Infrastructure Improvements

In the third simulation (alternative IV), the costs of commuting between the LP and MP regions have been reduced from 0.12 to 0.06 (–50 per cent). In many respects (unemployment, vacancies, wages), the results are similar to interregional infrastructure improvements (see Table 5.3). However, interregional infrastructure improvements not only induce additional interregional commuting flows but, maybe surprisingly, particularly induce intraregional commuting flows. The main explanation for this result is that interregional improvements induce firms to create additional vacancies in the regions that are better connected and the local labour force benefits most from additional job openings.

3.5 Comparative Statics with other Parameters

We have investigated the effects of changes of various exogenous variables (the regional productivity level, search costs, discount rate, bargaining strength β, utility of not working, destruction rate).[12] One of the main results is that changes in regional productivity levels have a strong effect on commuting flows. This result may explain the findings of Cameron and Muellbauer (1998) and Heyma and van Koppenhagen (2001) which show that temporal changes in regional commuting flows are much stronger than those in migration. Also, vacancies react much more strongly than unemployment to changes in regional productivity levels. Further, an increase in regional productivity always reduces local unemployment and increases the local vacancy rate, but may have adverse unemployment and vacancy effects on other regions. Nevertheless, wages in all regions increase as a result of a regional productivity improvement.

In contrast to the effects of changes in productivity, the effects of changes in search costs, discount rate, bargaining strength, the utility of not working and the destruction rate on the unemployment rates are of the same magnitude as the effects on the vacancy rates. The effects on commuting flows are negligible. Although the result that changes in regional productivity levels have a much stronger effect on unemployment than on vacancies is partly due to the choice of the 'search intensity parameters' k_{ij}, it makes intuitive sense. Firms are perfectly mobile (they may open and close vacancies in any region), whereas workers are immobile but search in all regions in competition with other job seekers. Because workers are able to search in adjacent regions, the effect of a change in the local number of vacancies is partly compensated by a change in the opposite direction in the number of vacancies in the adjacent regions.

4 CONCLUSION

In this chapter, we have described the functioning of a regional equilibrium model for the labour market. Regional labour supply is fixed, but vacancies, unemployment and wage levels are endogenously determined at the regional level given regional variation in productivity levels.

We have investigated the labour market effects of infrastructure improvements employing a multiregional equilibrium search model, which extends the seminal work of Pissarides (2000). One of the main advantages of this model is that firms react to changes in the labour market by changing the number of job openings. In contrast to the general practice in spatial interaction models of assuming that the number of jobs is given in all zones, we chose a formulation where the number of jobs increases as a result of new infrastructure. This gives the model a medium-run orientation: it allows for changes in the location of firms. However, the fact that changes in the location of households are not considered means that it is not a long-run model.

The main results are that an *intraregional* infrastructure improvement reduces local unemployment, but may increase unemployment in adjacent regions. In addition, such an improvement increases the local vacancy rate, but reduces the number of vacancies in adjacent regions. Infrastructure improvements *between regions* tend to reduce unemployment and increase vacancies in both regions. Vacancies are more sensitive to infrastructure improvements than unemployment. It also appears that wages are almost insensitive to infrastructure improvements; local infrastructure improvements may reduce the commute in other regions. Finally, we would like to emphasise that we have analysed exogenous changes in commuting costs. In principle, the effects may be interpreted as the negative effects of road tolls, although this requires a proper modelling of congestion (see Pilegaard, 2003). The model may be improved in a number of ways (see Pilegaard, 2003; Larsen, 2003). For example, Larsen (2003) includes the choice of the region as an endogenous variable whereas Pilegaard (2003) includes leisure. Future research should clearly focus on modelling of an endogenous labour force including the modelling of house prices.

NOTES

1 Free University, FEWEB, De Boelelaan, 1081 HV Amsterdam, the Netherlands; Email: jommeren@feweb.vu.nl. Piet Rietveld and Jos van Ommeren are affiliated to the Tinbergen Institute, Keizersgracht 482, 1017 EG Amsterdam, the Netherlands. We would like to thank Marcel Hoogzaad for assistance.

2 In the long run, the assumption of exogenous productivity levels may be hazardous, but in the medium run it is a plausible assumption.

3 An extension would be to assume that employed persons also search for jobs.

4 This assumption is quite strong, but must be viewed as a simplifying assumption that large shares of persons are not completely mobile due to residential moving costs.

5 A region is defined by a homogeneous environment. So, within the region all agents (workers and firms) face the same environment.

6 For a more extensive model that allows for searching in regions for which there is a zero probability of a job match, see van Ommeren and Rietveld (2002).

7 From a theoretical point of view, the assumption that k_{ij} is constant, and thus does not depend on the spatial labour market conditions, is undesirable. However, empirical studies largely support the assumption that search intensity (of job seekers and firms) is relatively constant compared to temporal and spatial changes in the UV ratio (Russo, 1996; Burda and Profit, 1996). For a model with varying search intensity, see Pilegaard (2003).

8 Note that k_{ij} and K_{ij} are closely related to each other. In the numerical simulations, we presume they are identical.

9 Given the properties of the contact function, f_{ij} is increasing in θ_{ij}. This makes sense. If the number of vacancies in j increases relative to the number of job seekers in i, the job seekers from this region are more likely to find employment in j.

10 This can be most easily seen when focusing on one regional economy. The wage rate can then be written as: $w = (1-\beta)(t+z) + \beta\frac{pcv}{u} + \beta p$.

11 In this case, the assumption that k_{ij} is given is not implausible.

12 The numerical results are not shown in this chapter, but they are available on request from the authors.

REFERENCES

Blanchard, O. (2000), *Macroeconomics*, 2nd edn, London: Prentice–Hall International.

Burda, M. and S. Profit (1996), 'Matching across Space: Evidence on Mobility in the Czech Republic', *Labour Economics*, 255–78.

Cameron, G. and J. Muellbauer (1998), 'The Housing Market and Regional Commuting and Migration Choices', CEPR Discussion Paper, no. 1945, London: Centre for Economic Policy Research.

Hazans, M., J. Earle and R. Eamets (2002), 'Labour Markets in the Baltic States', background paper for the *OECD Review of Labour Markets and Social Policies in the Baltic States* (forthcoming).

Heyma, A. and P. van Koppenhagen (2001), 'Verkenning van individuele pendel- en migratiebeslissingen', TNO, RRO, 025, Delft.

Lakshmanan, T.R., P. Nijkamp, P. Rietveld and E.T. Verhoef (2001), 'Benefits and Costs of Transport: Classification, Methodologies and Policies, *Papers in Regional Science*, **80** (2), 139–64.

Larsen, M. (2003), 'Location of the Labour Force in an Interregional General Equilibrium Model: An Applied Case', AKF, Institute of Local Government Studies, Denmark.

Newell, A. (2001), 'The Distribution of Wages in Transition Countries', IZA Discussion Paper No. 267.

OECD (2002), *Labour Markets and Social Policies in the Baltic States*, Paris: OECD.

Pilegaard, N. (2003), *Transport Demand in a CGE Model with Leisure Goods and Commuting*, PhD Thesis, Institute of Economics, University of Copenhagen.

Pissarides, C. (2000), *Equilibrium Unemployment Theory*, Oxford: Basil Blackwell.

Russo, G. (1996), *Firms' Recruitment Behaviour*, Amsterdam: Thesis Publishers.

van Ommeren, J.N. and P. Rietveld (2002), 'A Multiregional Equilibrium Search Model for the Labour Market', Free University, Research Memorandum.

6. International Migration to Germany: Estimation of a Time-Series Model and Inference in Panel Cointegration[1]

Herbert Brücker,[2] Boriss Siliverstovs[3] and Parvati Trübswetter[4]

1 INTRODUCTION

In this chapter, we analyse the macroeconomic determinants of international migration into Germany from a panel of source countries in the European Union (EU). Our focus on Germany is not purely arbitrary. Being one of the largest economies in the world, Germany serves as an important migration destination country: it is home to around 40 per cent of the EU citizens who live in other EU countries (Eurostat, 2000). Moreover, the analysis of the factors determining migration into Germany is greatly facilitated by the fact that the country is one of the few in the EU that consistently reports international migration flows and stocks on an annual basis by country of origin over a long span of time.

In general, the analysis of the economic determinants of international migration is hampered by the fact that institutional restrictions naturally hinder the effectiveness of the economic forces that have an impact on the migration decisions of economic agents. The EU forms an interesting exception in this respect, since it has eliminated the legal and administrative barriers to the movements of workers and other persons within the community to a large extent. In 1968, free movement was guaranteed to the citizens of the six founding members of what was then the European Economic Community (EEC) with a joint population of 185 million, and has since been extended to the 18 members of the EU and the European Economic Area (EEA) with a joint population of 375 million. Thus the EU and the EEA form a natural laboratory in which to study the economic determinants of international migration.

In this chapter, we consider migration to Germany from the five other founding members of the EU, where free movement was introduced in 1968, and three further countries, where free movement was introduced when they joined the EU in 1973. Hence it is assumed that for the present subsample of the migrant population, the decisions to emigrate to Germany were mostly voluntary and the emigration occurred without targeted government intervention of an either encouraging or discouraging nature over the relevant course of time.

In the empirical literature on macro migration functions, usually gross or net migration flows are explained by a set of variables. The choice of the explanatory economic variables is motivated by microeconomic theories of migration, where individuals form expectations on utility differences in the respective locations, which are determined by the income differentials between home and host countries as well as by the variables that reflect labour-market conditions in the respective locations; see e.g. Hicks (1932), Todaro (1969), and Harris and Todaro (1970). Moreover, many models include the existing migrant stock as a proxy for 'social network' effects which are expected to increase the propensity to migrate by alleviating the adaptation costs in the host country; see Stark (1991) and Epstein and Hillman (1998).

Hatton (1995) applies the recent advances in non-stationary time-series econometrics in estimating macro migration functions. Since macro-economic variables are widely acknowledged as non-stationary, the standard model in the migration literature can only meet the requirements of modern non-stationary time-series econometrics if migration flows and the explanatory variables are integrated of the same order. Largely in line with the literature, Hatton's migration function relates gross (net) migration rates to several explanatory economic variables as well as to the already existing migrant stock in the destination country. In contrast to the existing migration literature, he addresses the statistical properties of the data by testing for the order of integration of the economic variables. The finding that the relevant variables are found to be I(1) subsequently leads to the statistically supported hypothesis that these variables might form a cointegration set. Thus the resulting migration function of Hatton (1995) represents the long-run equilibrium relation between the migration flows on the one hand and the explanatory economic variables on the other.

Observe that the Hatton model (1995) implies that both migration flows and migration stock variables are I(1). It is, however, rather unlikely that both these variables are integrated of the same order, since migration flows essentially are the first difference of migration stocks. Hence we expect that if the migration stock variables are I(1), then the corresponding flow variables should be I(0), according to the definition. We therefore suggest in this chapter an alternative specification of the long-run migration function, where migration stocks are explained by income differential and employment variables. In this form of migration function the problematic issue of the same order of integration of migration flows and stock variables is no longer present.

The hypothesis that a long-run equilibrium between migration stocks and the explanatory variables exists can be motivated by the assumption that individuals differ with respect to their preferences and human capital characteristics, which in turn affect benefits and costs of migration. Consequently, for a given difference in expected income, the stock of migrants will eventually achieve equilibrium, where benefits and costs of migration are equalised for the marginal migrant.

Taking these considerations as a starting point, we formulate the objectives of this chapter as follows. First, we shall determine whether the properties of the data at hand can be reconciled either with the migration flow or the migration stock equation. To this end, we shall determine whether the order of integration of migration flows or migration stocks is compatible with that of the explanatory variables using both single time-series and panel data unit root tests. Second, we shall test whether the hypothesis of a dynamic equilibrium relationship between migration rates or, alternatively, migration stocks on the one hand, and macroeconomic variables such as per capita income differential and employment rates on the other, is supported by our data. Third, after testing for cointegration, we estimate the heterogeneous cointegration vectors in order to make inferences on the parameter estimates of the long-run relations between migration and the relevant explanatory economic variables.

The remainder of the chapter is organised as follows. Section 2 discusses the theoretical considerations behind the macro models of migration. Section 3 describes the database used. Section 4 presents the empirical results. The final section concludes.

2 THEORETICAL CONSIDERATIONS

A standard specification of the long-run migration function in the empirical literature has the following form (see e.g. Hatton, 1995):

$$\ln(m_{it}) = a_{1i} \ln\left(w_t^* / w_{it}\right) + a_{2i} \ln\left(e_t^*\right) + a_{3i} \ln(e_{it}) + a_{4i} mst_{it} + a_{5i} + a_{6i} time + u_{it}, \quad (6.1)$$

where $i = 1,\dots,N$ and $t = 1,\dots,T$ are the country and time indices, m_{it} denotes the gross migration rate as a percentage of the whole home population of country i, w_t^* the wage rate in the host country, w_{it} the wage rate in the home country i, e_t^* the employment rate in the host country, e_{it} the employment rate in the home country i, mst_{it} the migrant stock variables measured as a percentage of the whole home population of country i, and *time* stands for a linear deterministic time trend. Observe that the specification of the migration function in double logarithmic form is common in the literature (see e.g. Faini and Venturini, 1996, and Hille and Straubhaar, 2001), but is only one among many different functional forms that can be developed. On the basis of other assumptions about the utility function, Hatton (1995) also conceives a semi-logarithmic specification.

This parsimonious specification of the migration function has a long tradition in the literature. The choice of economic variables is primarily based on the classical contributions of Ravenstein (1989), Hicks (1932), Sjaastad (1962) as well as Todaro (1969) and Harris and Todaro (1970). The former studies suggest that differences in wages and other sources of income between the host and the source countries could be regarded as a primary determinant of migration decision, while the latter two papers introduce the role of labour markets in the decision-making process.[5]

More specifically, Hatton (1995) presents a migration model that is derived from the following theoretical assumptions. The utility of risk-averse individuals is determined by expectations on income levels in the respective locations. Utility is convex in the income differential. Uncertain employment opportunities affect the expectations on income levels in the foreign and home countries. Migration networks alleviate the costs of adapting to an unfamiliar environment, such that the costs from migration are expected to decline with the stock of migrants already existing in the host country. The time trend serves as a proxy for the variation in the costs of migration, which are expected to fall over time in the course of decreasing transport and communication costs.

Thus it is expected that the income differential and the host country employment rate have positive coefficients, while the coefficient of the employment rate in the home country has a negative sign. Moreover, positive signs are expected for the coefficients of the stock of migrants and of a deterministic time trend. In addition, the model predicts that the coefficient for the employment variables is larger than that for the income variables. Finally, since employment opportunities of migrants in host countries are below those of natives, it is expected that the coefficient for the employment rate in the host country is larger than that in the source country.

In this chapter we want to highlight a key assumption of the standard model in Equation 6.1 which is largely ignored in the literature. The model presumes that a log-linear relationship between the migration flow and the economic variables exists in the long-run equilibrium. This implies that migration ceases not before (expected) income levels between the host and the source country, as determined by the wage and the employment variables on the right hand side of Equation 6.1, have converged to a certain threshold level, which is determined by the fixed and variable costs of migration. In case of persistent differences in (expected) income levels, either the total population will eventually migrate or migration will not happen at all from the beginning.

Note that this is a consequence of deriving macro migration functions from the concept of a representative agent, i.e. of assuming that individuals are homogeneous. If we assume that individuals are heterogeneous, i.e. that they differ with regard to their preferences and their human capital characteristics, which in turn determine the benefits and costs of migration, (net) migration ceases when the benefits from migration equal its costs for a marginal migrant. Thus we achieve an equilibrium between migration stocks instead of migration flows and the difference in (expected) income levels in the respective locations. As an alternative to the standard model in Equation 6.1, we conceive therefore the following specification for the long-run migration function:

$$\ln(mst_{it}) = b_{1i} \ln\left(w_t^* / w_{it}\right) + b_{2i} \ln\left(e_t^*\right) + b_{3i} \ln(e_{it}) + b_{4i} + b_{5i} time + v_{it}. \quad (6.2)$$

The estimation of the migration functions in Equations 6.1 and 6.2 can be affected by spurious correlation problems, if the regressions involve integration of order one, I(1), variables (see the seminal paper by Granger and Newbold, 1974). The notable exception is the situation when I(1) dependent and explanatory variables form a cointegration set; see Engle and Granger (1987). From this point of view, Equation 6.1 should represent a cointegrating equation. Indeed, the Hatton (1995) paper provides the supporting evidence for this proposition.

However, the possible empirical caveat with the specification of Equation 6.1 is that the underlying assumption that all the variables should be I(1) might not be supported by other data sets. While there is general agreement that macroeconomic variables such as income levels and employment rates are rather well represented as I(1) processes, there still is limited evidence on the time-series properties of the migration flows and corresponding migrant stock variables. Particularly puzzling is the fact that both the migration flow and the migration stock variable are included in Equation 6.1. Since migration flows can be conceived as (almost) the first difference of migration stocks, they can hardly be I(1) variables if migration stocks are supposed to be I(1) variables as well. Thus we expect that the migration flow variable can be better approximated by an I(0) process if we find that migration stocks are I(1). In this case we suggest applying our alternative specification in Equation 6.1 for estimating the long-run migration function.

The purpose of the empirical section below is to test whether the specification of the migration function of Hatton (1995), which worked well in describing UK–US migration during the time period 1870–1913, is compatible with our data at hand, or whether we should conceive an alternative specification along the lines of Equation 6.2. Moreover, we estimate the long-run migration function in order to test whether the signs and the relative magnitudes of the coefficient estimates support our theoretical expectations.

3 DATA

Our sample comprises the migration data from eight European source countries to Germany: Belgium, Denmark, France, Italy, Ireland, Luxembourg, the Netherlands and the United Kingdom. The data on migration stocks and flows come from the Federal Statistical Office (Statistisches Bundesamt) in Germany; see Statistisches Bundesamt (2001). For the stock of migrants, we used the foreign residents as reported by the Central Register of Foreigners (Ausländerzentralregister) as a variable.[6] These data are available from 1967 to 2000. The stock of foreign residents is reported on 31 December (in some early years on 30 September). The number of foreign residents is slightly overstated by the Central Register of Foreigners, since return migration is not completely registered by the municipalities. Consequently, the figures for the stock of foreign residents have been revised twice in the wake of the population censuses of 1972 and 1987. Moreover, after German unification complete figures for Western Germany are no longer available. Since the number of foreigners in Eastern Germany has been fairly low, this does not affect the total figures much. The data on migration flows stem again from the Central Register of Foreigners. The migration stock and flow variables are calculated as shares of the corresponding home population. Population figures are derived from the World Bank World Development Indicators 2000 and OECD sources.

As a proxy for wages and other incomes, we use per capita GDP as reported by the Main Economic Indicators of the OECD. The employment rate is defined as one minus the unemployment rate. Unemployment rates have again been taken from the OECD Main Economic Indicators; where these were not available, data from national statistical offices were used. The ILO definition has been used for all unemployment rates.

4 EMPIRICAL RESULTS

As noted in Hatton (1995), the long-run migration model given in Equation 6.1 has performed well on his data. All variables appear to be I(1), and, moreover, they represent a cointegration set. Therefore the first thing to do, if we want to apply his model specification to our data, is to infer the order of integration of our country-specific variables. To this end, we use the

Augmented Dickey–Fuller (ADF) test for the individual time series and the panel unit root test suggested in Im, Pesaran and Shin (2003) (IPS test).

In the econometrics literature, the use of panel unit root tests has been justified by their significantly greater power when compared to univariate tests (see e.g. Levin, Lin and Chu, 2002). Indeed, panel unit root tests applied to a various economic time series, such as nominal interest rates in Wu and Zhang (1996), inflation rates in Culver and Papell (1999), and real exchange rates in Wu (1996) and Papell (1997), *inter alia*, often yield opposite results to those of the univariate unit root rests. In particular, Wu (1996) observes that he never was able to reject the unit root hypothesis in real exchange rates using univariate unit root tests (e.g. Augmented Dickey–Fuller and Phillips–Perron tests) at the conventional significance levels, whereas the panel unit root tests reject the null hypothesis of unit root even at the 1 per cent significance level. Hence it is useful to check whether the univariate and panel data unit root tests yield consistent results when applied to our data.

Table 6.1 reports the results of the ADF and IPS unit root tests performed on the host and home country-specific economic variables. The choice of the deterministic terms in the ADF regressions, i.e. the inclusion of an intercept or an intercept and a linear trend, was based on the following considerations for each variable separately: for those variables that clearly exhibit a trending behaviour, we included a linear trend in order to increase power against the possible trend-stationarity of the variable. These variables are the migrant stock and employment rate in Germany. For other variables, where no such clear-cut distinction can be made, we report the results of tests with both sets of deterministic components.

As expected, the results of the unit root tests suggest that the null hypothesis that our macroeconomic explanatory variables, i.e. the relative income ratio and the employment rates, follow I(1) processes cannot be rejected. We also cannot reject the null hypothesis that the migrant stock variables are I(1) processes as well. What is striking is that, even so, the univariate ADF test results applied to gross migration rates suggest that in some cases the null hypothesis of a unit root cannot be rejected; the more powerful panel data unit root tests yield the opposite conclusion. Thus we can reject the null unit root hypothesis for gross migration rates. Hence, on the basis of the unit root results, we conclude that our data seem to be incompatible with the specification of the long-run migration function suggested in Hatton (1995). The regression equation is unbalanced as the chosen dependent variable (gross migration rates), which has been found to be I(0), is explained by the non-stationary I(1) variables.

Table 6.1 Univariate and panel data unit root test results

		Belgium		France		Italy		Luxem-bourg		Nether-lands		Denmark		Ireland		UK		IPS test
$\ln(mst_{it})$	With trend	–2.36	0	–2.82	0	–2.03	4	–3.58*	0	–2.93	0	–3.92**	4	–0.86	0	–1.26	0	–1.12
$\ln(m_{it})$	Without trend	–2.95*	1	–3.46**	1	–2.27	1	–2.33	1	–2.55	1	–1.17	3	NA	NA	–3.09*	3	–2.99***
	With trend	–2.93	1	–3.33*	1	–3.07	1	–2.04	1	–2.67	1	–2.20	1	NA	NA	–3.65**	1	–2.06**
$\ln(e_{it})$	Without trend	–1.65	1	–1.44	1	–1.26	1	–0.75	3	–1.90	1	–1.74	1	–1.45	1	–1.65	2	0.08
	With trend	–0.96	1	–0.80	1	–2.89	1	–4.38**	2	–1.11	1	–1.22	1	–0.44	1	–0.67	2	1.95
$\ln(e_t^*)$	With trend	–3.02	1	–3.02	1	–3.02	1	–3.02	1	–3.02	1	–3.02	1	–3.02	1	–3.02	1	NA
$\ln(w_t^*/w_{it})$	Without trend	–1.42	0	–3.54*	0	–1.52	0	1.18	0	–1.50	0	1.09	5	1.85	0	–1.85	3	2.44
	With trend	–1.37	0	–3.10	0	–1.92	0	–0.22	1	–1.35	0	–0.76	5	–1.77	4	–2.80	3	1.49

Notes:
This table reports the Augmented Dickey–Fuller (ADF) and Im, Pesaran and Shin (IPS) test statistics with the selected augmentation lag length according to Campbell and Perron (1991). The critical values of the ADF test are reported after Hamilton (1994) for the sample size of 25 observations. They are –3.75, –3.00 and –2.63 for the corresponding 1, 5 and 10 per cent significance levels when only an intercept is included in the ADF test regression and –4.38, –3.60 and –3.24 when an intercept as well as a linear time trend are included. The signs ***, **, and * denote the significant test statistics at the 1, 5 and 10 per cent levels, respectively.

The IPS test statistics are reported in the last column of the table. The IPS test statistic has the standard normal asymptotic distribution. The one-sided critical values are –2.32, –1.64 and –1.28 for the 1, 5 and 10 per cent significance levels, respectively.

The data on gross migration rates are lacking for Ireland.

Thus, in order to reconcile the features of our data with the theoretical considerations, we utilise the long-run migration function specified in Equation 6.2 above. According to the unit root test results, all the variables of regression (6.2) seem to be I(1) and they should hypothetically form a cointegration set in order to avoid the 'spurious' regression effects. Under the assumption of cointegration, the remainder term v_{it} is assumed to be an I(0) variable.

We use two specifications of this cointegrating relation: without including a linear deterministic trend, i.e. $b_{5i} = 0$, and with a linear trend, i.e. $b_{5i} \neq 0$. In economic terms, the presence of a linear trend in our regression helps to account for the constant growth rate in the migration stock that has been caused by other factors than income differential and employment conditions. These socioeconomic factors that are not modelled explicitly reflect the decreasing moving costs over time caused *inter alia* by the increasing integration of the European economy.

Our next task comprises testing the hypothesis that the variables entering Equation 6.2 are cointegrated. We report two sets of the results of cointegration tests. The first set comprises the results of the two-step Engle–Granger cointegration procedure performed for the variables of every country. The second set of results comprises the panel cointegration group *t*-test statistics of Pedroni (1999) which aggregates the test statistics of the Engle–Granger procedure reported for every country in our panel.

Table 6.2 contains the results of the time-series and panel cointegration tests of the relation of interest given in Equation 6.2 for both specifications with and without a linear deterministic trend. For the specification without a trend, we reject the null hypothesis of no cointegration for the four countries out of the eight considered at the 10 per cent significance level and only once at the 5 per cent significance level. Here we see that the inclusion of the trend in the model resulted in the rejection of the null hypothesis in four cases at the 10 per cent level and for three countries at the 5 per cent significance level. The panel cointegration test of Pedroni (1999) rejects, however, the null hypothesis of no cointegration for both model specifications at the 5 per cent significance level.

The results of the cointegration tests suggest that every group of country-specific variables forms a cointegrated set. Given this, we intend to estimate and to make an inference on parameter estimates of the heterogeneous country-specific cointegrating relations. Unfortunately, the distribution of the OLS (Ordinary Least Squares) estimator of the cointegrating regression (which we employ in the two-step Engle–Granger method) is unknown for the general case due to the static nature of the cointegrating regression and unaddressed 'endogeneity bias'; see e.g. Patterson (2000) for details. Therefore we are unable to make a valid inference on the parameters of interest. Hence we estimate the cointegrating vectors by the method of canonical cointegrating regression (CCR for short) of Park (1992), which is the non-parametric method of transforming the variables in a way that eliminates the unfortunate properties of the OLS estimator. The CCR estimator has a standard normal asymptotic distribution and therefore makes the standard parameter inference possible.

Table 6.2 Cointegration test results

	Without trend		With trend	
Belgium	–3.94*	1	–4.45**	1
France	–1.75	1	–2.84	0
Italy	–2.92	4	–3.71	2
Luxembourg	–4.02*	1	–4.81***	5
Netherlands	–3.90	1	–3.84*	1
Denmark	–3.21	1	–4.33**	4
Ireland	–3.74	1	–3.07	4
UK	–4.12**	1	–3.09	1
Group *t*-test	–2.31**		–2.27**	

Notes:
The table reports the country-specific as well as the panel cointegration tests results. The test statistics of the Engle–Granger cointegration test along with the selected augmentation lag length according to the method suggested in Campbell and Perron (1991) obtained for every country. The 1, 5 and 10% critical values when only intercept and no trend were allowed in the model are respectively –4.73, –4.11 and –3.83, and when both intercept and trend were included, –4.65, –4.16 and –3.84, correspondingly; see Hamilton (1994). The signs ***, ** and * denote the significant test statistics at the 1, 5 and 10% levels, respectively.

The panel cointegration group *t*-test statistics of Pedroni (1999) have the standard normal asymptotic distribution. The one-sided critical values are –2.32, –1.64 and –1.28 for the 1, 5 and 10% significant levels, respectively.

The estimation results of cointegrating vectors are presented in Table 6.3, where the left (right) panel contains the slope parameter estimates of cointegrating equations when a linear deterministic trend has been included (omitted) in Equation 6.2. Recall that, according to the theoretical considerations discussed in Section 2, we expect positive signs for the difference in per capita GDP levels as well as for the employment rate in the host country. Note also that a negative sign is expected for home employment rates since they increase employment opportunities in the source country. However, several empirical studies find that home employment opportunities have actually increased migration (see Greenwood, 1975, for a review). One possible explanation for this phenomenon is that favourable employment opportunities at home might help to lift liquidity constraints that a potential migrant experiences there, and, in doing so, might prove to be a factor encouraging migration.

Table 6.3 Cointegrating relations

	With trend		
	$\ln(w_t^*/w_{it})$	$\ln(e_t^*)$	$\ln(e_{it})$
Belgium	0.151*	2.767***	–1.202***
	(0.08)	(0.45)	(0.27)
Denmark	–0.400**	4.914***	–2.164***
	(0.20)	(0.79)	(0.50)
France	0.583***	1.232	1.947*
	(0.12)	(0.82)	(1.13)
Ireland	1.242***	2.265	0.423
	(0.16)	(1.80)	(0.80)
Italy	0.001	2.298**	4.405**
	(0.05)	(1.01)	(1.80)
Luxembourg	0.279***	1.775***	1.886
	(0.05)	(0.60)	(2.17)
Netherlands	–0.151	1.623***	–0.357
	(0.10)	(0.51)	(0.33)
UK	0.871***	–0.149	–2.741***
	(0.10)	(1.71)	(1.05)
	Without trend		
	$\ln(w_t^*/w_{it})$	$\ln(e_t^*)$	$\ln(e_{it})$
Belgium	–0.255	–6.653***	0.265
	(0.28)	(1.27)	(1.00)
Denmark	–2.455***	–2.220	–4.510***
	(0.63)	(2.19)	(1.48)
France	0.677*	3.426	–8.037***
	(0.35)	(2.32)	(1.87)
Ireland	–0.848	–13.310*	–5.346
	(0.66)	(7.64)	(3.56)
Italy	0.115**	2.988***	–3.236***
	(0.05)	(1.03)	(1.10)
Luxembourg	0.017	–2.217*	–1.627
	(0.10)	(1.15)	(4.24)
Netherlands	–0.166	1.572***	–0.409
	(0.11)	(0.28)	(0.33)
UK	0.804***	–15.902***	1.904
	(0.21)	(2.37)	(2.17)

Note: The signs ***, ** and * denote the significant test statistics at the 1, 5 and 10% levels, respectively.

When comparing the estimation results for both model specifications, i.e. with and without trend, we notice that the regressions with a time trend yield more plausible results. In the model with the linear deterministic trend we find that five coefficients for the income ratio are significant at the 5 per cent level, four of which are positive. Interestingly enough, with the exception of the UK, all coefficients of the German employment variable have the expected positive sign. Five of the positive coefficients are significant at the 5 per cent level. Moreover, the coefficients of the employment variable are larger than the coefficients of the income variables in all cases where both variables have the expected positive sign. This is in line with the expectations that follow from the theoretical model. Finally, the home employment rate coefficient is found to be significant in five cases at the 10 per cent level, out of which three estimates have a positive and the remaining two a negative sign. Note that the inclusion of a linear trend has wiped out the implausibly high values of the long-run elasticities of the migrant stock with respect to the host country employment rate in the case of Ireland and the UK.

In the cointegrating regression without trend, the income ratio variable is significant for the four countries at the 10 per cent level, and in three cases it has the expected positive sign. The German employment rate variable is found to be significant in six cases at the 10 per cent level, and in only two cases does it have the expected positive sign. Finally, we find that the home employment rate variable is significant in only three cases at the 10 per cent level and has a negative sign in all significant cases.

5 CONCLUSIONS

In this chapter we have analysed the determinants of international migration from eight European source countries to Germany in the period 1967 to 2000. We chose these countries because they did not restrict emigration for most of the time period. This enables us to draw interesting conclusions on the economic forces underlying international migration.

The standard approach in the empirical literature presumes the existence of an equilibrium relationship between the migration rate and explanatory variables such as the difference in income and employment opportunities between the host and the home country; see Hatton (1995) as an example. In terms of modern non-stationary time-series econometrics, the migration function has to be modelled within a cointegration framework, which demands that both the migration rate and all the explanatory variables are non-stationary I(1) variables, and that a long-run equilibrium between the economic variables exists, i.e. that the variables in question are cointegrated. The statistical tests in the Hatton (1995) paper indeed suggest that for UK–

US migration between 1870 and 1913 the long-run migration function meets all the necessary requirements. However, following a well-established tradition in the empirical literature, the Hatton model includes migration flows and stocks in one equation, which theoretically cannot form a cointegrated set if migration stocks are I(1) variables on the one hand, and migration flows are first differences of migration stocks, i.e. I(0) variables, on the other. We therefore considered an alternative specification that avoids this problem by assuming that an equilibrium relationship between migrant stocks and the explanatory variables exists.

One the one hand, we find analogously to the Hatton (1995) paper that the difference in per capita GDP levels as well as the employment rates could be approximated by non-stationary stochastic processes. On the other hand, however, the hypothesis of a unit root is rejected for the migration rate in our data. This latter finding contrasts clearly with the results of Hatton (1995). This implies that the flow model is incompatible with our data, as the stationary migration rate and non-stationary variables such as the difference in per capita GDP and employment rates cannot be cointegrated, and thus cannot form a long-run dynamic equilibrium relationship. However, we find evidence supporting the existence of cointegration between the migration stocks and the key explanatory variables such as the difference in per capita incomes and the host and source countries' employment rates.

Our results generally support the theoretical hypothesis that a positive difference in per capita income between host and home country increases the long-run stock of migrants. However, the impact of employment rates in the home country on migration has turned out to be ambiguous in our sample.

NOTES

1 This chapter has benefited from comments by the three anonymous referees as well as by participants in the 15th European Advanced Studies Institute in Regional Science 'Emerging Market Economies and European Economic Integration', held in Eksjö, Sweden. We also thank Peter Pedroni for making his panel cointegration code available. Any remaining errors and shortcomings are ours.

2 Institute for Labour Studies, IZA and DIW Berlin, Königin-Luise Straße 5, Berlin, 14195, Germany, e-mail: hbruecker@diw.de

3 DIW Berlin, Königin-Luise Straße 5, Berlin, 14195, Germany, e-mail: bsiliverstovs@diw.de

4 Ludwig-Maximilians University Munich, Germany, e-mail: parvati.truebswetter@lrz.uni-muenchen.de

5 Microeconomic models of the migration decision have gone far beyond these classical contributions. *Inter alia*, these models analyse the role of financial constraints in the absence of perfect capital markets (see Stark, 1991), the impact of uncertainty about future wage and employment conditions on the migration decision in the presence of fixed migration costs (see Burda, 1995), and the choice of the optimal length of stay in a foreign country if migration is temporary (see Djajic and Milbourne, 1988). However, few of these

theoretical contributions have developed macro migration functions whose parameters can be estimated empirically.

6 Note that all residents in Germany are obliged to register themselves at the place of residence. The figures from the Central Register of Foreigners are based on the reports of the municipalities.

REFERENCES

Burda, M.C. (1995), 'Migration and the Option Value of Waiting', *Economic and Social Review*, **27**, 1–19.

Campbell, J.Y. and P. Perron (1991), 'Pitfalls and Opportunities: What Macroeconomists Should Know About Unit Roots', *NBER Macroeconomics Annual*, pp. 141–201.

Culver, S.E. and D.H. Papell (1999), 'Long-run Power Parity with Short-run Data: Evidence of a Null Hypothesis of Stationarity', *Journal of International Money and Finance*, **18**, 751–68.

Djajic, S. and R. Milbourne (1988), 'A General Equilibrium Model of Guestworker Migration', *Journal of International Economics*, **25**, 335–51.

Engle, R.F. and C.W.J. Granger (1987), 'Cointegration and Error Correction: Representation, Estimation and Testing', *Econometrica*, **55**, 251–76.

Epstein, G.S. and A.L. Hillman (1998), 'Herd Effects and Migration', CEPR Discussion Paper No. 1811.

Eurostat (2000), *Statistical Yearbook 2000*, Luxembourg: Eurostat.

Faini, R. and A. Venturini (1996), 'Migration and Growth: The Experience of Southern Europe', CEPR Discussion Paper No. 964.

Granger, C.W.J. and P. Newbold (1974), 'Spurious Regression in Econometrics', *Journal of Econometrics*, **2** (2), 111–20.

Greenwood, M.J. (1975), 'Research on Internal Migration in the United States: A Survey', *Journal of Economic Literature*, **13** (2), 397–433.

Hamilton, J. (1994), *Time Series Analysis*, Princeton, NJ: Princeton University Press.

Harris, J. and M. Todaro (1970), 'Migration, Unemployment and Development: A Two-sector Analysis', *American Economic Review*, **60**, 126–42.

Hatton, T.J. (1995), 'A Model of UK Migration, 1870–1913', *Review of Economics and Statistics*, **77**, 407–15.

Hicks, J.R. (1932), *The Theory of Wages*, London: Macmillan.

Hille, H. and T. Straubhaar (2001), 'The Impact of EU Enlargement on Migration Movements and Economic Integration: Results of Recent Studies', in OECD (ed.), *Migration Policies and EU Enlargement: The Case of Central and Eastern Europe*, Paris: OECD, pp. 79–100.

Im, K.S., M.H. Pesaran and Y. Shin (2003), 'Testing for Unit Roots in Heterogeneous Panels', *Journal of Econometrics*, **115**, 53–74.

Levin, A., C.-F. Lin and C.-S.J. Chu (2002), 'Unit Root Tests in Panel Data: Asymptotic and Finite-sample Properties', *Journal of Econometrics*, **108** (1), 1–24.

Papell, D.H. (1997), 'Searching for Stationarity: Purchasing Power Parity under the Current Float', *Journal of International Economics*, **43**, 313–32.

Park, J.Y. (1992), 'Canonical Cointegrating Regressions', *Econometrica*, **60** (1), 119–43.

Patterson, K. (2000), *An Introduction to Applied Econometrics: A Time Series Approach*, New York: Palgrave.
Pedroni, P. (1999), 'Critical Values for Cointegration Tests in Heterogeneous Panels with Multiple Regressors', *Oxford Bulletin of Economics and Statistics*, **61**, 653–70.
Ravenstein, E.G. (1989), 'The Laws of Migration', *Journal of the Statistical Society*, **59**, 214–301.
Sjaastad, L.A. (1962), 'The Costs and Returns of Human Migration', *Journal of Political Economy*, **70** (5), 80–93.
Stark, O. (1991), *The Migration of Labour*, Oxford and Cambridge, MA: Basil Blackwell.
Statistisches Bundesamt (2001), *Fachserie 18*, Wiesbaden.
Todaro, M.P. (1969), 'A Model of Labour Migration and Urban Unemployment in Less Developed Countries', *American Economic Review*, **59** (1), 139–48.
Wu, Y. (1996), 'Are Real Exchange Rates Nonstationary? Evidence from a Panel Data Set', *Journal of Money, Credit, and Banking*, **28** (1), 54–63.
Wu, Y. and H. Zhang (1996), 'Mean Reversion in Interest Rates: New Evidence from a Panel of OECD Countries', *Journal of Money, Credit, and Banking*, **28** (4), 604–21.

7. Regional Specialisation and Employment Dynamics in Transition Countries[1]

Iulia Traistaru and Guntram B. Wolff[2]

1 INTRODUCTION

Since 1990, Central and Eastern European countries (CEECs) have gone through a major structural adjustment following the trade reorientation towards Western markets and the transition to a market economy. In the early phase of the transition process, all CEECs experienced a sharp decline of GDP and substantial employment drops (Svejnar, 2002). Growth resumed after 1993, but it was followed in some countries such as Bulgaria and Romania by a second economic decline and further employment reductions. Furthermore, there have been strong sectoral shifts in employment structures, which have become more similar to the sectoral structures of advanced economies (Landesmann and Stehrer, 2002). Meanwhile, the patterns of structural change have been uneven across space and have thus led to increasing regional inequalities (Petrakos, 1996, 2000) and changing patterns of sectoral specialisation of regions and concentration of industries (Traistaru, Nijkamp and Longhi, 2002; Resmini, 2002).

While macro-structural changes have often been analysed, the spatial dimension of the structural adjustment process in the CEECs needs to be investigated in more depth. This chapter uncovers and explains regional employment change differentials in three CEECs, namely Bulgaria, Hungary and Romania. In particular, we assess the importance of sectoral specialisation and region-specific factors in explaining regional employment change differentials.

The importance and policy relevance of this analysis is twofold. First, highly specialised regions are more vulnerable to asymmetric shocks, since industry shocks may become region-specific shocks. While in the long term regions may benefit from specialisation via productivity growth, short-run adjustment costs could be high in the case of relocation of firms. Second, understanding determinants of regional growth differentials could facilitate the targeting of regional policy actions such as the European Union's structural funds.

Previous studies of the roles of national, industrial and regional factors in explaining regional employment change have established the following stylised facts. In a seminal paper, Blanchard and Katz (1992) show that in the USA a large proportion of movements in employment growth is common to all states. In the case of Europe, Decressin and Fatas (1995) show that most of the dynamics in employment growth are region-specific. This implies that region-specific shocks may be important in Europe. In the USA, Gracia-Milà and McGuire (1993) find that the industrial mix plays an important role in explaining regional employment growth differentials. In transition countries, the existing evidence is less conclusive: while region-specific factors seem to explain regional employment growth differentials in Poland, the inherited industry mix played the major role in countries such as Hungary and Slovakia (Boeri and Scarpetta, 1996). These results, however, occur in the early years of transition.

In this chapter, we use sectoral employment data at a regional level for the period 1990–99, and investigate regional differentials in employment growth in Bulgaria, Hungary and Romania. We apply a shift-share analysis using a three-factor decomposition suggested by Esteban (2000) and assess the role of sectoral mix (structural component), region-specific factors (differential component) and regional competitiveness (allocative component) in explaining regional differentials in employment change. To our knowledge, this is the first contribution to introduce empirical evidence concerning the role of these three components in explaining regional employment change differentials in transition countries. The results of the shift-share analysis indicate that, in these three countries, the variance of regional employment change is driven almost entirely by region-specific factors. Sectoral mix and regional competitiveness factors play only a minor role in explaining regional employment dynamics. Furthermore, we checked the robustness of these results using a shift-share regression analysis. The results found in the cases of Bulgaria and Romania are confirmed, while in the case of Hungary region-specific factors are not significant. The latter result is in line with the findings of Boeri and Scarpetta (1996).

The remainder of this chapter is organised as follows: section 2 discusses the three-factor decomposition methodology applied. Section 3 describes the data and summary statistics of regional employment growth and regional specialisation in Bulgaria, Hungary and Romania. The results we obtain from our shift-share analysis are presented and discussed in section 4. Section 5 presents the shift-share regression results. Finally, in section 6 we formulate the main conclusions of our findings as well as policy implications.

2 METHODOLOGICAL FRAMEWORK

Regional employment growth differentials can be analysed with the shift-share methodology. Despite reservations and criticisms, the shift-share approach is the most commonly used method to break down the regional employment dynamics into regional and structural factors (e.g. Patterson, 1991; Loveridge and Selting, 1998; Fothergill and Gudgin, 1982; Esteban, 2000).[3] Initially it was used to break down growth differentials between a region and the national average into two components: the growth differential due to a better/worse than national average performance of the region; and the growth differential due to the specialisation of the region in fast-/slow-growing sectors (Dunn, 1960). Esteban (1972) extended the two-factor decomposition to a sum of three components described as structural, differential and allocative. The structural component indicates the growth share due to the specialisation (industry mix) of each region. The differential component measures the part of growth due to region-specific factors. Finally, the allocative component measures the covariance of the two factors, and can be interpreted as regional growth deriving from its specialisation in those activities where the region is most competitive.

Notations and definitions of the variables used in the analysis of this chapter are given in Table 7.1.

Table 7.1 Notations and definition of variables

Variables	Definitions
g	employment growth rate at national level
g_r	employment growth rate in region r
g_i	employment growth rate in industry i
E	employment growth at national level
E_r	employment growth in region r
E_i	employment growth in industry i
E_{ir}	employment growth in industry i and region r
$S_{ir} = E_{ir} / E_r$	share of employment in industry i in region r in total employment of region r
$S_i = E_i / E$	share of employment in industry i at national level
$g_{ir} = \dfrac{E_{ir,t+1} - E_{ir,t}}{E_{ir,t}}$	growth rate of employment in industry i in region r

In order to disentangle the role of industry mix and region-specific factors in explaining the regional employment growth differentials, we compare each region with a benchmark region having sectoral employment growth rates and industry mix equal to the national average. The differences between the actual and the benchmark regions with respect to industry mix and sectoral employment growth capture the importance of these two factors in each region.

The difference between regional and national growth rates, as defined by Equation 7.1, can be broken down into three components:

$$g_r - g = \sum_i g_{ir} s_{ir} - \sum_i g_i s_i . \tag{7.1}$$

The growth differential due to the specific sectoral composition/specialisation of the region r, assuming that sectoral employment growth rates in each region are equal to the national average, is measured by μ_r:

$$\mu_r = \sum_i \left(s_{ir} - s_i \right) g_i . \tag{7.2}$$

μ_r is positive if the region is specialised ($s_{ir} > s_i$) in sectors with high positive employment growth rates at the national level and de-specialised ($s_{ir} < s_i$) in sectors with low positive employment growth rates. μ_r is maximum if the region r is specialised in the sector with the highest employment growth nation wide. μ_r is minimum if the region is specialised in the sector with the lowest employment change. Equation 7.2 can be rewritten as:

$$\sum_i s_{ir} g_i = g + \mu_r . \tag{7.3}$$

The term on the left-hand side (LHS) is the average employment growth in region r if regional and national employment growth rates coincide sector by sector.

The growth differential due to differences in the employment growth of industry i in region r compared to the national growth of i, π_r is given by Equation 7.4.

$$\pi_r = \sum_i s_i \left(g_{ir} - g_i \right) . \tag{7.4}$$

It can be rewritten as:

$$\sum_i s_i g_{ir} = g + \pi_r . \tag{7.5}$$

The LHS describes the growth rate of the region if it had the same sectoral structure. The variable π_r therefore describes the part of growth difference between the region and the national average, which can be attributed to region-specific factors.

The covariance between the two effects is given by Equation 7.6.

$$\alpha_r = \sum_i (s_{ir} - s_i)(g_{ir} - g_i). \tag{7.6}$$

It captures high employment growth in those regions where a combination of certain industries and the region-specific advantages lead to higher growth rates. With these equations it is easy to show that:

$$g_r - g = \mu_r + \pi_r + \alpha_r = \sum_i s_{ir} g_{ir} - \sum_i s_i g_i. \tag{7.7}$$

One way of measuring the role played by each of the shift-share components in explaining interregional differences in employment growth is to compute the relative weight of the variance of each component in overall observed variance. The variance of $g_r - g$ is:

$$\begin{aligned} \operatorname{var}(g_r - g) = {} & \operatorname{var}(\mu_r) + \operatorname{var}(\pi_r) + \operatorname{var}(\alpha_r) \\ & + 2[\operatorname{cov}(\mu_r, \pi_r) + \operatorname{cov}(\mu_r, \alpha_r) + \operatorname{cov}(\pi_r, \alpha_r)]. \end{aligned} \tag{7.8}$$

3 THE DATA AND SUMMARY STATISTICS

We use employment data at regional NUTS-3 level for Bulgaria, Hungary and Romania for the period 1990–99.[4] Our data set[5] contains employment data on sectors of economic activity and on manufacturing branches for 28 regions in Bulgaria, 20 regions in Hungary and 41 regions in Romania. The sectors of economic activity include agriculture, industry and services. Regional manufacturing employment is disaggregated on 14 manufacturing branches for Bulgaria, 12 manufacturing branches for Romania and eight manufacturing branches for Hungary. The data included in this data set have been collected from national statistical offices. Employment refers to persons employed in Bulgaria and Romania and employees only in Hungary. The GDP growth figures are taken from the EBRD (2001).

The average population size of NUTS-3 regions is similar in Hungary and Romania while in Bulgaria it is smaller. The average size of NUTS-3 regions has declined over the period 1990–99 in all three countries. Regional size differentials are highest in Hungary and smallest in Romania. Regional size differentials have increased in Bulgaria and decreased in Hungary and Romania.

Figures 7.1 to 7.3 plot the evolution of GDP and employment growth in the 1990s. Bulgaria has experienced large losses in GDP and employment since the beginning of transition (EBRD, 2001). While GDP per capita was more than US$1500 in 1990, it declined to US$1150 in 1994 and to similar values as in 1994 again in 1996. GDP and employment growth moved together during most of the 1990s. Only in 1999 did employment decrease, although GDP increased.

In Hungary, employment decreased over the period 1992–97. In the initial phase of transition, GDP decreased strongly, but positive growth resumed in 1994. With higher GDP growth rates since 1997 (almost 5 per cent), employment has increased again.

Over the period 1992–99, Romania continuously lost employment (see Figure 7.3). The loss was particularly high in 1993, a 3.8 per cent decrease relative to 1992, and in 1995, a 5.2 per cent decrease. Contrary to Bulgaria, the evolution of employment has not closely matched the real GDP growth. GDP declined sharply in the early 1990s; in the mid-1990s the economy recovered, entering a new recession in 1997/98. Since 2000, GDP has been growing again. The GDP growth was high in particular in 1995, coinciding with negative employment growth. This points to productivity gains during the mid-1990s.

All three countries have experienced considerable changes in their aggregate employment structure (see Table 7.2 and, for a more detailed analysis, Traistaru and Wolff, 2002).

The Bulgarian economy can be characterised by a huge process of deindustrialisation during the 1990s. The share of the industrial sector in total employment decreased dramatically during the 1990s, falling from over 45 per cent to 28 per cent in 1999. The share of industry in GDP also decreased from 33 per cent to 25 per cent (EBRD, 2001). At the same time, the shares of services and agriculture increased continuously during the 1990s. In absolute terms, the industry sector continuously lost employment during the 1990s. From 1990 to 1999, industrial employment decreased from 1.9 million to 0.9 million. The shrinkage of industrial employment was most dramatic in the initial phase of transition. Employment in the service sector decreased slightly from 1.47 million to 1.40 million, while employment in the agricultural sector increased from 0.75 to 0.79 million.

While in Bulgaria the industry sector has lost importance and the agricultural sector increased relatively to a share of around 26 per cent, in Hungary the service sector dominates the economy. Throughout the 1990s, its share increased from around 53 to 60 per cent. The industry sector held a constant share of around 35 per cent, while the agricultural sector slightly lost importance, approaching a share close to West European values. Employment growth was negative in all sectors until 1997. Since then employment has increased considerably in the construction, industry and service sectors. Thus after an initial phase of employment and GDP losses in Hungary, the economy has recovered.

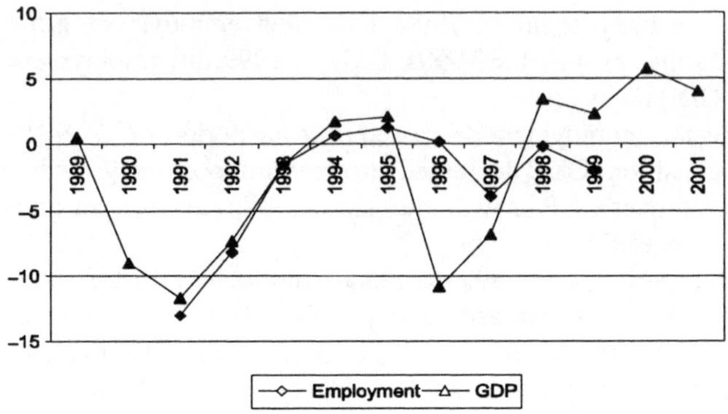

Figure 7.1 *Real GDP and employment growth in Bulgaria (%)*

Figure 7.2 *Real GDP and employment growth in Hungary (%)*

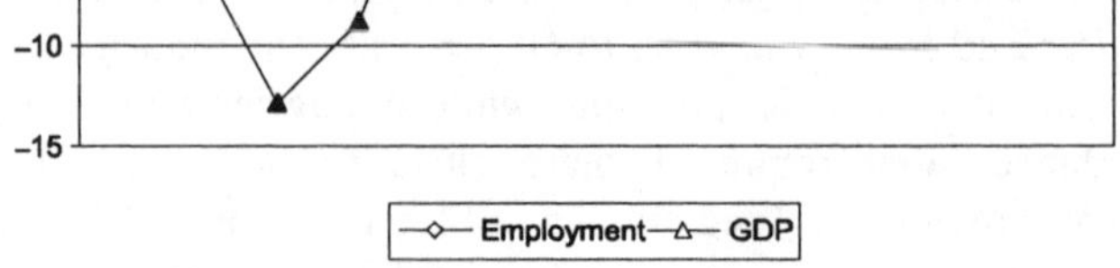

Figure 7.3 *Real GDP and employment growth in Romania (%)*

Table 7.2 Aggregate shares of employment in three sectors; the coefficient of regional variation in employment shares

	Bulgaria		Hungary		Romania	
	1990	1999	1992	1999	1992	1999
Employment shares						
Agriculture	0.185	0.258	0.100	0.054	0.312	0.396
Industry	0.455	0.289	0.366	0.350	0.404	0.312
Service	0.360	0.454	0.534	0.597	0.284	0.292
Coefficient of variation						
Agriculture	35.6	31.6	37.8	39.6	31.3	28.5
Industry	13.1	24.9	15.1	29.8	22.8	27.3
Service	15.6	19.8	14.1	16.0	19.0	23.0

The employment share of the industry sector in Romania declined by 8 percentage points (Table 7.2). This loss was matched by an increase in the employment share of the agricultural sector, which had a share of 40 per cent in Romanian employment in 1999. The variation in total employment is driven by all three sectors, the agricultural, industry and service sectors. While the agricultural sector remained at 3.4 million employed, the industrial sector lost more than 1 million workers, with the number of employed persons falling from 3.3 to 2 million during the 1990s. Service sector employment fell from 3.2 to 2.6 million. In 1994/95, employment in the service sector moved along with increasing GDP, while employment in the other sectors declined.

On a regional level we observe in all countries considerable differences in sectoral composition. The coefficient of variation reported in Table 7.2 reveals that differences in agricultural shares are the largest in all three countries. This is followed by the industry sector. In the case of the service sector, the regional differences are comparatively low in all three countries.

The maps (Figures 7.7–7.9 in the Appendix) show the spatial variation of employment growth during the 1990s. In Bulgaria, the capital region and eastern regions (Varna, Shumen, Targoviste, Sliven, Yambol) had the best performance, while regions situated in the north (such as Vidin, Razgrad) and south (Kurdjali, Haskovo) had the worst performance. For example, regions such as Vidin and Razgrad lost more than 20 per cent of their initial employment in the course of the 1990s. In Hungary, regional differentials in employment growth are also substantial. In particular, regions situated in the north-east (such as Borsod–Abauj–Zemplen and Nograd) experienced an employment decline of 30 per cent, while regions situated in the centre (Pest,

Fejer) and west (Györ–Moson–Sopron) did relatively well. In Romania the best-performing regions are those situated in the centre and north-east, while the worst are former mining areas (Hunedoara, Gorj) and regions situated in the south-east (Constanta, Braila, Calarasi). With the aim of uncovering the role played by geography and proximity to Western markets in employment dynamics, we use the following taxonomy suggested by Resmini (2002): regions bordering the European Union (BEU), regions bordering other EU candidate countries (BAC), regions bordering countries outside the EU enlargement (BEX), and non-border regions (INT). The composition of the four groups is given in Table 7.7 in the Appendix.

Table 7.3 Average employment shares and average growth rates for different regions

	Employment shares			Employment growth		
	Agriculture	Industry	Services	Agriculture	Industry	Services
Bulgaria[a]						
BEU	0.24	0.36	0.40	9.17	–15.64	–8.86
BAC	0.30	0.33	0.37	2.44	–10.33	–1.43
BEX	0.30	0.34	0.36	–3.99	–8.61	–1.75
INT	0.26	0.35	0.38	–0.15	–6.62	0.05
Hungary[b]						
BEU	0.09	0.47	0.45	–11.30	0.79	–3.14
BAC	0.09	0.39	0.52	–10.63	–4.68	–3.00
BEX	0.12	0.34	0.54	–10.46	–2.85	–3.61
INT	0.09	0.39	0.52	–11.09	–2.69	–1.54
Romania[b]						
BEU	none	none	none	none	none	none
BAC	0.46	0.28	0.26	–0.17	–6.87	–2.86
BEX	0.44	0.30	0.26	–0.04	–6.23	–1.81
INT	0.35	0.38	0.27	0.13	–6.36	–2.39

Notes:
a = 1990–99, b = 1992–99. BEU = regions bordering the EU15, BAC = regions bordering other candidate countries, BEX = regions bordering third countries, INT = non-border regions.

Table 7.3 shows average sectoral employment shares and employment growth rates over the period 1990–99 for the above four groups of regions in each of the three countries. In Bulgaria, employment in services had the highest share in all four groups of regions. In particular, regions bordering

Greece (Blagoevgrad, Smolyan, Kardjali) had the highest average employment share in services at 40 per cent. This category of regions had also the highest employment growth rate in agriculture and the highest employment decline in industry. In Hungary, employment in services had the highest share in all four categories of regions. Regions bordering countries outside the EU enlargement (Croatia, Serbia and Montenegro, Ukraine) had the highest share of employment in services and regions bordering Austria (Györ–Moson–Sopron, Vas) the lowest. Regions bordering Austria had the highest share of employment in industry, suggesting the presence of manufacturing exporting firms. In these latter regions there was a clear increase of employment in industry while employment in agriculture decreased by 11 per cent. In Romania, border regions were predominantly agricultural while in non-border regions employment share in industry was the highest. The highest employment decline took place in industry. In comparison with Bulgaria and Hungary, in Romania employment decline rates were relatively low.

Summing up, there are similarities and differences in the three countries with respect to employment, sectoral shares and employment growth. The average employment size of a region in the three countries varies. While in Bulgaria and Hungary the average regional employment is around 120 000 and 130 000 people respectively, in Romania 230 000 people work in every region on average. Hungary had a fairly different sectoral structure in comparison with Romania and Bulgaria. While Bulgaria and especially Romania had a relatively large agricultural sector, Hungary's economy was dominated by the services sector. Furthermore, Bulgaria and Romania experienced a sharp decline in employment in the industry sector, while Hungary had a comparatively constant sectoral structure. Regions differ largely in terms of employment size in Hungary, where the coefficient of variation increased during the 1990s. In Romania, the coefficient of variation for regional employment size is only half the size of Hungary and decreasing. Regions in Romania have thus become more similar. In Bulgaria, regional variation was somewhat higher than in Romania, and increased during the 1990s. In Hungary, regional employment size variation increased in the course of the 1990s. For the sectoral employment shares there was less regional variation in Hungary compared to Romania and Bulgaria except for the agricultural share. Regional variation in employment growth rates was highest in Bulgaria, especially in the mid-1990s. In Hungary this variation was relatively low in the late 1990s but was quite high in 1996, especially in the industrial sector. Overall, one can conclude that the three investigated countries differ substantially in terms of sectoral composition of their economies. Also the evolution of the variation in regional employment sizes shows a different pattern. Regional employment differentials increased in

Hungary and Bulgaria and decreased in Romania. Regions differ in terms of their sectoral shares; this variation is lowest in Hungary. Regional employment growth variation is substantial in all three countries, especially in the early phase of transition. Proximity to Western markets is associated with industry specialisation in Hungary and services specialisation in Bulgaria. Proximity to other accession countries and countries outside the EU enlargement is associated with specialisation in services in Bulgaria and Hungary and specialisation in agriculture in Romania. Non-border regions are specialised in services in Bulgaria and Hungary and industry in Romania.

4 DETERMINANTS OF REGIONAL EMPLOYMENT CHANGE

This section presents the results of the regional employment growth decomposition into three components as described in section 2. Our aim is to assess the importance of the industry mix, regional factors and allocative factors in explaining regional growth differentials. To this purpose, we calculate the variance shares of the respective components in the overall variance of the regional employment change differentials.

4.1 Shift-share Results

Bulgaria

In Bulgaria, region-specific factors play the predominant role in explaining regional growth variation. π has the largest share of variance in all years, as shown in Figure 7.4. The sectoral/industry mix factor, μ, explains little or nothing, while α, the allocative component, has a variance share between 5 and 38 per cent. Figure 7.4 illustrates that region-specific factors played the major role in explaining employment growth differentials, whereas the different composition of industries in the regions explained only little of the overall variance.

The fact that regional factors are the predominant source of regional growth variation is quite surprising in view of the fact that the three sectors included in the analysis are expected to have very different growth potentials and different responsiveness to shocks. In the previous section we showed that there is considerable variation in the regional shares of sectors in total regional employment. Regional employment growth differentials, however, are driven by factors specific to a region, and not by sectoral structure differentials. The importance of regional factors declined from 1993 to 1996 and had a second maximum in 1998. It is interesting to note that the regional component attained its two maxima in times when GDP growth was positive. Thus especially in times of booms, which coincided with times of expanding employment in Bulgaria, some regions grew faster than others. Economic growth was thus uneven across space. This result is in line with Petrakos and Saratsis (2000), who show for Greece that regional inequalities are pro-cyclical, increasing in times of economic booms and decreasing in times of recessions.

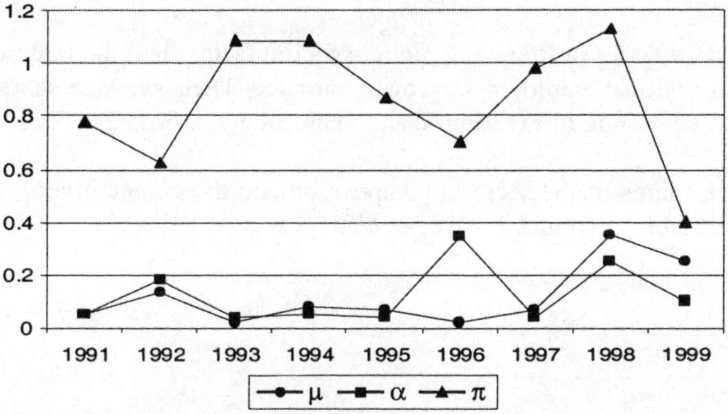

Figure 7.4 The evolution of variance shares over time in Bulgaria

Hungary

Region-specific factors constitute the largest share of regional employment growth variance in Hungary. π's variance share is around 100 per cent, declining to 60 per cent in 1998, where the covariance between the three factors gained some importance (Figure 7.5).

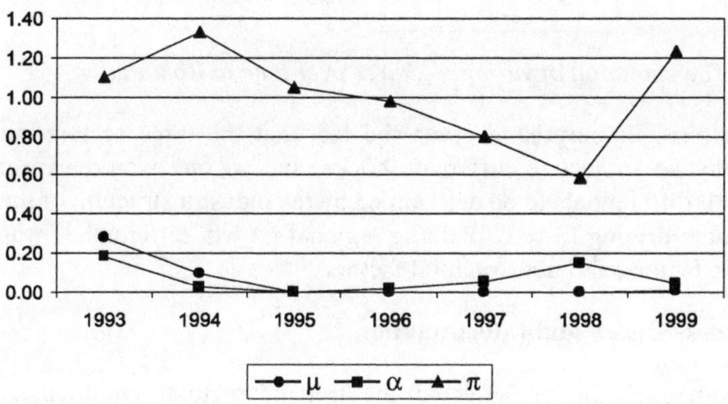

Figure 7.5 The evolution of variance shares over time in Hungary

Over the entire period the importance of π decreased by 40 percentage points, but it increased again in 1999. Again we believe that the result is remarkable since the three sectors considered have certainly had very different shares in each region. Although the sectors may be subject to very different shocks, which cause regions to grow at different speeds, regional differences in growth performance appear to be almost entirely driven by region-specific factors.

Romania

Over the period 1993–99 in Romania, region-specific factors had the largest share in overall regional employment growth variance. Their variance share increased at the beginning of the sample and declined again in 1999 (Figure 7.6).

The variance shares of the sectoral composition and the competitiveness factor remained stable at around 3 to 18 per cent.

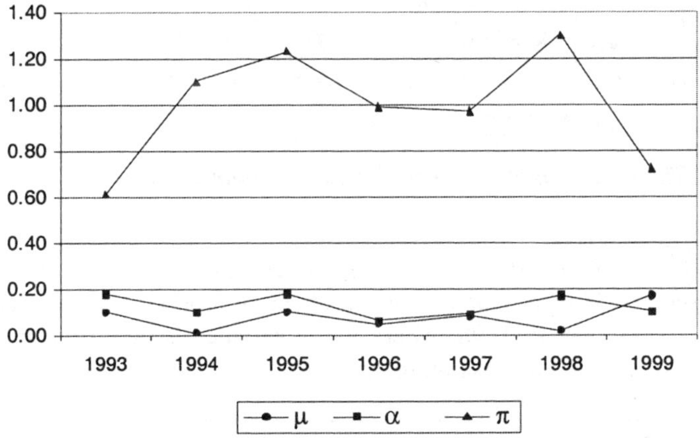

Figure 7.6 The evolution of variance shares over time in Romania

Again this result is surprising given the fact that the three sectors we considered may be subject to different shocks, and so one would expect regional growth differentials to be determined by the industry structure of the region. The main driving force explaining regional growth differentials was region-specific factors, and not structural factors.

4.2 Robustness Check and Interpretation

In the preceding section we assessed the role of sectoral employment composition in explaining regional employment growth differentials in three transition countries. We find that the sectoral mix does not play a major role in accounting for regional employment dynamics in Bulgaria, Hungary and Romania. Highly aggregated data may bias our results. Therefore, as a robustness check, the above analysis was applied to Hungarian data with a 1-digit industrial classification with 12 sectors. The results stayed qualitatively the same, indicating that our high level of aggregation with three sectors does not drive our results. Furthermore, for all three countries, we implemented the shift-share analysis for a 2-digit classification of the manufacturing sector. Our data set includes regional manufacturing employment disaggregated on 14 branches in the case of Bulgaria, 12 branches in the case of Romania and eight branches in the case of Hungary. (See Figures 7.10, 7.11 and 7.12 in the Appendix.) The results are qualitatively identical to those presented above.

Our research indicates that in the three transition countries, the sectoral employment structure in a region does not explain regional growth patterns. The results of the shift-share analysis rather suggest that by far the largest part of regional employment growth differentials can be attributed to the fact that the sectors in a region grew slower or faster than the national average. This is surprising given the regional differentials of sectoral shares. These broadly defined sectors are possibly subject to quite different shocks, leading on a regional level to diverging growth performances.[6]

Our analysis, however, implies that in Bulgaria, Hungary and Romania the sectoral composition of the regions does not play a major role. There are at least two explanations for this. First, the sectors may be strongly interrelated. This implies that if one sector is affected by a shock,[7] all the other sectors in the respective region will benefit or suffer, meaning that strong inter-sector (industry) spill-over effects are present. Second, there may be very few idiosyncratic shocks affecting only one specific sector, whereas many region-specific shocks affect regions as a whole. Both views justify the analysis of regions on an aggregate level.

5 REGRESSION ANALYSIS

The traditional shift-share analysis is widely used in regional science. However, this method has a number of drawbacks. One of the main criticisms of this method is that it does not allow us to draw statistical inferences and the method is not very robust to the choice of regional, sectoral and temporal limits. In order to address these concerns and go beyond the above-mentioned drawbacks, we further check the robustness of our results using a shift-share regression analysis as suggested by Patterson (1991).[8] We decompose employment growth in sector i, region r at time t into a business cycle (time) component, a regional component and a structural component. The business cycle component is captured by time dummies, the regional component by region dummies and the structural component by sector dummies. In addition, one can account for the effect of higher than average initial specialisation in a certain sector. The equation to be estimated is given by:

$$g_{ir,t}w_{ir,t-1} = \alpha_t w_{ir,t-1} + \beta_i w_{ir,t-1} + \gamma_r w_{ir,t-1} + \mu_i \left(s_{ir,0} - s_{i.,0}\right) w_{ir,t-1} + \varepsilon_{irt} \quad (7.9)$$

The growth rate $g_{ir,t}$ is given as the difference of the log employment. $w_{ir,t-1}$ is a weight to account for the problem of 'shipbuilding in the midlands', which is the effect of an industry starting from very little employment, thus generating very high growth rates. High growth rates (outliers) are, however, weighted very strongly in OLS regressions. Therefore the weight is computed as $w_{ir,t-1} = L_{it,t-1}/L_{..,t-1}$. α_t is a matrix of time dummies, β_i is a matrix of sector dummies and γ_r is a matrix of regional dummies. The term $\mu_i(s_{ir,0} - s_{i.,0})$ gives the effect of specialisation in sector i in region r relative to the national average sectoral shares. A negative coefficient can be interpreted as structural convergence, meaning that regions with higher than average specialisation in sector i in the initial period will lose employment in this sector, while a positive coefficient means that specialisation in that sector increases. The estimation of Equation 7.9 poses the problem that the regressors are perfectly multi-collinear. In this case one can either drop one regressor for each set of dummy variables and then interpret the coefficients relative to this missing dummy or one can impose identifying restrictions, which is the avenue we take here. We impose the following three restrictions: (a) $\sum \alpha_t w_{ir,t-1} = 0$, (b) $\sum \beta_i w_{ir,t-1} = 0$, and (c) $\sum \gamma_r w_{ir,t-1} = 0$. This implies that the coefficients for the time, sector and regional dummies must be interpreted relative to each other. If, for example, one sector grows faster than the others, it will have a positive coefficient. This holds even if all sectors lose employment; thus the coefficient is a coefficient of relative performance.

As shown in Table 7.4, in Bulgaria the regions Blagoevgrad and Razgrad performed significantly worse than the national average. In addition, the coefficients of the regional dummies are jointly different from zero, as indicated by the F-test for the null H_0: $reg1 = 0, \ldots, reg28 = 0$ result significant at the 1 per cent level. Thus regions do perform differently from the national average. Employment growth changed significantly over time. Remarkable is the year 1996, which was characterised by a huge employment loss relative to the other years (in which employment growth was also sometimes negative as was pointed out in Figure 7.1). The agricultural sector relative to the other sectors gained employment while the industrial sector experienced strong declines in employment. Initial specialisation in agriculture and services led to structural convergence to average national sectoral employment shares. Thus we can conclude that, after controlling for the sectoral composition effects, regions had a quite differing employment growth relative to national average growth. Employment growth in general was driven by aggregate restructuring of the economy and by the strong time effects of the recession of 1996/97. This result also holds for non-weighted regressions.

Table 7.4 Results for the restricted regression: Bulgaria

Variable	Coefficient	t-value	Variable	Coefficient	t-value
Blagoevgrad	–0.20	–5.34	1991	0.07	2.23
Bourgas	0.01	0.22	1992	0.14	4.26
Dobrich	0.06	0.57	1993	0.22	6.73
Gabrovo	–0.03	–0.35	1994	0.23	7.13
Haskovo	0.01	0.14	1995	0.25	7.87
Kardjali	–0.03	–0.23	1996	–0.91	–28.87
Kustendil	0.08	0.61	1997	–0.04	–1.28
Lovech	0.05	0.40	1998	0.02	0.47
Montana	0.02	0.14	1999	0.03	0.99
Pazardjik	0.07	0.66			
Pernik	–0.08	–0.90	Agriculture	0.09	3.40
Pleven	0.01	0.14	Industry	–0.08	–3.98
Plovdiv	0.01	0.21	Services	–0.01	–0.55
Razgrad	–0.27	–6.46	Structural agriculture	–1.22	–2.14
Russe	0.09	0.83	Structural industry	0.09	0.14
Shumen	–0.04	–0.37	Structural services	–0.66	–2.60
Silistra	–0.09	–0.93	Constant	0.00	–1.62
Sliven	0.12	0.90			
Smolyan	0.00	–0.02			
Sofia	0.03	0.74			
Sofia region	–0.02	–0.22			
Stara Zagora	0.01	0.14			
Targoviste	0.13	0.83			
Varna	0.03	0.62			
Veliko	–0.02	–0.31			
Vidin	–0.12	–1.38			
Vtratza	0.08	0.68	Obs	756	
Yambol	0.09	0.69	F(40,715)	34.5	

Table 7.5 Results for the restricted regression: Hungary

Variable	Coefficient	t-value	Variable	Coefficient	t-value
Baranya	–0.026	–0.74	1992	–0.062	–7.18
Borsod–Abauj–Zemplen	–0.010	–0.4	1993	–0.077	–9.3
Budapest	–0.047	–0.93	1994	–0.037	–4.45
Bacs–Kiskun	0.000	0	1995	–0.064	–7.81
Bekes	–0.001	–0.02	1996	–0.032	–3.85
Csongrad	–0.008	–0.26	1997	0.186	22.69
Fejer	0.051	1.33	1998	0.084	11.95
Gyor–Moson–Sopron	0.030	1.01			
Hajdu–Bihar	–0.015	–0.51	Agriculture	0.010	0.31
Heves	–0.001	–0.02	Industry	–0.012	–0.63
Jasz–Nagykun–Szolnok	–0.002	–0.06	Services	0.002	0.12
Komarom–Esztergom	0.039	0.76	Structural		
Nograd	–0.025	–0.34	agriculture	–1.430	–1.33
Pest	0.017	0.71	Structural		
Somogy	–0.017	–0.36	industry	–0.382	–0.99
Szabolcs–Szatmar–Bereg	–0.029	–0.87	Structural		
Tolna	0.004	0.07	services	0.366	1.66
Vas	0.021	0.49	Constant	0.000	–1.06
Veszprem	0.014	0.36	obs	420	
Zala	0.006	0.13	F(30, 389)	28.38	

As Table 7.5 indicates, in the case of Hungary the regions' dummies are jointly and individually insignificant. An F-test for the weighted restricted model H_0: $reg1 = 0,\ldots, reg20 = 0$ gave a p-value = 0.99. We also estimated a non-weighted model with $w_{irt} = 1 \forall i,r,t$ and could not reject the H_0 of zero coefficients. Thus we conclude that the performance of regions after controlling for sectoral composition and initial specialisation is the same relative to other regions. The F-test for the time dummies in the weighted model clearly rejected a zero effect. The structural convergence effect is different from zero with a p-value of 0.059, while the sectoral effects are not different from zero. Employment growth thus differed considerably from year to year, as has already been seen in Figure 7.2. In Hungary, employment declined until 1997 and then it increased. In the non-weighted model, the effect of the sectors is clearly different from zero with a p-value of 0.00. Thus we conclude that in Hungary employment growth in the 1990s was driven by aggregate structural change. In addition, sectors performed differently, with agriculture losing significantly relative to the other sectors and industry and services gaining employment relative to agriculture. If we account for the relative importance of each observation by weighting them, it appears that especially initial sectoral composition of a region as compared to the national average accounts for growth. The sectors per se do not differ. Regions with a higher than average initial specialisation in agriculture and industry converged to the national average, while initial specialisation in the services sector consolidated, leading to a higher share of services in regional employment.

As Table 7.6 shows, in Romania some regions performed significantly differently from the rest of the country. In particular, we find that Bucuresti and Constanta grew more slowly than the rest of the country, after controlling for their industry structure and initial specialisation. An F-test of joint significance of the regional factors allows us to reject the H_0 of all regional dummies equal to zero at a 12 per cent level of significance. Thus regional factors matter, especially in some selected regions. The time effects are important determinants of employment growth. The years 1994, 1996 and 1998 were ones with relatively high employment growth, while 1995 and 1999 were years with lower than average growth. Agriculture was performing relatively well while the industrial sector lost employment significantly. Initial specialisation of a region in agriculture leads to lower than average growth in agriculture and thus to structural convergence to the average national shares.

Our regression analysis thus only partly confirms the results we obtained with the traditional shift-share analysis. For Bulgaria and Romania we find that regional factors do matter, even after controlling for sectoral composition effects. In Hungary, differences in employment growth across regions cannot significantly be attributed to purely regional effects. In addition, our regression analysis confirms the results shown in section 3. Bulgaria and Romania are characterised by a large aggregate structural change, especially a process of de-industrialisation and, in particular in the case of Romania, a process of re-agrarisation. The aggregate composition of the Hungarian economy, on the other hand, stayed broadly constant. The coefficients of sectors' dummies are not significant. Furthermore, the regression analysis accounted for the evolution over time. We find that Bulgaria experienced particularly large employment declines in 1996 and 1997 relative to the other years. Hungary had significantly lower employment growth in the early years of transition up to 1997, while Romania had more volatile growth rates, doing poorly in 1995 and 1999 relative to the other years. Beyond this standard analysis we also tested for

Table 7.6 Results for the restricted regression: Romania

Variable	Coefficient	t-value	Variable	Coefficient	t-value
Alba	0.002	0.06	1993	0.008	1.33
Arad	–0.022	–0.89	1994	0.036	5.66
Arges	–0.003	–0.18	1995	–0.046	–7.04
Bacau	–0.014	–0.78	1996	0.025	3.68
Bihor	–0.012	–0.66	1997	0.001	0.22
Bistrita–Nasaud	0.025	0.64	1998	0.031	4.56
Botosani	0.015	0.51	1999	–0.056	–8.37
Braila	–0.007	–0.22			
Brasov	0.003	0.12	Agriculture	0.037	6.56
Buc	–0.061	–4.68	Industry	–0.042	–8.31
Buzau	–0.002	–0.06	Services	0.005	0.92
Calarasi	0.002	0.06	Structural		
Caras–Severin	0.003	0.09	agriculture	–0.150	–1.76
Cluj	–0.020	–1.29	Structural		
Constanta	–0.029	–1.75	industry	–0.015	–0.14
Covasna	0.039	0.76	Structural		
Dambovita	–0.022	–1	services	–0.010	–0.11
Dolj	–0.005	–0.29			
Galati	–0.011	–0.59			
Giurgiu	0.027	0.62			
Gorj	–0.015	–0.57			
Harghita	0.015	0.44			
Hunedoara	–0.023	–1.02			
Ialomita	0.014	0.36			
Iasi	–0.006	–0.38			
Maramures	–0.007	–0.33			
Mehedinti	0.031	0.87			
Mures	–0.002	–0.09			
Neamt	–0.002	–0.09			
Olt	0.001	0.02			
Prahova	–0.024	–1.44			
Salaj	0.050	1.11			
Satu Mare	0.006	0.21			
Sibiu	0.018	0.64			
Suceava	0.000	–0.03			
Teleorman	0.018	0.67			
Timis	–0.014	–0.83			
Tulcea	0.007	0.15			
Valcea	0.002	0.07	Constant	0.000	–5.27
Vaslui	0.016	0.57	obs	861	
Vrancea	0.008	0.26	F(51, 809)	12.88	

structural convergence. Do regions with an initial high specialisation in one sector increase this specialisation? We find that in Bulgaria regions with specialisation in agriculture and/or services experienced a decrease in this specialisation, and thus approached the national averages. In Hungary we do not observe this effect. In Romania, the agricultural sector had a tendency to converge to national averages. Thus, regional fixed effects matter in Bulgaria and Romania, while in Hungary they are not statistically significant.

6 CONCLUSIONS AND POLICY IMPLICATIONS

In this chapter we used employment data at regional level for the period 1990–99 and applied a shift-share analysis to explain regional employment growth differentials at sectoral level in three transition countries, namely Bulgaria, Hungary and Romania. The sectors included in our analysis are agriculture, industry and services. Our research results suggest the following conclusions and policy implications:

1. We find both commonalities and particularities in the patterns of regional employment growth in the three above-mentioned transition countries. In the period 1990–99 the industrial sector declined everywhere, most strongly in Bulgaria and Romania, while the services sector grew in Bulgaria and especially in Hungary. Bulgaria and Romania experienced a growing share of employment in agriculture. Regional disparities in employment increased in Bulgaria and Hungary and decreased in Romania.
2. Despite different patterns of regional disparities we find that in all three countries regional variance in employment growth was characterised mostly by region-specific factors. An additional shift-share analysis using data for regional employment in manufacturing branches pointed to similar results. Employment growth differentials appear uniform across sectors and vary across regions. Regional industry mix does not play an important role in explaining regional growth differentials.

Several hypotheses can be put forward to explain these results. First, the three sectors analysed in this chapter are interrelated at regional level. This implies that, if one sector is affected, the other sectors in the region will be affected as well. Second, the nature of shocks seems to be region-wide rather than industry-specific/sector-specific.

3. A further robustness check of the above results using a shift-share regression analysis confirmed our previous findings in the cases of Bulgaria and Romania. In the case of Hungary, we find that on average,

other things being equal, employment growth was the same across regions. In this case, regional employment growth was driven by aggregate structural change.

4. We tested in addition for structural convergence and found that in Bulgaria regions specialised in agriculture or services experienced a decrease in this specialisation, and thus converged to the national average. No structural convergence was found in the case of Hungary. In Romania, regions specialised in agriculture seemed to converge to national averages.

NOTES

1 We thank Ian Gordon, Roger Vickerman, Ronald Moomaw, Johannes Bröcker, Anna Iara, Johannes Ricke, seminar participants at ZEI, University of Bonn, participants of the conference 'Emerging Market Economies and European Economic Integration', organised by the Nordic section of the Regional Science Association, participants at the University of Pittsburgh, European Union Centre, participants of the ACCESSLAB workshop in Budapest, and participants at the annual conference of the Regional Studies Association in Pisa for many helpful comments. Remaining errors are ours. Financial support from the European Union's Fifth Framework Programme is gratefully acknowledged.

2 Corresponding author: Centre for European Integration Studies (ZEI), Walter-Flex Str. 3, D-53113 Bonn, Tel: +49/228/73-1887, e-mail: guntram.wolff@gmx.de

3 One of the points of reservation raised is its lack of an underlying theory (Houston, 1967). One additional major criticism is that the method is deterministic. We believe that, despite its deterministic nature, the method allows us to give an accurate description of actual employment changes. Furthermore, we do not seek to make statements about individual regions, for which a statistical significance test is necessary, but our analysis aims at looking at variance shares of the different components over the entire cross-section.

4 In Hungary and Romania, data were only available for the period 1992–99.

5 The data set REGSTAT was generated in the framework of the project P98-1117-R undertaken with financial support from European Communities PHARE ACE programme 1998.

6 Consider the following thought experiment: the occurrence of a particularly long and severe winter should affect the production of the agricultural sector, which should lead to significant lay-offs in employment. Regions with a high agricultural sector should be affected much more by this winter than regions with virtually no agricultural sector.

7 A shock may be of a short-term nature but it can also represent long-term structural change of the regional and sectoral structure of the transition economies.

8 For an application of this method to German data, see Möller and Tassinopoulos (2000).

REFERENCES

Blanchard, O. J. and L. Katz (1992), 'Regional Evolutions', *Brookings Papers on Economic Activity*, pp. 1–75.

Boeri, T. and S. Scarpetta (1996), 'Regional Mismatch and the Transition to a Market Economy', *Labour Economics*, **3**, 233–54.

Decressin, J. and A. Fatas (1995), 'Regional Labor Market Dynamics in Europe', *European Economics Review*, **39** (9), 1627–55.

Dunn, E.S. (1960), 'A Statistical and Analytical Technique for Regional Analysis', *Papers and Proceedings of the Regional Science Association*, **6**, 97–112.

EBRD (2001), *Transition Report 2001*, London: European Bank for Reconstruction and Development.

Esteban, J. (1972), 'A Reinterpretation of Shift-Share Analysis', *Regional and Urban Economics*, **2**, 249–61.

Esteban, J. (2000), 'Regional Convergence in Europe and the Industry Mix: A Shift-Share Analysis', *Regional Science and Urban Economics*, **30**, 353–66.

Fothergill, S. and G. Gudgin (1982), Unequal Growth, Urban and Regional Employment Change in the United Kingdom, London: Heinemann.

Garcia-Milà, T. and T. McGuire (1993), 'Industrial Mix as a Factor in the Growth and Variability of States' Economies', *Regional Science and Urban Economics*, **23**, 731–48.

Houston, David (1967), 'The Shift and Share Analysis of Regional Growth: A Critique', *Southern Economic Journal*, **1067** (33), 557–81.

Landesmann, M. and R. Stehrer (2002), 'The CEECs in the Enlarged Europe: Convergence Patterns, Specialization and Labour Market Implications', *WIIW Research Report, The Vienna Institute for Economic Comparative Studies*, **286**.

Loveridge, S. and A.C. Selting (1998), 'A Review and Comparison of Shift-Share Identities', *International Regional Science Review*, **21**, 37–58.

Möller, Joachim and Alexandros Tassinopoulos (2000), 'Zunehmende Spezialisierung oder Strukturkonvergenz? Eine Analyse der Sektoralen Beschäftigungsentwicklung auf Regionaler Ebene', *Jahrbuch für Regionalwissenschaft*, **20** (1), 1–38.

Patterson, Murray G. (1991), 'A Note on the Formulation of a Full-Analogue Regression Model of the Shift-Share Method', *Journal of Regional Science*, **31** (2), 211–16.

Petrakos, G. (1996), 'The Regional Dimension of Transition in Eastern and Central European Countries: An Assessment', *Eastern European Economics*, **34** (5), 5–38.

Petrakos, G. (2000), 'The Spatial Impact of East–West Integration', in G. Petrakos, G. Maier and G. Gorzelak (eds), *Integration and Transition in Europe: The Economic Geography of Interaction*, London: Routledge.

Petrakos, G. and Y. Saratsis (2000), 'Regional Inequalities in Greece', *Papers in Regional Science*, **79**, 1–18.

Resmini, L. (2002), 'Specialization and Growth Prospects in Border Regions of Accession Countries', ZEI Working Paper, Centre for European Integration Studies, University of Bonn, B02–17.

Svejnar, J. (2002), 'Transition Economies: Performance and Challenges', *Journal of Economic Perspectives*, **16** (19), 3–28.

Traistaru, I. and G.B. Wolff (2002), 'Regional Specialization and Employment Dynamics in Transition Countries', ZEI Working Paper, Centre for European Studies, University of Bonn, B02-18, 1–32.

Traistaru, I., P. Nijkamp and S. Longhi (2002), 'Regional Specialization and Concentration of Industrial Activity in Accession Countries', ZEI Working Paper, Centre for European Studies, University of Bonn, B02-16.

APPENDIX

Table 7.7 Regions as classified in Resmini (2002)

	BEU	BAC	BEX	INT
BG	Blagoevgrad; Kardjali; Smolyan	Vidin; Vtratza; Dobrich; Montana; Pleven; Russe; Silistra	Bourgas; Kustendil; Pernik; Haskovo; Yambol	Varna; Veliko Tarnovo; Gabrovo; Lovech; Pazardjik; Plovdiv; Razgrad; Sliven; Sofia; Sofia region; Stara Zagora; Targoviste; Shumen
HU	Gyor–Moson–Sopron; Vas	Komárom–Esztergom; Zala; Borsod–Abaúj–Zemplén; Nógrád; Hajdú–Bihar; Szabolcs–Szatmár–Bereg; Békés; Csongrád	Baranya; Somogy; Bács–Kiskun	Budapest; Pest; Fejér; Veszprém; Tolna; Heves; Jász–Nagykun–Szolnok
RO		Constanta; Calarasi; Giurgiu; Teleorman; Dolj; Mehedinti; Olt; Arad; Timis; Bihor; Satu Mare	Botosani; Iasi; Suceava; Vaslui; Galati; Tulcea; Caras-Severin; Maramures	Bacau; Neamt; Braila; Buzau; Vrancea; Arges; Dambovita; Ialomita; Prahova; Gorj; Valcea; Hunedoara; Bistrita–Nasaud; Cluj; Salaj; Alba; Brasov; Covasna; Harghita; Mures; Sibiu; Mun. Bucuresti (incl. Ilfov)

Note: BEU = regions bordering the EU15, BAC = regions bordering other candidate countries, BEX = regions bordering with third countries, INT = non-border regions.

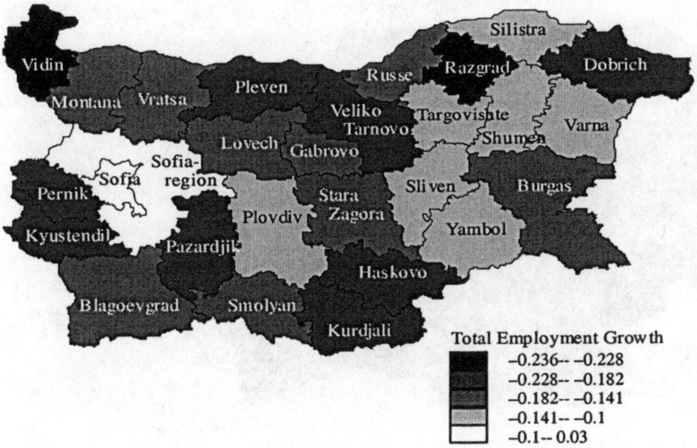

Note: Negative values indicate employment losses.

Figure 7.7 Regional employment growth over the entire period investigated in Bulgaria, 1990–99

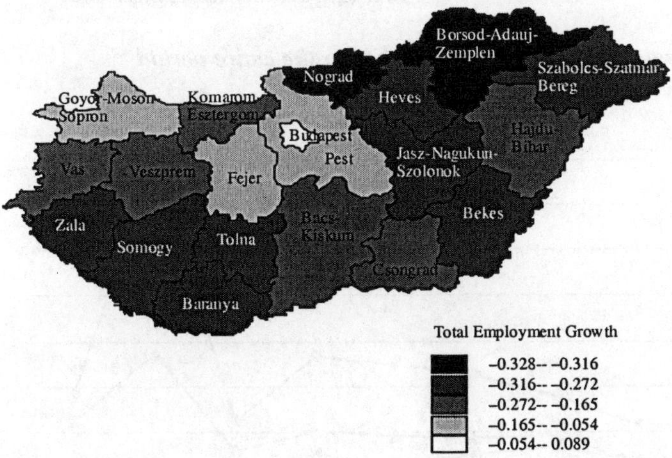

Note: Negative values indicate employment losses.

Figure 7.8 Regional employment growth over the entire period investigated in Hungary, 1992–99

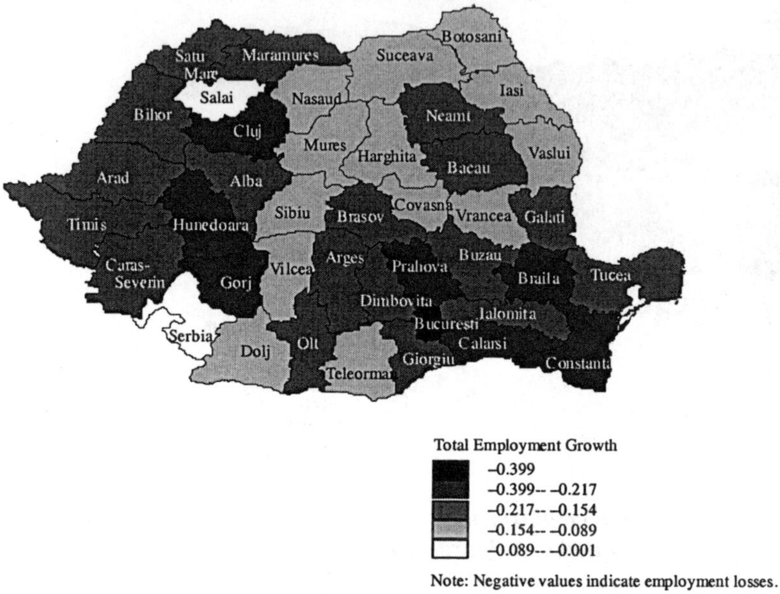

Figure 7.9 ***Regional employment growth over the entire period investigated in Romania, 1992–99***

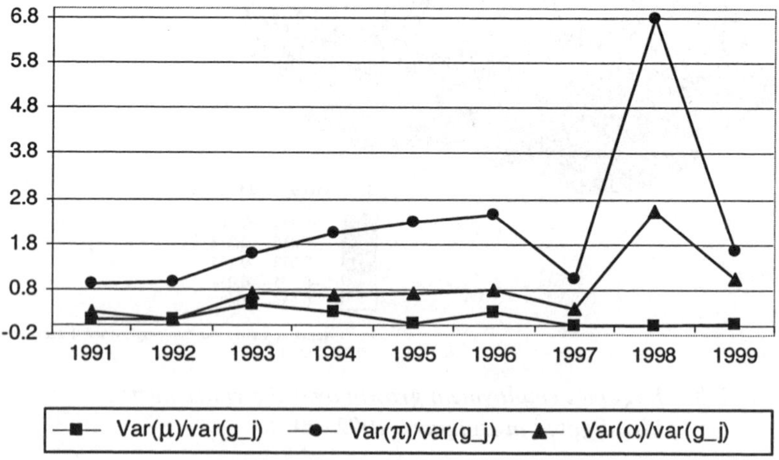

Figure 7.10 ***The evolution of variance shares over time in Bulgaria for the manufacturing sector***

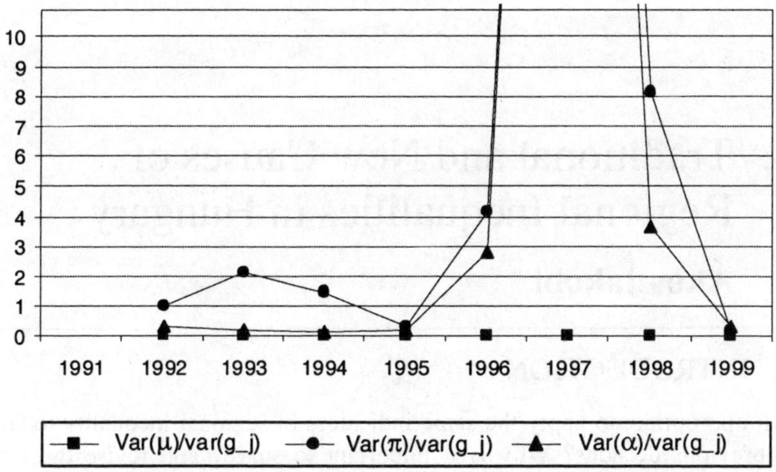

Figure 7.11 *The evolution of variance shares over time in Romania for the manufacturing sector*

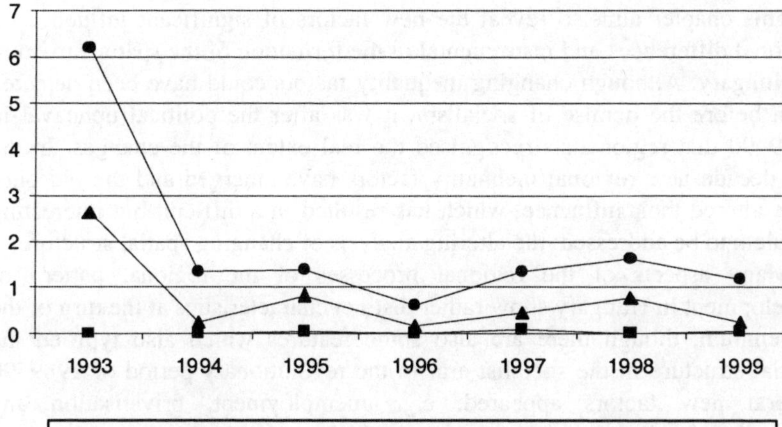

Figure 7.12 *The evolution of variance shares over time in Hungary for the manufacturing sector*

8. Traditional and New Causes of Regional Inequalities in Hungary

Ákos Jakobi

1 INTRODUCTION

Is it appropriate to apply the same indicators of regional inequality today as in previous decades? Why is it important to survey and revise the set of factors and indicators regularly? In what context have the regional inequality patterns changed during the period of the turn to a market economy? These questions are obviously important for researchers analysing regional inequalities in a dynamic way.

This chapter aims to reveal the new factors of significant influence on regional differences and instrumental in the formation of the spatial structure of Hungary. Although changing inequality factors could have been detected even before the demise of socialism, it was after the political upheaval in 1989–90 that regionalists recognised the real extent of the changes. In the last decade new regional inequality factors have emerged and the old ones have altered their influence, which has resulted in a difficult but interesting problem to be addressed: the altering analysis of changing spatial structure.

Many aspects of the regional processes of the regional pattern of development in Hungary show rather distinct characteristics at the turn of the millennium, though there are also some features which also typified the spatial structure in the socialist era. In the revolutionary period of 1989–90 several new factors appeared, e.g. unemployment, privatisation and expanding foreign direct investments, which were previously unknown in Hungary. The novelty of these factors, however, has faded away. The period since the political and economic upheaval seems to be long enough for them to leave their imprint on regional inequalities. Nevertheless the strong influence of the traditional elements must not be ignored.

According to the considerations outlined above, the factors influencing regional differences can be classified as follows: (1) traditional factors, which had the same effects on regional inequalities in the past as they will probably have in the future, (2) transformed factors, which were on the scene in the past, too, but have a different kind of influence on inequalities at present, and (3) new factors, which either did not exist formerly or did not have any influence on regional inequalities, but exert a strong regional impact nowadays.

Looking further back at the past 20–30 years, traditional, transformed and new factors could always be recognised among the causes of actual regional differentiation. Up to now, however, during the period of socioeconomic transformation the factors may have altered in different ways: some new factors have changed into transformed or traditional ones, some have disappeared completely or traditional factors have retained their original form and sphere of influence.

The chapter deals with 'factors' as causes or determinants of regional inequalities. Sometimes they seem like expressions of inequality, which suggests that a basic social difference is given, with several different components in the form of factors. In that case causes of differences in social development would be noted by all observers. This study applies a different approach by putting the factors and not the social development at the forefront. Accordingly, regional differences are regarded as spatial inequalities of the factors themselves. 'Indicators' are used in the chapter as representatives and measures of inequality factors. Occasionally it was easier to demonstrate inequality by applying a specific indicator, knowing meanwhile that the inequality is actually related to the factor itself.

The aim of the study is to systematise the factors of inequality already well known from the pertinent literature; on the other hand it tries to reveal the transformation of the role of the various factors by new investigations. The chapter also tries to direct attention to the changing role of regional inequality factors and to the completely new state of regional disparities, thus proving the hypothesis that most of the relevant processes of the previous decades have different effects on spatial structures after 10–12 years of a market economy.

2 THE CONCEPTUAL FRAMEWORK

Richardson (1969), Isard (1975) and Bartke (1995), whose results have been adopted and improved in this research, studied the uneven development of economies in space and the theoretical basis of regional inequalities. Without any detailed discussion we accept the argument that inequality does not merely mean the opposite of equality but also differences in quality. By adding to the background of the problem the dimension of time, we have the main guidelines of our research.

It is obvious that the determining processes and characteristics of regions are subject to continuous transformation, creating links between former periods of development and progress in the future. According to theoretical assumptions, the processes in the background of regional disparities are developing, declining, appearing or fading away over the course of time.

To decide whether a certain inequality factor is a new or a customary one, long enough time-series and historical information is needed on the conditions of spatial differences and especially on the size and diffusion of the factor itself. To simplify, by using the dynamic analysis of the data series, different development paths can be connected to the various inequality factors. By making static segments (cross-sections) in time on the graph showing the path of the factor, it can be determined where the factor is situated in its 'life cycle'.

From a geographical point of view the importance of an inequality factor can be determined on the basis of its social and regional spread. The diffusion theories of the last decades have formulated the main principles supported by practical examination. In the beginning – taking a regional economic perspective – the spatial diffusion of a new phenomenon was regarded as a feature of economic space (Hägerstrand, 1967; Hoover, 1971). Regional development and differences were later put into the spotlight of innovation-diffusion theory (Brown, 1981). Innovation diffusion was defined as a feature's spreading process in time and space starting from a few points (places), and in close connection with regional development. In other words, the changing extent of regional development differences can also be approached by examining the diffusion of socioeconomic parameters (Nemes-Nagy, 1998). It is important to note that the notion of innovation is neutral on the scale of values, although the everyday language treats it – with good reason – as positive. A newly arising element, however, can be judged negative as well. If that is the case, at least from this prior condition we can expect different development paths by examining regional inequality factors.

The progress of diffusion can be divided into four phases, representing consecutive parts of a saturation progress. The S-shape model of innovation diffusion (Figure 8.1) consists of the phases of beginning, diffusing, thickening and saturating.

The model explains the changing level of diffusion well, although the theory of saturation does not take into account the decreasing and disappearing effects and trends. The wave-movement model of innovation diffusion allows a factor to show decreasing diffusion after having passed the maximum level of saturation (Figure 8.2). The static (spatial) and dynamic (in time) cross-sections of the model are represented in the three-axes system of distance, time and acceptors, showing a wavelike shape retreating after the point of highest saturation. The factors which influence regional inequalities are of changing importance in both time and space, giving a useful basis for determining whether a factor is a traditional or a new one.

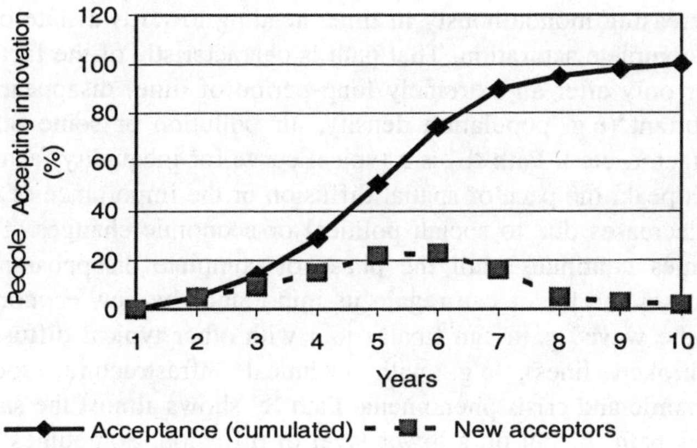

Source: Valente (2001).

Figure 8.1 Generalised empirical curve of innovation diffusion

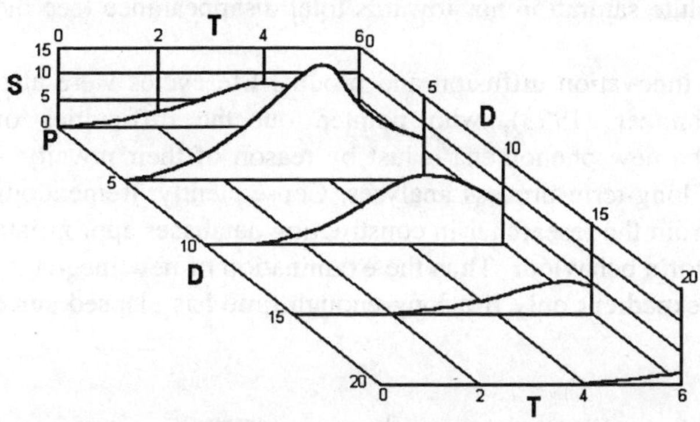

Note: T: time, D: distance, S: saturation, P: point of origin.

Source: Nikodémus (1991).

Figure 8.2 Wave-movement model of innovation diffusion

By looking at the various paths starting from the same point, one can find several common characteristics as well as some differences originating from various effects. Theoretically, the factors are converging in the phase of complete saturation or complete disappearance (in a long enough period of time), while the extent of their spatial diffusion is increasing or decreasing over the course of time (Figure 8.3).

Path 'a' corresponds to the saturation model. In this case the diffusion of the factor is increasing monotonously in time, heading towards a state of a higher-level or complete saturation. That path is characteristic of the factors which never (or only after an extremely long period of time) disappear or become unimportant (e.g. population density, air pollution or some other environmental factor, etc.). Path 'b' is a typical curve for inequality factors. After reaching a peak, the pace of spatial diffusion or the importance of the factor usually decreases due to social, political or economic changes. This process sometimes continues until the phase of complete disappearance, while in other cases the factor can regain its importance by new economic changes. Then the waved path can finally join with other typical diffusion courses (see broken lines), e.g. with technical infrastructure, social institutions, dynamic and crisis phenomena. Path 'c' shows almost the same characteristics as path 'b' but on a lower level of diffusion. Sometimes the judgement of a factor can be altered straight after its appearance, which results in a waved diffusion path reaching a lower level of spread (e.g. informatics and some features of the information society). Since most inequality factors are changing continuously, their typical path is heading neither towards absolute saturation nor towards total disappearance (see the dotted lines).

Spatial diffusion, innovation diffusion and product life cycles were also dealt with by Rechnitzer (1993), who pointed out the difficulties of modelling because the new phenomena – just by reason of their novelty – cannot be subject to long-term process analyses. Consequently, tremendous efforts are required from the researcher in constructing databases appropriate for revealing the factor's behaviour. Thus the examination of new inequality factors seems to be expedient only if a long enough time has elapsed since their appearance.

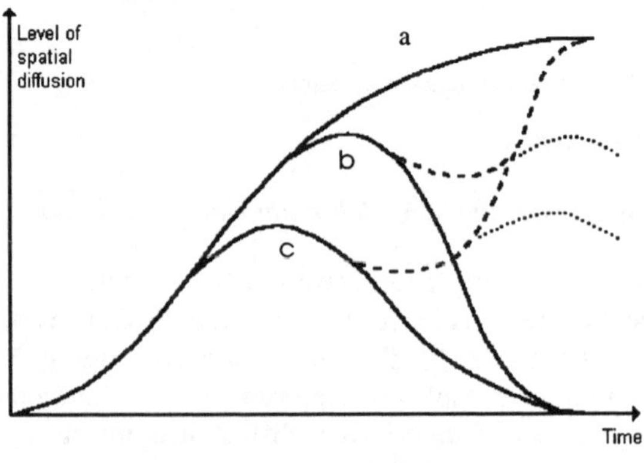

Figure 8.3 Theoretical courses of the diffusion of regional inequality factors in time (types a, b, c)

3 OBSERVING THE CHANGING NATURE OF INEQUALITY FACTORS

An easy and convenient way of getting information about the changing nature of a regional inequality factor is to use indirect methods. The following section describes how inequality factors come to light, alter or disappear in the scientific literature, in the statistical sources and in the devices applied by the regional development policy (Table 8.1).

> A basic task of regional development is to establish what kind of factors are influencing the economic growth of a region and which one has to be blamed for an eventual decline. All the regional examinations called attention to the fact that the regional development cannot be explained by considering only one or several factors; therefore the complete set of elements and their joint system of impact should be examined. (Rechnitzer, 1993, p. 20)

This is particularly important in the research aimed at formulating the principles and the direction of development on the basis of a regional progress report.

The publications and the documents on regional development can provide us with an image of regional inequalities of selected years, and of the 'traditional' and 'new' factors prevailing at that time. With the progression of time the decreasing importance of traditional factors, and also the loss of novelty of ageing factors and the emergence of new, formerly completely unknown ones, can be expected.

We cannot go back in time enough to explore the whole life cycle of every regional inequality factor. Perhaps it is worth starting our survey in the 1970s, when the National Settlement-network Development Plan (NSDP) (1007/1971. Govt. decree) was approved. This document provided the framework for the treatment of regional inequalities for a long period of time. (Among the predecessors of this decree we find plans for the period 1949–51 or the Survey of National Settlement-network Development in 1963.) The NSDP attributed the regional disparities basically to the inequalities of settlements,[1] due to their different functions and sizes. The elaborated strategy of the document outlined the ideal or attainable state of affairs until the 1980s and 1990s. The importance of the plan is due to the fact that levelling regional disparities has been brought into sight as a key target of regional policy based on the settlement hierarchy. Those who created the plan were the first to recognise the importance of regional thinking and to introduce measures against spatial disparities in Hungary.

Table 8.1 Comparison of the main traditional, transforming and new inequality factors in time

	1970s, beginning of the 1980s	End of the 1980s	Beginning of the 1990s	End of the 1990s
Traditional	Public utility supplies, institution supplies (NSDP 71) Classical complex indicators Rural industrialisation	Settlement hierarchy	Classical elements of complex examination (NRDP 98)	Natural environmental factors
Transforming	Employment, education, demography, migration etc. Living conditions	Natural conditions, traditional organisations Industry	Industry, structural depression Income disparities Geographical location	Industry (machinery) Foreign capital Unemployment
New	Settlement hierarchy (NSDP 71) Declared regional equalisation (NSDP 71) Technical innovations	Technological innovations (computing, electronics) 'Second economy' Foreign capital	Stimulation from foreign capital Unemployment	Informatics, information society

According to the NSDP, a significant improvement in social and financial conditions was only possible by moving upwards in the settlement hierarchy. Though the regional development policy declared the aim of reducing regional inequalities, in reality multiple handicapped regions started to take shape. While the equalisation of counties was under way, the differences among settlements increased. The decreasing inequalities also had a great effect on the diffusion of new technical, economic, constitutional and other innovations. In the diffusion of these different new elements the dependence on the hierarchy of settlements was quite strong. In the 1980s the NSDP was – due to the criticism of professional and wider circles – modified, then in the decision of December 1980–85 the Parliament passed proposals on the long-term tasks of regional and settlement development, and in 1986 – by the 2015/1986 Govt. decision – the programme concerning the definition of socially backward regions. This programme set as an aim to moderate the 'unjustified' differences in social and economic conditions, and marked out a group of factors to identify the multiple backward regions. These factors are therefore the actual determining indicators of regional inequalities; those are, however, not newly discovered.

There were multifactoral examinations in the 1970s of regional handicaps at the level of communities and small regions, which should be mentioned as an analysis of the ruling inequality factors in those times (Beluszky, 1976). In their first research the authors described the inequalities of the villages using 28 indicators (e.g. those giving the facts and figures of demography, migration, employment, consumption, infrastructure and education); later this research rose to the level of small regions characterised by 66 indicators (including new ones such as the level of urban functions, accessibility and public utility supplies).

In an attempt to widen the range of indicators, and after the adaptation of innovation-oriented regional policy, a great number of researchers turned to examine the potential innovative factors and their spatial diffusion and inequalities as well. Publications were made following international tendencies (Zmud, 1982; Rogers, 1983) on subjects such as diffusion of agricultural innovations (Enyedi and Rechnitzer, 1987) and technical innovations (Nemes-Nagy and Ruttkay, 1987), which were factors influencing regional differences at the same time.

The regional differences of the 1980s were basically under the influence of the formerly known factors. Industrial development, which had had an obvious role in regional equalising since the 1960s and 1970s, was still a determining factor in moderating regional differences due to the industrialisation of rural areas. Nevertheless, strikingly new and in the future more influential factors started to emerge because of the new technical and technological innovations and also as a consequence of the improving socioeconomic transformation. It should be noted that although the importance of electronics, telecommunications and computer technologies was increasing worldwide, their effects on Hungarian regional disparities were insignificant at that time. This is also reflected in the statistics: the number of manual loaders – taken as typical physical workers – was six times greater than that of those employed in computing, a rate that shows rather small diffusion of computerisation (Nemes-Nagy and Ruttkay, 1987).

As a part of social and economic innovations, the 'second economy' – with its small enterprises – is considered to be the most significant new space-shaping innovative factor in the decade (Pomázi, 1988). This successful factor of dynamics modified the former geographical idea of determining regional development on the basis of natural resources and traditional establishments. Meanwhile the diffusion of these trends was still influenced by formerly powerful declared factors (e.g. types of settlements).

The alteration of regional inequality factors had already begun at the end of the 1980s, even before the political transformation. Such a circumstance strengthened entrepreneurial activity due to increased legal opportunities, and also the appearance of foreign capital. Since 1972 there had been opportunities to invest foreign capital in joint ventures, but the amount of investments was insignificant until 1987, so that this did not play such a big role in modifying regional differences. The gradually liberalised legal background (first law on companies 1987, on foreigners' investments in Hungary 1988, on joint ventures 1988, law on transformation 1989, law on privatisation 1990) made it possible to found more and more joint ventures and to attract increasing amounts of foreign direct investment to Hungary.

Foreign direct investment spread widely in the country and became one of the most determining elements of dynamism after recovery from the shock just after the change of regime. The recognition of its role happened in the early years and remained an important subject for analysis in the 1990s as well (Nagy, 1995; Enyedi, 1996).

Besides these new factors of dynamism, those of crisis appeared too. Unemployment, widening differences of income and deepening depression of whole industrial branches appeared as new phenomena. The so-called structural depression of industrial zones and the critical branches have revalued the role of traditional industry (Bartke, 1993). The previously unknown unemployment and the related problems of employment appeared as entirely new factors and threw light on new elements of spatial structure (Schwertner, 1992).

In the middle of the last decade new studies appeared describing the new regional structure in general terms. These works tried to determine the reasons and structure of regional inequalities after the upheaval by using complex analyses and a wider range of indicators. In these papers some new factors arose among the main and determining factors of regional disparities (Csatári, 1996). The multifactoral models filtered indirectly into the National Regional Development Plan (1998) as well, and also into the decision on beneficiary regions (e.g. into the determination of permanently backward regions). The two factors, backwardness and success, were also important for the settlements searching for their way in the market economy.

At the end of the 1990s or rather at the beginning of the new century, a new worldwide innovation and its adapting society should be mentioned as new factors of inequality: informatics and the information society. The analysis of communication systems and information flow in spatial terms is not a new aspect of analyses (Cooper and Zmud, 1986; Rechnitzer, 1990). On this basis a new direction for analysis of the information society seems to be emerging (Nagy, 2002) and regional policy is taking it increasingly into account.

As a comparison of factor types and periods, Table 8.1 shows a summarised picture of inequality factors of the recent past. According to the information gained from the above-mentioned documents and other regional development sources, the main tendencies of the changing importance can be easily traced and detected in the form of a cross-tabulation.

In the first period under examination lots of inherited factors were on the scene, which were actually typical inequality factors of the whole socialist era. These were mainly outlined in the first period of the regime, namely in the 1950s and 1960s, and became part of the main 'five year plans' of those decades. These factors could be found in the spatially important NSDP plan, too, which stabilised and supplemented their role. The significance of this permanently stationary condition of factors reveals two typical life-courses. One is for the general or classical elements of regional disparities, e.g. public utility supplies and institution supplies, which stayed as stable traditional inequality factors for decades. The NSDP brought a new kind of inequality factor, too, the settlement hierarchy, which remained unchanged and for that reason traditional until the end of the 1980s. This kind of factor disappeared as the new democratic conventions came to light. (If we look back to the theoretical models (see Figure 8.3), the life-course of this factor can be perfectly traced in the curves.)

At the end of the 1980s, just before the economic, social and political upheaval, the ruling processes were already so influential that most of the inequality factors must have gone through a transformation or appeared as new ones. This period preceded the evolving economic and social reforms leading to the unusual situation in the 1990s with hardly any factor being able to keep its traditional role. The transition brought to the surface a great number of new phenomena (e.g. foreign direct investment, unemployment), which were obviously new inequality factors on the first occasion, but with the progression of the transition to a market economy they became more and more familiar and represent transformed structural factors.

It can be concluded that during the examined period some events of overriding importance controlled the fate of the inequality factors. A small part of them retained their traditional position; the number of new factors was seldom too high, while the greatest part of the set was made up of the altering type. These tendencies and rates were almost stable throughout the examined period, which suggests that the same can be expected in the future.

4 PROCESSES OF THE NEW MILLENNIUM

The recent trends in research and the emerging new factors due to the rapidly changing processes unambiguously require that the regional inequalities of the contemporary socioeconomic space should be analysed by taking approaches different from the previous ones. If we want to determine the present range of processes and indicators, we have to apply a broader interpretation of the reasons behind the changes by extending the scope of research to a long-term perspective.[2] In our case the indicators which describe the socioeconomic processes of the millennium should be practically surveyed beginning from the early 1990s.

Many factors which have emerged since the second part of the 1980s and were new at that time became widespread after the change of regime. They did not appear overnight, but have developed as the result of a chain of logical processes (Rechnitzer, 1993; Korompai, 1995). The new factors such as foreign direct investment and unemployment were realised by the social scientists quite soon, and, what is more important, exerted their influence on the regional inequalities almost immediately. The effect of several factors, however, was not felt immediately after the political change but only after a relatively long time.

Among the old and the new or newly appearing socioeconomic characteristics of the millennium four groups of factors can be distinguished:

1. Traditional factors, which have had the same effects on regional inequalities for decades
2. Factors which have existed for a long time but whose impact on regional inequalities is different from that in previous times
3. Factors with a considerable past, having, however, greater influence on regional differences in the last short period of time
4. New factors which have been on the scene and affected regional differences of the society and economy only for a short time.

4.1 Traditional Factors: Are There Any Today?

According to our definitions, traditional factors are those that have long existed with the same kind of influence. Approaching the present state from the perspective of time, it is not hard to find old factors; it is more difficult, however, to determine whether they have the same influence as before. The major problem is that the revolutionary transformation at the end of the 1980s and beginning of the 1990s was so deep and shocking that almost all segments of life were affected. New institutions and political and legal systems were formed, and new processes emerged, all of them having a widespread and inescapable impact.

If we were to insist on the narrowest interpretation we would not find any traditional factors; since every effect exerting an influence on the society and economy is changing, none of them could be considered invariable. One can also claim that any alteration of the society results in an alteration of inequality factors: in this perspective the changing objects of the factors inevitably modify the factors themselves as well. Therefore we can expect a positive feedback with a multiplicative effect.

Even if we consider the changes in factors in a broader sense, we cannot easily find traditional factors. We still have to decide whether a factor is changing or traditional, and that is a question for sophisticated research. Even in this case the determination of the critical threshold of alteration is rather subjective. If the measure of change was quite small (the spatial rearrangement or the intensity of the factor's diffusion was insignificant), then the factor could be treated as a non-changing traditional one.

Looking for the very slow transforming factors, it is worth examining environmental, natural or geographical ones in relation to social processes. Some of them are changing in a shorter timescale (e.g. pollution) but we can find very slowly altering ones, too (e.g. with regard to the country or population density). In the latter case it is a stable factor in the Hungarian structure of space. On the other hand the geographical site has, contrary to other geographical factors, a very different meaning today.

4.2 The Transformed Factors

We can read about factors changing in accordance with the altering socio-economic processes in many documents in the relevant Hungarian literature. Small wonder that in the new millennium most factors belong to this group.

After the political transformation, which brought radical changes in the 1990s, the society and the economy 'got used to' numerous inequality factors, which appeared on the scene or became important at the beginning of the decade. At the end of this decade unemployment (Kertesi and Köllő, 1998) and widespread foreign direct investment (Hrubi, 2000) were most frequently cited among the transformed factors. The economy experienced substantial changes in many senses. After the rapid economic upheaval the various sectors and branches of the slowly stabilising sphere of production followed rather different courses. A significant part of the old branches remained in continuous decline until the new millennium; others, however, (e.g. manufacturing of machinery) soon recovered and contributed to the new wave of regional development. The diverging paths of the dynamic and crisis-hit branches led to a reappraisal of the regional differentiating role of industry in accordance with the concept of permanently transformed inequality factors. The industrial structure and specialisation had a significant influence on regional competitiveness under the conditions of the altered socioeconomic milieu (Jeney and Szabó, 2001). The role of agriculture has also altered, although the specialisation within this branch is not an essential element of regional disparities as far as competitiveness is concerned (Kiss, 1998).

As was mentioned above, geographical location also has a transformed influence on regional disparities with substantial effects on inequalities both in the past and today, though in a different sense. Previously the proper location has always been important and mostly the same elements were as decisive in the past as they are today (e.g. traffic connections, natural resources etc.); however, there were some changes, too. After the fall of the iron curtain the formerly neglected western border regions of Hungary became of more interest to investors; hence after a few years the inflow of FDI was perceptible in the region. These counties were not so affected by the socialist industrialisation; therefore they could avoid the structural crisis of obsolete industries. As an advantage after the upheaval, the western regions started to develop a new structure of industry almost free from the burden inherited from the socialist era. Along with the change of export orientation, the western counties have gained while the eastern ones lost a number of commercial partners.

4.3 The Emerging Factors of Today and of the Future

It is hard to distinguish disparity factors requiring a longer period to evolve from those appearing suddenly, since factors generally cannot be connected to exact moments of time (except, for example, a patent for an innovation). It is an equally hard and rather subjective task to distinguish the altering from the slowly shaping factors, since slow formation can also be interpreted as a slow change. Applying an arbitrary, but to some extent certainly objective, principle, we can consider as slowly shaping factors those that appeared well before the second half of the 1990s but have no substantial influence on regional processes.

According to that principle, we must go back at least to the date of the socioeconomic upheaval in 1989–90 in order to examine the origin of the new factors with longer precedents. An important result of the system change was the emergence and diffusion of democratic order in public affairs. Besides the formal and legal transformation, a much slower social and economic democratisation has begun. While the society's mentality, disposition and attitude adjusted themselves to the new conditions only after a fairly long time, citizens realising the new perspectives opened by democracy started to take advantage of them as soon as possible. In the first years after the change, several non-profit organisations were founded and civil activities started to become stronger. When non-profit organisations had recognised the opportunities and had captured the awareness and support of society, their role and influence on local affairs became more and more obvious. By the end of the decade the civil organisations reached a level that allowed them to be treated as a dynamic factor of regional development. We can suppose that the more intensive civil activity is (for example in the form of proliferating non-profit organisations), the more mature democratic society may become.

A new kind of factor can be discovered in the different level of regional policy subsidies from public sources. These practical tools of development policy took shape in the 1990s and influenced directly or indirectly (depending on types of subsidies) the conditions of the examined region (Nemes-Nagy et al., 2000).

Thinking ahead to the next decade, the preparation for membership of and accession to the European Union will certainly add new components to the present ones. The EU and the accession countries have rather small effects on each other's sets of inequality factors; on the other hand it is obvious that some of the actions of the EU will substantially affect regional inequalities. The EU has set up and provides pre-accession sources which have an influence on disparities (e.g. PHARE, SAPARD etc.). Some of them have served preferential areas such as border regions (CBC), although their effect on equalising regional differences has been quite small.

After accession we can expect marked changes in the composition of inequality. It will be almost as important an upheaval as was the demise of socialism, and new questions will be posed by the introduction of the EU NUTS-2 level regions. Today some of the features influence regional inequalities on distinct regional levels only.[3] At present it is not usual to compare Hungarian efficiency with that of European regions, but later, in the EU, Hungarian regions and counties will compete in several fields with EU regions. It is becoming more and more important, and after the accession to the EU it will be absolutely necessary, to think not just in a Hungarian but also in a European context.

4.4 New Processes and Factors

Information and the knowledge society as a distinctly new socioeconomic concept, motivation factor and value system burst upon the scene, though not without preliminaries, in the 1990s; it is a consequence of the social evolution caused by accelerated technological development. The commercial opening of the Internet in 1992 brought really important changes into the previously almost closed world of research institutes and technology-developing laboratories. The innovation spread at an unprecedented rate, and has required a completely new way of thinking, which proved to be an extremely useful instrument and also created new opportunities. Although computers and mobile phones were in use much earlier and information and knowledge have always been important, the substantial change was due to all these elements being associated with the main production factors (besides labour force and capital), thus gaining much more importance than simple tools.

The term 'information society' has been used by researchers since the 1960s (Umesao, 1963; Porat, 1977) and has appeared in many contexts ranging from utopian to matter-of-fact scientific approaches. It has had the highest occurrence among the key words of publications in recent years (Fichman, 1992; Masuda, 1988; Castells, 1998; Trujillo, 2001).

With the increase in the available knowledge about the information society more and more demand has emerged for measuring the new processes and for comparing different experimental units. Since neither the term 'information society' nor the related phenomena are precisely determined, and no comprehensive definition exists, researchers have tried to work out experimentally on their own basis of examination an indicator of the development level of the information society.

Since the term is a complex one, no simple indicator can be found to characterise it; therefore multi-variable methods have had to be elaborated. These complex analyses apply indicators that were formerly also important in affecting similar processes, and new indicators that have recently become indispensable. For example, the calculations and the methodology of World Times and International Data Corporation (2001) use 23 different indicators in a complex index of the information society. Among the indicators we find those representing the phases of invention, innovation, diffusion and adaptation of the innovation chain. Some new indicators were also introduced – new factors to be analysed – among others, software versus hardware spending, home Internet users per household, e-commerce spending per total Internet users and mobile phone ownership per capita. A similar experiment in methodology was the elaboration of the knowledge imperative index by Ramachandran (1999), who formulated a new collection of indices representing the development of a knowledge society (which is considered to be slightly different from an information society).

The easiest and therefore the primary aim of examination was the identification of national conditions not on any spatial aspect but on a wide base of disciplines (e.g. informatics, sociology and economics). Since it was soon recognised that a basically new set of factors is influencing social differences, their spatial interpretation became inevitable. Due to the novelty of the factors, regionalists often struggle with lack of data, and can therefore make only general models and measurement experiments of their own; no widespread consensual measure or methodology has yet evolved. (On regional differences in the development of the information society there are only some initial research experiments in Hungary, which also reflects the new character of this factor (Nagy, 2002)).

5 TWO EXAMPLES OF FACTOR CHANGE

Many examples could be cited to demonstrate the transformation of inequality factors in the previous decade, but only two of them will be introduced here. One is the indicator of personal income, a typical example of living standard; the other is social: unemployment. These factors have been selected due to their different and interesting paths in the 1990s and because of their substantial role in modifying regional differences.

5.1 Income Differences as Regional Inequality Factors

Personal income is one of the most exact indicators of social well-being; perhaps only gross domestic product (GDP) is better. However, GDP can be spatially not so well disaggregated as personal income; thus the latter is more suitable for research concerning the levels of micro-regions (NUTS-4) or settlements (NUTS-5). Income is perhaps the best representative of winner and loser regions; hence it is worth using in regional disparity analysis.

Personal income differences have been favourite topics of research since the basic data set became available (Förster and Tóth, 1997; Milanovic, 1998). The personal income tax system was introduced in Hungary in 1988, right at the end of the socialist era. Until then the system of income distribution by the government prevailed. The state-owned enterprises employed the overwhelming majority of citizens, who could be controlled in a direct way by the planned economy. The slow formation of the private sector – since ownership of a firm was allowed from 1982 – induced a reform of the income tax system which has brought about significant changes both in the national economy and in the personal living standard. At that time there was no income tax, and income as an important inequality factor could only be measured by using other indirect sources.

The transition to a market economy brought about some new tendencies. In this process – which appeared first of all in the sharp regional socio-economic divide – the transformation of the political system, the functions of the market economy, the new system of economic organisation, the changed direction of foreign trade, the opening borders and the obvious adaptation to the European economic space were emerging as joint influences. All these phenomena gave a new importance to the regions and localities, thus strengthening the impact of the geographical dimension.

In the assessment of regional income differences by Nemes-Nagy et al. (2001) it has been proved that during the 1988–99 period the first five years had a much greater impact on regional income inequalities than the following ones. Using the method of shift-share analysis, it was found that the relative income position of NUTS-3 regions had been more strongly influenced by regional dynamics than by the health of the economic structure of settlements. In numerous cases regions with higher income remained winners, while the differences among them increased. The distance between poor and rich regions also increased, and the regional disparities in taxable personal income became obvious and rather important (Major and Nemes-Nagy, 1999).

The following formula has been used in the calculations for the five regional levels:

$$h = \frac{\sum_{i=1}^{n} |f_i - x_i|}{2}, \tag{8.1}$$

where:

h = the value of the index (per cent)
f_i = the share of region i in the total income of the country (per cent)
x_i = the share of region i in the total population of the country (per cent).

(The result of this equation is also known as the Hoover index or dissimilarity index, while the expression 'Robin Hood index' is used for income inequality calculations. Original source: Hoover, 1941.) As can be seen in Table 8.2, the value of the index increases in every type of region, which means that more and more income should have been redistributed from the richer to the poorer regions in order to achieve less inequality. The gap between rich and poor is increasing mainly due to the different paces of adopting the new rules of a market economy and to the vanishing subsidies of the socialist state.

Table 8.2 Robin Hood index of taxable personal income at different regional levels

Year	Budapest* (n = 2)	Regions (NUTS-2) (n = 7)	Counties (NUTS-3) (n = 20)	Micro regions (NUTS-4) (n = 150)	Settlements (NUTS-5) (n = 3100)
1988	7.1	7.6	7.7	9.1	10.8
1989	7.5	8.1	8.2	9.8	11.7
1990	8.3	8.6	8.7	10.7	12.9
1991	7.5	8.0	8.2	10.6	13.3
1992	9.6	9.3	9.8	12.0	14.8
1993	9.9	9.6	10.2	12.6	15.1
1994	9.9	10.0	10.4	12.9	15.5
1995	9.5	9.7	10.1	12.6	15.2
1996	9.0	10.1	10.3	12.7	15.2
1997	9.3	10.5	10.7	13.2	15.4
1998	9.4	11.0	11.2	13.2	15.5
1999	9.7	11.1	11.2	13.6	15.8

Note: * Budapest versus rest of the country.

Source: Major and Nemes-Nagy (1999).

Behind the obvious tendencies demonstrated by the figures in Table 8.2, the spatial pattern of personal taxable income shows an even more interesting picture. At the beginning – in the 1980s – the capital city, Budapest, the greater cities and some distinctly industrial (mainly heavy-industrial) towns were found among the wealthy ones. This was due to their major share in public and other institutions and state-owned enterprises (see NSDP, 1971) and – especially in cities with a small population but important heavy industry – this situation resulted from the state subsidies. After the upheaval the bigger cities and Budapest remained as winners in the competition, whereas the highly industrialised ones became losers. The winners gained qualified labour forces by migration and were free of the burden of structural problems, while losers suffered from the decline of industries with products no longer marketable. As a result the income standard of the local citizens has dramatically changed and the above-mentioned regional income disparities have increased.

There are of course numerous reasons for changing income disparities among the competing cities and regions. An instructive and edifying way of getting ahead was the local policy of creating a favourable climate for enterprises to invest and settle in the region. It was easier to attract firms into regions that had inherited no structural problems and had proper human resources (a qualified and cheap workforce). The infrastructure and the geographical location were also among the main attracting factors. Examples can be given, such as Székesfehérvár (pop. 108 000), which has introduced a favourable local industrial tax system, and furthermore could take advantage of its perfect traffic location and highly qualified workforce; Százhalombatta (15 000), Tiszaújváros (19 000) and Paks (20 000), which were specialised in strategic and valuable industrial branches; Győr (130 000), which enjoys a perfect traffic location on the highway axis of Budapest–Vienna towards Western Europe; and Telki (1000) and Solymár (7500), representing the small but rich settlements in the agglomeration of Budapest, attracting well-off citizens in the recent wave of suburbanisation.

In conclusion, regional income disparities should be discussed in different ways during the two halves of the 1988–2002 period. Before 1990 income (taxable personal income) was a new – or in other interpretations transforming – factor; at the beginning of the decade it obviously turned out to be transforming, and at the end of the 1990s it can be explained as traditional or transforming, because in several respects the regional structures and the regional disparity patterns have stabilised since the middle of the 1990s.

5.2 Unemployment as a Regional Inequality Factor

Our second topic to be analysed is the indicator of unemployment. This social problem was unknown in Hungary before the political upheaval in 1989–90: in the socialist era it was treated as a taboo; unemployment was not officially acknowledged. It was not unusual to employ more people than was rational; this was called 'inside-gate unemployment'. After the demise of socialism the latent non-workers became practically unemployed and formed the first group of registered unemployed people. After the spread of economic decay and in the run-up to the deep depression, many private and state enterprises had to dismiss their workers. This affected first the countryside establishments of the companies, and later the headquarters too. This shock was an effect of the transition to a market economy, and meant therefore the return to a normal state.

After a radical increase of unemployment, the economy started to recover. The main reasons for unemployment have slowly altered; among others the lacking competitiveness of regions, enterprises or individuals can be mentioned. The regional differences in unemployment started to reflect the regional differences in the level of development and of economic success. The spatial extent of unemployment has also altered over time: at the beginning only a few counties were significantly affected by this problem (see Figure 8.4), whereas after the deepening decay all of them – except for

Budapest – had an unemployment rate higher than 10 per cent. As time passed more and more counties – by 2002 half of them – were able to reduce their rate below this level.

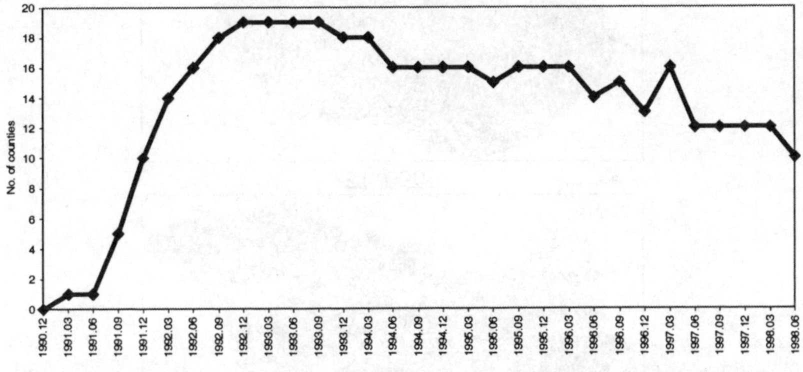

Figure 8.4 Number of counties with more than 10 per cent unemployment, December 1990 – June 1998

The regional differences show the new characteristics of unemployment. If we calculate the dissimilarity index of regional inequality we get rather interesting results (see Figure 8.5).

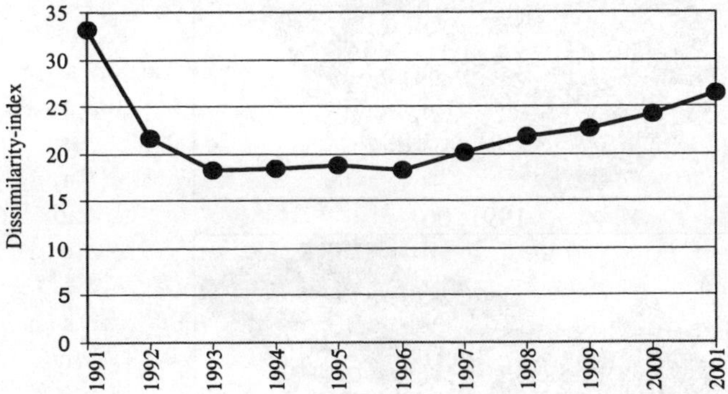

Figure 8.5 The regional inequalities of unemployment, 1991–2001

In our calculations we compared the regional dispersion of unemployed persons (f) and the population (x) by using the formula for the dissimilarity index (see Equation 8.1), where:

h = the value of the dissimilarity index (per cent)
f_i = the share of region i in the total number of unemployed (per cent)
x_i = the share of region i in the total population of the country (per cent).

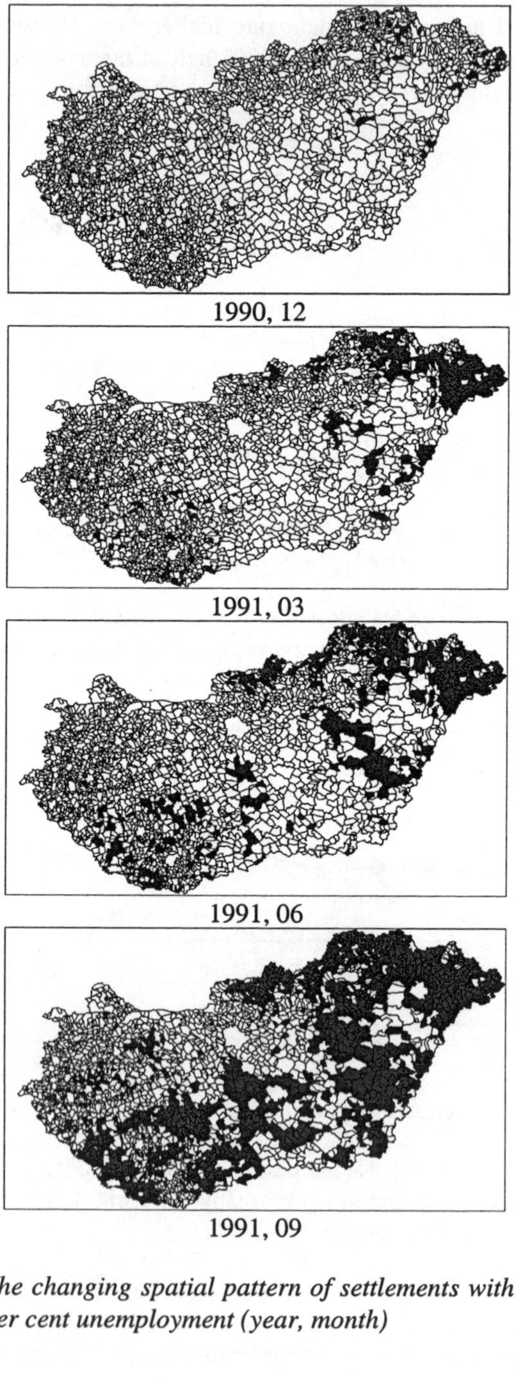

Figure 8.6 The changing spatial pattern of settlements with more than 10 per cent unemployment (year, month)

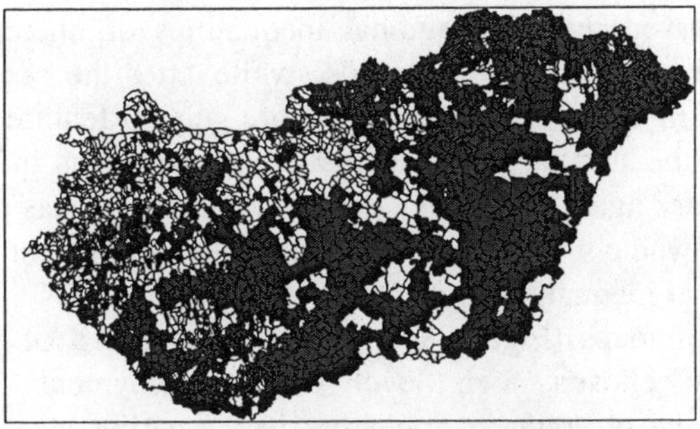

1991, 12

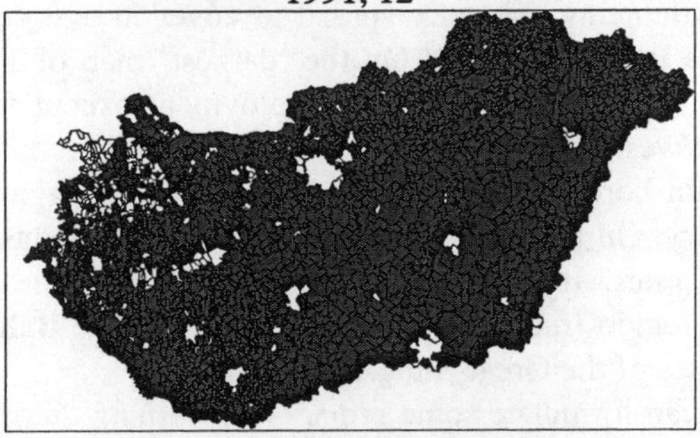

1993, 03

1996, 03

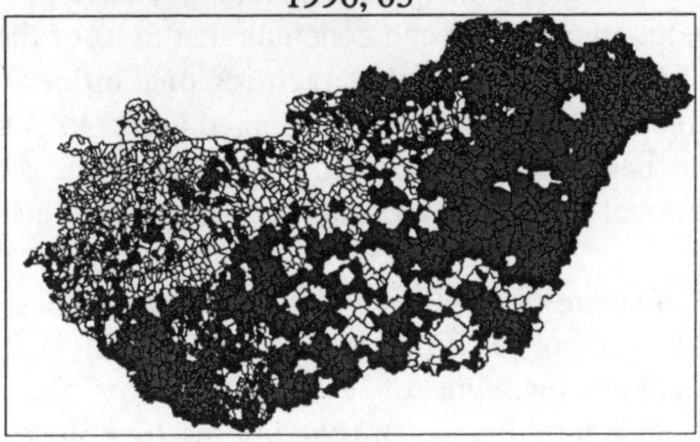

1999, 09

It can be observed that the regional inequalities of unemployment were higher at the beginning of the decade, while after the rapid diffusion of unemployment in 1991–92 it became a more general feature throughout the country. After the turning point of 1993 the differences in unemployment started to increase again, but with a different content (as has previously been explained). Nowadays Hungary deals with unemployment not as a new factor of regional inequalities but as an altering one.

The series of maps (Figure 8.6) presents the spread of unemployment. The arbitrarily chosen high level of unemployment (10 per cent) demonstrates how the process appearing in the earlier years in the eastern and smaller settlements gradually spread to cover in one year most of the settlements (see maps for 1991). On the 'darkest' map of 1993 almost the whole country shows considerable unemployment except for some larger cities and some western counties. After this the map starts to lighten: first of all some western border settlements and the Budapest agglomeration show signs of recovery. On the map for 1999 many more settlements show lower unemployment rates. It is important to pinpoint here the Northwestern–Transdanubian region (including the settlements at Lake Balaton) and some of the larger cities of the Great Hungarian Plain.

Finally we can formulate some remarks concerning the inequality factor of unemployment. It can be concluded that this factor took a changed course in the 1990s. For this reason it should be treated differently in the examination of the first part of the decade and the millennium. Unemployment also has an important role today, so it is worth using this indicator in social development calculations.

6 CONCLUSION

According to the foregoing calculations and 'soft' experiments, it can be definitely stated that regional inequality factors may have different meanings at various moments in time. We can conclude that most of the factors had or still have an altering tendency as far as their regional influence is concerned, but there are some stable ones as well. It seemed useful to classify inequality factors – on the basis of their behaviour and influence over time – into groups of traditional (unchanged), altering (changing) and new (young) factors.

The regional inequalities of the new millennium could be best revealed by using appropriate and up-to-date statistical sources. It is important to be aware of the actual meaning of every inequality factor, since their interpretation is subject to change. Answering the first question posed at the beginning of the chapter, it can be stated that most factors of the previous decades must be revised if they are to be used in today's examinations. It can be a valuable recommendation to apply a changing set of indicators in both regional policy and regional analyses, as appeared for example in the information published by Eurostat. Several national and international professionals work on developing up-to-date databases, which can be used to assemble new factor sets and also as sources to search for and to analyse factor characteristics.

It was also shown that formerly unknown, quite new inequality factors can appear as well; these new factors should also be integrated into the set of today's inequality indicators, since our principal aim is to understand the actual state of spatial differences. This led to the answer to the second question: a regular revision of our factors is needed to obtain a correct regional image of an area.

The spatial structure of Hungary has been changed in many ways. This has been reflected not only in the altering inequality factors, but also in the emerging basic elements of space. New axes, lines, centres and peripheries etc. have formed, though some of them have been inherited from previous eras. This duality is characteristic of the regional structure of the millennium, which should be – due to permanently changing influencing factors – re-appraised and redrawn again and again.

NOTES

1 The Hungarian regional structure of administration consists of counties (NUTS-3) and settlements (NUTS-5). For regional development purposes the level of regions (NUTS-2) and the level of micro-regions (NUTS-4) have also been introduced. There are no administrative units such as municipalities which could be placed between settlements and small regions.

2 Such alterations may in a narrow interpretation refer to temporary changes. In a broader context, alterations comprise long-term and lasting changes.

3 For example, among the educational institutions the universities should be treated at the regional (NUTS-2) level, the secondary schools on the county level (NUTS-3) and the elementary schools on the level of micro-regions (NUTS-4).

REFERENCES

Bartke, I. (1993), 'The Main Factors of Regional Structural Crisis at the End of the 80s' (A regionális szerkezeti válság főbb tényezői a nyolcvanas évek végén), in Kovács K. (ed.), *Település, Gazdaság, Igazgatás a Térben* (Settlement, Economy, Administration in Space), Pécs: MTA RKK.

Bartke, I. (1995), *Regional Development* (*Területfejlesztés*), Budapest: Eötvös Kiadó.

Beluszky, P. (1976), 'Regional Disadvantages in the Life Conditions of the Population – Disadvantageous Regions in Hungary' (Területi Hátrányok a Lakosság Életkörülményeiben – Hátrányos Helyzetű Területek Magyarországon), *Földrajzi Értesítő*, **25**, 301–12.

Brown, L.A. (1981), *Innovation Diffusion: A New Perspective*, London: Methuen.

Castells, M. (1998), *The Informational City – Information Technology, Economic*

Restructuring and the Urban-regional Process, Oxford: Basil Blackwell.
Cooper, R.B. and R.W. Zmud (1986), 'Information Technology Implementation Research: A Technological Diffusion Approach', *Management Science*, **32**, 554–71.
Csatári, B. (1996), 'Some Characteristics of the Hungarian Sub-Regions' (A magyarországi kistérségek néhány jellegzetessége), Kecskemét: MTA RKK ATI.
Enyedi, Gy (1996), 'Regional Processes in Hungary in the Period of Transition' (Regionális folyamatok Magyarországon az átmenet időszakában), Hischer Rezső Szociálpolitikai Egyesület, Budapest.
Enyedi, Gy and J. Rechnitzer (1987), 'Spatial Diffusion of Innovations in Hungarian Agriculture' (Az Innovációk Térbeli Terjedése a Magyar Mezőgazdaságban), *Tér és Társadalom*, **2**, 31–48.
Fichman, R.G. (1992), 'Information Technology Diffusion: A Review of Empirical Research', *Proceedings of the Thirteenth International Conference on Information Systems*, ICIS, Dallas, pp. 195–206.
Förster, M.F. and I. Gy Tóth (1997), 'Poverty, Inequalities and Social Policies in the Visegrad Countries', *Economics of Transition*, **5** (2), 505–10.
Hägerstrand, T. (1967), *Innovation Diffusion as a Spatial Process*, transl. Allan Pred, Chicago: University of Chicago Press.
Hoover, E.M. (1941), 'Interstate Redistribution of Population, 1850–1940', *Journal of Economic History*, **1**, 199–205.
Hoover, E.M. (1971), *An Introduction to Regional Economics*, New York: Alfred A. Knopf.
Hrubi, L. (2000), 'The Changing of Economic Spatial Structure in Hungary' (A Gazdasági Térszerkezet Változásai Magyarországon), in Gy Horváth and J. Rechnitzer (eds), *Magyarország Területi Szerkezete és Folyamatai az Ezredfordulón* (*Regional Structure and Processes in Hungary at the Millennium*), Pécs: MTA RKK, pp. 237–64.
Isard, W. (1975), *Introduction to Regional Science*, Englewood Cliffs, NJ: Prentice-Hall.
Jeney, L. and P. Szabó (2001), 'The Changing of Hungarian Industry in the Mirror of Concentration and Specialisation Indices' (A Magyar Ipar Változása a Koncentrációs és Specializációs Indexek Tükrében az 1990-es Években), in *A Magyar Földrajzi Konferencia Tudományos Közleményei* (*Scientific Reports of the Hungarian Geographical Conference*), (CD), Szeged.
Kertesi, G. and J. Köllő (1998), 'Regional Unemployment and Wages in the Years of Transition: The Altering of Wage-structure' (Regionális Munkanélküliség és Bérek az Átmenet Éveiben: A Bérszerkezet Átalakulása Magyarországon), *Közgazdasági Szemle*, **7–8**, 621–52.
Kiss, J. (1998), 'The Role of the Economy's Departmental Structure in Hungary's Regional Differentiation' (Az Ágazati Gazdaságszerkezet Szerepe a Regionális Differenciálódásban Magyarországon), *Tér és Társadalom*, **1–2**, 138–62.
Korompai, A. (1995), 'Future-researching Bases of Regional Strategies' (Regionális Stratégiák Jövőkutatási Megalapozása), *Regionális Tudományi Tanulmányok*, **1**, 3–106.
Major, K. and J. Nemes-Nagy (1999), 'Regional Income Inequalities in the 90s' (A Területi Jövedelemegyenlõtlenségek a Kilencvenes Éveben), *Statisztikai Szemle*, June, 397–421.
Masuda, Y. (1988), 'The Information Society as a Postindustrialised Society' (Az Információs Társadalom mint Posztindusztriális Társadalom), Budapest: OMIKK.

Milanovic, B. (1998), *Income Inequality and Poverty during the Transition from Planned to Market Economy*, Washington, DC: The World Bank.

Nagy, G. (1995), 'The Role and the Spatial Diffusion of Foreign Capital in Hungary' (A Külföldi Tőke Szerepe és Térbeli Terjedése Magyarországon), *Tér és Társadalom*, **1–2**, 55–82.

Nagy, G. (2002), 'Regional Differences on the Threshold of the Information Age' (Területi Különbségek az Információs Korszak Küszöbén), *Területi Statisztika*, **1**, 3–25.

Nemes-Nagy, J. (1998), 'Space in Social Researches' (A Tér a Társadalomkutatásban), Hilscher Rezsõ Szociálpolitikai Egyesület, Budapest.

Nemes-Nagy, J. and É. Ruttkay (1987), 'Some Geographical Characteristics of Technical Innovation in Hungary' (A Műszaki Innováció Néhány Földrajzi Jellemzője Magyarországon), *Tér és Társadalom*, **2**, 19–30.

Nemes-Nagy, J., Á. Jakobi and N. Németh (2001), 'Regional and Settlement Structure Components of Income Inequalities' (A Jövedelmi Egyenlőtlenségek Térségi és tel. szerkezeti összetevői), *Statisztikai Szemle*, **10–11**, 862–84.

Nemes-Nagy, J., Á. Kullmann, A. Fekete and P. Szabó (2000), 'The "State" and "Market" Routes of Regional Development in the 1990s' (A Területi Fejlődés „állami" és „Piaci" Útjai az 1990-es Években), *Területi Statisztika*, **3**: 203–20.

Nikodémus, A. (1991), 'The Problem of Spatial Diffusion and Opportunities of Application' (A Térbeli Diffúzió Problémája és Alkalmazási Lehetőségei), *Földrajzi Értesítő*, **1–2**, 7–25.

NSDP (1971), 'National Settlement-network Development Plan' (Országos Településhálózat-fejlesztési Koncepció), 1007/1971, Governmental decree.

Pomázi, I. (1988), 'Regional Inequalities of the Diffusion of Small Enterprises in Hungary' (A Kisvállalkozások Elterjedésének Területi Egyenlőtlenségei Magyarországon), *Földrajzi Értesítő*, **1–4**, 177–91.

Porat, M. (1977), 'The Information Economy', US Department of Commerce, Office of Telecommunications, Washington.

Ramachandran, R. (1999), *The Knowledge Imperative Index*, Kuala Lumpur: NITC.

Rechnitzer, J. (1990), 'Regional Diffusion of Computing in Hungary' (A Számítástechnika Területi Terjedése Magyarországon), Ts–2/2 Program Iroda, Budapest-Győr.

Rechnitzer, J. (1993), 'Differentiation or Catching up' (Szétszakadás vagy Felzárkózás), Győr: MTA RKK.

Richardson, H. (1969), *Regional Economics*, London: Weidenfeld and Nicolson.

Rogers, E.M. (1983), *Diffusion of Innovations*, 3rd edn, New York: The Free Press.

Schwertner, J. (1992), 'Regional Characteristics of Unemployment' (A Munkanélküliség Területi Jellemzői), *Munkaügyi Szemle*, **12**, 27–31.

Trujillo, M.F. (2001), 'Diffusion of ICT Innovations for Sustainable Human Development', www.payson.tulane.edu/research.

Umesao, T. (1963), 'On Information Industry', in Y. Ito (1991), 'Birth of Joho Shakai and Johoka Concepts in Japan and Their Diffusion Outside Japan', *Keio Communication Review*, **13**: 3–12.

Valente, T.W. (2001), *Models and Methods for Diffusion of Innovation*, Budapest: XXI Sunbelt INSNA.

World Times and International Data Corporation (2001), 'ISI Countries and Current Ranking', http://worldpaper.com/2001/xjan01/ISI/2001%20Information%20Society%20Ranking.html

Zmud, R.W. (1982), 'Diffusion of Modern Software Practices: Influence of Centralization and Formalization', *Management Science*, **28**, 1421–31.

9. From Publicly Encouraged Networks to Cluster Formation in Pärnu's Holiday Industry

Urmas Kase,[1] Tiit Kask,[2] Heli Müristaja[3] and Garri Raagmaa[4]

1 INTRODUCTION

Tourism is one of the fastest growing sectors in the world economy. Tourism and supporting industries provide a large range of extra outcomes such as increasing openness, innovativeness and entrepreneurialism of the region, a better and more attractive living environment, etc. Activities carried out by expanding 'fun' industries, spas and the like, in order to attract tourists, create a favourable environment for businesses and investors and foster a positive image of the region. Tourism promotion can therefore be considered as a very efficient tool in regional development.

> Small states and nations must seize every opportunity that could bring them either political, economic or other benefits. We should take advantage of every chance that could increase our national wealth and profit our citizens. That would benefit them either politically, economically or another way.
>
> Tourism is one of such activities providing sufficient extra income for small nations and helping upswing economic balance of small states. It does not require substantial economic investments, but all the more good organisation, far-sighted promotion and enough will to advance it. But making one country popular as a tourism country requires appropriate preparation for years, starting with putting in order every single home and household and ending with relevant far-reaching steps taken by the government. (Velner, 1939)

However, tourism favours certain types of areas, concentrating its structures and facilitating the most important resources from the point of view of attractiveness and demand. Consequently, tourism creates territorial imbalance between those areas that have been endowed with environmental or cultural attractions and those that have not. The area chosen for this case study, the town of Pärnu in Estonia (see Figure 9.1), belongs to the first group with its marvellous beach, over 160-year-old spa traditions and cosy milieu dominated by low-rise wooden architecture and villas. Therefore Pärnu is the best (Estonian) destination to use to monitor how a tourism cluster forms and the processes involved.

Figure 9.1 Location of Estonia and Pärnu

As expected, tourism enterprises of less desirable regions are not only looking at how areas with a rich cultural heritage or natural beauty become profitable. There is a range of alternative strategies which can help such regions to promote their image. They may organise cultural events and even create 'élitist' environments for certain target groups of consumers. Again, Pärnu serves as a good example with its rich cultural life and rather aggressive promotion of tourism during the last decade.

Tourism development should consider the interests of a wide range of actors and stakeholders; it overlaps significantly with general regional development and requires a well-integrated approach: natural preconditions, historical industrial structures, cultural heritage and enterprise culture as basic factors playing an important role together with social structures and administration.

Therefore we found it useful to apply a network versus cluster approach to this study and to analyse the activities of public authorities throughout history in more detail, paying particular attention to the 1990s, a period of major changes, when the authorities of the town of Pärnu played a decisive role in its tourism industry development.

This chapter consequently has two main goals: first, to follow the structural development of holidaymaking and related service industries using Wasson's product life cycle model, which is adjusted to a tourist destination, concentrating on supply and relations between suppliers in the destination (Wasson, 1974); and second, to analyse the activities of the public sector in network/cluster formation relying on Porter's (1990) diamond as a conceptual basis.

Statistical data used in this study have been gathered from the Statistical Office of Estonia and Pärnu Town Government. Students of the University of Tartu Pärnu College carried out a survey, which was financed by the Pärnu Town Government, in April–May 2002.

2 CONCEPT OF A TOURISM DESTINATION AND ANALYSIS OF THE LIFE CYCLE ON THE BASIS OF WASSON'S MODEL

A tourism destination is a region travellers have decided to visit and where they intend to spend a significant part of their available time (Gee and Choy, 1989). It is not just a place for transit or stopover that a tourist has to pass through to arrive at the designated destination. Based on the product concept, a destination is a symbiosis of various tourism products. These may be services as well as natural or man-made attractions. It has been said that a destination is a mosaic of different elements, all of which have their different life cycles (Goncalves et al., 1997). Choice of destination is dependent on tourists' needs, wishes and to a large extent their psychographic characteristics.

The spa life cycle theory worked out by Butler has most frequently been used to analyse a destination's life cycle (Ioannides, 1995), which is based on local people's participation in provision of products and services. This chapter uses the product life cycle curve, developed by Wasson, to analyse a tourism destination. The curve may, with some modifications, be used to evaluate all products, including a tourism destination's life cycle (Wasson, 1974). Wasson's complete product life cycle comprises five phases – from market development or destination introduction, continuing to rapid growth and competition until market saturation and finally reaching decline (see Appendix 1).

Phase 1 or market development is a period when supply in the destination exceeds demand and expenses to develop the destination exceed revenues. Suppliers are mostly local entrepreneurs, and local people are extremely interested in having visitors. This phase enjoys low-key competition – within the destination as well. Identities are determined during this phase and its relative length is in turn determined by the product's level of complexity – the more complex the product, the longer the first phase. Well-trained tour operators of the distribution channel network, who assist in solving visa problems or any other travel-related issues, facilitate product availability. Heavy discounting may occur in this phase.

Phase 2 is the rapid growth phase. Distribution channels have been developed and potential consumers have accepted the product or destination. Demand exceeds supply and sales increase. Profits attract new suppliers on the market (both local and foreign investors). 'Growth phase is oriented towards supply and profits are increased by launching new products on the market, whereas discounting ends and product prices have come to a halt at unit elasticity – attempting to maximise profits' (Witt and Mountinho, 1989).

Phase 3 is characterised by 'competition turmoil'. More and more companies provide similar products, hoping for the existence of unused consumer potential and therefore profit as well. Demand still exceeds supply in this phase, but its growth rate is in decline. Suppliers should mainly focus on customer orientation – marketing gains importance in the daily activities of the destination and market research is begun. Based on customers' needs and requests, market segments that are still viable are pinpointed and packages and programmes of all kinds are offered. Characteristic of this phase is that a number of non-viable suppliers withdraw from the market, and the leavers are those who could not cope with the changing environment and who did not have a sufficiently loyal customer base to guarantee income.

Phase 4 is characterised by slack demand. Products are considered mature and there is not much growth potential if opportunities to enter new markets or win over competitors' clients are not considered. Companies that have survived the fourth phase have usually carried out market research, drawn marketing plans and planned marketing activities. Price competition reduces opportunities to make profits in the saturated maturity phase and usually there are no newcomers to the market in this situation.

Regardless of all activities, products and destinations may reach phase 5 or the decline phase. The most characteristic indicator of this phase is decline in demand. Supply exceeds demand and expenses in product supply are considerably higher than income from sales. A saving rule marks the decline phase: overcoming the phase requires strong orientation towards customers, renewal of familiar products and giving them new added value.

2.1 Napa's Success Story

The following is an analysis of the case of Napa Valley as a tourism destination. It was selected for its progressive development strategy, which might be followed in the development of Pärnu as a destination.

For over 150 years, vineyards have been part of the Napa Valley scenery. This lush growing region is located at the north-eastern tip of San Francisco Bay in Northern California. Because of its proximity to the Bay, the region has numerous microclimates that provide perfect conditions for the growing of grapes. The Napa wine industry's progress can be tracked through five distinct periods (The Cluster Consortium Strategy in Action Report, 1999).

1. The establishment of the industry, from 1838 to 1900. Explorer George Yount planted the first Napa vineyards in 1838. During the following ten years, Yount was joined by other settlers who recognised the region's excellent grape-growing potential, and in 1848 the town of Napa came into being.
2. The decline of the valley, due to the damaging infestation of phylloxera, followed by Prohibition (1920–33).
3. The renaissance and recovery after the repeal of Prohibition. The year 1943 was important in the valley's development, when industry leaders formed a vintners' forum that would allow winemakers a regular opportunity to exchange ideas on grape growing and winemaking amidst a convivial atmosphere of shared camaraderie, good food and wine.
4. Tremendous expansion throughout the 1980s. Beginning in the early 1980s, the growers' and vintners' associations joined forces on projects of common interest, devoting much of their time to an active marketing programme. The 1980s also marked the birth of the tourism cluster in the region. The first bed and breakfast was established in 1982, a number which grew to over 150 by 1990. Wineries also opened their doors for tastings, furthering the appeal to the tourist sector.
5. The 1990s focused on refinement of the product, as well as emphasising the development of ancillary clusters.

The challenge today lies in ensuring the continued growth and improvement of the region's wines, while also developing other clusters, in a constant effort to improve the region's economic well-being.

A key value essential to Napa Valley residents' concept of a high standard of living involves limited physical growth in order to maintain the agricultural heritage of the area. At the same time, residents seek well-paying employment, which will generate enough money to improve the area's standard of living.

Napa's total visitor numbers have climbed very slowly in the past several years, an annual increase of 2 per cent. Eleven per cent of these visitors were international. The constraint on increase of visitors is the lack of space to accommodate them. As the supply of rooms and convention space cannot increase to meet demand, the price that each room garners has risen significantly.

Average daily rates of hotel rooms in Napa were 40 per cent higher than national averages in 1995. Therefore, while the number of tourists is stagnating, the revenues collected are still on the rise. Another significant statistic to note is that Napa virtually doubled its tourism revenue in five years without significantly increasing its supply of meeting rooms and overnight sleeping rooms. The total employment generated by travel spending rose from 6100 people in 1992 to 8300 in 1997.

Napa has transformed a seasonal tourist industry into a year-round industry by directing marketing at Bay Area visitors looking for a weekend getaway, as well as attracting convention traffic.

2.2 Concise History of Tourism Development in Pärnu

The life cycle of Pärnu as a resort town is over 160 years, which is divided into four sub-cycles. The number of visitors to Pärnu has been used as a significant factor to characterise its life cycle. The four sub-cycles of the Pärnu resort are the periods:

1837–1914
1927–39
1946–91
1991–

The first three periods differ from the last period by volume and quality, therefore they are described separately (see Figure 9.2) and the last period is covered in more detail in the following sections.

The year 1838 was the starting point of the health resort tradition in Pärnu as the first bathing establishment was opened by private enterprise. However, the overall economic slump in the 1870s, low image, bad connections, and low quality and small number of services provided for bathing guests did not give Pärnu a flying start as a resort known all over the Baltic Sea region. Instead of competing with other established resorts in the region Pärnu first had to sort out its priorities as a local treatment centre.

As the economy continued to nosedive in the 1880s, local decision makers were forced to find new ways of sustaining employment and income for the local community – it was time for the resort to become one of the local development priorities. The town purchased the otherwise doomed bathing establishment in 1889, and a new organisation was set up with its expenses to be covered by the town. In no time visitor numbers picked up, and no wonder – the beach area, parks and avenue network were developed, a variety of new and high-quality services were offered and a partnership of the private and public sectors was not far from exemplary (Eerme, 1939).

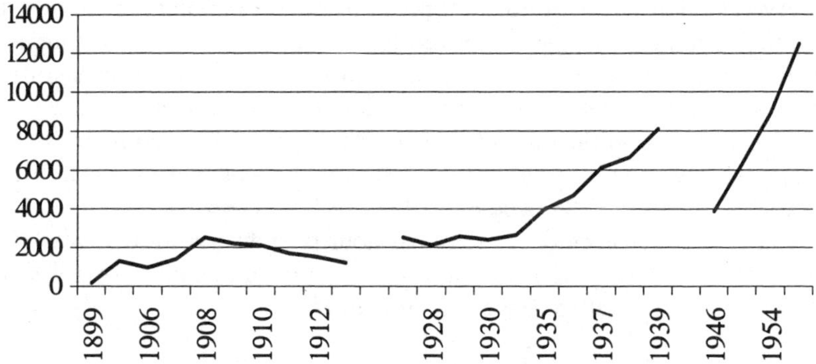

Figure 9.2 Number of summer visitors and customers of rehabilitation centres in 1899–1956

By the beginning of the twentieth century Pärnu as a tourism destination had passed the introductory phase and growth phase and achieved success. By the year 1908 the peak of the period was reached. At the same time a tough competitor to the resort business had appeared – a processing industry. At the end of the year 1900 the largest cellulose factory in Russia, Waldhof, started operations (Kivimäe et al., 1998). The developing industry endangered the resort business – wastewater from Waldhof rendered the river and sea stinking and lifeless and wastewater threatened to turn the Bay of Pärnu into a dead sea (see Figure 9.2). The years of the First World War ruined the resort and halted its development.

By the end of the 1920s the pre-Second World War traditions were in full swing and by the end of the 1930s Pärnu had established itself as one of the best-known resorts in the Baltic Sea region. When it celebrated its 100th anniversary, the resort as such was run by the town as a large-scale municipal business with a large part of the investments being provided by the town, and thus most of the decisions concerning the resort development were made by the town government and council as well. The number of summer visitors grew year by year but never reached the maturity phase – the Second World War, which began in 1939, interrupted the resort activities at their peak (see Figure 9.2).

From 1948 Pärnu was gaining fame as a health and summer resort of Soviet Union-wide importance, with most of the decisions being made in Moscow and the local level left to do the 'subcontracting'. The volume of tourists increased rapidly, fostered by an extensive Soviet market. In the summer season the population doubled and for the most part the visitors arrived from Leningrad (St Petersburg) and Moscow. Precise numbers for this period are absent but the introductory phase is characterised by steep growth (see Figure 9.2). According to the SU classificator, Pärnu belonged in the ranks of climate and mud resorts and was one of the most significant in the Soviet Union. Even in this period demand exceeded supply as the market was huge but accommodation limited. In 1956 there were three sanatoria with a total of 830 beds (Pärnu was ready to admit 14 000 customers per year). In 1971 the sanatorium Tervis opened with 125 beds and at the end of the 1980s Pärnu had four public sanatoria with approximately 1780 beds. In addition, a whole host of guesthouses and bed and breakfasts of various authorities, including the armed forces, was located here. The estimated number of visitors to Pärnu was about 300 000.

After Estonia regained independence in 1991, the system of sanatoria which was administered by the trade unions broke down (Veinpalu, 1998). The number of customers receiving treatment slumped as the Russian market disappeared. Some buildings were returned to their previous owners; some remained in town ownership. All treatment establishments began offering accommodation services. Entrepreneurs opened a wide range of new hotels, catering and entertainment facilities. This period will be treated in more detail in the following sections.

3 TOURISM CLUSTER – WHAT IS IT AND HOW DOES IT DIFFER FROM A NETWORK?

The impact of tourism on a destination's economy may be treated on two levels: (1) in a narrower sense, tourism involves transportation, accommodation services (including catering) and attractions; (2) in a broader sense, tourism is the sum of all activities and services provided for tourists by a tourism-generating country while travelling back and forth, and staying at the destination.

Tourism in a broader sense includes infrastructure and milieu. A well-maintained physical infrastructure (air and surface transport, seaports, telecommunications, tourist information centres, signage, institutional facilities and amenities) is crucial to the development of the tourism industry. Owing to tourism activities and actions designed for visitors, the life quality and business environment might be considerably better than without these activities. Tourism guarantees openness for cities and localities without additional costs for the public sector or business community, and allows marketing and exports of local products without significant additional costs.

A cluster is a geographically proximate group of interconnected companies and associated institutions in a particular field, linked by commonalities and complementarities (Porter, 1998). The term 'agglomeration' or 'geographical concentration' of industry is used where the concentration is 'over and above' the normal pattern of industrial concentration in that industry. The more competitive and entrepreneurial the environment, the greater the growth potential and agglomeration tendency.

In some cases networks and clusters are linked (see Table 9.1), and then networks are the 'essence' of functioning clusters, but linkage is not necessary because networks can occur among firms situated anywhere, whereas clusters refer to location-specific characteristics and coincide more closely with regional, state or national government development agendas (Chapman, 2000).

Table 9.1 *Differences between clusters and networks*

Networks	Clusters
Networks allow firms access to specialised services at lower costs.	Clusters attract needed specialised services to a region.
Networks have restricted membership.	Clusters have open membership.
Networks are based on contractual agreement.	Clusters are based on social values that foster trust and encourage reciprocity.
Networks make it easier for firms to make complex products.	Clusters generate demand for other firms with a variety of similar and related capacities.
Networks are based on cooperation.	Clusters generate both cooperation and competition.
Networks have common business goals.	Clusters have collective visions.

Source: Rosenfeldt (1995).

There are three main elements of clusters that emerge from the literature on the subject. These can be described as:

- Spatial co-location (geographical agglomeration).
- Economic interactivity (vertical and horizontal integration, networks, innovation).
- Social capital (collaboration, trust, competency and knowledge transfer).

Clusters can be located in smaller city regions as well as within large metropolitan areas. Experience has shown, however, that regions with traditional, declining industries and a relatively low skills base find it most difficult to restructure their economy and redefine their fields of expertise.

Regional economic growth of a cluster is based on the sum of: geographic proximity, experience, trust and collaboration (Harrison, 1992). An effective cluster embodies groups of firms that frequently meet, interact and conduct business and have developed high levels of mutual trust, hold a shared vision and learn from each other – all of which produce dynamism and synergy (Rosenfeldt, 1995). Social glue binds clusters together (Porter, 1998).

Several authors such as Porter (1998, 2000), Krugman (1995), and others claim that clusters offer a competitive advantage for single firms through three main factors: productivity, innovation and new business formation.

A tourism cluster can be described as a combination of the following elements (Porter, 1990; Smeral, 1998) (see Figure 9.3):

- Factor condition (natural and cultural resources, capital and infrastructure).
- Demand (market structure and size, tourists' habits and open-mindedness, new products and standards, share of business trips).
- Quality and structure of supply (range, level of specialisation and functioning network).
- Market and distribution channels of the organisation, strategies and goals.

Tourism industries are normally characterised by low-technology components. However, environment and milieu as well as links to the public sector can be considered even more important. There are some aspects of clusters that make them particularly relevant in tourism research:

- Increasing market concentration through horizontal integration in the travel industry.

- Economies of scale in the travel industry primarily via chains and packaging.
- Innovation via information technology and branding, allowing major production chains to practise wider market segmentation by supplying mass markets and tailor-made niche markets.
- Outsourcing (Ioannides and Debbage, 1998).

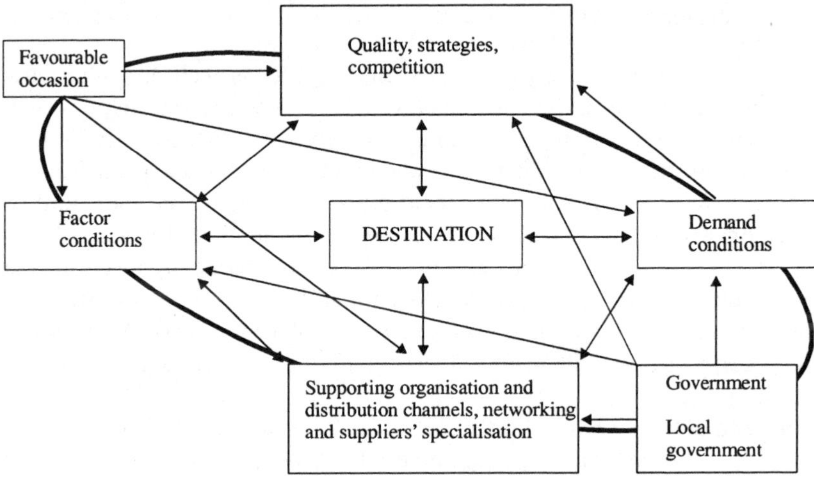

Figure 9.3 Conceptualising a tourism cluster (after Porter) and the focus of this study

According to structuration theory (Giddens, 1984), focusing on mutual interaction, the impact of people (entrepreneurs) and on the social system, the social system as such (tourism cluster in this case) does not have its so-called 'own' goals and depends mostly on decisions made by people (entrepreneurs, civil servants). These subjects within the cluster attempt to maximize their benefits.

Social networks (Porter, 1990) are regulated by rules and norms (contracts, ethics, oral agreements) and both natural and human resources influence their functioning. Rules, norms and resources influence the behaviour of the people (entrepreneurs). For practical reasons, to maximize profit, gathering and renewing social capital is far more important. At the same time, tourism enterprises are normally very diverse and face a range of extra problems such as seasonality (e.g. during a low season more cooperation and during a high season fair competition and (product) innovation), extreme dependence on the media, economic ups and downs, and the image of the destination region.

3.1 The Case of Chattanooga Tourism Clusters

The following is a brief look at the development of clusters in the Chattanooga resort located in the south-east of Tennessee, USA. Pärnu could learn from its experience in rehabilitation-related issues (Chattanooga Area Chamber of Commerce, 2001). According to 2000 Census data, Tennessee businesses, particularly corporations, have some of the highest taxes per person in the USA. The unfavourable situation in taxation policies forced local authorities and the private sector to make extra efforts.

Chattanooga Area Chamber of Commerce asked Michael Porter of Harvard University to analyse this region's economy. Porter's concept of locational advantage is 'the idea that you need to understand what you have that's unique and use it as a base to grow the economy, look at the things you do here, and do well, then get the word out to other people who do those things. I think that's right on target.' Dr Porter's analysis offered cluster groupings, the key industries that form the backbone of the region's economic base. After that the Chamber took Dr Porter's clusters and began a series of meetings – totalling eight hours per cluster – to help industry representatives examine the strengths and weaknesses within each cluster. They also added some clusters that were not part of Dr Porter's original analysis. In addition four clusters (Medical Devices, Health Services, Insurance, Retirement Services) began to identify areas where services and industries overlapped, creating the emerging Rehabilitation Practice, Research and Technology cluster.

As far as creating a new common vision is concerned, Chattanooga has long been able to sell itself as a great place to visit and live. Now the work on clusters can be used to sell Chattanooga as a great place to do business, particularly in the rehabilitation field. Vision – in just a few short years, visitors stepping off the plane at Chattanooga's airport might be greeted with a sign that says: 'Welcome to Chattanooga: The Rehabilitation Capital of the World'. Chattanooga is perfectly poised to become an international centre for businesses associated with the rehabilitation of medical conditions and injuries because of the infrastructure already in place. Most clusters are maturing into self-sufficiency, which is exactly what was intended. More than a dozen cluster subcommittees meet regularly to address industry-specific issues and actions. Each cluster meets as a whole every quarter for lunch. The Chamber provides logistics and communications support.

The Health Services, Retirement Services, Rehabilitation and Insurance clusters are now working together to establish some parameters that might facilitate the development of a research institute focusing on patient outcomes. Chattanooga is home to both the Siskin and HealthSouth facilities, two of the leading rehabilitation hospitals in the US south-east. In the hospitality and tourism cluster, significant progress is being made on two fronts. One group is now studying possible improvements to local signage, while another is awaiting the results of a survey concerning consumer profiles. The signage group hopes to make Chattanooga more visitor friendly, helping to guide people more efficiently to real attractions. They hired the research firm Ethridge & Associates of Memphis to measure consumer profiles. This firm was used by the Tennessee State Department of Tourism in developing the 'Tennessee Sounds Good To Me' campaign. The research firm is measuring such important statistical information as visitor's length of stay in Chattanooga, how many times they visit, and how much money they spend – this is a good indicator of the overall impact of the visitor on the market. The results serve as a platform for an overall marketing plan for the tourism destinations in the area.

Some facts about the importance of the role of universities (taking into consideration the role of University of Tartu Pärnu College in the framework of Pärnu cluster's development): on the threshold of what may prove to be the most exciting and innovative decade in its history, the University of Tennessee at Chattanooga (UTC) is poised for growth. In coordination with the Chattanooga Regional Growth Initiative (CRGI), a special regional development institution established by the local chamber of trade and industry, UTC provides graduate certificate programmes in key fields, including Engineering Quality Management, Internet Application Programming, Computer Networking, Project Management, and, most recently, Information Technology.

3.2 From Networking to Cluster Formation – Pärnu Town Government as a Promoter

In the early 1990s – as in the 1890s and the 1920s – the town had to take the lead in order to get Pärnu on the right track as a resort once again. The Eastern markets were gone, the Western markets were yet to be found, the ownership disputes were unresolved – these were some of the difficulties of the first couple of years. The key issue was how the town could once again become the owner of the resort facilities as it had been before the Second World War. It took some years and, after complicated negotiations with different interest groups, the municipalisation process was completed in 1994.

The municipal enterprise Pärnu Tourism Development (PTD) was founded in 1992 (Appendix 2). This institution replaced a former similar unit, but was staffed by new people and obtained independent status. On its creation, the PTD was the only such institution in Estonia. During the first years a network of 12–15 firms cooperating under the umbrella of the PTD was established. The core of this network is currently functional. However, until recently no official organisation or union of city or county tourism firms has been established (Raagmaa, Kask and Rein, 2000).

In 1992–95 the key concepts of Pärnu as a tourism destination were determined: tradition, heritage, continuity, trust and contemporary marketing in accordance with which the private and public sectors learned to cooperate. Through international cooperation coordinated and initiated by the public sector, Pärnu also became the tourism know-how centre of Estonia. In 1992–94 Canadian tourism lecturers taught at Pärnu Business School, thus founding a solid basis for the University of Tartu Pärnu College – the number one tourism school in Estonia at the moment.

In 1995 the main stress was laid on an annual event – as a reason to visit Pärnu and also as a general marketing tool. First of all, Pärnu had become an attractive tourism destination for domestic tourists and a well-known international project partner. In 1996 Pärnu made news by initiating its Summer Capital status, which has been a successful marketing device ever since. Since 1996, marketing has been based on an annual theme and relevant events. By participating in many projects throughout the Baltic Sea region the destination generated more trust and reliability on the international tourism development level.

Tourism development in Pärnu was based on activities of localised firms, enthusiastic people in the public sector and institutions. A local umbrella combining all sectors and running the town and the county as an integrated destination has not been founded so far. This keeps destination development initiatives largely in the hands of the public sector and makes the private sector passive, i.e. minding their own business mostly. Overheated local politics and ever-changing authorities made the local public sector a bit hesitant and less focused, causing friction for the local business environment and making cooperation between sectors problematic. It also caused setbacks to the local image. An estimate of summer visitors to Pärnu in 1995–2001 is shown in Figure 9.4.

In the years 1929–39 foreign tourists accounted for 30–40 per cent of the total number of tourists. The period in focus is characterised by a similar 30 per cent ratio of foreign tourists in the total number of visitors (in 2002 foreign visitors accounted for 40 per cent of the total number). The country origin of tourists is also similar: over 60 per cent of tourism is generated by Finland, followed by Sweden and Germany, and Latvia. The overwhelming majority of visitors from Finland is due to the relative proximity of that market, good accessibility, the favourable exchange rate of the Finnish mark into Estonian kroons (later the favourable exchange rate of euros) and the fact that people understand Finnish – there is no language barrier. The reason for the visit of over 60 per cent of foreigners was holidaymaking, followed by combining treatment and holiday (in rehabilitation centres) and visits. A total of 14 per cent of foreign visitors to Pärnu were there in transit, i.e. they stopped over for two to three hours, had a short sightseeing tour in town, had lunch, went shopping. About half of the tourists were aged 31–59 and 37 per cent were below 30. The average length of stay was 5.3 days. Foreigners spent on average US$90 per day in the summer of 2000.

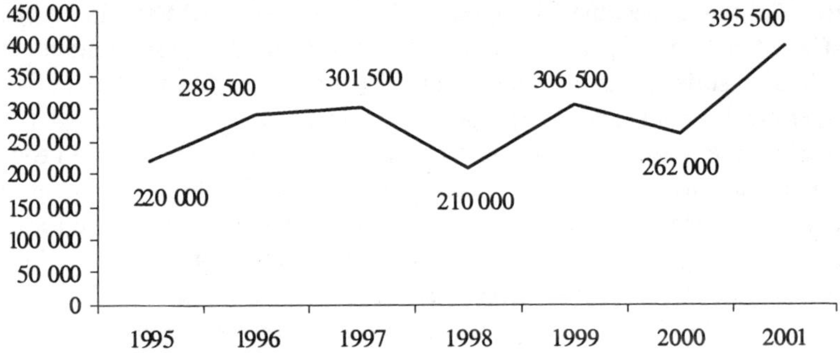

Figure 9.4 Number of summer visitors in 1995–2001

The number of Estonian summer visitors is largely determined by the weather: the year 1998 and the summer of 2000 were relatively rainy and this left its mark on the number of visitors. An increase in 2001 is connected to the celebrations of the 750th anniversary of the town. For this reason there were more sights in town (a temporary medieval town model) and more entertaining events. In 1999 claims were made that Pärnu had reached a saturation phase among Estonians (Müristaja, 2000) (in 1998 because of bad weather the number of visitors plummeted and the number of visitors in 1999 had not recovered much compared to that of 1997). One of the causes of such an effect may have been a loss of enthusiasm for Pärnu. No new ideas were employed to sell Pärnu and summer events had remained the same year in year out. In terms of a destination's life cycle, this indicates that Pärnu reached a certain saturation phase among Estonians, which may be followed by a new rise due to successful development activities, or a plunge in the case of unsuccessful development activities or absence thereof (see Figure 9.4). Following the results of the two succeeding years (2000 and 2001), we can say that an increase is continuing and the celebration of the 750th anniversary had a considerable impact on the rise in the number of visitors.

When we analyse changes in the volume of visitors both among foreigners and Estonians (see Figure 9.5), we can claim that a slight saturation phase is developing among foreigners – the number of visitors has remained almost stable for three years. There are two choices in developing the destination: (1) search for new markets (Russia, Sweden, Norway and Germany, besides Finland), and (2) follow the Napa example in which qualitative development prevails over quantitative and the target is larger expenditures by fewer tourists.

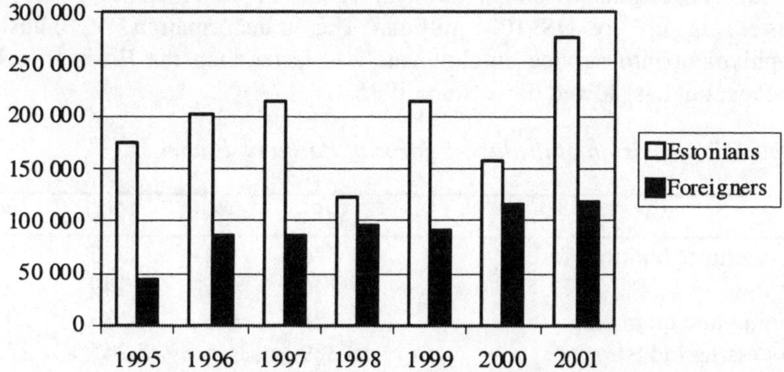

Figure 9.5 *Comparison of the share of Estonians and foreigners in 1995–2001*

3.3 The Tourism Sector in Pärnu According to the Statistics

Despite the status of a fairly well-known resort town, Pärnu had an economic structure like every 'normal' industrial town in the Soviet Union. The occupational structure shows a share of secondary jobs close to 50 per cent of total employment in 1989 (see Table 9.2).

During the general economic transition from the centrally planned state economy to a market-driven private economy, both occupational and size structures of enterprises changed all over the country. The share of the primary and secondary sectors has been decreasing and the share of the tertiary sector, particularly financial and business services and trade, has significantly increased.

Pärnu differs from other Estonian towns by having a concentration of service and leisure industry (Pärnu has 400 000 annual visitors, being nationwide destination number two after the national capital city Tallinn) and the employment numbers seem to indicate an opposite trend in a purely statistical sense. However, we cannot overlook an indirect impact and statistical grey areas: for example the health treatment guests are not included in the national accommodation statistics because the primary activity of the facilities in question is to provide health treatment. All in all, the service and leisure industry acounts for far more than 7 per cent of employment – Pärnu is among the most seasonally sensitive destinations among the larger towns in Estonia.

Due to successful tourism development in the 1990s, a number of new hotels and restaurants opened, and a variety of new cultural events took place throughout the year, causing changes in the occupational structure of Pärnu. The estimated annual turnover of the so-called Pärnu 'Take care cluster' is up to US$100 million. The transformation of industrial employment into service employment was faster than the Estonian urban average, but has slowed down since 1996.

Table 9.2 Division of the labour force of Pärnu by branches

	1989	%	2000	%
Agriculture, hunting, forestry	1 576	5.2	295	1.6
Fishing	140	0.5	149	0.6
Mining and quarrying	28	0.1	33	0
Processing industry	10 389	34.5	5 245	27.5
Electricity production and water supply	208	0.7	281	1.1
Construction	3 500	11.6	1 569	8.7
Trade; maintenance of vehicles and household appliances	2 056	6.8	3 195	15.9
Hotels and restaurants	1 244	4.1	884	4.2
Transportation, stocking and communication	2 136	7.1	1 628	8.5
Financial intermediation	224	0.7	211	0.8
Real estate, rental and business activities	564	1.9	989	2.6
Public administration and national defence, mandatory social insurance	1 768	5.9	1 177	5.5
Education	1 748	5.8	1 329	7.7
Health care and social welfare	2 356	7.8	1 377	8.0
Other community, social and personal services	2 184	7.3	842	1.2
Total number of employees in town	30 112		19 425	

In any case, total employment in the tourist sector was still a few times lower than in manufacturing, which continues to be a major employer in Pärnu. The share of manufacturing decreased quickly until the mid-1990s because of new, more productive technologies. Since then, several textile and food processing companies have been expanding their production as well as employment, so that Pärnu had about twice as high an employment rate in textile and food processing industry as the Estonian average by 2000. Construction and real estate also have a higher employment rate than the Estonian average.

4 CLUSTER ANALYSIS – SURVEY RESULTS

Based on initial data, five clusters with some overlapping were found in Pärnu (Pärnu County Government, 2001):

1. Leisure and service industry (take care cluster), covering summer visitors, conferences, fairs and health resort
2. Textiles and sewing
3. Forestry and timber
4. Fishery and food industry
5. Logistics.

Consequently, on the basis of these brief facts we can say that the tourism industry has become deeply rooted in the economy of Pärnu. However, manufacturing industries are still the most important employers in the town and their share is even larger taking into account directly measured GDP and wages.

Hypothetically, the Pärnu tourism cluster probably approached a strategic networking stage or even a competition stage where outside investors take advantage of a well-established cluster. In that the available statistics are probably not entirely correct, these new hypotheses should be rechecked using other sources of data which are more closely related to administrative units (e.g. Revenue Office data).

A wide-scale survey was carried out in March 2002 among businesses of the Pärnu tourism cluster. It researched processes in the social structure and focused on the above-mentioned factors indicated in Porter's figure (see Figure 9.3). It was a qualitative survey – both a questionnaire and an interview were used.

All responses were dealt with anonymously and the outcome was used only for generalisation. The sample involved 170 tourism-related enterprises: accommodation, health treatment, shops, catering and other service businesses. Finally a total of 61 businesses responded; the response rate amounted to 35.6 per cent of the sample. The spread of the respondents according to sphere of activity is given in Figure 9.6.

The enterprise survey was designed to define cross-sectoral flows, co-operation and partnership and response of enterprises to public policies. Before the survey a list of factors likely to be characteristic of the Pärnu tourism cluster was compiled:

1. The Pärnu tourism enterprise cluster in relation to outside markets: share of small enterprises within the cluster interacting with global partners (airlines, hotel chains, car rentals).
2. Collective associations/organisations to carry out joint marketing.
3. Various spheres being represented (means of reaching goals could seem too different to allow successful cooperation).
4. Enterprise structures to respond to changing demand.
5. Cooperative mindset.
6. Opportunities for new start-ups (demand for new services, milieu, legislation).
7. Competition vs. cooperation (competition focusing on cooperation).
8. Community-based factors: infrastructure, information distribution, some attractions not based on business but affecting attractiveness of the destination.
9. Readiness to learn from mistakes made by others vs. 'ruthless copying'.
10. Members of the cluster changing and rotating constantly (enterprises have rather a short lifespan).
11. Fluctuating workforce shift between the sectors of the cluster.

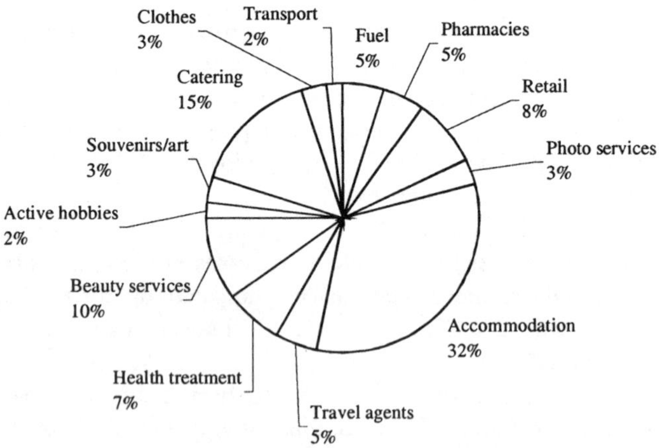

Figure 9.6 Field of activity of the responding businesses in the tourism cluster

The theoretical part of the chapter analyses the essence of the tourism cluster. One of the main tasks of the survey in question was to discover the main factors influencing the decision made by the enterprises to operate in Pärnu. Also, the role of the municipality in developing the decisive factors was dealt with. The following analysis covers mainly the second group of questions, dealing with the enterprises' relations and interaction with other enterprises.

The crucial factor was the entrepreneur's place of residence (46 per cent), followed by Pärnu being an attractive environment and market (17 per cent of respondents, both local inhabitants and tourists). The environment and milieu (23 per cent) were decisive for the accommodation and catering enterprises. For other enterprises the market and workforce were also important. All in all the above can be considered as resources (8 per cent) (funds, assets, facilities, know-how and good-will). Infrastructure seems to be an issue in which the local municipality is expected to be most active, but environment, safety and demand fluctuation (seasonality) also seem to concern businesses. Analysis of response distribution shows that, seen from the entrepreneurs' point of view, Pärnu as a destination is in its introductory phase – major entrepreneurs are local people and foreign capital has arrived in Pärnu only through large hotels and tour operators which bring Finnish tourists and provide them with services (tour operators have not made direct investments and only use Pärnu to make money).

- We live here. The environment is not really favourable as Pärnu experiences the toughest competition in tourism.
- Where, apart from Pärnu, is it easiest to attract tourists?
- In 1998 this market (bowling) was completely empty. No other alleys were in existence. The people who opened the new bowling hall were our first customers; they started playing at our hall and got the idea. It is pleasant to see our idea developing.
- The environment/milieu is special in Pärnu; tourists are very interested in Pärnu.
- Especially for our company Pärnu is good for having tourists – the summer's turnover helps us to survive the winter.
- Pärnu is beautiful – water, sun, sand.

Within the cluster, competition and cooperation among the enterprises have distinctive roles. Eighty-nine per cent of the respondents were of the opinion that competition exists in Pärnu and only 11 per cent saw no competitors at all. The latter enterprises provide active recreational services and sell souvenirs and art. Some spheres feel especially heavy pressure from businesses based on foreign capital.

- The main competitor in our sphere is a large Finnish tour operator. They have outwitted the market.

Accommodation and catering competition was considered very varied as well – there are different actors in the market providing similar services, yet adding their own personal touch to stand out.

The question about the methods of market division was answered by half of the respondents (53 per cent), pointing to their ongoing sales work. The rest of the respondents were dominated by the market division either occasionally (20 per cent) or by outsmarting competitors (17 per cent).

- We have increased quality and thus won more customers.
- Cooperation with competitors is inevitable in tourism.
- The market is common; the winner is the one who can provide better service.
- My target group has from the very start been families with children or middle-class people who want a really good rest. I also do not take busloads of people and my prices are not affordable for everybody. I have invested a lot and put my heart into it.
- Continuity in sales by outsmarting. Any agreements with competitors are out of the question; everybody should manage on their own.

When the respondents were asked to estimate the cooperative mindset in Pärnu, more than 60 per cent considered the overall atmosphere to be cooperative. But about a quarter of the respondents did not see any opportunity for cooperation.

- There is no need for more cooperation; we work separately.
- It depends on whom to cooperate with. Larger hotels are willing to; smaller ones believe if they work together with anyone similar they will lose clients. They have not understood that if everybody kept together they would enlarge their market share.
- It is not unambiguous. In general you should be the initiator. Nobody has asked me but I have asked others for information, e.g. if they have vacancies and at what price, what they offer, if I can send my customers to them as my house is full, etc. I have communicated because of my beauty service and mud baths and asked for price lists; and when my guests arrive and want a more exciting day, not everyone from England or America is fortunate enough to have a mud bath. You have to push and beg. No one has come of their own accord.

Local tourism enterprises were asked to estimate whether under the circumstances of tougher competition their activities are more focused on the core activity (specialisation). More than half of the respondents agreed with the statement and only 15 per cent did not see any specialisation. Less competition clearly means less specialisation as, among the above, the 15 per cent was dominated by those enterprises who did not see any competitors (see above), i.e. active service providers, souvenir and art sellers, more 'no specialisation' responses coming from the complementary sector (filling stations, retail, photos, etc.). The strongest specialisation trend was found in the accommodation, travel service and beauty service sectors.

- A kind of definite image has formed and some certain details that others do not have. Different from others.
- Sauna service is not often provided in hotels and I can order beauty service and massage here. People come from throughout the country to my jacuzzi. I am making efforts to please them.
- For example, a hairdresser's salon is not just a salon but Wella Expert Salon. We represent a large product range in Pärnu. A beauty salon is not just a beauty salon but a curative cosmetics surgery, where our speciality is treatment of scars in many ways. A service has to be made special.
- Competition regulates the market, specialising is linked to the Tervis sanatorium; elderly couples who do not want accommodation in Tervis stay with us; also we have Finnish families.
- We are not a classic accommodation provider, we are not specialised in anything, we make no effort to have them, we do not change ourselves into something different, we do not change, they just know and come; for us it is ancillary business.

Even though the local market is open for new providers and suppliers, 20 per cent of the respondents were of the opinion that the market is penetrable for newcomers, but 73 per cent regarded the local market as rather hard to enter (summer seems to offer more opportunities for new providers, but survival in winter could be problematic). The respondents would gladly see more newcomers among the souvenir sellers and providers of transportation services.

- I think there are niches to work in and develop (tour operator).
- I cannot tell if it is easy (to penetrate the market), but they keep coming.

Respondents were asked to rate the activities of the local administration from 1 to 5 points. More than half of the respondents assessed the work done as good or very good, but 40 per cent did not rate it higher than satisfactory. The average turned out to be 3.5. Among the main setbacks were mentioned the bad state of the local infrastructure (potholed streets with no streetlights) and the municipality was recommended to pay more attention to essential matters. The latter were considered to include the local (business) environment and infrastructure. Some were of the opinion that to some extent the town seems to place visitors before the local inhabitants, as the majority of events almost overlap in terms of time, causing large crowds in town.

- The town has not paid much attention to local working people; it is only addressing tourists. Events should also consider local people and be more dispersed, not only at weekends, because local workers get tired and cannot work all summer like robots. If they had better conditions of relaxation they would be able to smile more.

The communication and interaction between the entrepreneurs and the local administration was not found to be satisfactory either. Some respondents expressed their view that the municipality could use more tourism-related staff. At present, only one person is in charge of tourism development matters along with all international relations. More emphasis should be laid on safety and welfare; for example, more playgrounds would be welcome.

The promotion work carried out by the town was lauded, but some respondents warned of running out of fresh ideas and consequently slowing down. Construction of ramps on the pavements was brought up as a good example of the authorities regarding Pärnu as a health resort. The entrepreneurs also had a high opinion of the events celebrating the 750th anniversary in 2001. The international PR and promotion was rated highly, with the example of Pärnu being a member of ESPA (European Spa Association) and EFCT (European Federation of Conference Towns).

On the to-do list, training programmes for the local tourism-related entrepreneurs were at the top, with either partial or even full financial coverage from the municipality. Entrepreneurs also wished to be more involved in twinning activities with other towns in order to be able to learn from the entrepreneurs of other countries.

Finally, the executive managers were asked to assess their relations with the local tourism branch. The closest relation was expressed by the souvenir sellers, travel agents and tour operators, and accommodation providers. The majority of health treatment and beauty service providers were focusing on tourists. It was strange that providers of active recreational services did not regard themselves as linked to the local tourism branch.

5 CONCLUDING REMARKS

Following the comparison of clusters and networks in Table 9.1, it is possible to state that the cluster is the operational structure of tourism in

Pärnu: relations between enterprises are competitive, and efforts are made to differ from each other by specialisation rather than comprehensive cooperation and, based on agreements, reduce expenses by using wholesale firms as suppliers. The binding glue of the structure is social values and necessity to survive (seen from the entrepreneurs' point of view the destination is still at its beginnings. Considerable foreign investments have not been made yet). Enterprises feel the need to have partnership relations as well as competitive relations, but often they cannot find the best partners or they feel that such relations are not important at all. Competition has so far outrun cooperation.

In terms of development of the destination, the Pärnu town government has played a key role so far, but an umbrella organisation representing entrepreneurship and non-profit organisations does not yet exist. The town government attempts to involve the business community in decision-making, but the survey revealed that such a relationship is unequal and business people's wishes are not seriously considered. This, in turn, should force entrepreneurs to concentrate in a common organisation to voice their opinions and needs more powerfully.

The reason for such a situation is that Pärnu as a destination is undergoing a rapid development phase in its life span and is fairly close to the tough competition phase. First, distribution channels have evolved and potential customers have accepted the product or destination. Second, more enterprises offer similar products, expecting to seize unused consumer potential and profit as well. Third, demand growth rate shows a declining tendency. The main focus of suppliers should be client-oriented – marketing gains an increasingly important role and market research is begun.

We may argue that the employment structure of Pärnu is shifting to a more service-oriented direction. However, at the same time some sort of reindustrialisation in several traditional branches is taking place. Also, we may say that, from publicly encouraged networks, enterprises already form quite a complex and interrelated rapidly expanding tourism cluster, which is already networking actively nationwide and internationally.

There are several signs that reflect the mature clustering of tourism and leisure industry enterprises in Pärnu. The tourism industry has been expanding for several years without any significant assistance from public authorities. Enterprises are networking internationally; both local ones and outsiders are expanding and investing extensively in real estate and new services.

NOTES

1 Institute of Geography, University of Tartu, Vanemuise, 51014, Tartu, Estonia. Fax. +37 2737 5825; Tel. +37 2737 5817; e-mail: urmas_k@mv.parnu.ee, http://www.geo.ut.ee.
2 Institute of Geography, University of Tartu, Vanemuise, 51014, Tartu, Estonia. http://www.geo.ut.ee.
3 University of Tartu, Pärnu College, Ringi 35, Pärnu 80012, http://www.pc.ut.ee.
4 University of Tartu. Pärnu College, Ringi 35, Pärnu 80012, Estonia. Tel. +372 44 50520, Fax +372 44 50530, GSM +372 56 495 438 E-mail: garri@ut.ee, http://www.pc.ut.ee.

REFERENCES

Chapman, P. (2000), 'Assisting Cluster Development and Networking in Regional Economies of South Australia', Centre of Labour Research, Adelaide: Adelaide University.

Chattanooga Area Chamber of Commerce: News, Info & Links (2001). http://chattanooga-chamber.com/newsandinfo/headline.php3?id.html, 16 November 2001.

Eerme, K. (1939), 'Pärnu ja ta kuurort', Pärnu.

Gartner, C.W. (1996), *Tourism Development: Principles, Processes and Policies*, New York: Van Nostrand Reinhold.

Gee, Y.C., C.J. Makens and J.L.D. Choy (1989), *The Travel Industry*, New York: Van Nostrand Reinhold.

Giddens, A. (1984), *The Constitution of Society: Outline of the Theory of Structuration*, Berkeley: University of California Press.

Goncalves, F. Da C.V. and P.M.R. Aguas (1997), 'The Concept of Life Cycle: An Application to the Tourist Product', *Journal of Travel Research*, Fall, **35** (1), 12–22.

Harrison, B. (1992), 'Industrial Districts: Old Wine in New Bottles', *Regional Studies*, **26** (5), 469–83.

Ioannides, D. (1995), 'Planning for International Tourism in Less Developed Countries: Toward Sustainability?' *Journal of Planning Literature*, **9** (3), 235–59.

Ioannides, D. and K.G. Debbage (1998), *The Economic Geography of the Tourism Industry*, London: Routledge.

Kivimäe, J., A. Kriiska, I. Põltsam and A. Vunk (1998), 'Merelinn Pärnu', Pärnu.

Krugman, P. (1995), *Development, Geography and Economic Theory*, Cambridge: MIT Press.

Müristaja, H. (2000) 'Pärnu linna turismipotentsiaali hindamine ja arendamine', Diplomitöö. Pärnu.

Pärnu County Government (2001), 'Pärnu goes Europe 2000+', Report.

Porter, M.E. (1990), *The Competitive Advantage of Nations*, London: Macmillan.

Porter, M.E. (1998), 'Clusters and the New Economics of Competition', *Harvard Business Review*, November–December, 77–90.

Porter, M.E. (2000), 'Location, Competition, and Economic Development: Local Clusters in a Global Economy'. *Economic Development Quarterly*, **14** (1), 15–34.

Raagmaa, G., T. Kask and A. Rein (2000), 'Tourism in City Marketing and Regional Development: The Success Story of Pärnu, Estonia', in *The Proceedings of*

ERSA's XII Summer Institute – Tourism Sustainability and Territorial Organisation, Faro: University of Algarve.

Rosenfeldt, S.A. (1995), *Industrial Strength Strategies: Regional Clusters and Public Policy*, Washington: Aspen Institute.

Smeral, E. (1998), 'The Impact of Globalisation on Small and Medium Enterprise: New Challenges for Tourism Policies in European Countries', *Tourism Management*, **19** (4), 371–80.

The Cluster Consortium Strategy in Action Report (1999), http://www.nedlac.org.za/research/fridge/satourrep/index.html, 4 June 2002.

Veinpalu, E. ja L. (1998), 'Pärnu kuurort 150', Tallinn:

Velner, A. (1939), 'Turism ja kodukorrastamine omavalituste ülesannetena', *Loodushoid ja turism*, **1** (4), 181–7.

Wasson, C.R. (1974), *Dynamic Competitive Strategy and Product Life Cycles*, St. Charles, IL: Challenge Books.

Witt, F.S. and L. Mountinho (1989), *Tourism Marketing and Management Handbook*, New York: Prentice Hall.

APPENDIX 1

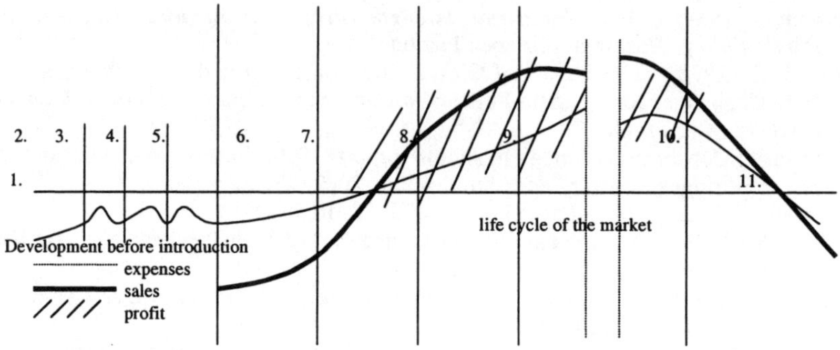

1. creation of the destination concept
2. development
3. development of pilot project
4. semi-commercial piloting
5. business activities commence and local initiative is facilitated
6. market development
7. rapid growth phase
8. competition turmoil
9. saturated maturity phase
10. decline
11. termination

Source: Gartner (1996).

Figure 9.7 The product life cycle model by Wasson

APPENDIX 2

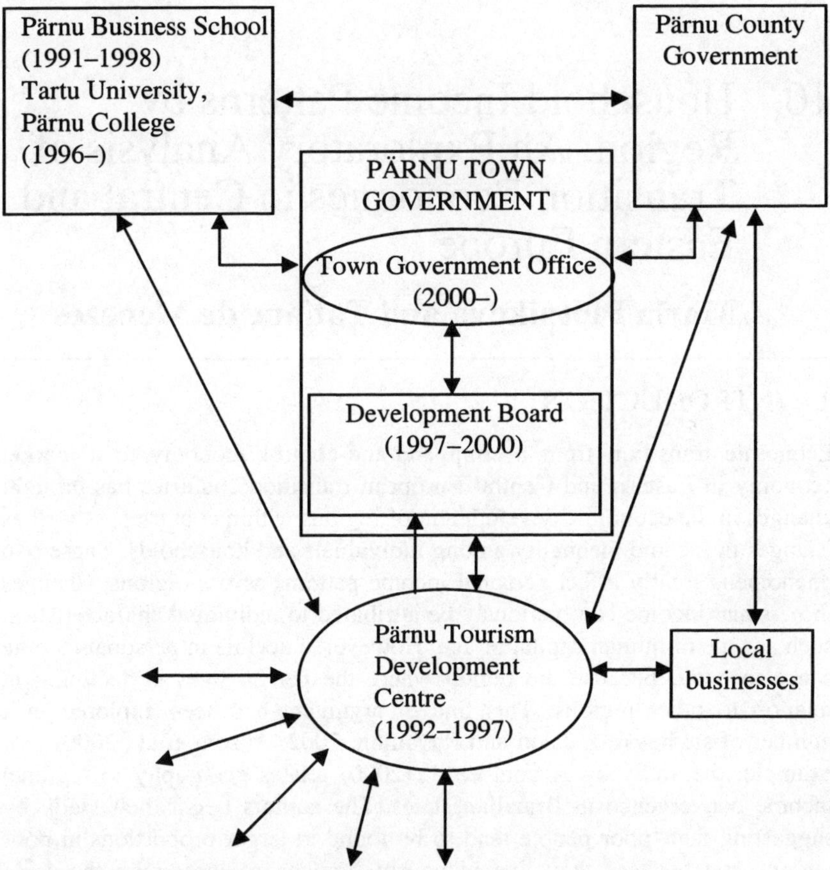

Figure 9.8 Pärnu tourism cooperation network, 1992–2000

10. Household Income Patterns by Region: An Exploratory Analysis of Transition Economies in Central and Eastern Europe

Maria Plotnikova and Tatiane de Menezes

1 INTRODUCTION

Economic transition from a command-and-control economy to a market economy in Eastern and Central European transition countries has brought changes in the economic development of regions within countries, as well as changes in income inequality among individuals and households. These two phenomena jointly affect personal income patterns across regions. Changes in personal income can obviously be attributed to individual characteristics, such as type of human capital or age. However, a decline in personal income can also occur because the region where the person lives is declining in relation to other regions. This line of argument has been explored in a number of studies (e.g. Jalan and Ravallion, 2002; Azzoni et al., 2000). For example, the study by Azzoni et al. (2000) relates geography to regional income convergence in Brazilian states. The authors begin their study by suggesting that 'poor people tend to be found in larger proportions in poor regions just because they live in poorly supplied regions: with the same personal characteristics, such people would be in a better situation if they lived in a richer region' (Azzoni, 2001, p. 1).

This line of reasoning is of particular relevance for understanding the emerging income disparity in Eastern Europe. The demise of central planning in the transition countries has led to the collapse of the planned and controlled regional patterns of growth seen during the earlier regime. The literature on transition generally examines poverty issues separately from the issues of changing regional economic landscape. This chapter attempts to bring the two issues together. It aims to explore the patterns and determinants of household income differences, in particular the regional component of income differences. The work is exploratory in nature and analyses the two issues using the transition countries of Hungary, Bulgaria, Estonia and Latvia. Using cross-section data from a World Bank household survey for these countries, it provides a descriptive, graphical analysis of regional income differences by age cohorts as well as a regression analysis of household income.

We now briefly discuss the relevant areas in the transition literature motivating this study, in particular the literature on inequality and spatial patterns. A very important element of transition documented in many studies is the increasing income inequality in transition countries. Fleming and Micklewright (1999) provide an extensive survey of income inequality studies in transition economies. They note that countries such as Poland, Hungary and the Czech Republic experienced a smaller increase in inequality than the former Soviet Union and the southern group of European transition countries. The Gini coefficient increased by 3 per cent in Hungary over the 1989–97 period and by 6 per cent in Poland between the years 1989 and 1996. This is a small increase compared to an 11 per cent annual increase between 1993 and 1994 in Russia, where the value of the average pension fell by half between 1992 and 1996. As a group, however, the EU frontrunners surpassed the majority of their Western European neighbours in levels of inequality measures (reported in Fleming and Micklewright, 1999).

It has also been documented that the emerging differences have a spatial pattern. The OECD reports the emergence and persistence of regional disparities in unemployment following a shift to a market economy throughout Central and Eastern Europe (OECD, 2000).

A study by Forster, Jesuit and Smeeding (2002) links regional and labour-related disparities by measuring intra-regional inequality versus inter-regional income inequality using regional versus national poverty lines in four Central and Eastern European countries. They find that the contribution of intra-regional inequality to overall inequality is larger than that of inter-regional inequality.

Bachtler and Downes (1999) suggest that the disparities are connected to the four spatial patterns of macro development: core–periphery (including capital city region versus the rest of the country), the East–West pattern, urban–rural, and industrial problem areas. Underlying these spatial patterns are the causal processes of spatial economic restructuring in response to new market demands. One of the important processes from a regional perspective is selective integration with the rest of Europe and the border countries. The general argument is that border regions and urban agglomerations may be transforming themselves faster than the 'hinterland' (Kratke, 1999).

On a related note, Pavlinek and Smith (1998) identify differential influx of local and regional foreign investment as one of the causal processes for regional differentiation. The literature describes the 'maquiladora'-type foreign/multinational firms that primarily use local labour and not capital and hence are not 'embedded' in the local economy. The authors argue that such maquiladora enterprises do not contribute to regional integration but, moreover, can contribute to poverty traps as the low wages are the primary reason for locating the enterprise in the transition country. They may use labour inefficiently in terms of skill match and contribute to the erosion of human capital by employing workers with high skills in low-skilled jobs.

While we do not offer causal explanations, we try to account for differences in the level of income by controlling for group effects. A crucial part of our analysis is controlling by regions to capture inter-regional income differences. This study attempts to decompose the two dimensions of income differences, regional and those attributed to individual or household characteristics, in order to offer more detail about the nature of the emerging pattern of differences. To do this, we use two complementary techniques: (1) graphical analysis of income difference by regions and (2) regression analysis of household income. While one can describe the trends and differences in household incomes by regions and countries using graphs at an aggregated level, regression analysis at a disaggregated level is a means to account for factors explaining these trends and differences.

In the following section we describe the data and introduce the regional income differences by means of graphical cohort analysis and follow on to regression analysis in Section 3. In Section 4 we summarise the results and suggest directions for further research.

2 DESCRIPTIVE ANALYSIS

In this section we briefly describe the data source and then focus on the graphical analysis.

2.1 Data

The data come from the World Bank Household Survey conducted in a number of countries, including the Central and Eastern European countries, and organised in the Household Expenditure and Income Data for Transition Economies (HEIDE) database. The particular countries in this study were selected because they are all European transition countries with survey data that have not already been adjusted for regional differences.[1] The territorial definitions of regions of HEIDE data correspond to the administrative divisions of the respective countries at the time the survey was taken. See Figures 10.1 and 10.2 for maps of the countries and regions studied as well as for the regional GDP per capita as a percentage of the EU average for 1995.

The available data consist of a detailed set of variables on household expenditure, income and assets. The survey also provides a limited set of variables of individuals; in particular, age, sex, education and employment status. The data for Hungary are for 1993, those for Bulgaria and Estonia are for 1995 and the Latvian data are for 1997. The Household Survey used in this analysis is available only for one year.

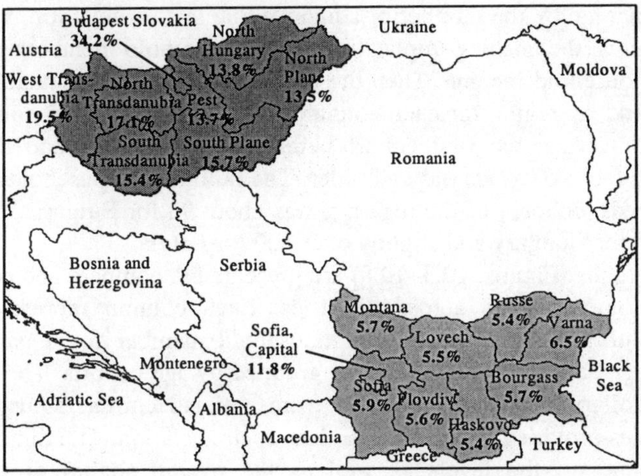

Source: Eurostat Regio Database.

Figure 10.1 *Hungary and Bulgaria: regional GDP per capita as percentage of EU average, 1995*

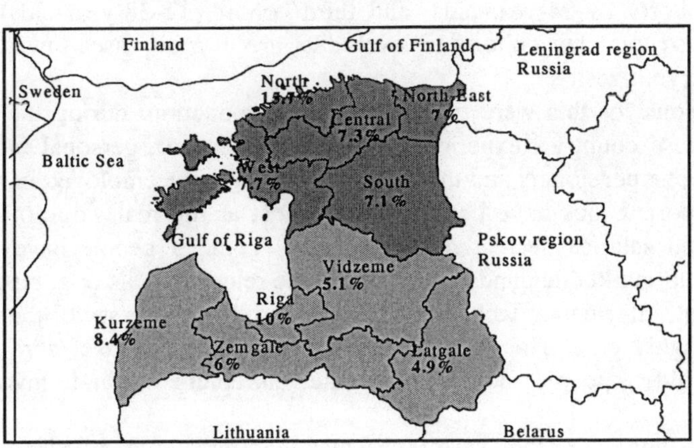

Source: Eurostat Regio Database.

Figure 10.2 *Estonia and Latvia: regional GDP per capita as percentage of EU average, 1995*

2.2 Graphical Analysis of Cohort Income by Region

Household survey data were averaged by region and by age cohort for each country. Since the data contained only household income and not individual income, the per capita household income was calculated by dividing household income by the number of adults. While this formulation is due to data constraints, the ensuing implication is that household members equally share total household income. Then the per capita income was averaged by age cohort and by region for each country. We constructed eight cohorts at seven-year intervals, the first cohort being 18–24-year-olds and the last cohort being those 67 years old and older. The number of households in the unit of analysis, cohort i of the region j, was about 90 for Bulgaria, 150 for Estonia, 260 for Hungary and slightly over 100 for Latvia.

The six graphs (Figures 10.3–10.8) are presented to compare and contrast regional income patterns across countries. Each column represents the average monthly income of an adult household member for a particular region and age cohort. The columns are grouped by age cohorts. The values are in US dollars and were converted from national currencies using the exchange rates provided in the HEIDE data documentation. The dimensions of comparison are the levels as well as the overall shapes of income distributions across cohorts.

What we see across the four countries is that the distributions are skewed to the left. Considering how the cohorts were constructed, younger people tend to be part of wealthier households. Incomes increase rapidly between the first cohort (18–24-year-olds) and third cohort (32–38-year-olds) and then decrease for latter cohorts to levels that are in most cases lower than those of the youngest.

The reasons for this were outlined in the introduction: during the time analysed these countries experienced a rapid increase in personal income inequality. The pensioners and those who continued to be employed in state-budget-supported jobs have been suffering most as the real value of their pensions and salaries decreased dramatically. Younger people have been responding to market demands by acquiring the relevant skills (e.g. business management, information technology) and taking the private sector jobs that are more highly paid. The young also may be inclined to take more risks than the older people do and become entrepreneurs and investors themselves.

It is also apparent from the graphs that there are large differences by regions within countries and across countries.

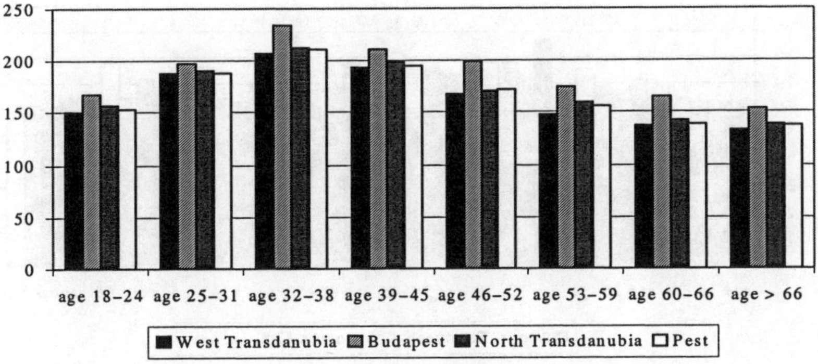

Figure 10.3 *Hungary, four higher-income regions: cohort-average monthly income of adult household member (US$), 1993*

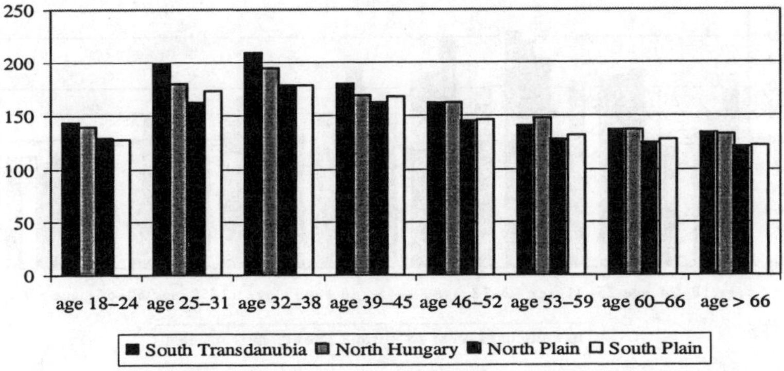

Figure 10.4 *Hungary, four lower-income regions: cohort-average monthly income of adult household member (US$), 1993*

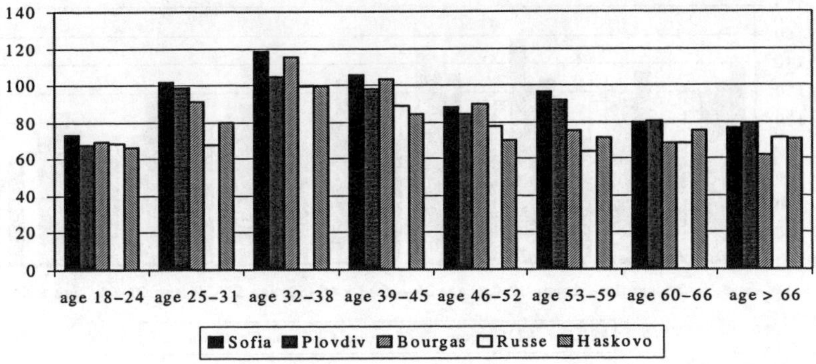

Figure 10.5 *Bulgaria, five higher-income regions: cohort-average monthly income of adult household member (US$), 1995*

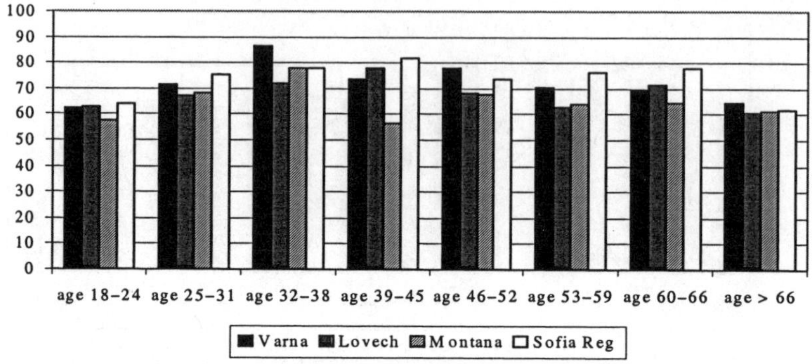

Figure 10.6 *Bulgaria, four lower-income regions: cohort-average monthly income of adult household member (US$), 1995*

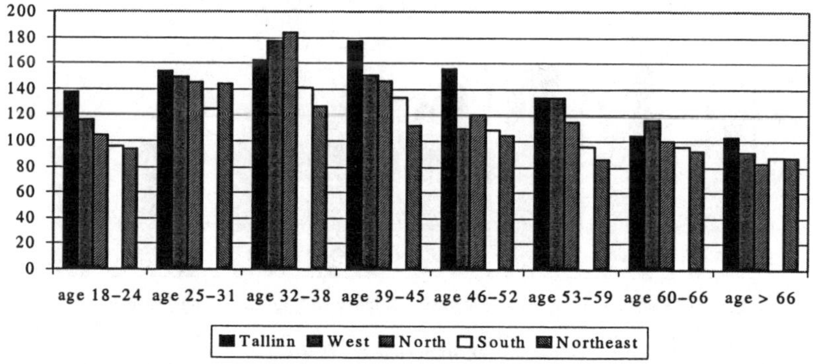

Figure 10.7 *Estonia: cohort-average monthly income of adult household member by region (US$), 1995*

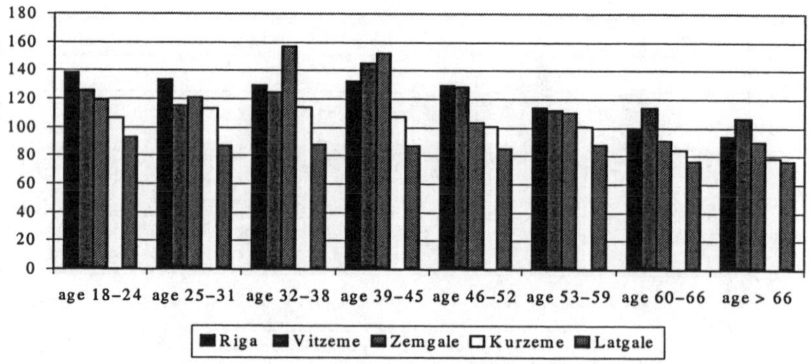

Figure 10.8 *Latvia: cohort-average monthly income of adult household member by region (US$), 1997*

For all countries the region containing the capital consistently has one of the highest income levels. What is interesting to note is that this is not necessarily the case for the highest-earning cohort (32–38-year-olds) (e.g. in Estonia and Latvia the capitals are clearly not the highest income regions for this group). Another cross-country trend apparent from visual inspection is that, with the possible exception of Hungary, the distribution of income across cohorts for lowest-income regions tends to vary less than that for highest-income regions.

In terms of comparison, in Hungary the inter-regional differences appear to be smaller than in other countries. In Bulgaria incomes appear more stable across the older cohorts than in other countries. Estonia and Latvia exhibit a high degree of variation both across regions and across cohorts. In Estonia the North region appears to have the most dramatic changes across cohorts. In Latvia the Latgale region is far behind other regions, exhibiting effectively no variation in income across cohorts.

3 REGRESSION ANALYSIS

While cohort-income graphs may be useful in demonstrating the effects of transition on generations, their application is limited with regard to explaining what factors account for income differences. It is possible that income differences between two regions or between cohorts may be explained, for example, by differences in the education and employment sectors. Therefore we conduct regression analysis of household income to control for demographic characteristics and identify the remaining regional effects. The unit of analysis is a household.

The regression analysis in this study is aimed at accounting for intra-regional vs. interregional differences in household income. The postulated relationship is that income is a function of individual, household and regional characteristics.

$$\begin{aligned} \textit{Household income} = {} & \beta_0 + \beta_1 age_i + \beta_2 age_i^2 + \beta_3 edu_i + \beta_4 household\_size_i \\ & + \beta_5 female_i + \beta_6 employment\_sector_i \\ & + \beta_{7-10} income\_source_i + \beta_{11} urban/rural \\ & + \beta_{12-18} region_i + \varepsilon_i . \end{aligned}$$

In addition we included a number of interaction terms between the discrete variables and continuous age variable in an effort to account for differences in effect by age.

In the following section a more detailed description of the variables included in the analysis is given.

3.1 Variables Included in the Analysis

The dependent variable is total disposable household income, which includes wages, self-employed income, and government aid payments. It also includes in-kind income (e.g. wages paid in terms of production of the employer/enterprise rather than money wages). The in-kind compensation may be important during transition and is a legacy of the command-and-control economy. Enterprises may be forced to pay wages in-kind when they do not receive payment from customers, or other enterprises. Since the dependent variable is household income it is necessary to control for household size because there may be a number of income earners.

We are including workers and non-workers because non-wage-income components may be important, such as pensions. To account for this, we control for the source of the largest share of total household income: wage-earner, self-employed, pensioner, public assistance recipient (such as disabled) and other source of income. The 'private versus public employment' variable is included in order to determine whether there is a wage premium for working in an emerging private sector. Since private enterprises are created in view of economic opportunities as a result of pent-up demand for scarcely supplied goods and services under the command-and-control system, it is reasonable to expect that there will be a premium for working in a private sector. The household variable for private/public employment was set at 1 if at least one household member was employed in the private sector. (The public/private survey category was not available for Hungary.)

Individual characteristics included in the analysis are education, gender, age and age squared. In the HEIDE database education is a categorical variable corresponding to four levels of educational attainment: primary, secondary (completed high school), vocational or professional (typically less than university degree), and university or higher (five or more years of university education). Primary education is not a significant category and we expect little variation by the secondary and vocational categories. Therefore we created a variable for the presence of higher education in the household.

The age variable used is slightly different from the typically used age of household head. In transition countries there are often two or more income earners in a household (the legacy of a housing shortage under the former economic system). Reported household heads are not necessarily the earners of the highest share of the household income. In two- or multi-generational families the reported head is typically the older parent, who earns less than the adult children. Therefore we created an age variable that reflects the age of the household head if the household head is employed. If the household head is not employed, the age variable reflects the age of the next employed household member (HEIDE data-set order of spouse, children, parents and 'others'). If there is more than one child or parent employed, their average age is taken.

We operationalise the gender variable by creating a dichotomous variable corresponding to female-headed households.

To capture differences in earning between urban and rural locations, we control by the type of location: towns/urban areas (urban = 1) versus rural areas. Note that the urban category excludes the capital, while the effect of the capital is expected to be accounted for by controlling for regions.

Regional controls

The reason for including dichotomous variables as regional controls is that we expect there to be regional effects that influence income, which cannot be operationalised with the available data and are therefore not explicitly accounted for in the analysis. The dichotomous variables are coded so that comparison is not to the omitted category but to the average of the rest of the regions.

To capture possible differences by categories with respect to age, we use several interaction variables, notably the region–age interaction. Graphical analysis indicated differences in income–age distribution by regions (higher incomes for younger cohorts in richer regions). This implies that the slopes of the income functions may be different by regions and an interaction term would control for that. While we control for many other factors in regression analysis, it is possible that there are residual effects that are not accounted for. Similarly there may be an age-related urban–rural dichotomy, so we also include the age–urban interaction.

We would like to stress that the set of explanatory variables might not be exhaustive as the choice of variables was constrained by data availability. In particular, an industry sector classification would be a useful addition to the survey data. For example, service sector workers and their incomes may be different from those in other occupational categories. Earnings in the service sector may be higher during the transition period because there was underprovision of services prior to transition. Another industry undergoing dramatic changes in the transition period is agriculture. Under the current classification, farmers would be found under the categories self-employed and wage-earners. The self-employed category is potentially problematic because it includes very different groups of workers – farmers, emerging entrepreneurs, small traders, and possibly marginalised groups with no steady income. One way to separate the entrepreneurs and traders is to include the self-employed–age interaction, assuming that the entrepreneurs and traders tend to be young people in the transition economy.

3.2 Regression Results

The regression parameters were estimated using OLS robust to the presence of heteroscedasticity. Note that the estimated coefficient (beta) has been standardised. The correlation matrix calculated for the explanatory variables prior to estimation indicated no significant collinearity between explanatory variables. The omitted variable test was conducted (Ramsey RESET type test in STATA 7.0). It indicated that there are omitted variables. Referring back to our discussion of data limitations at the end of section 3.1, the presence of omitted variables is not surprising. The tables of results for each country are given in the Appendix.

Effects of education, age and gender

Education positively affects income in all cases. Effect of age was accounted for by the age and age-squared variables. The age variable may be interpreted as work experience in this analysis because we are accounting for pensioner status and we are excluding individuals under 18 from the analysis. In contrast to the negative relationship between income and age displayed on the two-variable cohort income plots, age in the regression analysis has a positive effect on income in Hungary and Bulgaria. This is because in regression analysis we control for other factors, notably pensioner status and education, which almost certainly accounts for the positive effect of the age variable. Since younger households are more educated than older households, the positive association between young age and income on a two-variable cohort income plot is explained by higher levels of education in regression analysis. Despite these explanatory factors, age and income are still found to be negatively related in Estonia.

A negative estimated coefficient for the predominantly female household variable indicates that women tend to earn less than men, holding other characteristics constant. The effect is negative for all countries.

Effects of sector of employment and type of income source

Employment in the private sector has the highest premium in Bulgaria and the lowest premium in Estonia.

The omitted category for type of income source variable was 'wage-earner'. As expected, pensioner status negatively affects income. And, as expected, receiving public assistance was associated with lower income, as was the 'other income' category. The 'self-employed' variable had a positive effect across countries. In Hungary it was the age effect that mattered with, as expected, older people worse off when self-employed.

Rural–urban differences

Effects of urban location are positive, as expected (except in the case of Latvia, where it was not statistically significant). What is more interesting is the negative effect of urban location–age interaction. The older people are worse off in an urban area, presumably because in the rural area they do not 'retire' from farming activities or they can supplement their pension by farming.

Regional differences

Regional controls are included to account for the residual effects after the effects of individual and household characteristics have been accounted for. There are statistically significant effects for regional controls in every country's regression, notably in Bulgaria. This suggests that there are unaccounted effects associated with regions. There are also interesting results with respect to regional differences by age. In many instances regions that have a positive regional effect also have a negative region–age interaction, suggesting that region-specific income 'bonuses' decrease with age. However, in some cases there are no pronounced age differences by regions, as in the case of Estonia.

4 CONCLUSION AND SUGGESTIONS FOR FURTHER RESEARCH

The regression results largely confirm the trends in graphical exposition with respect to regional effects in the sense that regions with low absolute income tend to have negative estimated regional control effects. At the same time our findings on regional effects and region–age interaction point to the need for further, more complex analysis with respect to regional and locational effects on income. A natural extension would be to check for the presence of spatial effects in smaller territorial units.

An immediate point for future research would be to check whether income patterns are similar for all poor, middle-income and richer regions across countries. An appropriate tool would be quantile regression, which looks at the relationship between income and explanatory variables at different levels of income.

An important part of future work would be to extend the analysis to Western Europe and subsequently provide an effective comparison between the EU and the accession countries as a group and individually. The larger question to be answered is whether the EU accession countries are individually and as a group different from the current EU members.

To enhance understanding of the degree of regional differentiation one can compute regional inequality measures such as Theil inequality coefficients. A possible research direction in this regard is to explore the link between regional inequality and economic growth. This would require time-series data or, alternatively, linking these micro-data with aggregate time-series data.

The regional versus individual/household characteristics explanation for income has important implications for public policy intervention with respect to choice of regional policies versus social policies. Differences in per capita income by region should not automatically lead to implementation of regional policies. In some cases income differences by region can be explained by differences in individual and household characteristics, making a case for social policies.

NOTE

1 Other European transition countries for which HEIDE data were available were Poland and Slovakia. However, Polish data have already been adjusted for regional differences while others have not. Slovakian data were lacking essential variables, making them not comparable with those of the rest of the countries.

REFERENCES

Azzoni, C. (2001), 'Economic Growth and Regional Income Inequality in Brazil', *Annals of Regional Science*, **35**, 133–52.

Azzoni, C., N. Menezes-Filho, T. A. de Menezes and R. Silveira-Neto (2000), 'Geography and Income Convergence among Brazilian States', Inter-American Development Bank, Research Network Working Paper #R-395.

Bachtler, J. and R. Downes (1999), 'Regional Policy in the Transition Countries: A Comparative Assessment', *European Planning Studies*, **7**.

Fleming, J. and J. Micklewright (1999), 'Income Distribution, Economic Systems and Transition', Innocenti Occasional Papers, no. 70, May, Inequality and Poverty in Transition Program, The World Bank.

Forster, M., D. Jesuit and T. Smeeding (2002), 'Regional Poverty and Income Inequality in Central and Eastern Europe: Evidence from the Luxembourg Income Study', Luxembourg Income Project, Working Paper No. 324, www.lisproject.org.

Household Expenditure and Income Data for Transition Economies, http://www.worldbank.org/research/transition/house.htm.

Jalan, J. and M. Ravallion (2002), 'Geographic Poverty Traps: A Micro Model of Consumption Growth in Rural China', *Journal of Applied Econometrics*, **17**, 329–46.

Kratke, S. (1999), 'Regional Integration or Fragmentation? The German–Polish Border Region in a New Europe', *Regional Studies*, **33** (7), 631–41.

OECD (2000), 'Disparities in Regional Labor Markets Employment', *Outlook 2000*, Paris: OECD.

Pavlinek, P. and A. Smith (1998), 'Internationalization and Embeddedness in East-Central European Transition', *Regional Studies*, **32** (7), 619–38

APPENDIX: REGRESSION RESULTS

Table 10.1 Regression results, Bulgaria

Dependent variable: Household income		
Explanatory variables	Standardised coefficient	t-statistic
Age of primary earner(s)	0.143	1.96
Age squared	–0.042	–0.57
Education	0.114	8.98
Household size	0.259	12.21
Female-headed household	–0.07	–8.44
Private employment sector	0.169	6.53
Main source of income: pension	–0.188	–9.64
Self-employed	0.167	8.41
Other public assistance recipient	–0.094	–11.40
Other source of income	–0.148	–14.51
Urban location	0.207	3.97
Urban location*age interaction	–0.181	–3.75
Sofia	–0.331	–5.01
Sofia*age interaction	0.208	3.29
Bourgas	–0.216	–3.77
Bourgas*age interaction	0.204	4.07
Varna	–0.065	–1.33
Varna*age interaction	0.120	2.66
Lovech	–0.078	–1.64
Lovech*age interaction	0.103	2.39
Montana	0.148	3.67
Montana*age interaction	–0.067	–1.76
Plovdiv	0.35	0.56
Plovdiv*age interaction	–0.141	–2.26
Russe	–0.065	–1.33
Russe*age interaction	–0.259	–3.09
Sofia Region	–0.078	–1.64
Sofia Region*age interaction	–0.026	–0.60

Adjusted R-squared 0.37
Number of observations 4453

Table 10.2 Regression results, Hungary

Dependent variable: Household income		
Explanatory variables	Standardised coefficient	t-statistic
Age of primary earner(s)	0.565	9.67
Age squared	–0.574	–13.03
Education	0.222	17.83
Household size	0.458	3.72
Female-headed household	–0.110	–15.44
Main source of income: pension	–0.318	–26.91
Self-employed	0.042	1.06
Self-employed*age interaction	–0.187	–3.25
Other source of income	–0.180	–26.68
Urban location	0.132	5.10
Urban location*age interaction	–0.055	–2.47
West Transdanubia	–0.051	–1.11
West Transdanubia*age interaction	0.042	1.03
Budapest	–0.157	–3.35
Budapest*age interaction	0.068	1.70
North Transdanubia	–0.061	–1.52
North Transdanubia*age interaction	0.025	0.67
Pest	–0.042	–0.94
Pest*age interaction	0.012	0.32
South Transdanubia	–0.044	–1.06
South Transdanubia*age interaction	–0.035	0.95
North Hungary	0.058	1.69
North Hungary*age interaction	–0.052	–1.65
North Plane	0.189	6.26
North Plane*age interaction	–0.085	–3.19
Adjusted R-squared 0.57		
Number of observations 7858		

Table 10.3 Regression results, Latvia

Dependent variable: Household income		
Explanatory variables	Standardised coefficient	t-statistic
Age of primary earner(s)	0.036	1.24
Age squared	0.043	1.58
Education	0.132	9.44
Household size	0.194	15.55
Female-headed household	–0.027	–2.86
Private employment sector	0.062	7.49
Main source of income: pension	–0.073	–7.02
Self-employed	0.189	4.87
Public assistance recipient	–0.030	–5.75
Other source of income	–0.020	–3.16
Urban location	0.004	0.75
Riga	–0.182	–6.18
Riga*age interaction	0.138	5.81
Kurzeme	0.027	0.97
Kurzeme*age interaction	–0.014	–0.62
Vidzeme	0.018	0.44
Vidzeme*age interaction	–0.028	–0.91
Zemgale	–0.058	–0.84
Zemgale*age interaction	0.025	0.54
Adjusted R-squared 0.148		
Number of observations 7689		

Table 10.4 Regression results, Estonia

Dependent variable: Household income		
Explanatory variables	Standardised coefficient	t-statistic
Age of primary earner(s)	–0.169	–2.94
Age squared	0.051	0.96
Education	0.180	10.99
Household size	0.269	18.37
Female-headed household	–0.052	–5.60
Private employment sector	0.043	2.96
Main source of income: pension	–0.243	–19.80
Self-employed	0.064	3.61
Public assistance recipient	–0.135	–3.42
Other source of income	–0.163	–4.06
Urban location	0.034	2.38
Tallinn	–0.176	–3.08
Tallinn*age interaction	0.023	0.44
North	–0.035	–0.68
North*age interaction	0.054	1.18
West	–0.035	–0.68
West*age interaction	–0.038	–0.75
North-East	0.188	3.64
North-East*age interaction	–0.072	–1.60
Adjusted R-squared 0.33		
Number of observations 4658		

PART THREE

Fiscal, Financial and Environmental Policy Issues

11. Assessing Fiscal Policy in Romania with Special Focus on Fiscal Sustainability[1]

Doina Maria Radulescu

1 INTRODUCTION[2]

Compared to other transition countries such as the Czech Republic, Hungary and Poland, Romania still faces major macroeconomic problems, which shed a dark shadow on the country's image. Particular challenges arise from the inconsistent fiscal policy pursued, characterised by ad hoc measures and a stop-and-go pattern of reforms, which have led to increasing deficits and economic imbalances. This chapter aims to analyse the development of Romanian fiscal policy during the 1990s, with the main emphasis on the aspect of sustainability of the budget situation. First, this study presents the underlying causes of the domestic and external disequilibrium during the 1980s and describes the major economic developments that occurred during the transition period. They form the necessary background for the subsequent policy analysis. Second, the evolution of budget revenues (mainly taxes) and expenditures is highlighted, taking into account the problem of quasi-fiscal subsidies and payment arrears that led to very large quasi-fiscal deficits. In the next step, a macroeconomic model is introduced to assess the degree of fiscal sustainability, starting with the intertemporal government budget constraint. Using official statistics from Romanian institutions and ministries as well as from the IMF and World Bank, the overall deficit for the entire government, including central and local governments and other institutions belonging to the non-financial public sector, is computed. The research findings suggest that Romania has followed an unsustainable fiscal policy in the transition period, particularly up to 1996. In the first half of the 1990s, the government financed the deficit partly through seigniorage and tried to deal with immediate pressures, preventing social dissatisfaction but neglecting the long-term targets. The situation has improved slightly in recent years, but nevertheless, there is still much to be done in this area.

2 ROMANIA'S ECONOMY DURING THE TRANSITION PERIOD

For a correct assessment of Romanian fiscal policy, it is important to consider first the evolution of the country's economy, starting with central planning during the 1980s and continuing with the presentation of some macroeconomic data for the transition period. Romania's economy declined over the course of the 1980s, a fact that can be attributed both to the failures of central planning and to Ceausescu's mismanagement of the economy, as he planned and succeeded in repaying Romania's external debt by the end of the 1980s. The policy, aimed at achieving near complete self-sufficiency in all areas of production, accompanied by rigid control of the exchange rate and limitation of imports, created and artificially maintained a foreign account surplus. However, the price of this success was a sharp decline in consumption on the part of the Romanian population and only a little growth in traditional export sectors due to trying to achieve growth in the industrial goods sector. This policy strategy also led to the depletion of domestic energy resources and induced costly dependence on imports of raw materials and energy (OECD, 1998, p. 1). Industrial and urban infrastructure began to decay and the situation was worsened by massive state expenditures on largely ceremonial infrastructure and industrial projects that were never completed. Therefore, it is not surprising that social unrest grew throughout the 1980s, culminating in the revolution in December 1989 (Poirot, 1996, pp. 1060–61; EU, 1997, p. 21). Although foreign economic constraints were not present in the form of inherited debt, the debt repayment efforts of the communist regime meant that Romania had to start from scratch with economic reforms, in contrast with other socialist countries where such reforms were implemented even before 1989. Accordingly, Romania started its transition period with a considerable gap in its legal, economic and social infrastructure *vis-à-vis* market economies (Poirot, 1996, p. 1059; Hunya, 1998, p. 242; EU, 1997, p. 21). At the beginning of the 1990s, dramatic external events such as the Gulf War and Yugoslavia's breakdown also negatively influenced the country's economic situation.

In 1990, the government initiated a policy aimed at improving living conditions for the population, a policy that was, however, ill designed and proved unsustainable in the long run. The exchange rate was maintained at unsustainably high levels, price controls remained in place and the workweek was shortened. Because growth in consumer demand was not matched by an increase in production, labour productivity, investment and real output fell. Since no tax structure had replaced the old system of collecting revenues directly from firms, enterprise arrears to the government rose sharply. Attempting to avert the complete collapse of the industrial sector, the government directed the National Bank of Romania (NBR) to write off enterprise debts against bank deposits (Poirot, 1996, pp. 1064–6). Moreover, the trade surplus of 1989 had become a US$3 billion trade deficit because the authorities gave way to pressure to consume 'tradables', which led to rising imports and which was financed through depletion of Romania's hard currency reserves. NBR credits to state firms were granted on a universal basis without regard to any individual firm's competitiveness. Interest rates remained negative in real terms and the situation of an inflationary spiral arose. One of the policy mistakes made by the government of the time concerned the disposition of land and lack of clear property rights on land. In December 1991, the Romanian parliament again directed the NBR to provide the equivalent of US$1.35 billion at a nominal rate of 28 per cent in the form of a global six-month credit to all enterprises. After the election in September 1992 the leu was devalued by more than 300 per cent against the US dollar, unemployment rose from 3.0 per cent in 1991 to 8.2 per cent in 1992, GDP growth declined from -5.6 per cent in 1990 to -8.8 per cent in 1992 and inflation reached an annual rate of more than 200 per cent (see Table 11.1) (EBRD 1999, 2000, 2002; Poirot, 1996, pp. 1066, 1068, 1069). During 1993, a major change was brought about by the introduction of VAT, while 1994 was the year the treasury bills market was initiated and a Securities and Exchange Commission established.

The strategies followed during the first five years of the transition process failed to establish a functioning market mechanism as a device for allocating resources. The result was a decreasing output performance and collapsing export markets. Efforts designed to use the exchange rate as an anti-inflationary anchor failed and restrictive credit and monetary policies did not achieve the expected results because of growing enterprise arrears. These arrears were financed by the monetarisation of debt such that monetary and fiscal policies had no anti-inflationary effect (Poirot, 1996, p. 1071).

The risks of the gradualist strategy adopted by the authorities materialised in 1995. In order to support energy-intensive industries and allow them to import their production inputs, foreign exchange was allocated to these favoured sectors on the basis of a non-market 'official' exchange rate and accordingly rationed in the other sectors (OECD, 1998, p. 2). The impact of the exchange rate on domestic prices was direct only in the case of imported manufactured products but was managed by a regulated price mechanism for raw materials and energy. On the one hand, consumers were spared some of the impact of cost increases and currency devaluation; on the other hand, producers had to be helped by subsidisation, as they could not set prices based on costs. This subsidisation placed growing pressure on the budget and finally also led to higher inflation (Hunya, 1998, p. 247). Among the unsustainable policies the government implemented was the artificial

Table 11.1 General economic data for the Romanian economy, 1992–99

	1992	1993	1994	1995	1996	1997	1998	1999
Output and expenditure	(Percentage change in real terms)							
GDP	–8.8	1.5	3.9	7.1	3.9	–6.1	–5.4	–3.2
Gross fixed investment	11.0	8.3	20.7	6.9	5.7	–3.0	–18.1	–5.1
Exports of goods and services	–36.6	11.1	19.0	17.0	2.0	11.4	–	9.7
Employment	(In per cent of labour force)							
Unemployment (end-year)	8.2	10.4	10.9	9.5	6.6	8.9	10.3	11.8
Prices and wages	(Percentage change)							
Consumer prices (annual average)	210.4	256.1	136.7	32.3	38.8	154.8	59.1	45.8
Interest and exchange rates	(In per cent per annum, end-year)							
Deposit rate (average)	–	42.5	49.5	36.5	38.1	51.6	38.3	45.4
Lending rate (average)	–	86.4	61.8	48.6	55.8	63.7	56.9	65.9
Exchange rate (annual average) (Lei per US dollar)	308	760	1655	2033	3083	7168	8875	15 333
External sector	(In millions of US dollars)							
Current account	–1564	–1174	–428	–1774	–2584	–2137	–2917	–1296
Trade balance	–1420	–1128	–411	–1577	–2494	–1980	–2625	–1092
Foreign direct investment (net)	73	87	341	417	415	1267	2079	1025
External debt stock	3240	4249	5509	6484	8345	9502	9902	9091

Sources: EBRD (2000, 2001, 2002).

stabilisation of the exchange rate. The spread between the official exchange rate and the market-oriented rate used by foreign exchange offices reached 30–40 per cent in the final quarter of 1996 (OECD, 1998, p. 38). Considered overall, the policy failures during 1995–96 had two dimensions: false targeting of indirect policy instruments and proliferation of administrative policy interventions.

After the elections in November 1996, a new government was formed which favoured a liberal market economy. As a result, prices (except those of fewer than 20 goods, including energy as well as goods and services in the field of public utilities (EU, 1998, p. 23) and the exchange rate were completely liberalised, leading to a jump in inflation (Hunya, 1998, p. 251; OECD, 1998, p. 37). The restructuring process led to company closures and increased social tensions. Due to the fact that laid-off workers had to be offered unemployment benefits and the liquidation of enterprises also entailed additional costs, budgetary expenses increased (EU, 1998, p. 9). However, even the newly elected parties did not succeed completely in implementing the privatisation process (EBRD, 1997, p. 197).

The year 1998 brought both further reforms and economic recession. The authorities introduced protectionist measures such as an import tax of 6 per cent (Troschke, 1998, p. 72). Enterprises were not able to take advantage of the low labour costs and lost market share *vis-à-vis* cheaper and better import products. Due to downgrading by rating agencies and the effects of the Russian crisis, the country had difficulties in gaining the financial resources needed to cover the current account deficit (EU, 1998, p. 9). It was also in 1998 that a law stating that the NBR was no longer allowed to finance the budget deficit was promulgated. However, because of the insufficiently developed capital markets, the bank could still grant 180-day loans at the market interest rate in order to help the government overcome temporary deficits.

In 1999, the external position was strengthened by the exchange rate. The authorities continued the economic programme, including tight fiscal corrections and the closure of a large insolvent bank (Bancorex) (IMF, 2000b, p. 18).

During the year 2000 continued tax and other economic reforms started to show results, reflected in growing output performance based mainly on rising exports. However, Romania is likely to be the only country in Central and Eastern Europe (CEE) to continue to have high inflation (EBRD, 2000, p. 50; IMF, 2000b, p. 15). To correctly assess what direction the transition process will take, it is important to examine the policies the new government formed after the elections in November 2000 and led by Prime Minister Adrian Nastase. The newly elected government aimed at accelerated economic growth mainly from foreign investment, growth of small and medium-sized enterprises and privatisation. However, it is still important to note that Romania faces a substantial gap in its institutional set-up *vis-à-vis* other market economies, which poses a major problem and also needs to be addressed in the future by a proper design of such institutions. As the stand-by agreements with the IMF and World Bank rely on the achievement of further progress with reforms, in order to continue to rely on these financial resources and to meet the criteria for EU accession the government will probably have no other choice but to continue with economic reforms.

3 FISCAL POLICY IN ROMANIA DURING THE 1990s

The main budget entities in Romania include the state, the social security fund, covering old-age pensions and invalidity benefits, and local government administration responsible for local services (excluding health and education) and for social assistance. In addition, there are also a number of smaller funds which cover some areas of social support (such as unemployment compensation and the farmers' pension fund) (OECD, 1998, p. 47). To understand the fiscal problems in Romania, the political economy perspective appears to be fundamental (Croitoru and Tarhoaca, 1999, pp. 11–12; Albu and Pelinescu, 1999, pp. 2–3). In an analysis of Romanian policy, a link can be seen between election cycles and the evolution of fiscal policy, such that the transition period can be divided into three stages corresponding to three different legislature periods.

3.1 The Evolution of Fiscal Policy from 1990 until 1992

At the beginning of the 1990s, fiscal policy was officially tight. Fiscal deficits amounted to only 0.4 per cent of GDP according to the NBR. The main purpose of the newly pursued policy was to reduce the size of the government and its role in the economy (OECD, 1993, p. 64). In 1991 and 1992, the projected budget deficits increased as subsidy expenditures accelerated with inflation. Nevertheless, the 1992 budget looked even better than expected. The main reason for the satisfactory budget position actually derived from increasing enterprise taxation as a result of inflation, which was able to offset the negative effects of declining output. Despite tax reform, the budget still depended to a large extent on profit taxes from state enterprises, which accounted for about 15 per cent of government revenues. The surprising fact that companies were still able to pay the profit tax was attributable to the distorted accounting system (inventories were valued at historic cost using the FIFO method, resulting in paper profits in times of high inflation and inappropriate depreciation expenses which resulted in underestimated costs) and the prevailing, sometimes triple-digit, inflation. In order to respond to cash-flow pressures, enterprises reduced their investment spending or incurred inter-company arrears. These arrears actually represent one of the major causes of fiscal deficits in Romania. Since these inter-enterprise arrears also led to tax arrears towards the government, a policy aimed at forcing enterprises to meet their tax payments would be an important step toward a more comprehensive fiscal policy (Tanzi, 1993b, p. 17).

A problem posed by rising arrears is that they can endanger the reform process and distort available economic information such as relative price changes. Concerning arrears of state enterprises, these actually represent a future liability of the government and covering these fiscal deficits also entails a moral hazard problem: if enterprises expect the bailout policy to be continued in the future, they will be induced to continue running arrears. In Romania, gross inter-enterprise arrears (representing overall arrears before adjusting for bilateral payables and receivables) were almost 18 times higher at the end of 1991 than at the end of 1990. The roots of these arrears lie in the previous government policy aimed at repaying external debt during the 1980s. In order to generate large fiscal surpluses, the government levied high taxes on enterprises such that these firms did not have enough resources to finance themselves; they incurred losses financed through bank credits, which became, in time, unserviceable. These arrears appeared then as bad debts in banks' balance sheets. When transition started, the authorities decided to write off these bad debts against government bank deposits. Later on, when banks tightened their eligibility requirements in granting credits, enterprises started to build up arrears among themselves in order to facilitate the financing of current operations. The moral hazard problem, due to the lack of financial discipline, was still not adequately addressed (Clifton and Khan, 1993, pp. 681–7). Since state company managers were able to obtain a good price for their enterprises, it was rational for them to accumulate large amounts of debt in the form of tax arrears, as they knew the State Ownership Fund (SOF) would later cancel these arrears when the enterprise was to be sold. Moreover, another explanation for accumulating overdue tax debts was the fact that the effective interest rate paid by a firm on delayed tax payment was almost always more attractive than an alternative source of financing. Finally, the complicated tax collection system makes tracking non-payment of taxes very difficult (Borc, 1999, p. 8). To the extent to which such arrears were tolerated and barter trade flourished, the capacity of enterprises to meet their tax liabilities was eroded. In the end, the best solution that will lead to diminishing arrears will be enterprise privatisation as well as enforcement of bankruptcy procedures (Clifton and Khan, 1993, pp. 690–92, 695; Fisher and Gelb, 1992, p. 71).

3.2 The Evolution of Fiscal Policy from 1993 until the November 1996 Elections

In 1993, the government tried to improve financial discipline: enterprises that incurred arrears were penalised and the issuing of subsidised refinancing credits was no longer the obligation of the National Bank of Romania. Two years later, the amount of subsidies increased due to the policy followed by the authorities of stimulating economic growth by expanding fiscal expenditure. On one hand, subsidies were directed to the agricultural and energy sectors, while, on the other hand, these subsidies were partially financed by taxes levied on light industry and trade.

The fiscal policy conducted reflects the role of the government in implementing the privatisation process. State-owned, loss-making enterprises were bailed out by the State Ownership Fund (SOF), which distributed revenues from privatisation among state enterprises that still faced financial problems. In the election year, the authorities even encouraged large state enterprises to incur tax arrears in order to finance artificially high wage growth and production. All these indirect instruments of fiscal policy, targeted in the wrong direction, led to economic tensions reflected in the macroeconomic imbalances of that period (Hunya, 1998, p. 245).

The problem of quasi-fiscal expenditures culminated during 1996. These quasi-fiscal subsidies were provided by means of concessionary interest rates (i.e. at the discount rate of 35 per cent for structural credits to agriculture and energy-intensive sectors and 0 per cent interest to banks in financial distress) while market-based interest rates amounted to about 55 per cent. Another type of quasi-fiscal subsidy was created by supporting an overvalued exchange rate or trading restrictions; thus, exports were subjected to an implicit tax, while imports received a subsidy. In particular, the price of energy imports was lowered. A measure for this type of quasi-fiscal subsidy can be the difference between the 'official' exchange rate and the market-oriented exchange rate used by foreign exchange offices. In 1996 the premium obtained by these offices was about 16 per cent. Overall, the subsidy value of the artificial exchange rate can be approximated to almost 0.5 per cent of GDP (OECD, 1998, p. 55). The economic situation in 1996 was also worsened by continued enterprise losses and payment arrears. Overall gross arrears in the economy reached 39.5 trillion lei (36 per cent of GDP) at the end of 1996 (OECD, 1998).

3.3 Fiscal Policy Reforms from 1997 to 2000

Fiscal adjustment started in 1997, when most of the above-mentioned activities ceased following the exchange and interest rate liberalisation. Financing the deficit became more difficult as a result of higher interest payments and complicated conditions on international capital markets (EU, 1998, p. 13). The most important changes in the course of the year related to the elimination of most of the subsidies to agriculture (which was partly offset by a budget provision of 0.4 per cent of GDP in new lending to small land-owners) and industry. The tax shortfall in the field of personal and labour income taxes mirrored the declining earnings in the economy. The sustainability of the fiscal situation started to be questioned due to the rapid increase in the public debt to GDP ratio, although the current ratio was not too high. The government also passed a new law allowing ministries to exert direct control over highly indebted companies from the SOF through a 'debt for equity swap' in order to recover their claims. Additionally, through the forced execution of bank accounts by which bank accounts were seized to satisfy debt payments, the government hoped to reduce the arrears of the main utility providers (EU, 1999, pp. 25–6).

Unfortunately, even in the course of 1999, fiscal policy was still governed by non-economic criteria such as the interests of different pressure groups, which induced politicians, for example, to adopt legislation granting generous fiscal facilities for small and medium-sized enterprises (Croitoru and Tarhoaca, 1999, p. 2). Moreover, the country is still characterised by the presence of a large public sector responsible for important off-budget expenditures for industrial and bank restructuring. In this situation, expenditure cuts[3] may lead to the need to reform the social security system as well as the public administration, fields that are extremely politically sensitive (EBRD, 2000, p. 51). Additionally, the reform of the taxation system,[4] making it become an instrument for achieving sustainable economic development, is going to be a major objective.

A crucial aspect of the fiscal policy pursued during the 1990s is the relatively high reliance on taxes to finance large budget expenditures. Consequently, the tax burden, measured as the ratio of annual tax liabilities to annual value added, increased from 39 per cent in 1996 to 42 per cent in 1997 and ultimately to 52 per cent in 1998. The high tax burden overwhelmed private enterprises, undermining their savings and thus future growth possibilities (Croitoru and Tarhoaca, 1999, pp. 7–8).

At the beginning of 2000, important steps in the area of tax reform were taken by lowering tax rates and widening the tax base. Nevertheless, arrears to the government have continued to grow. Regarding the evolution of economic and fiscal policies during the first months of 2001, it is important to note that, for the first time since the start of transition, the budget included significant outlays for investment purposes that will help improve the country's infrastructure. Additionally, the privatisation process was starting to accelerate.

4 EMPIRICAL REASSESSMENT OF FISCAL SUSTAINABILITY IN ROMANIA IN THE 1990s

4.1 Fiscal Sustainability: Basic Theoretical Aspects[5]

In order to assess the country's fiscal sustainability, we can compare the country's primary balance (representing the government balance less interest payments) with the primary balance under which the ratio of debt to GDP is stabilised at its current level. Thus, if the interest rate is higher than the growth rate, the primary balance would have to be in surplus in order to stabilise the mentioned ratio (IMF, 1998, p. 98). Fiscal sustainability is focused among other things on securing economic growth as well as intragenerational equity. For this purpose, the structure and the level of both the state income and state expenditure should enable sustainable growth. A large percentage of consumption expenditures or subsidies paid to enterprises and transfers paid to households, which distort incentives, can hinder economic growth and endanger full employment. Therefore, fiscal sustainability is achieved if the discounted value of all primary surpluses is matched by the value of government debt (Wissenschaftlicher Beirat, 2001, pp. 7–8, 15). A specific method used to assess the degree of fiscal sustainability in the literature is for example the one employed by the OECD. This concept has as a starting point the deficit of the consolidated state budget, which is computed as the difference between the overall state expenditures and the total state revenue plus the interest on state debt. In this framework, special attention can be paid to the primary balance, defined as the difference between total expenditures and total income. A primary deficit means that the state is financing part of its expenditures through debt. Such a policy cannot be sustained for ever, since it would lead to exploding indebtness. (Wissenschaftlicher Beirat, 2001, p. 11). Trying to attain fiscal stabilisation is often justified by the fact that the Ricardian equivalence hypothesis does not usually hold (Buiter and Tobin, 1979). According to this thesis, the increase in government savings is completely offset by non-governmental saving. However, there are several restraints, such as the lack of forward-looking behaviour by private savers or borrowing constraints, which lead to the failure of the Ricardian hypothesis (Sinn and Nachtkamp, 1981, p. 303; Croitoru and Tarhoaca, 1999, p. 5).

The applied framework includes the central government budget, including all local government budgets and extra-budgetary accounts as well as the central bank profit and loss account, since the government shifted certain fiscal expenditures to the balance sheet of the central bank.[6] Therefore, the authors start by applying the following consolidated budget deficit constraint, where the left-hand side represents the funding requirements and the right-hand side the different sources of financing (Budina and van Vijnbergen, 1996, 1997):

$$\begin{aligned} &D + iB_{-1} + iDC^{g}_{-1} - iDEP^{g} + ((1+\hat{E})(1+i^{*}) - 1)B^{*}_{-1}E_{-1} \\ &= \Delta B + \Delta(B^{*}E) + \Delta DC^{g} - \Delta DEP^{g}, \end{aligned} \tag{11.1}$$

where

D = public sector primary deficit
B = domestic debt taken from the government's accounts (held by other institutions than the central bank, i.e. commercial banks)
iB_{-1} = interest payments on domestic debt
DC^{g} = domestic credit to the government (taken from the accounts of the central bank)
iDC^{g} = interest payments on domestic credit to the government
$iDEP^{g}$ = interest payments on government deposits at the National Bank of Romania (NBR)
$((1+\hat{E})(1+i^{*})-1)B^{*}_{-1}E_{-1}$ = interest payments, expressed in terms of domestic currency, on foreign debt
ΔB = domestic debt issue
E = real exchange rate
$\hat{E}$ = real exchange rate change (per cent depreciation)
$\Delta(B^{*}E)$ = foreign borrowing
ΔDC^{g} = changes in domestic credit to the government
ΔDEP^{g} = changes in government deposits held at the NBR.

Changes in the value of government foreign liabilities, as well as changes in the value of interest payments on foreign debt, can be broken down into the following components:

$$\Delta(B^{*}E) = E_{-1}\Delta B^{*} + B^{*}_{-1}\Delta E + \Delta B^{*}\Delta E \tag{11.2}$$

$$((1+i^{*})(1+\hat{E}) - 1)B^{*}_{-1}E_{-1} = (1+\hat{E})i^{*}B^{*}_{-1}E_{-1} + B^{*}_{-1}\Delta E, \tag{11.3}$$

where ΔB is the level of change in the real exchange rate. Accordingly, inserting Equations 11.2 and 11.3 into the Equation 11.1, we obtain:

$$D + iB_{-1} + iDC^{g}_{-1} - iDEP^{g}_{-1} + (1+\hat{E})i^{*}B^{*}_{-1}E_{-1} = \Delta B + \Delta B^{*}E_{-1} \\ + \Delta B^{*}\Delta E + \Delta DC^{g} - \Delta DEP^{g}. \quad (11.4)$$

Furthermore, the central bank profit and loss account can be derived using the central bank balance sheet. The left-hand side of Equation 11.5 represents the change in 'net interest free' central bank liabilities to the private sector, whereas the right-hand side represents the change in the bank's assets, net of its profits.

$$\Delta M - \Delta C^{p} = \Delta DC^{g} - \Delta DEP^{g} + \Delta NFA^{*}E - \Delta NW, \quad (11.5)$$

where

ΔM = change in currency in circulation plus change in required reserves (money base) held by commercial banks at the central bank
ΔC^{p} = change in refinancing credit to the commercial banking sector
$\Delta NFA^{*}E$ = change in central bank's net foreign assets in domestic currency
ΔNW = central bank profits = change in its net worth.

Moreover,

$$\Delta NW = iDC^{g}_{-1} - iDEP^{g}_{-1} + iC^{p}_{-1} + ((1+i^{*})(1+\hat{E}) - 1)NFA^{*}_{-1}E_{-1}. \quad (11.6)$$

Adopting Equations 11.5 and 11.6, the central bank profit and loss account can be expressed as

$$iDC^{g}_{-1} - iDEP^{g}_{-1} + iC^{p}_{-1} + ((1+i^{*})(1+\hat{E}) - 1)NFA^{*}_{-1}E_{-1} = \Delta DC^{g} \\ - \Delta DEP^{g} + \Delta(NFA^{*}E) - \Delta M + \Delta C^{p}. \quad (11.7)$$

Using Equations 11.2 and 11.3, replacing B^{*} by NFA^{*} and substituting into Equation 11.7 gives us the central bank profit and loss account written in the following way:

$$iDC^{g}_{-1} - iDEP^{g}_{-1} + iC^{p}_{-1} + (1+\hat{E})i^{*}NFA^{*}_{-1}E_{-1} = \Delta DC^{g} - \Delta DEP^{g} \\ + E_{-1}\Delta NFA^{*} + \Delta E\Delta NFA^{*} - \Delta M + \Delta C^{p}. \quad (11.8)$$

The following integrated government and central bank budget constraint is obtained by integrating Equation 11.8 with Equation 11.4. Due to the fact that the assets of one entity represent the liabilities of the other entity, the items $iDC^{g}_{-1} - iDEP^{g}_{-1}$ and $\Delta DC^{g} - \Delta DEP^{g}$ will cancel out:

$$D + iB_{-1} - iC^{p}_{-1} + (1+\hat{E})i^{*}(B^{*}_{-1} - NFA^{*}_{-1})E_{-1} = \Delta B \\ + E_{-1}(\Delta B^{*} - \Delta NFA^{*}) + \Delta E(\Delta B^{*} - \Delta NFA^{*}) + \Delta M - \Delta C^{p}. \quad (11.9)$$

4.2 Empirical Results

The results of the empirical analysis are summarised in Tables 11.2 and 11.3 and Figure 11.1. The second row in Table 11.3 shows the annual figure for the total public deficit for the period 1992–99 calculated in Table 11.2. The overall public deficit includes both the government budget deficit and the NBR deficit, which includes the quasi-fiscal operations undertaken by the government through the accounts of the central bank. Additional quasi-fiscal deficits, such as the bad loans of commercial banks taken over by the government, are part of the figure for the government deficit computed in the eighth row of Table 11.2.

The total public deficit gradually declined over the investigated period. The deficit amounted to 10.9 per cent of GDP in 1992, 7.2 per cent of GDP in 1996 and finally reached 4.3 per cent of GDP in 1999. This decreasing trend is also illustrated in Figure 11.1. The NBR deficit, including the quasi-fiscal operations of the government (the shaded part of the columns), has shrunk in the course of time. Moreover, if we look at the figures for the conventionally defined state budget deficit (the first row of Table 11.3) in the official statistics (as collected by Economist Intelligence Unit, Datastream), Romania appears to have a much smaller deficit size (4.4 per cent of GDP in 1992, 4.9 per cent of GDP in 1996 and 2.5 per cent of GDP in 1999). Yet these figures can be misleading since they do not take into account the quasi-fiscal deficits. However, even considering these additional deficits, the budget balance has gradually improved in recent years. This is a positive trend and ideally should be sustained in the future.

On the other hand, a worrying fiscal situation prevails due to the difference between the growth rate and the net interest rate (see rows 7, 8 and 9 of Table 11.3). As the theory of fiscal sustainability[7] generally asserts, the increase in primary deficits is not detrimental, as long as the GDP growth rate exceeds the net interest rate. However, in the case of Romania, the foreign net interest rate in particular remained higher than the GDP growth rate in the investigated years (the former rate amounted to 7.9 per cent in 1992, 5.0 per cent in 1996 and 3.8 per cent in 1999 while the latter amounted to –8.8 per cent in 1992, 3.9 per cent in 1996 and –3.2 per cent in 1999. This situation, linked with the rather rapidly increasing size of domestic and public debt, can still call into question the sustainability of Romania's fiscal position. At the beginning of the 1990s, the country started its economic transition with virtually no debt,[8] and the ratio of foreign debt to GDP reached a level higher than 25 per cent in 1999. It should be noted that over the period until 1997 the Romanian government was able to raise financial means domestically at negative real interest rates, due partly to high inflation, but starting in 1998 real interest rates became positive.

Looking again at the figures for the total public deficit in 1996 and 1997 (7.2 per cent and 7.4 per cent of GDP respectively), these numbers can be partly explained by the government's decision to take over the bad debts of two banks in financial distress (Banca Agricola and Bancorex) and to recapitalise them. Furthermore, a second bailout for these banks was necessary in 1999, thus adding to the amount of quasi-fiscal deficits that year (IMF, 2001, p. 70).

Summing up, it can be concluded that high interest rates, exceeding the country's growth rate, still endanger the sustainability of the country's fiscal position, while the declining inflation rate and the shrinking overall public sector deficits show that there is further hope for improvement. The mistakes made by policy makers in the first half of the 1990s, when they acted with only a short-term horizon, trying to deal with immediate pressures and avoid social dissatisfaction instead of pursuing long-term targets aimed at sustainable economic growth, contributed significantly to the rise of the quasi-fiscal deficits which culminated in 1997. To overcome this situation, lower quasi-fiscal deficits leading to lower interest rates would be needed (Daianu, 1999, p. 21). Lower interest rates facilitate economic growth and reduce the burden created by repaying foreign debt. Some steps in this direction have recently been taken by the government. However, the pace of reforms combined with a coherent fiscal policy needs to be sustained in the future.

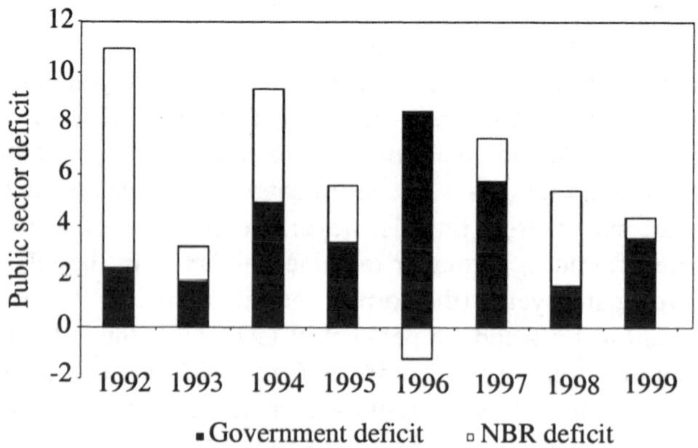

Source: see calculations from Table 11.2.

Figure 11.1 Total public deficits for Romania, 1992–99

Table 11.2 Total public deficits for Romania, 1992–99

Nominal deficit as a percentage of GDP	1992	1993	1994	1995	1996	1997	1998	1999
1. Net change in monetary base: $\Delta M - \Delta C^p$	8.32	0.59	3.22	0.2	–2.00	7.02	1.13	5.17
1.1 Change in monetary base: ΔM	7.70	8.21	4.25	3.43	1.76	4.86	1.2	4.95
1.2 Change in refinancing credit: ΔC^p	–0.62	7.62	1.03	3.23	3.76	–2.16	0.07	–0.22
2. NBR's net foreign assets: *NFA*	3.55	1.89	–0.51	–1.32	–1.4	5.74	–1.29	4.08
3. Change in government net foreign liabilities: ΔB^*	5.44	3.46	4.06	2.92	4.73	2.33	–0.23	–3.86
4.1 Change in government domestic debt: ΔB	0.72	1.00	1.68	1.13	3.11	3.81	3.18	7.09
4.2 Change in government deposit at NBR: ΔDEP^g	3.85	2.63	0.84	0.71	–0.62	0.41	1.33	–0.28
I. Government deficit (= 3 + 4.1 – 4.2)	2.31	1.83	4.9	3.34	8.46	5.73	1.62	3.51
II. NBR deficit (= 1 + 2 + 4.2)	8.62	1.33	4.47	2.23	–1.22	1.69	3.75	0.81
III. Total public sector deficit (= 1 + 2 + 3 + 4.1)	10.93	3.16	9.47	5.57	7.24	7.42	4.24	4.32

Sources: Budina and van Wijnbergen (1996); NBR Annual Reports – Statistical Appendix 1998, 1999, 2000; *World Debt Tables* (1998, 2000); IMF, Romanian National Commission for Statistics (1996, 1998); own calculations.

Table 11.3 Assessing the fiscal stance of the Romanian economy, 1992–99

	1992	1993	1994	1995	1996	1997	1998	1999
State budget deficit	4.4	1.7	4.2	4.1	4.9	3.6	2.8	2.5
Total public sector deficit	10.9	3.2	9.4	5.6	7.2	7.4	4.2	4.3
Public debt to GDP ratio	20.3	34.2	20.9	21.7	29.1	32.9	30.1	37.4
Foreign debt to GDP ratio	16.6	16.1	18.4	18.8	24.1	26.9	22.8	25.3
Domestic debt to GDP ratio	3.7	18.1	2.5	2.9	5.0	6.0	7.3	12.1
Inflation rate (end of period)	199.2	295.5	61.7	27.8	56.9	151.4	40.6	54.8
Real growth rate (n)	–8.8	1.5	3.9	7.1	3.9	–5.1	–4.8	–3.2
Foreign net interest rate $r^*(1–T^*)$	7.9	5.3	3.4	3.4	5.0	4.2	3.5	3.8
Domestic net interest rate $r(1–T)$	–26.0	–34.7	–0.4	–0.4	–0.4	–0.2	0.1	0.1

Notes:
[*] T = 38 per cent company income tax rate until 1999; KPMG (2002).

Sources: Budina and van Wijnbergen (1996, 1997); WIIW database; Economist Intelligence Unit database; National Bank of Romania (1998, 2000) – Annual reports, Romanian Ministry of Finance; IMF Staff Country Report No. 98/123; Romanian National Commission for Statistics (1996, 1998); *World Debt Tables* (1998, 2000); own calculations.

5 CONCLUSION

This chapter has discussed several aspects of fiscal policy in Romania. The country's economic development during the transition period is described, as a necessary background for the subsequent policy analysis. Major aspects of the conducted fiscal policy are highlighted, such as the aspect of quasi-fiscal deficits and enterprise arrears. The applied model tries to find a measure for these hidden deficits from the central bank profit and loss account, which is integrated with the central government budget constraint, in order to compute the overall budget deficit for the economy. The empirical part of the discussion focuses on the question of fiscal sustainability. The figures for the state budget deficit are very large, especially for the period 1994–97, while high debt ratios prevailed in the period 1996–99. They can be worrying in so far as the country's growth rate is exceeded by the domestic and foreign interest rates, in which circumstances the debt burden cannot be diminished over time. However, the total public deficit has declined in recent years and declining inflation shows that there is some hope for recovery.[9] Additionally, the government could implement measures aimed at achieving a more sustainable economic development. These measures include stricter rules forcing enterprises to meet their tax payments, enforcement of bankruptcy procedures, and the further development and reform of the tax system. These policies, along with the establishment of an efficient public finance system, could improve the overall economic situation and lead to steady economic growth.

NOTES

1 An earlier version of this chapter appeared in the journal *Post-Communist Economies*, **15** (2), 2 June 2003, pp. 259–75, http://www.tandf.co.uk/journals/carfax/14631377.html under the title 'An Assessment of Fiscal Sustainability in Romania'.

2 The paper was presented at the 15th ERSA Summer Institute on 'Emerging Market Economies and European Economic Integration', Eksjö, Sweden, 10–16 June, 2002.

3 Regarding the expenditure side of the budget, the first years of the transition period brought about large increases in fiscal and quasi-fiscal expenditures; a tighter policy leading to a better fiscal sustainability was, however, started in 1997 (IMF, 2001, pp. 56, 57). In the first years of the decade, the expenditure item 'transfers and subsidies' reached about 23 per cent of GDP. Subsidies were mainly granted to agriculture and to energy-intensive industry by means of directed credits. To this end, the NBR contracted external debt, mounting from 0 per cent of GDP in 1992 to 4.8 per cent in 1996. Additionally, non-performing loans appeared to be a major item in the balance sheets of state-owned banks.

4 The main steps that have to be taken in reforming the Romanian tax system include: simplifying and improving the transparency of the tax system (widening the tax base, especially for VAT and profit tax; reducing the number of exemptions etc.), improving the tax administration and collection system, moving from direct to indirect taxes in order to stimulate investments in the private sector and decentralisation of budget revenues (Romanian Ministry of Finance, 2000a). With regard to VAT, which is currently applied at a rate of 19 per cent, one can say that the VAT system has undergone a positive

development. Nevertheless, there are still some critical issues requiring clarification. The scope of applied exemptions is too broad; the timing of the tax point and the time of reimbursement or the carry-forward option are major factors that can adversely affect the companies' cash flow; frequent changes to laws because of ambiguous provisions and the unstable economic climate create a heavy burden on taxpayers (Veghelyi, 1998). Broadening the base of VAT by reducing the number of exemptions could offer a source of additional revenues that could compensate for losses resulting from rate reductions. An additional important tax is the profit tax of 25 per cent with a provision allowing losses to be carried forward for five years. Income from export activities however, is just subject to a reduced rate of 5 per cent. Last but not least, the global personal income tax must be mentioned. The global taxing system in effect since 1 January 2000 implies the accumulation of all incomes realised by a person through one year, both in and outside the country, irrespective of the income source. Global income includes wage income, income resulting from independent activities, interest, and income from the transfer of goods. Salary tax rates are calculated on a progressive scale, with a top salary rate of 40 per cent that applies to salaries in excess of 5 785 000 lei per month (approximately US$300) (Romanian Ministry of Finance, 2000a). Concerning withholding taxes, interest on State Treasury National Housing Agency bonds and on-sight deposits is exempted from tax payment. The tax on distributed dividends is 5 per cent.

5 The applied model is taken from Budina and van Wijnbergen (1996, 1997) as well as Buiter (1996), and the empirical calculations are extended to the years 1997–99.

6 Focusing on seigniorage revenue to finance government deficits was also possible due to the central bank acting as a monetary and quasi-fiscal agent of the state. The National Bank of Romania offered quasi-fiscal outlays in the form of subsidised credits, access to an overvalued exchange rate, or imposition on commercial banks of reserve requirements bearing below-market interest rates. Additional hidden deficits arose when the central bank committed itself to bailing out banks in financial distress. Therefore, in assessing the evolution of fiscal policy, it is important to consider the general government, including central and local governments, off-budget funds such as the social security fund, and the central bank accounts. In this context note that it will be the unknown (fiscal) deficit rather than the measured budget deficit that will influence policy makers and the public (Tanzi, 1993a, pp. 698, 700).

7 See studies carried out by Solow (1956), Blinder and Solow (1973), Wenzel (1994), Wenzel and Wrede (2000). The model applied is a neo-classical growth model of government activity in a growing economy including the government budget constraint. Under certain assumptions, such as large capital intensity, it can be proven that in a unitary economy, a steady state with positive public debt and positive primary deficit can be asymptotically stable. Additionally, it can be shown that this steady state can also fulfil the golden rule.

8 In 1990, the foreign debt amounted to US$1133 million (see *World Debt Tables*), while GDP was 39 791 million (using an average exchange rate of leu 21.56 = US$1; see NBR data) such that the foreign debt to GDP ratio was only 0.003 per cent.

9 Nevertheless, payment arrears and subsidised prices, especially for energy products, both leading to quasi-fiscal deficits, may still be a problem.

REFERENCES

Albu, L. and E. Pelinescu (1999), 'Sustainability of the Public Debt and Budget Deficit', http://www.worldbank.org.ro/eng/news/conf/.

Blinder, A.S. and R.M. Solow (1973), 'Does Fiscal Policy Matter?', *Journal of Public Economics*, **2**, 319–37.

Borc, C. (1999), 'Why are Domestic Interest Rates so High?' http://www.worldbank.org.ro/eng/news/conf/.

Budina, N. and S. van Wijnbergen (1996), 'Fiscal Deficits, Monetary Reform and Inflation Stabilisation: the Case of Romania', Tinbergen Institute Discussion Paper, TI 96–113/4, pp. 1–37.

Budina, N. and S. van Wijnbergen (1997), 'Fiscal Policies in Eastern Europe', *Oxford Review of Economic Policy*, **13** (2), 47–64.

Budina, N. and S. van Wijnbergen (2000), 'Fiscal Deficits, Monetary Reform and Inflation Stabilisation in Romania', World Bank Policy Research Working Paper, No. 2298, http://wbln0018.worldbank.org/Research/workpapers/nsf.

Buiter, W. (1996), 'Aspects of Fiscal Performance in Some Transition Economies under Fund Supported Programmes', *CEPR Discussion Paper Series*, No. 1535.

Clifton, E.V. and M.S. Kahn (1993), 'Inter-Enterprise Arrears in Transforming Economies: The Case of Romania', *IMF Staff Papers*, **40** (3), 680–99.

Croitoru, L. and C. Tarhoaca (1999), 'Fiscal Policy in Romania', http://www.worldbank.org.ro/eng/news/conf/.

Daianu, D. (1999), 'Structure, Strain and Macroeconomic Dynamic in Romania', http://www.worldbank.org.ro/eng/news/conf/.

Fisher, S. and A. Gelb (1992), 'Issues in the Reform of Socialist Economies', in V. Corbo, F. Coricelli and J. Bossak (eds), *Reforming Central and Eastern European Economies: Initial Results and Challenges*, Washington: The World Bank, pp. 67–82.

Hunya, G. (1998), 'Romania 1990–2002: Stop–Go Transformation', *Communist Economies and Economic Transformation*, **10** (2), 241–58.

Poirot, C. (1996), 'Macroeconomic Policy in a Transitional Environment: Romania', 1989–1994, *Journal of Economic Issues*, **30** (4), 1057–75.

Sinn, H.-W. and H.H. Nachtkamp (1981), 'Die konjunkturellen Wirkungen der Schuldenstrukturpolitik', *Finanzarchiv*, **29**, 279–305.

Solow, R.M. (1956), 'A Contribution to the Theory of Economic Growth', *Quarterly Journal of Economics,* **70**, 65–94.

Tanzi, V. (1993a), 'The Budget Deficit in Transition – A Country Note', *IMF Staff Papers*, **40** (3), 697–707.

Tanzi, V. (1993b), 'Financial Markets and Public Finance in the Transformation Process', in V. Tanzi (ed.), *Transition to Market – Studies in Fiscal Reform.* Washington: International Monetary Fund.

Troschke, M. (1998), 'Rumänien', Osteuropa Institut München (ed.), pp. 65–73.

Veghelyi, M. (1998), 'Main Features of VAT in Romania', *VAT Monitor*, **9** (3), 67–79.

Wenzel, H.-D. (1994), 'Staat und Wachstum – Grundlegende Zusammenhänge zwischen staatlicher Aktivität und gesamtwirtschaftlicher Kapitalbildung', in J. Engelhard and H. Rehkugler (eds), *Strategien für nationale und internationale Märkte*, Wiesbaden: Gabler, pp. 351–78.

Wenzel, H.-D. and M. Wrede (2000), 'Public Debt in a Federation – Growth and Stability', *Jahrbücher für Nationalökonomie und Statistik*, **220** (1), 95–107.

Wissenschaftlicher Beirat beim Bundesministerium der Finanzen (2001), 'Nachhaltigkeit in der Finanzpolitik – Konzepte für eine langfristige Orientierung öffentlicher Haushalte', *Schriftenreihe des Bundesministeriums der Finanzen*, No. 71.

Official Statistics

EBRD (1997), *Transition Report 1997*, London: European Bank for Reconstruction and Development.

EBRD (1999), *Transition Report 1999*, London: European Bank for Reconstruction and Development.
EBRD (2000), *Transition Report 2000*, London: European Bank for Reconstruction and Development.
EBRD (2001), *Transition Report 2001*, London: European Bank for Reconstruction and Development.
EBRD (2002), *Transition Report 2002*, London: European Bank for Reconstruction and Development.
Economist Intelligence Unit database.
EU (1997), *Stellungnahme der Kommission zum Antrag Rumäniens auf Beitritt zur EU*, Brussels: European Commission.
EU (1998), *Agenda 2000, Regular Report from the Commission on Romania's Progress towards Accession*, Brussels: European Commission.
EU (1999), *Agenda 2000, Regular Report from the Commission on Romania's Progress towards Accession*, Brussels: European Commission.
EU (2000a), 'Romania – Screening Results', Chapter 10 – Taxation, Brussels: European Commission.
EU (2000b), *Agenda 2000, Regular Report from the Commission on Romania's Progress towards Accession*, Brussels: European Commission. http://www.imf.org/external/pubs/ft/scr/2991/cr0116.pdf.
IMF (1998), 'Progress with Fiscal Reform in Countries in Transition', International Monetary Fund, *World Economic Outlook*.
IMF (2000a), *World Economic Outlook: Focus on Transition Economies*, in International Monetary Fund, October.
IMF (2000b), IMF Staff Country Report No. 00/159, 'Romania: 2000 Article IV Consultation', December.
http://www.imf.org/external/pubs/ft/scr/2000/cr00159.pdf.
IMF (2001), IMF Country Report No. 01/16, 2001 'Romania: Selected Issues and Statistical Appendix'.
KPMG (2002), Corporate Tax Rate Survey.
OECD (1993), *Romania: An Economic Assessment*, Paris: OECD.
OECD (1998), *Romania*, Paris: OECD Economic Surveys.
Romanian Ministry of Finance (2000a), 'Politica fiscala', Ministerul Finantelor – Directia Impozite Indirecte.
Romanian Ministry of Finance (2000b), 'Sistemul impozitelor si taxelor din Romania', Ministerul Finantelor.
WIIW (Wiener Institut für Internationale Wirtschaftsvergleiche), database.
World Bank (2000), *World Debt Tables*.

12. FDI Inflows to the Transition Economies in Eastern Europe: Magnitude and Potential Determinants

Andreas Johnson

1 INTRODUCTION

1.1 Background

The last two decades have seen a strong increase in FDI flows. It is the transnational companies (TNCs) that are responsible for the majority of these flows. Since the Second World War the majority of the flows have taken place between the developed economies but during recent years the share of the flows going to the developing economies and the transition economies in Eastern Europe has increased. The general attitude towards FDI has changed from the suspicious, negative view that was prevalent from the 1980s to the present situation, where almost all economies allow foreign investment and most of them actively encourage inflows of FDI.[1] While this shift in attitude was gradual for the developing economies, it was more dramatic for the transition economies. As will be described in more detail below, the transition economies very quickly changed their legal frameworks from a situation in which FDI was extremely restricted to one in which potential host countries now actively compete for inflows.

However, irrespective of the type of economy, the reasons for the present optimistic view of FDI are the acceptance of the advantages provided by foreign investment and the failure of inward-looking economic policies and restrictive attitudes to FDI inflows. Examples of advantages that can be provided through FDI include inflow of capital, management skills, job creation, increased exports and transfer of technology. FDI might also have indirect positive effects on the efficiency of the host economy through improved competition. It is believed that these advantages outweigh the possible drawbacks, such as a loss of economic independence when a large part of the production is controlled by foreigners and increasing industrial concentration when a TNC achieves a dominant position in an industry.[2]

Inflow of capital has been vital for the transition process in Eastern Europe. This region[3] is replacing an economic system based on central planning with a system based on market economy and democracy. While developing economies historically needed inflows of capital in order to start building an industry, the transition economies are in a very different position. These economies were already industrialised when the transition process started. The problem for these economies is rather to replace an outdated capital stock through inflows of FDI. There exists a great demand for new capital to be used in the restructuring of enterprises in order to create a competitive market economy that will be able to compete in the Common Market after accession to the EU has been gained. FDI should, however, be evaluated not only by its quantitative effects but also through its qualitative effects. It has been shown that FDI has a potential to transfer technology to the host country; see for example Sjöholm (1999). This ability can play a very important role for the transition economies in reducing the technology gap between these economies and the developed economies. The other advantages of FDI mentioned above naturally also apply to the transition economies.

It can thus be concluded that FDI provides many potential advantages to the transition economies. But what factors are important for the volume of FDI that an economy receives? Can economic policies affect the volume of flows? Are FDI inflows into the transition economies determined by the same factors that are believed to be important for developed economies, or do the special economic conditions in the transition economies result in other determinants being important?

1.2 Objectives

The chapter has two objectives. The first is to illuminate the magnitude of FDI inflows in the transition economies of Eastern Europe. This is done through presenting data for FDI into these economies since the beginning of transition. The second objective is to analyse what conditions in the host country economies have had an impact on the inflow of FDI.

1.3 Outline

Section 2 starts by describing the conditions for FDI during the period of planned economy and how the policy towards FDI changed when the transition process started. Data for the inflows of FDI during the transition period are presented. Section 3 presents the theoretical framework used in this study. On the basis of this framework, determinants that are believed to be important for the volume of FDI inflows to the region are selected. In

Section 4 the selected determinants will be discussed in detail and Section 5 concludes.

2 THE MAGNITUDE OF FDI IN THE TRANSITION ECONOMIES

This section starts by describing (subsection 2.1) the conditions for FDI inflows into Eastern Europe during the period of planned economy until the eve of transition. This is followed by subsection 2.2, which describes and presents data for the FDI inflows that have occurred since the transition to a market economy system began. Subsection 2.3 provides an indication of where the flows of FDI to the region are coming from. Subsection 2.4 focuses on the outward flows of FDI from the transition economies. The final subsection discusses the level of FDI in the transition economies.

2.1 The Heritage of an Administrative Economic System

Before the transition from an administrative economic system to a market-dominated economy system started in Eastern Europe, the inflows of FDI into this region were at a minimal level. The economic system and the belief in economic self-sufficiency, as well as the restricted policy adopted towards activities of foreign companies, kept both FDI and trade with countries outside the sphere of planned economies at a minimum. McMillan (1993a) suggests that it was the economic system itself rather than the specific FDI policies that deterred inflows of FDI. The system of central planning and administratively set prices and wages simply created an environment that severely constrained the manoeuvring possibility of potential foreign TNC entrants. However, there existed differences in degree between individual economies. The Soviet Union itself was the most centralised and collectivised economy, and other economies were less centralised. Hungary, for example, had already started to experiment with economic reforms during the 1960s, and at the beginning of the 1970s joint-venture laws that allowed FDI were introduced; see Gutman (1993). It should also be pointed out that while the planned economies of Eastern Europe in general had a very negative attitude towards FDI, they were at the same time attracted to the technology transfer that it might bring about, as pointed out by McMillan (1993b).

Naturally, to achieve any inflows of FDI the host country must have a regulatory framework that allows foreign direct investments. It is necessary to distinguish between this type of framework and policies that are designed to actively encourage FDI inflows. The former might be called an 'enabling framework' while the latter might be referred to as incentive policies. Before transition began, most Eastern European economies lacked such an enabling framework. This fact, together with the negative attitudes to activities of foreign enterprises discussed above, resulted in a stock of inward FDI that was at a minimum level when transition began.

2.2 FDI Inflows During the Transition Period

The start of the transition process led to a complete turnaround of FDI policy. The East European governments started to eliminate the existing disincentives through the establishment of new foreign investment laws creating enabling frameworks. This has developed into a situation where all transition economies are now actively encouraging inflows of FDI through incentive policies such as reduction of corporate taxes, tax holidays and provision of social amenities. There have been substantial inflows of FDI during the 1990s.

To get a more complete picture it could be rewarding to include a short description of the global development of FDI. The changes in the flows of FDI going to the transition economies can then be compared to the development in the rest of the world. Therefore, Table 12.1 presents some basic data on FDI stocks including the world total as well as data for different types of economies and regions. The last row presents the stock of FDI in Central and Eastern Europe as the percentage share of the world total. The intention is to provide an overview of both the global and the regional development since the start of the transition process.

Table 12.1 Inward stocks of FDI (millions of US dollars)

Region	1990	1995	2000	2001
World	1 871 594	2 911 725	6 258 263	6 845 723
Developed countries	1 382 978	2 021 303	4 124 261	4 504 122
Developing countries	484 954	849 915	2 002 173	2 181 249
Central and Eastern Europe (CEE)	3 661	40 508	131 829	160 352
CEE share of world total (%)	0.2	1.4	2.1	2.3

Source: UNCTAD (2002), Annex Table B.3.

Table 12.1 clearly shows the dominance of the developed economies as far as the total stock of FDI is concerned; in 2001 around 66 per cent of the world stock of FDI was located in developed economies. It can also be seen from the table that the world stock of FDI grew by approximately 266 per cent from 1990 to 2001.

Turning to the transition economies, it is clear that they have a small but increasing share of the total FDI stock. At the start of the transition in 1990 the total inward stock of FDI in Central and Eastern Europe (CEE) was less than 1 per cent of the world total. Reasons for this extraordinary situation were discussed in the previous subsection.

However, the growth rate of 4280 per cent of the FDI stock in Central and Eastern Europe between 1990 and 2001 was much higher than the global rate of increase and the transition economies increased their share of the total stock of FDI to 2.3 per cent in 2001. Of course this large increase for the transition economies is mostly explained by a very low initial level. Still, a comparison between the growth of FDI stocks in the world and in the transition economies from 1995 to 2001 reveals that the latter group had a much higher increase of 296 per cent compared to a global growth of 135 per cent. Thus the transition economies have a small share of the total stock but are in the process of catching up due to a larger share of total flows.

A disaggregation of total FDI inflows to individual transition economies is necessary in order to allow for country comparisons.[4] Table 12.2 presents inflows of FDI for individual transition economies during the 1990s.

According to Table 12.2, Hungary and the Czech Republic were the most successful economies in attracting FDI inflows during the first years. Poland was slower in attracting FDI inflows but in 1996 inflows into this economy overtook the flows into Hungary and the Czech Republic. Studying the total inflows into the selected economies, there was a large increase in the inflows in 1995. A closer inspection of the table reveals that almost three-quarters of this increase was accounted for by the Czech Republic and Hungary. In the case of Hungary there are indications that the increase was a result of a large number of privatisations in 1995, as suggested by the discussion in section 4.3.

Table 12.3 uses the data presented in Table 12.2 to calculate FDI inflows per capita for the same time period and economies. This is done in order to take the size of the economies into account.

From Table 12.3 one can conclude that economies located close to the European Union such as the Czech Republic and Hungary have been more successful in attracting FDI than some of the more distant economies such as Russia or Ukraine.

Table 12.2 FDI inflows into selected transition economies (millions of US dollars)

Country	1992	1993	1994	1995	1996	1997	1998	1999	2000
Bulgaria	41	40	105	98	138	507	537	789	1 003
Croatia	13	102	110	109	486	347	835	1 445	1 086
Czech Rep	983	563	749	2 526	1 276	1 275	3 591	6 234	4 943
Estonia	80	156	212	199	111	130	574	222	324
Hungary	1 471	2 328	1 097	4 410	2 279	1 741	1 555	1 720	1 090
Latvia	..	50	279	245	379	515	303	331	400
Lithuania	..	30	31	72	152	328	921	478	375
Poland	284	580	542	1 134	2 741	3 041	4 966	6 348	8 171
Romania	73	87	341	417	415	1 267	2 079	1 025	1 051
Russia	..	..	..	1 460	1 657	1 679	1 496	1 103	–496
Slovakia	100	107	236	194	199	84	374	701	2 058
Slovenia	113	111	131	183	188	340	250	144	110
Ukraine	..	..	151	257	516	581	747	489	594
Total for selected economies	3 158	4 154	3 984	11 304	10 537	11 435	18 228	21 029	20 709

Notes:
'..' indicates that data are not available.
Negative figure indicates disinvestment; foreign-owned facilities have been closed down.

Source: EBRD (2002), Table A.3.9, selected economies.

Table 12.3 Per capita FDI inflows into selected transition economies (US dollars)

Country	1992	1993	1994	1995	1996	1997	1998	1999	2000
Bulgaria	4.8	4.7	12.5	11.7	16.6	61.1	65.5	96.2	123.8
Croatia	2.9	22.2	23.9	23.2	108.0	75.4	185.6	321.1	236.1
Czech Rep.	95.4	54.7	72.7	245.2	123.9	123.8	348.6	605.2	479.9
Estonia	52.3	104.0	141.3	132.7	74.0	86.7	410.0	158.6	231.4
Hungary	142.8	226.0	107.5	432.3	223.4	170.7	154.0	172.0	109.0
Latvia	..	19.2	111.6	98.0	151.6	206.0	126.3	137.9	166.7
Lithuania	..	8.1	8.4	19.5	41.1	88.6	248.9	129.2	101.4
Poland	7.4	15.1	14.0	29.4	71.0	78.6	128.3	164.0	211.1
Romania	3.2	3.8	15.0	18.4	18.4	56.1	92.4	45.6	47.1
Russia	..	..	..	9.8	11.2	11.4	10.2	7.6	neg.
Slovak Rep.	18.9	20.2	44.5	35.9	36.9	15.6	69.3	129.8	381.1
Slovenia	56.5	55.5	65.5	91.5	94.0	170.0	125.0	72.0	55.0
Ukraine	..	..	2.9	5.0	10.1	11.5	14.9	9.8	12.0

Notes:
'..' Indicates that data are not available.
'neg.' Indicates disinvestment.

Sources: Calculated based on EBRD (2002), Table A.3.9 and population data from EBRD, various issues.

Studies of FDI inflows have pointed to the large differences in the amount of FDI that the transition economies managed to attract during the first years of the transition process; see for example McMillan (1993a), Meyer (1995) and Lankes and Venables (1996). Table 12.3 suggests that these differences in attractiveness have continued during the second half of the 1990s. Therefore, there should now be substantial differences in the stocks of FDI that the transition economies have managed to attract. Whether this is indeed the case can be answered by Table 12.4, which presents cumulative inflows of FDI in total as well as per capita to selected transition economies. The rightmost column presents data for the inward stock of FDI as a share of GDP. The countries have been ranked according to cumulative FDI inflows per capita.

The data presented in Table 12.4 describe the amount of FDI that individual transition economies have attracted. According to the third column of the table, it is Poland that has received the largest absolute volume of inflows of FDI, followed by the Czech Republic and Hungary. Despite its size, the Russian economy has only the fifth largest stock of FDI.

Table 12.4 Measures of the ability to attract FDI for selected transition economies

Country	Cumulative FDI inflows 1989–2001 per capita (US$)	Cumulative FDI-inflows 1989–2001 (millions of US$)	FDI inward stock as share of GDP in 2000 (%)
Czech Rep.	2 615	26 960	42.6
Hungary	2 137	21 751	43.4
Estonia	1 727	2 351	53.2
Croatia	1 315	5 858	27.1
Latvia	1 138	2 670	29.1
Slovakia	1 042	5 629	24.2
Slovenia	934	1 847	15.5
Poland	890	34 426	21.3
Lithuania	813	2 826	20.6
Bulgaria	491	3 961	26.4
Romania	356	7 928	17.7
Belarus	132	1 315	11.9
Ukraine	84	4 104	12.1
Russia	47	6 762	7.7
Uzbekistan	30	768	..

Note: '..' indicates that data are not available.

Sources: EBRD (2002), Table A.3.9 and UNCTAD (2002), Annex Table B.6.

However, measuring FDI per capita provides a somewhat different picture. According to this measure it is the Czech Republic that has the highest inflow of FDI while Poland ends up somewhere in the middle and Russia turns out to be among the least successful economies in attracting FDI. Estonia, on the other hand, is among the most successful attractors of foreign investment. But what really stand out through a per capita comparison are the large differences among individual economies. The Czech Republic and Hungary have managed to attract around three times more FDI inflows than Poland, almost six times more FDI than Bulgaria and Romania and as much as 30 times more than Russia or Ukraine.

The FDI stock measured as a share of GDP reinforces the indication that there are huge differences in the success of attraction of FDI between different economies. With an FDI stock constituting 53.2 per cent of its GDP, Estonia is the most successful economy, followed by Hungary and the Czech Republic. A comparison with Russia is striking: Russia's inward stock constituted as little as 7.7 per cent of GDP in 2000.

It can thus be concluded from this study of recent data that the large differences in FDI inflows between individual transition economies that existed during the earlier part of the 1990s have continued during the second half of the 1990s. Section 4 will suggest and discuss possible explanations for these huge differences in the transition economies' abilities to attract FDI.

2.3 Geographical Sources of FDI Flows to the Transition Economies

An interesting question is where the foreign investments to the transition economies are coming from: which are the most important source countries? Table 12.5 presents the most important geographical sources for FDI inflows to the region during the year 2000.

It must be remembered that Table 12.5 only depicts the FDI flows of one particular year and should be treated accordingly. However, some indications of the sources of FDI inflows can still be found. The six most important geographical sources of FDI in 2000 have been included in Table 12.5. Japan has been added to these six due to that country's importance for the world economy. The Netherlands had significant flows to many of the transition economies, as had the USA. Austrian flows were important mostly for the Czech Republic, Croatia and Slovakia. Sweden was responsible for 7.5 per cent of the FDI flows to the selected economies. Still, Sweden was a very important investor in Estonia and Latvia, with more than 40 per cent of the FDI inflows. The flows of FDI from France were rather insignificant except for Poland and Romania. Germany was an important investor in many of the transition economies. It seems clear that Japan plays a very minor role for investments in the region. With the exception of the United States, the foreign investments in the region are dominated by European economies. Together the five European economies included in the table accounted for 55 per cent of the total flows to the region in 2000; when Japan and the United States are included the figure rises to around 71 per cent.

Table 12.5 Geographical sources of FDI inflows into selected transition economies (per cent of total inflows) in 2000

Country	Austria	France	Germany	Japan	Netherl.	Sweden	USA
Bulgaria	8.1	2.6	6.5	0.1	1.5	0	3.4
Croatia	16.4	0.3	7.8	..	4.6	2.5	11.4
Czech Rep.	20.4	3.7	22.0	1.4	21.9	2.8	3.2
Estonia	neg.	1.8	3.3	0.3	4.3	46.2	0
Hungary	1.2	4.0	18.0	0.9	29.5	2.6	13.5
Latvia	neg.	0	28.1	0	1.8	40.4	7.0
Poland	3.5	38.2	neg.	1.0	9.4	11.7	20.7
Romania	7.4	11.9	32.5	0	26.5	neg.	neg.
Russia	0.5	2.2	7.7	2.4	13.8	5.8	28.0
Slovakia	12.7	0.8	35.7	..	33.5	..	3.2
Ukraine	..	..	1.3	..	10.3	..	7.7
Total	6.8	17.0	9.1	1.1	14.6	7.5	15.3

Notes:
'..' indicates that no data are available.
'neg.' indicates disinvestment.

Source: Constructed from UNCTAD (2001), Annex Table A.I.5.

2.4 Outward Flows of FDI from the Transition Economies

One characteristic of most of the developed economies is that they simultaneously have both substantial inflows and outflows of FDI. Developing economies tend to have larger inflows than outflows. What about the transition economies? Table 12.6 presents data for the outward flows of FDI from the transition economies. A negative sign indicates disinvestment; production facilities abroad owned by the transition economy have been closed down.

Table 12.6 shows that the transition economies are more similar to the developing economies than the developed economies as far as outgoing FDI is concerned. The outflows of FDI from the transition economies are insignificant compared to the inflows, with the exception of Russia. It is noticeable that economies that have had large inflows of FDI, such as Hungary, Poland and the Czech Republic, also dominate the outflows of FDI from the region.

Table 12.6 Outward flows of FDI from selected transition economies (millions of US dollars)

Country	1995	1996	1997	1998	1999	2000	1995–2000
Russia	358	771	2597	1011	1963	3050	9750
Hungary	43	–3	431	481	249	532	1733
Poland	42	53	45	316	31	126	613
Czech Rep.	37	153	25	127	90	118	550
Estonia	2	40	137	6	83	157	425
Lithuania	1	..	27	4	9	13	54
Ukraine	10	–5	42	–4	7	1	51
Latvia	–65	3	6	54	17	8	23
Romania	3	2	..	–9	16	–11	1
Bulgaria	–8	–29	–2	..	17	–2	–24
Slovakia	8	52	95	146	–372	23	–48
Total for selected economies	431	1037	3403	2132	2110	3915	13 028

Note: '..' indicates that data are not available.

Source: UNCTAD (2001), Annex Table B.2.

An explanation for the small outflows of FDI from the region could be that the transition economies still lack enterprises that are competitive enough and have the knowledge to be able to benefit from investing abroad. As time passes the competitiveness should improve and the outward flows of FDI from the region should increase.

The substantial outflows from Russia merit a comment. It is unlikely that all of these flows constitute FDI. A more realistic interpretation of these flows of capital is that some of them constitute portfolio investments resulting from capital flight out of Russia. Due to measurement problems they have been included as outward flows of FDI. However, as suggested by EBRD (2000), there has also been Russian foreign direct investment in some of the former Soviet republics in order to exploit natural resources.

2.5 The Level of FDI

Linked to the above description of flows is the question of whether investments into the region have been as large as could be expected. At the beginning of the transition period many experts anticipated huge inflows of FDI into Central and Eastern Europe. It has been proposed that the actual level of FDI in the Eastern European countries is disappointingly low. This opinion is shared by McMillan (1993a), Meyer (1995, 1998) and Sinn and Weichenrieder (1997). But what is meant by 'too low FDI levels'? The argument of these studies is based on the observation that FDI flows to other emerging market economies in other parts of the world such as South East Asia were much higher than the flows to Central and Eastern Europe. No empirical analysis is used to support the argument that FDI flows are too low. In contrast to these studies is Brenton et al. (1999). This study differs from the earlier ones in that it tries to determine empirically whether the stock of FDI in the region is reasonable. The study uses a gravity model approach to provide long-term estimates of FDI levels for the Eastern European economies. Brenton et al. (1999, p. 118) conclude that 'the stock of FDI in CEEC countries diverges little from the normal pattern we would expect after controlling for the main determinants of FDI stocks throughout the world.' The determinants that are taken into account include GDP, economic policy in the host country and distance.

Table 12.7 tries to contribute to this discussion by presenting data for the inward stock of FDI as a share of GDP in 1995 and 2000 for individual economies and country groups.

For individual economies there are large variations in the share of FDI in GDP, among both transition and developed economies. Russia, Japan and the USA have particularly low shares. However, division of countries into groups provides data that are more consistent. The figure for the developed economies' country groups is very low. Most likely, this figure is lowered by the inclusion of the United States and Japan. The inward stock of FDI as a share of GDP in the European Union in 2000, on the other hand, is 30.3 per cent. According to the table it is the economies of South East Asia that have the largest stocks of FDI compared to GDP. This is in line with the arguments of the studies mentioned earlier.

What about Central and Eastern Europe? This region has a low figure of only 18.9 per cent in 2000. In fact, even the group of least developed economies had a larger stock of FDI. Based on the data presented in Table 12.7, the transition economies do seem to have attracted low inflows of FDI.

Comparing 1995 to 2000, it is striking that the stock of FDI as a share of GDP has increased for every country or country group included in Table 12.7. However, of the country groups, Central and Eastern Europe has the highest increase from 1995 to 2000. Even though this region might only have achieved a low level of inward FDI stock compared to other country groups, Table 12.7 further strengthens the conclusion that the transition economies of Eastern Europe are in the process of catching up.

Table 12.7 Inward stock of FDI as a share of GDP in 1995 and 2000

Individual economies/groups	Inward FDI stock as a share of GDP in 1995	Inward FDI stock as a share of GDP in 2000
Transition economies		
Czech Republic	14.1	42.6
Poland	6.2	21.3
Romania	3.2	17.7
Russia	1.6	7.7
Ukraine	2.5	12.1
China	19.6	32.3
Developed economies		
France	12.3	19.9
Germany	7.8	24.1
Japan	0.6	1.1
Sweden	12.9	36.1
United Kingdom	17.6	30.5
USA	7.3	12.4
Country groups		
South East Asia	18.9	36.4
Developing economies	15.3	30.9
European Union	12.9	30.3
Africa	15.6	25.5
Developed economies	8.9	17.1
Least developed economies	11.3	19.4
Central and Eastern Europe	5.4	18.9

Source: UNCTAD (2002), Annex Table B.6.

3 THEORETICAL FRAMEWORK

This section provides a theoretical framework for the last half of the chapter. The intention is that the chosen framework (Dunning's OLI-paradigm – ownership, location and internalisation) should be helpful in identifying host-country determinants that can explain the large differences in FDI inflows to the transition economies that were identified in section 2. Subsection 3.1 provides a short discussion of the development of the theories of FDI. Subsection 3.2 provides a short description of John Dunning's OLI paradigm that has been chosen as a framework for this study. Subsection 3.3 selects host-country determinants that are believed to be important for FDI inflows.

3.1 General Theories of FDI

This section has no ambition to provide an all-inclusive description of existing FDI theories. Readers who are interested in a more thorough discussion are referred to Cantwell (1991) and Meyer (1998), both of which provide useful descriptions of the development of different FDI theories.

There are several loosely defined 'schools' of FDI theories that attempt to provide explanations for the phenomenon of FDI. All theories of FDI have been developed during the post-war period. Two examples of earlier theories are the so-called capital markets approach, which treated FDI as portfolio investments (Aliber, 1970), and the development cycle theory, which is loosely based on Vernon's theory of the production cycle (Vernon, 1966). Most of the early theories have by now been discarded or significantly modified as the development of the world economy, as well as empirical studies, has found them to be unsuitable as explanations for foreign investment.

A theory that has managed to remain influential is Stephen Hymer's theory of firm-specific advantages (Hymer, 1976). His argument is that, to overcome the information advantage that domestic enterprises have over foreign firms, a foreign firm that contemplates investment must have some offsetting firm-specific advantage. Examples of such advantages can be scale economies, brand name, managerial skills or superior technology. John Dunning developed Hymer's ideas, leading to the so-called OLI paradigm of FDI.

3.2 The OLI Paradigm

The attempt that has come closest to success in providing a general theory of FDI and has been chosen for this study is Dunning's OLI paradigm. The paradigm was first presented in Dunning (1977). According to the OLI paradigm a firm's decision to invest in a foreign country is determined by the existence of three types of advantages, namely ownership, locational and internalisation advantages; hence the acronym OLI. In order for FDI to take place all three advantages must be present simultaneously. To cancel out the disadvantage of operating in a foreign country a firm must have an ownership advantage, such as superior technology. Ownership advantages can be moved between different locations and can therefore be transferred to a foreign country. For FDI to take place, it must be profitable for the firm to internalise the ownership advantage, rather than leaving the market to take care of the transaction. If an internalisation advantage is missing, the firm will serve the foreign market through exports or licensing rather than through investing in order to produce locally. There must also exist some kind of locational advantage that is specific to the geographical location and that will trigger the actual investment. An example of a locational advantage is supply of cheap labour or a large local market demand. Locational advantages can never be transferred to another location.

3.3 Locational Advantages in Eastern Europe

To allow the focus to be put on the host economies in Eastern Europe, ownership and internalisation advantages are excluded from the analysis. Therefore this study only chooses potential host-country determinants of FDI among variables that can be said to constitute locational advantages according to Dunning's terminology. For this study it is therefore taken as given that the TNCs that invest in Eastern Europe possess both ownership and internalisation advantages. The actual investment is therefore determined by variations in locational advantages among the host economies.

Many studies have been done on determinants of FDI, although only a limited number of them have dealt with Eastern Europe due to short time series and other data problems. Table 12.8 presents determinants of various kinds that have been used in empirical studies of all kinds of regions and their expected relationship to FDI inflows into the host economy.

The intention of Table 12.8 is to help to identify variables that can be argued to constitute locational advantages among the multitude of determinants that have been used in empirical studies. These variables have been designated by a dot in the second column. The remaining variables either constitute ownership or internalisation advantages or are variables that are difficult to specify according to the OLI paradigm. These variables have been designated by a dot in the third column. The rightmost column presents the expected relationship between each determinant and FDI flows.[5] The exchange rate, policies of government and trade flow variables have been assigned either plus or minus signs since the effects of these variables could be either positive or negative.

The focus of this chapter on host-country conditions implies that ownership and internalisation advantages are not discussed. It is argued that the locational advantages presented in Table 12.8 all constitute potential host-country determinants of FDI inflows.

Among the many locational advantages that are listed in Table 12.8, which would be most important for the transition economies in Eastern Europe? As far as advantages that could explain the differences in the amount of FDI attracted to the various Central and Eastern European economies are concerned, transition performance is an obvious candidate. Economies that have come far towards turning into a market economy should be able to attract more FDI than economies that are lagging behind in the transition process.

Table 12.8 Determinants of FDI used in empirical studies

Determinant	Potential locational advantage	Other advantage	Expected relationship to FDI inflows
Agglomeration	•		+
Capital costs	•		–
Cost of borrowing	•		–
Country risk	•		–
Cultural proximity		•	+
Exchange rates		•	–/+
Firm size	•	•	+
Firm profits	•		+
GDP per capita	•		+
Geographical distance		•	–
Information cost	•		–
Infrastructure	•		+
Labour costs	•		–
Market size (GDP)	•		+
Market size growth (GDP growth)	•		+
Non-tariff barriers	•		+
Policies of government	•		–/+
Population	•		+
Rates of return		•	+
Tariff barriers	•		+
Trade flows		•	–/+
Transition performance	•		+

Source: Compiled by the author.

Another determinant that should be important for the magnitude of FDI inflows to the transition economies is privatisation. Foreign investment has been an important source for the new capital that is needed in the privatisation and restructuring process of the large number of state-owned firms in the transition economies. Both the type and speed of the privatisation process in individual economies should affect the amount of FDI that the host country receives.

Based on empirical work, it is clear that market size should be an important determinant of the inflows of FDI for all types of economies, including transitional ones, since this variable is used in almost all studies and mostly turns out to be statistically significant.

Therefore, the following three host-country determinants have been selected for a more detailed study:

- transition performance
- privatisation
- market size.

These three host-country determinants are discussed in section 4. The intention is to analyse whether these determinants can help to explain the large differences in the amount of FDI that individual transition economies have managed to attract.

4 HOST-COUNTRY DETERMINANTS OF FDI IN THE TRANSITION ECONOMIES

4.1 Approach

The aim of this section is to discuss the three host-country determinants that were selected in section 3.3, namely transition performance, privatisation and market size. Can differences in these determinants explain the large variation of FDI inflows to the individual economies in the region that was described in section 2? The discussion in this section is based on Table 12.4 and the intention is to try to explain the differences in this table. A non-technical approach is used. The economies that are highly ranked according to FDI inflows in Table 12.4 should have something in common in their performance as measured by the selected determinants. An assessment of each individual determinant is carried out to try to determine its potential effect on the variations in FDI inflows.

4.2 Transition Performance

An explanation for the large differences in FDI inflows can be the substantial variations in the speed and success of the transition process in individual economies. Transition is the replacement of one economic system by another, in the present case the replacement of an administrative economic system by a market economy system. The transition process in Eastern Europe was briefly described above. It is debatable whether this process as of 2003 has been completed or not. But this question might in itself be wrong. Roland (2000, p. xix) argues that 'nobody can tell for sure how transitional the transition is or whether the countries engaged in this process will end up transformed into successful capitalist economies.' However, it is very obvious that some countries such as Hungary and Poland have come much farther towards market economies than others such as Russia and the Ukraine. The fact that Russia only recently (1999) has turned a trend of decreasing GDP into an increase is one indication that this economy is lagging behind other economies such as Poland in the transition process.

A successful transition improves the conditions for engaging in profitable economic activities in the economy. The further a host economy has moved from being a planned economy into being a market economy, the easier it will be for a TNC to operate profitably. This implies that the conditions for foreign enterprises should improve and their incentives to invest should become stronger as the transition process progresses.

What factors are usually taken into account when judging the progress of an economy's transition process? The EBRD tries to assess transition progress in individual economies by constructing transition indicators. These indicators include measures of large- and small-scale privatisation of enterprises, restructuring of enterprises, price liberalisation, trade liberalisation, infrastructure, legal reform and the exchange system as well as financial indicators such as banking reform and interest rate liberalisation. The highest possible score for an indicator represents the standards and performance of advanced industrialised economies. The higher the score on a transition indicator, the closer the transition economy is to a market economy.

Which of these indicators would be important for a foreign firm contemplating investment in a transition economy? Not all of the available indicators might be relevant for a TNC. Price liberalisation should be fundamental; the TNC of course wants to be able to set its own prices. A situation where prices are controlled by the government would restrict the foreign firm's ability to operate. Since FDI implies production by the TNC in the host country, trade liberalisation and the foreign exchange system is also very important. The TNC wants to be able to export the goods it produces and also import intermediate goods to use in its production without restrictions of various kind such as tariffs. It is also important that there exist well-established financial institutions providing full banking services and securities markets. The existence of a developed and effective commercial law is necessary for the operations of a TNC.

Therefore, the following transition indicators are suggested to be important for TNCs:

- price liberalisation
- trade and foreign exchange system
- financial institutions
- commercial law.

The approach is to calculate an average of these four selected indicators presented in EBRD (2001) for the transition economies. The intention is that this constructed measure should represent the attractiveness of a host country for a foreign firm contemplating investment. Economies that have a high average have come close to a market economy and should therefore be more attractive for foreign investment. Hence, they should also receive large inflows of FDI. Table 12.9 presents the average of the transition indicators for the selected economies.

Table 12.9 Transition performance and FDI inflows

Country	Cumulative FDI inflows per capita 1989–2001 (US dollars)	Constructed measure of transition progress
Czech Republic	2 615	3.4
Hungary	2 137	3.8
Estonia	1 727	3.6
Croatia	1 315	3.2
Latvia	1 138	3.2
Slovakia	1 042	3.0
Slovenia	934	3.4
Poland	890	3.4
Lithuania	813	3.4
Bulgaria	491	3.2
Romania	356	3.2
Belarus	132	2.0
Ukraine	84	2.6
Russia	47	2.6
Uzbekistan	30	2.2

Source: Compiled from EBRD (2002).

Interpretation of the constructed measure of transition progress is somewhat arbitrary. As has been explained, the measure is an average of four different indicators. These indicators all range from 1 to 4 and they are given quite detailed interpretations by the EBRD.[6] These interpretations differ between the indicators. For example, a '3' on price liberalisation means that substantial progress has been made on price liberalisation while a '3' on trade and foreign exchange system implies removal of almost all quantitative and administrative import and export restrictions. However, for our purposes a '4' on the measure of transition progress represents approximately the same standard as in a developed economy while a '1' indicates little progress from the standard of an administrative economy.

According to Table 12.9, it is Hungary that has come closest to the standards of a developed economy. As expected, Belarus, Russia, Ukraine and Uzbekistan have the longest way to go to become market economies. In general, there seems to be a correlation between the amount of FDI inflows and the constructed measure of transition progress.

Table 12.10 Private sector share of GDP and FDI inflows

Country	Cumulative FDI inflows per capita 1989–2001 (US dollars)	Private sector share of GDP in 2001 (%)	Private sector share of employment in 2001 (%)
Czech Republic	2 615	80	70
Hungary	2 137	80	..
Estonia	1 727	75	..
Croatia	1 315	60	..
Latvia	1 138	65	..
Slovakia	1 042	80	75
Slovenia	934	65	..
Poland	890	75	72
Lithuania	813	70	..
Bulgaria	491	70	80.8
Romania	356	65	..
Belarus	132	20	..
Ukraine	84	60	..
Russia	47	70	..
Uzbekistan	30	45	..

Note: '..' indicates no data are available.

Source: EBRD (2002).

Another way of measuring the degree of transition towards a market economy might be to study the development of the private sector share of GDP. The private sector share gives a rough indication of how far the transition process has come in an economy. Table 12.10 presents the private sector share of GDP in the transition economies.

The best two economies in attracting FDI, the Czech Republic and Hungary, also have the largest private shares of GDP. The least successful economies tend to have smaller shares. In general, there seems to be a correlation between the amount of FDI inflows and the size of the private share, even though it is far from perfect.

This subsection has provided indications that there is a positive relationship between an economy's progress in transition and the amount of FDI that it has received. This fact should help to explain the success of such countries as Hungary and the Czech Republic and the failure of Russia and the former Soviet republics.

4.3 Privatisation

Private ownership is a cornerstone of a market economy. Therefore privatisation of state-owned enterprises constitutes a fundamental part of the transition process. Privatisation is important in order to increase the efficiency of the existing companies through new management that will introduce more efficient production processes and make sure that the goods produced are in line with what is actually demanded. However, the success of privatisation is affected by how privatisation programmes are designed. The choice of privatisation process affects the amount of FDI since privatisation can take place through direct sales to foreign TNCs. In general, the privatisation process starts by setting up a state agency responsible for the programme. This agency will first make sure that proper legislation is enacted. It then has to identify the enterprises to be privatised as well as decide on the share structure. The most delicate decision, and the decision that determines the impact on FDI inflows, is that on how to distribute the shares to new owners.

In developed economies, it is not uncommon that citizens take part in privatisations and buy shares in the state-owned firms. However, the domestic savings in the transition economies are far too small to make more than a very marginal contribution in filling the demand for new capital involved in the privatisation processes. Privatisation has to be solved in some other way. There are several different alternatives, such as direct sales to outsiders, voucher-based mass privatisation or so-called management and employee buyouts. Holland and Pain (1998) study the ten EU accession economies plus Croatia and find that the different methods of privatisation used in individual economies are fundamental for the size of the inflows of FDI. They find that the alternative that has the largest effect on FDI inflows is sales to outside owners.

However, it is difficult to assess the impact of privatisation on FDI inflows for individual economies. Most of the transition economies have used more than one alternative for privatisation. Therefore it is difficult to divide the transition economies according to chosen privatisation alternative. It is also difficult to get hold of data measuring the amount of privatisation that has taken place through sales to foreign firms.

For the purposes of this section, a comparison between Hungary and Poland might be instructive in showing the importance of privatisation for FDI inflows. As can be seen in Table 12.11, Hungary managed to attract substantial inflows at the beginning of the transition process, while Poland did not. Hungary had fast privatisation during the early years while the process was more gradual in Poland. According to EBRD (2001), large-scale privatisation in Hungary began as early as 1990. This should be an important explanation for the differences in inflows during the first years. However, the inflows into Hungary reached a peak in 1995 and then decreased sharply and stabilised at a lower level. This is most likely an indication of the one-off effect of privatisation: when privatisation has been completed, an important motive for FDI inflows disappears. This is supported by the data for Poland, which also show a strong increase in inflows a few years later, delayed due to a slower pace of privatisation.

Table 12.11 Inflows of FDI (millions of US dollars) and privatisation revenues for Hungary and Poland

Country	1992	1993	1994	1995	1996	1997	1998	1999
Hungary								
Inflows of FDI	1 471	2 328	1 097	4 410	2 279	1 741	1 555	1 720
Privatisation revenues*	3.9	8.7	12.7	20.8	23.4	27.4	28.5	29.6
Poland								
Inflows of FDI	284	580	542	1 134	2 741	3 041	4 966	6 348
Privatisation revenues*	0.4	0.9	1.7	2.6	3.6	5.1	6.4	7.7

Note: * cumulative, as % of GDP.

Source: EBRD (2001), Table A.3.9 and Country assessments.

Is it possible to reinforce this argument with other data? Table 12.11 presents the inflows of FDI to Poland and Hungary that were reported in Table 12.2 along with the revenues from privatisation as a share of GDP.

During 1995, Hungary had a large increase in inflows of FDI. What happened to privatisation revenues during this year? In 1995 the cumulative privatisation revenues in Hungary as a share of GDP almost doubled. After 1995, the inflows of FDI to Hungary decreased and the privatisation revenue share of GDP started to increase at a slower rate. Studying the same data for Poland allows a similar interpretation. There seems to be a strong positive relationship between the amount of FDI inflows and the privatisation revenues. Adding the least successful economies such as Russia and the Ukraine to Table 12.11 would support this conclusion further.

Based on the analysis in this subsection, it is concluded that privatisation can explain many of the differences in the amount of FDI that the transition economies have attracted.

4.4 Market Demand

An important motive for a transnational firm to perform a direct investment abroad is so-called market seeking. A market-seeking firm invests in a foreign market in order to meet the existing local demand for products. As was mentioned in section 3.3, variables measuring market demand have turned out to be significant in almost all studies of host-country determinants of FDI. Examples of such studies are Culem (1988), Grosse and Trevino (1996) and Brenton et al. (1999). The most common variable that is used to measure market demand is GDP in absolute value or per capita. Some studies use the growth rate of these variables. The general result of earlier empirical studies is that greater market demand has a significant positive effect on the size of FDI inflows. There are two possible influences of market demand on FDI inflows. The first is naturally the size of the market, as it can be measured by absolute GDP. The second influence can be argued to come from the 'quality' of the market demand. A measure of this quality can be represented by GDP per capita. A higher GDP per capita implies a larger local demand for more advanced types of goods of a higher quality.

Based on the reasoning above, it can be concluded that, in general, the size of any given economy's absolute GDP should have a large effect on the size of the inflows of FDI. However, the question is whether differences in absolute market size are helpful in explaining the differences in FDI among the transition economies. If absolute market size alone were a good explanation for FDI inflows, there would not be any substantial differences in the size of the inward stock of FDI as a share of GDP between individual economies. Table 12.4 in itself is an indication that absolute market size fails to explain entirely the differences in FDI inflows among the transition economies.

Is it possible that the quality of market demand has explanatory power for the observed differences? Higher GDP per capita should mean that most TNCs face a larger local demand for their products. Table 12.12 presents cumulative FDI inflows per capita and GDP per capita for the selected transition economies.

With the exception of the observation for Slovenia, Table 12.12 indicates that there does seem to be a correlation between the quality of market demand as measured by GDP per capita and FDI inflows per capita. Economies that have a low GDP per capita, such as Romania, Russia and Ukraine, also tend to have had low inflows of FDI per capita during the 1990s.

Table 12.12 Cumulative FDI inflows and GDP per capita (US dollars)

Country	Cumulative FDI inflows per capita 1989–2001	GDP per capita 2000
Czech Republic	2 615	4 984
Hungary	2 137	4 745
Estonia	1 727	3 761
Croatia	1 315	4 206
Latvia	1 138	3 032
Slovakia	1 042	3 556
Slovenia	934	9 106
Poland	890	4 108
Lithuania	813	3 237
Bulgaria	491	1 548
Romania	356	1 636
Belarus	132	1 274
Ukraine	84	634
Russia	47	1 784
Uzbekistan	30	264.3

Source: EBRD (2002).

GDP per capita can be interpreted as a measure of how advanced the host-economy demand is. More advanced transition economies should be able to attract more FDI since the TNCs will find it easier to sell their products in these markets. Therefore, it can be concluded that the quality of market demand can be helpful in explaining the differences of FDI inflows to the transition economies of Eastern Europe.

5 CONCLUDING REMARKS

The presentation of data in section 2 proves that the large differences between individual transition economies' ability to attract FDI inflows during the earlier part of transition have continued during the second half of the 1990s. This has resulted in the large differences in FDI stocks among the transition economies that were presented in section 2. The Czech Republic, Hungary and Estonia are the most successful economies in attracting foreign investments. Russia, along with most of the former Soviet republics, has only managed to attract minimal amounts of investment. The most successful transition economies have attracted around 30 times as much FDI per capita as the least successful economies.

Regarding possible explanations for these large differences, the chapter suggests that transition performance, the privatisation process and the quality of market demand measured as GDP per capita constitute host-country determinants that should explain a substantial amount of the differences in FDI inflows.

As far as future research is concerned, the most obvious research project would be econometric studies trying to find determinants of FDI inflows to the region. The fact that it is only a little more than ten years since transition began has implications for empirical studies of FDI inflows to the region. Data for FDI inflows are not available before the beginning of the 1990s, resulting in a current time series no longer than ten years. This means that empirical studies based on the currently available data need to use panel data techniques. As the quantity (and quality) of the data increases, conditions for empirical studies of the region should improve.

NOTES

1 UNCTAD (2002) reports that out of all changes in FDI policies in various countries during 2001, 93 per cent were intended to improve the conditions for foreign investment.

2 However, the advantages might be diminished by inappropriate economic policies such as tax holidays, which may result in higher costs than benefits, or export processing zones (EPZs), which may fail in their intention to establish links between the foreign investor and the local economy.

3 This chapter deals with European transition economies. There are different ways to determine which economies should be included. The Appendix provides a definition contrived by the EBRD that includes as many as 27 countries divided into three major groups.

4 Earlier studies that provide useful overviews of the volume of FDI into individual transition economies include Meyer (1995) and Hunya (2000).

5 This is based on *a priori* theoretical reasoning; there might exist empirical studies that find other results.
6 For a complete description, see EBRD (2001).

REFERENCES

Aliber, R. Z. (1970), 'A Theory of Foreign Direct Investment', in C.P. Kindleberger (ed.), *The International Corporation*, Cambridge, MA: The MIT Press, pp. 17–34.
Brenton, P., F. Di Mauro and M. Lucke (1999), 'Economic Integration and FDI: An Empirical Analysis of Foreign Investment in the EU and in Central and Eastern Europe', *Empirica*, **26**, 95–121.
Brenton, P. and D. Gros (1997), 'Trade Reorientation and Recovery in Transition Economies', *Oxford Review of Economic Policy*, **13** (2), 65–76.
Cantwell, J.A. (1991), 'A Survey of Theories of International Production', in C.N. Pitelis and R. Sugden (eds), *The Nature of the Transnational Firm*, London: Routledge, pp. 16–63.
Culem, C.G. (1988), 'The Locational Determinants of Direct Investments among Industrialised Countries', *European Economic Review*, **32**, 885–904.
Dunning, J. H. (1977), 'Trade, Location of Economic Activity and the MNE: A Search for an Eclectic Approach', in P.-O. Hesselborn, P.-M. Wijkman and B. Ohlin (eds), *The International Allocation of Economic Activity*, London: Macmillan, pp. 395–418.
European Bank for Reconstruction and Development (2000), *Transition Report 2000: Employment, Skills and Transition*, London: EBRD.
European Bank for Reconstruction and Development (2001), *Transition Report 2001: Energy in Transition*, London: EBRD.
European Bank for Reconstruction and Development (2002), *Transition Report 2002: Agriculture and Rural Transition*, London: EBRD.
Grosse, R. and L. Trevino (1996), 'Foreign Direct Investment in the United States: An Analysis by Country of Origin', *Journal of International Business Studies*, **27** (1), 139–55.
Gutman, P. (1993), 'Joint-ventures in Eastern Europe and the Dynamics of Reciprocal Flows in East–West Direct Investments: Some New Perspectives', in P. Artisien, M. Rojec and M. Svetlicic (eds), *Foreign Investment in Central and Eastern Europe*, Basingstoke: Macmillan.
Holland, D. and N. Pain (1998), 'The Diffusion of Innovations in Central and Eastern Europe: A Study of the Determinants and Impact of Foreign Direct Investment', NIESR Discussion Paper No. 137, National Institute of Social and Economic Research, London.
Hunya, G. (2000) 'Home Country Patterns of Foreign Direct Investment in Central and East European Countries', *Russian and East European Finance and Trade*, **36** (2), 87–104.
Hymer, S. (1976), *The International Operations of National Firms: A Study of Foreign Direct Investment*, Cambridge, MA: The MIT Press.
Lankes, M.-P. and A.J. Venables (1996), 'FDI in Economic Transition: The Changing Pattern of Investments', *Economics of Transition*, **4** (2), 331–47.
McMillan, C. (1993a), 'The Role of Foreign Direct Investment in the Transition from Planned to Market Economies', *Transnational Corporations*, **2**, 97–119.
McMillan, C. (1993b), 'Foreign Direct Investment Flows to the Soviet Union and

Eastern Europe: Nature, Magnitude and International Implications', *Journal of Development Planning*, **23**, 305–25.

Meyer, K. (1995), 'Foreign Direct Investment in the Early Years of Economic Transition: A Survey', *Economics of Transition*, **3**, 301–20.

Meyer, K. (1998), *Direct Investment in Economies in Transition*, Cheltenham, UK and Northampton, MA, USA: Edward Elgar.

Roland, G. (2000), *Transition and Economics: Politics, Markets and Firms*, Cambridge, MA: The MIT Press.

Sinn, H.-W. and A. Weichenrieder (1997), 'Foreign Direct Investment, Political Resentment and the Privatization Process in Eastern Europe', *Economic Policy*, **12**, 177–210.

Sjöholm, F. (1999), 'Technology Gap, Competition and Spillovers from Foreign Direct Investment', *Journal of Development Studies*, **36** (1), 53–73.

UNCTAD (2001), *World Investment Report 2001: Promoting Linkages*, Geneva: United Nations.

UNCTAD (2002), *World Investment Report 2002: Transnational Corporations and Export Competitiveness*, Geneva: United Nations.

Vernon, R. (1966), 'International Investment and International Trade in the Product Cycle', *Quarterly Journal of Economics*, **80**, 190–207.

APPENDIX

According to the EBRD, the following 27 countries should be included among the European transition economies:

Central Eastern Europe and the Baltic states:
Croatia
Czech Republic
Estonia
Hungary
Latvia
Lithuania
Poland
Slovak Republic
Slovenia

South-Eastern Europe:
Albania
Bosnia and Herzegovina
Bulgaria
FR Yugoslavia
FYR Macedonia
Romania

Commonwealth of Independent States:
Armenia
Azerbaijan
Belarus
Georgia
Kazakhstan
Kyrgyzstan
Moldova
Russia
Tajikistan
Turkmenistan
Ukraine
Uzbekistan

13. Sustainable Development and Evaluation: An Introduction

Uwe Schubert and Bernd Schuh

1 INTRODUCTION

This contribution is aimed at persons with an interest in development policy in Europe, particularly in accession countries, where some of the concepts and approaches prevalent in the EU touched upon here might not be generally and sufficiently known to enable them to cope with the challenges ahead. Part of the problem dealt with is also still rather new for 'old hands' in EU policy discussion. This is particularly true of the core consideration in this chapter, i.e. the link between a rather new goal of the Union which aims at 'sustainable development' and the need to evaluate policies, programmes and projects in member countries from this perspective. This elementary review does not offer the reader any new and original research results by the authors, nor can it claim to be a comprehensive review of an already voluminous and still rapidly growing body of literature. The discussion of the issues presented here is as non-technical as possible; readers with a deeper interest in some of the issues will find a couple of key references to pursue the matter further. Given the necessary brevity of the contribution to a volume of this kind, the choice of significant topics discussed (and omitted) tends to be rather subjective; the references given might assist the reader to complement his/her own understanding of the topic.

The Role of the Concept of Sustainable Development in the European Union

The concept of sustainable development (SD) is closely linked with the evolution of environmental policy in Europe. In the 1980s and increasingly in the 1990s criticism of the environmental policy system became louder. Prominent among these critical aspects were the following points:

- The policies designed were dominated by short-run considerations.
- Policies were lacking embeddedness in a general socio-economic context.

- The singularity of legal and concrete environmental action often implied inconsistencies in the entire policy system.
- The lack of an overriding policy criterion which would overcome these drawbacks in the design and evaluation of social, economic and environmental policy became evident.

The report by the Brundtland Commission in 1987 (WCED, 1987) was a historical milestone in the creation of a new paradigm that had the potential to overcome some of the deficiencies in the prevalent policy systems and implementation realities in Europe. The process of acceptance of this new policy guiding principle was significantly supported by a rising volume of scientific literature in various fields dealing with environmental questions, in the realms of both natural and socio-economic sciences. The process of search for and growing acceptance of the paradigm of 'sustainable development' culminated in its inclusion in the Amsterdam Treaty of the European Union. In §52 this principle was added to the list of objectives of the EU, side by side with the aim of achieving international competitiveness and internal social cohesion. It is now part of the constitutional law of all member states and constitutes an essential part of the EU body of law which is also the basis of the 'Acquis' to be finally signed by all the accession states to the Union. All the member states are now in the process of formulating strategies for the implementation of the sustainability principle.

In this process several queries have arisen, which make it difficult to formulate strategies, programmes and policies. Prominent among these are:

- The definition of what is actually meant by sustainable development is not entirely clear.
- The operationalisation of the principle encounters many difficulties, partly because of the fuzziness of its definition.
- The principle warrants integration into a more general 'sustainability management' system, which usually entails a significant volume of institutional reform. In particular, the 'policy coordination' and consistency postulate implied by the principle is difficult to implement within a given 'departmentalised' institutional frame.
- To what extent can the principle be used to derive specific and definitive rules of action (such as infrastructure investments, etc.)?
- How should evaluation studies of development-related policies and programmes be structured and which methods are available for this purpose?

This chapter attempts to shed light upon some of these questions. (The institutional framework issue and the problem of the creation of an appropriate management system will not be discussed here; the reader can find some interesting ideas e.g. in Jänicke et al., 1999, and Lafferty, 1996.) Given the volume of literature in this field, a complete survey cannot be delivered and is thus not intended, as already mentioned.

The chapter proceeds by briefly introducing some attempts to define 'sustainable development' in an operational manner. This introduction is followed by a short discussion of the elements of a dynamic perspective which is implied by the term 'development'. In the sequel the question of to what extent the application of the principle of sustainable development could lead to consistent actions (programmes, policies, investments) is dealt with. A discussion of the role and the implied task of evaluating sustainable development strategies and measures follows. It will first concentrate on the question of what is meant by 'evaluation' and then approach the problem of linking this concept with policy in general and with sustainable development policies in particular. It will be shown that certain qualities postulated for evaluations in this context lead to suggesting some evaluation methods which might be able to meet this challenge. Generally speaking no claim is made to cover all possible evaluation scenarios, but the major aim is to collect the information necessary to represent cause–effect relations in various ways (which is a basic necessity in order to overcome the problem of fuzziness and complexity connected with the concept of sustainable development).

2 THE DEFINITION OF SUSTAINABLE DEVELOPMENT

Many attempts have been made to define sustainable development in a coherent and operational way. In this section a few selected definitions are given, which contain the main issues discussed, each one of them emphasising particular elements.

Brundtland Report

'Sustainable Development is development that meets the needs of the present without compromising the ability of future generations to meet their own needs' (WCED, 1987).

This definition is based on a concept of 'needs' that is not elaborated further, however. But it is clear that the 'resources' on which the satisfaction of needs critically depends are the central element in this definition. Their further development (particularly anthropogenic resources), maintenance and enhancement (particularly natural resources) constitute the core of these considerations. This formulation has become the most widespread version and is quoted regularly.

UNEP (United Nation Environmental Program)

'Sustainable Development means improving the quality of human living within the carrying capacity of the supporting eco-system' (IUCN/UNEP/WWF, 1991).

The characteristic elements of this definition are the 'quality of living' and the 'carrying capacity'. Improving the quality of living is a more demanding postulate than the mere satisfaction of needs mentioned above. The carrying capacity as a constraint on improving the quality of living introduces the entire ecosystem explicitly as the relevant resource base to be considered.

Gothenburg European Council

'Sustainable Development requires dealing with economic, social and environmental effects in a mutually reinforcing way' (EU Commission, 2001).

This definition spells out explicitly which resources need to be taken into account, i.e. natural, economic and human capital. Emphasis is placed upon 'win–win' constellations, i.e. such actions that imply synergies that lead to improvement (or least no deterioration) in all resources.

Process-focused Sustainability Concepts

Within these approaches sustainable development is understood to be process-related rather than output-related. Therefore these concepts concentrate on the question of how to foster the paths towards this goal. Specific characteristics of the process seem therefore to be more than or at least as important as the setting up of a final goal (see e.g. Turner, 1993; Nijkamp, 1990, 1997).

Difficulties in the application of the principle clearly arise because of some drawbacks of the concept of sustainable development. Some of these are:

- The definition of sustainable development is not clear enough and leaves important issues open or fuzzy. Even the very basic meaning of 'development' needs to be spelled out (see section 3) and 'sustainability' has many aspects that need pinning down (see sections 4 and 5).
- A few deficiencies are, for example, what happens in the case of trade-offs between different resource changes (in non-win–win situations), what can be done in the case of non-renewable natural resources, etc.
- The principle needs to be operationalised. It does not in itself provide any specific clues about variables to be included in the analysis and

their indicators for which data have to be collected, etc.
- The institutional framework needs to be adapted (particularly for better policy integration).
- A system of monitoring and evaluation needs to be set up.

The brief sketch presented above suggests clearly that analyses of any kind dealing with sustainable development need to carefully specify the starting point, i.e. the definition chosen, the criteria and their indicators selected and the data required for an empirical analysis. This implies that, given the manifold possibilities alluded to, the results of analyses undertaken are not easily comparable. To overcome these deficits, attempts have been made to arrive at operational concepts and to standardise the approaches. A few of these efforts are briefly mentioned in the next section.

3 STEPS TOWARDS OPERATIONALISATION

The Three Pillars Model (see e.g. Munasinghe, 1993)

This approach emphasises the importance of the inclusion of ecological, economic and social aspects into an analysis of sustainable development (following the logic of the EU Gothenburg Declaration). The stocks to be considered, and upon which criteria have to be defined, can be clustered into 'three pillars' (see Figure 13.1) corresponding to the three categories mentioned.

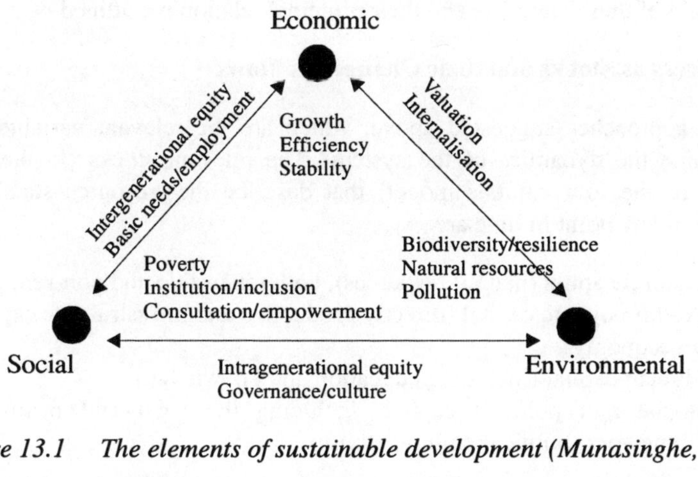

Figure 13.1 The elements of sustainable development (Munasinghe, 1993)

A variant of the three pillars concept is the 'The Four Capitals Model', in which 'Social Capital' is introduced as a separate stock to be considered. It reflects the importance attributed to the institutional framework of a society, including the human relations determining the effectiveness and satisfaction of the citizens in a democratic society in relevant decision-making. (This concept is utilised, e.g., by GHK consultants in their evaluation of the EU structural funds' contribution to sustainable regional development.)

4 DYNAMICS AND THE STATIONARY STATE

Development is clearly a dynamic concept (see also the discussion in section 5). This 'moving on' of a society has different aspects that need to be considered. These constitute, e.g., the (most likely) multiple objectives to be pursued if development is to occur, as well as the constraints that need to be taken into account. A central element of any dynamics striven for is the existence of sufficient resources (the most important constraints), allowing the pursuit of the objectives mentioned above. The resources identified as key in the concept of sustainable development are natural as well as anthropogenic resources, as mentioned in the previous section (these are the 'three pillars' or the 'four capitals').

These resources are not independent of each other; their relation constitutes an essential element in the attempt to formulate and implement strategies, programmes and policies to reach a sustainable development path for a society. Evidently they are also of paramount importance in the evaluation of such efforts, independently of the point in time of the process of pursuing the development goals (see section 6). A brief and basic overview of these elements and their principal relation is outlined next.

Resources as Stocks and their Changes as Flows

In the approaches suggested above, which are the relevant variables that determine the dynamics of the system? The relevant stocks (in the three pillars or the four capitals model) that describe the 'resource state' of a society at any point in time are:

- Natural capital (natural resources), both renewable and non-renewable.
- Anthropogenic capital (directly productive and infrastructure capital of an economy).
- Human capital (including education and knowledge).
- Social and political capital (including the legal and institutional framework, political culture, etc.).

How do these stocks (resources) change? The relevant flows are:

Net Change in Stock = Net Investment = Gross Investment – Depreciation

Note that investment can also be negative, e.g. the exploitation of natural resources leads to a reduction of the stock. If investment just replaces depreciation, obviously the net change of the stock equals zero and the stock remains constant.

Changing the stocks implies a decision about the flows that can be controlled by society, e.g. the rate of exploitation of the natural resources or investment in anthropogenic capital. In principle these decisions determine the quantity of investment as well as the areas into which capital is to be invested.

The essential relation between the anthropogenic capital and nature is sketched in Figure 13.2.

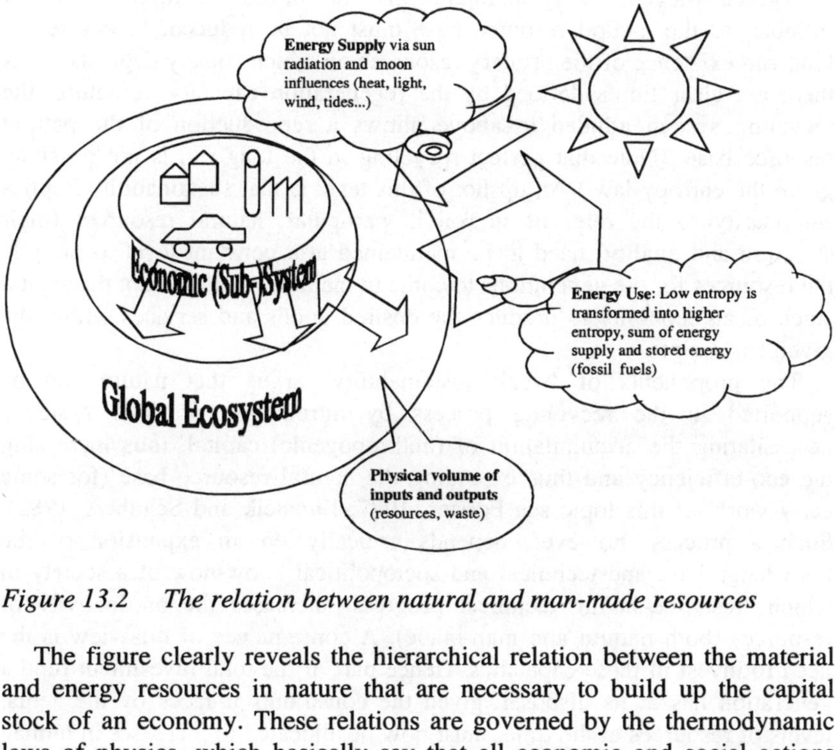

Figure 13.2 The relation between natural and man-made resources

The figure clearly reveals the hierarchical relation between the material and energy resources in nature that are necessary to build up the capital stock of an economy. These relations are governed by the thermodynamic laws of physics, which basically say that all economic and social actions depend on materials and energy (these actions simply constitute transformation processes in terms of physics). No such transformation can be 100 per cent efficient; thus there is always some residual, a by-product (which in terms of economics we call waste) of the process which is passed on to other elements (air, water, land, etc.) of the ecosystem. The law of thermodynamics also states that in these transformation processes no mass or energy used as an input is lost. This implies, as shown in the figure, that nature has developed a recycling system and that in quantitative terms the stock of mass and energy on earth does not change. But in qualitative terms it does! In the course of the transformation processes mentioned, the physical, chemical and organisational (entropic) structure and form of the resources change. The ecosystem adapts to these changes, in a way that is not necessarily beneficial for human society (or for many other living beings).

The question arises as to what extent natural and anthropogenic resources are substitutes for each other. Opinions on this subject vary widely among scientists. The 'school of strong sustainability' (see e.g. Daly, 1973: Georgescu-Roegen, 1971) maintains that substitution is in principle not feasible, as the natural resource base must not be reduced, to ensure the long-run existence of the primary resources on which society depends. Thus there are clear limits defined by the regeneration capacity of nature; the recycling system alluded to above allows a reproduction of the natural resource base. (Note that perfect recycling in the long run is not possible, given the entropy law.) An upshot of this tenet is that sustainability implies stationarity of the relevant stocks; in particular, natural resources (their structure and quality) need to be maintained at a constant level to provide the resources for the generations to come to maintain and/or adapt the capital stock of an economy to produce the desired goods and services within the given constraints.

The proponents of 'weak sustainability' argue that nature can be supported in the recycling process by introducing artificial systems, necessitating the accumulation of (anthropogenic) capital, thus increasing the eco-efficiency and thus extending the natural resource base (for some early work on this topic see Forster, 1977; Luptacik and Schubert, 1982). Such a process, however, depends critically on an expansion of the knowledge base and technical and sociopolitical know-how of a society in which 'resource-saving technical progress' increases the productivity of resources (both natural and man-made). A consequence of this view is the need to invest in these capacities. Hence part of the total investment fund a generation has at its disposal, given the constraints it faces by the actual levels of resources at the time, must now be allocated to increases in human and social/political capital stocks to enhance and achieve a better, or at least equal, resource endowment for the next generation. Note that stationarity, i.e. a constant level of all relevant capital stocks, is not feasible in this approach, as the task of increasing resource productivity implies continuous increases in the (multiple) man-made capital stocks mentioned (see also

Ramsey, 1928).

The operationalisation concepts presented above ('three pillars' and 'four capitals') thus are clearly based on the concept of 'weak sustainability'. It should be noted, however, that even this already more limited approach still allows considerable variations in how to derive an allocation rule for each generation to make the appropriate investment decisions. Needless to say, the view taken also has a crucial influence on the monitoring and evaluation of the specific development strategies, programmes and investments chosen and implemented. A short discussion on some of these issues is presented in the following section.

5 THE ECONOMIC CONCEPT OF WELFARE AND SUSTAINABLE DEVELOPMENT

Linguistically, 'development' means a move to something 'better'. In terms of standard normative economic theory does this mean: maximise welfare for all generations (given the resource and other relevant constraints)? Can this be operationalised as a better way of defining the objective of society to strive for maximised consumption for all generations (again given the constraints)? Or is the best way of viewing the task to be solved as 'making the best of a given potential' limited by the availability of all resources, thus implying a capacity-building goal?

Basically we may distinguish between those two extremes of definitions of SD. Consequently these definitions will lead us to different solutions with respect to possible investment decisions for the present and the future.

5.1 Sustainable Development as Welfare Measurement

Under this heading SD is understood as welfare maximisation over time. In due course development in this sense will be expressed as a stated goal function – in the case of both an ex-post and an ex-ante measurement of SD. Following this train of thought, it becomes evident that there will be only a single optimal solution for allocating resources between present and future generations. In principle (given all the information about the preferences of the next generations, etc.), this means that the calculation of the optimal level of investments in the relevant stocks of resources is feasible. Note that such an assumption leads consequently to an evaluation procedure which simply checks on the achievement of this single optimal goal, which in practice is however rather elusive in terms of measurement, and will therefore reduce the complexity of real-world situations considerably. Still, if such an approach is adopted, policy makers will only need this simple information in order to take decisions accordingly.[1]

5.2 Sustainable Development as Capacity Building

SD in this context implies that passing on flexible stocks into the future will secure this goal, so that the next generations can adjust according to their own preferences (assumed to be unknown in detail now). It usually entails the formulation of constraints and specific targets in a political process in which the next generations must have an advocate.

The underlying assumed qualities of reality in this context are that uncertainty, irreversibility and complexity are a vital part of our life and have to be taken into account in decision making and consequently in the evaluation of our actions. (Uncertainty is to be distinguished from risk.[2] While risk follows the formula of probability distributions by possible value of damage, uncertainty implies a lack of information on either of those entities, or even both.)

Irreversibility – according to Krutilla (1967) – implies that changes in the natural environment caused by economic activities may not be reversed by activities of production using manufactured capital. This fact leads to profound doubts about the concept of endless substitutability of man-made and natural capital. Man-made capital (as e.g. repair measures to the environment) cannot endlessly substitute natural capital, as ecosystem characteristics will only allow for that up to a certain point (i.e. critical threshold) beyond which the situation of the system will change forever. Consequently, for example, the concept of an optimal pollution standard, which may be negotiated between parties in- or outside the market, has to be critically reviewed in this context.

Complex systems are defined in epistemological terms as those that cannot be captured adequately by a single type of representation or analytical perspective (Stengers, 1987; O'Connor, 1994). This is discussed in more detail below, but to put it briefly here, this complexity leads to certain qualities with respect to interventions in the systems (i.e. decisions about the allocation of resources over time in our case), thus questioning the assumption of a single optimal solution and the way that an optimal level of investment could be determined. The basic conclusion will be that – unlike the above-mentioned approach – there are multiple allocation possibilities, and therefore a ranking of these possible alternatives with regard to specified multiple criteria (characterising SD) seems to be more likely to measure this attempt at an allocation plan than indicate a unique optimal solution.

Summarising the brief discussion above, is there some light at the end of the tunnel leading to acceptable (a far cry from optimal!) ways of formulating strategies for SD? In our view a few principles of a practicable approach can be formulated, but a consistent, generally usable way to address all the issues raised cannot be offered at this point in time. Which features should such an approach have? Some of the suggestions can be listed here:

- Sustainable development as a societal goal is not directly equivalent to maximising welfare for all generations from now on. As the preferences of the following generations cannot be known, constraints on the present resource use have to be imposed which imply that sufficient resources will be available in the future. These constraints must be formulated by the present generation in a participatory political process taking on board the most recent state of science, thus reducing uncertainty and increasing the knowledge about probabilities involved with risky decisions. Questions of irreversibility merit particular attention in this context. These constraints, hence, will have to be adapted continually as new knowledge is actively acquired.
- Where does welfare maximisation enter in this process? The imposition of constraints on resource allocation decisions offers the chance of the existence of a feasible range of alternatives between which to choose. Among these, each generation can select those which best meet their preferences, given the new set of constraints which have evolved as a result of the decisions of the past generation and the current state of the art in relevant science. Again these decisions about alternative development paths and the proper choice of instruments will have to cope with risk and uncertainty (for a critical review of the limits of traditional economic models in this respect see e.g. Pezzey, 1997).
- The political process warranted, based on recurrent feedback loops, needs solid foundations. Among these are an acceptance of the principle of SD by each generation and the legal and institutional framework which allows an effective political process. An important instrument for this aim is the continuous evaluation of this framework as well as the decisions taken, involving all elements needed in decisions about long-run development (objectives, constraints, programmes, policies, projects, etc.).

The next section will focus on the task of evaluating actions to promote sustainability, which was identified as a crucial task in the preceding discussion. Then follows a section that discusses choice of methods, assessment and evaluation, focusing on the two above-mentioned extremes of SD. On the one hand, following the idea of SD as a welfare concept, traditional economic evaluation methods such as cost–benefit analysis (see e.g. Hanley and Spash, 1995) are briefly mentioned. On the other hand the evaluation of SD actions following the concept of capacity building requires methods that are demanding in respect of both the underlying theoretical assumptions and the ability to deal with the conditions of uncertainty, irreversibility and complexity. It will be those methods that we shall discuss in more detail in the following section.

6 EVALUATION

Evaluation, not only in a political context, has become one of the buzzwords of economic and social action. It is usually accompanied by a general attitude of public policy implying necessary control and responsibility (social and ecological). The concept hence implies quite a range of tasks, such as obtaining information on improvement possibilities, justification of action and decision support. Given this wide range of tasks, the scope of definitions and methods has led to a lot of misuse of the concept as such and its intuitive meaning. There seems to be a similar difficulty to that in the case of the sustainability concept, where fuzziness of definition has caused a true inflation (and abuse) of interpretations and task formulations. Evaluation practice often suffers from these drawbacks. Thus the results are often not satisfactory, either for the contractor or for the client of an evaluation study. In the paragraphs to follow, a contribution towards more clarity is intended and some basic considerations for the use of evaluation in a policy context will be briefly touched upon.

Therefore we shall start with definitions of the terms involved, i.e. policy, evaluation and the evaluation of political action. We will then show the problems connected with evaluation in a policy context – particularly if sustainable development should be the goal to be pursued. This will lead to the definition of some minimum requirements for a method to be applied.

6.1 The Role of Evaluation in Public Policy

Policy and political action are embedded in a political process, which is defined (by political scientists) by three realms: polity, politics and policy (see e.g. Jänicke et al., 1999). It is clear that it is policy which is of interest for assessment and evaluation of success or failure.

Policy is to be seen as a multi-stage feedback concept, containing the following elements:

- Problem perception
- Agenda setting
- Policy formulation
- Decision making
- Implementation

- Evaluation
- Termination.

Evaluation thus clearly constitutes an essential element – it should obviously be a necessary part of any political action, possibly to take place in several stages of a full policy cycle. The question remains as to what exactly is meant by evaluation and how to do it properly.

Within the political process, to cope with all the tasks implied, evaluation according to Jänicke et al. (1999) is more than the assessment of the results of political action (appraisal) – as before elections; it is something different from a check-up of regulations and laws and it is more than a simple assessment of the cost-effectiveness of public spending by the financial control body of the state. Policy evaluation is basically the examination of the effects (i.e. the outcomes and impacts) and effectiveness of the political measures and programmes and their efficiency with respect to the inputs employed. It thus implies the comparison of a specific policy with one (or more) alternative(s).

Figure 13.3 'unravels' the relationship between a policy measure and its ultimate impact on human behaviour and the environment into a number of key elements. It illustrates how effect and effectiveness questions fit into a wider policy evaluation framework, which seeks to answer a broader set of evaluative questions.

More precisely, then, in this context, how can evaluation be defined? Evaluation is generally speaking the assessment of the value (or utility) of a subject to be investigated. This subject can take many forms – e.g. an innovation, a programme, a project or service (see e.g. Robson, 2000).

It follows from this definition that more is at stake than just assessing the value in order to measure whether something is 'good' or 'bad' or whether a goal has been reached or not or whether something is 'better' or 'worse' than an alternative. As the term evaluation already indicates (stemming from the Latin verb 'valere' – to be worth, to be liable), there is always a more general value judgement involved in a comparison of alternatives. Evaluation thus involves comparisons according to specific criteria (defining the utility aimed at) on the basis of information which has been gathered especially for this purpose. Hence the principal task is to aim at more rationality in decision making and planning by structuring all the relevant aspects of the decision.

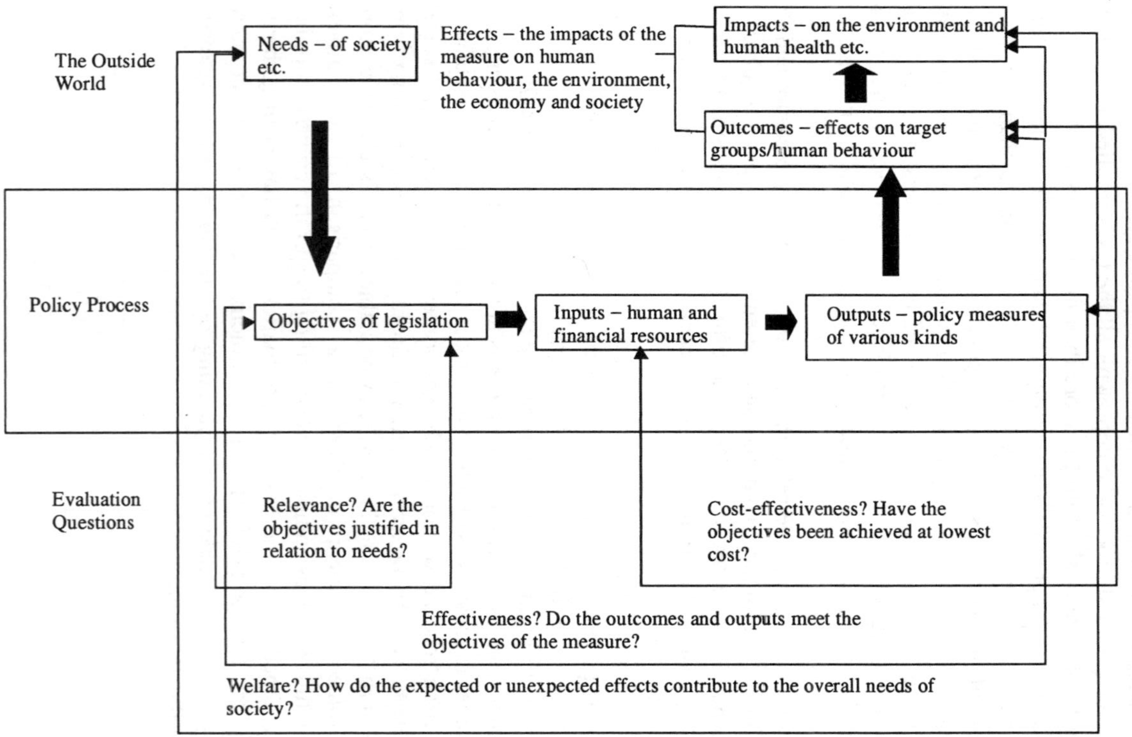

Source: EEA (2001).

Figure 13.3 Policy evaluation

6.2 Key Elements of Evaluations

Assessment of the value/utility of a subject

'When you can measure what you are speaking about, and express it in numbers, you know something about it; when you cannot measure it, when you cannot express it in numbers, your knowledge is of a meagre and unsatisfactory kind.' Lord Kelvin (cited in Samuelson and Nordhaus, 1989) has pointed out quite accurately the basic problem connected to this part of evaluations – i.e. the difficulty of finding operational measures for such complex concepts as utility and the full value of something – let alone the problem of expressing these findings in a quantitative way – thus making it compatible with comparisons in the next step. When assessing the value of something the major challenge is to transform as much information as possible from reality into a form which is accessible for our sensitive apparatus (i.e. computing capacity, senses). This postulate hence implies:

- Identification of cause–effect relations
- Choice of different scales/measuring rods
- Choice of different time scales where effects become visible
- Measuring psychic values such as satisfaction and happiness.

Comparison

This is the central task of evaluation. It is often forgotten and/or done implicitly, thus leading to major biases when interpreting the final results. Still, when talking about comparisons of facts and measures, four major philosophical concepts have to be taken into account (see e.g. Martinez-Alier et al., 1997):

- Strong commensurability, according to which there exists a common measure of the different consequences of an action, based on a cardinal scale of measurement.
- Weak commensurability, according to which there exists a common measure based on an ordinal scale of measurement.
- Strong comparability, according to which there exists a single comparative term by which all different consequences can be ranked.
- Weak comparability, according to which values are irreducibly plural and cannot be uniquely ordered along a single scale.

It should be noted in this context that incommensurability (i.e. to take into account all the different dimensions of a decision problem without any monetary reductionism) does not imply incomparability. It could be assumed that although there is no common measure based on an ordinal scale of measurement, there could be acceptance of the existence of conflicts between all different consequences of an action.

This task and the implications following from these concepts will be of major concern in this section.

Combining the two elements invoked above – i.e. political action on the one hand and evaluation on the other – it becomes clear that there is no such thing as 'the' policy evaluation. Evaluation of a policy measure consists of the assessment of its value in relation to specific criteria on the basis of information which has been collected and analysed especially for this purpose. The goal is to examine the 'right of existence' of a political intervention. This implies identifying success stories which should be reproduced as well as finding out about mistakes and failures to be avoided in the future.

6.3 Types of Evaluation

Evaluations can be necessary, as mentioned above, in all phases of the policy cycle and with many different foci. A classification of types of evaluation needs to distinguish with respect to:

- The focus: process-centred, effect-centred, efficiency-centred, output-centred.
- The time: before setting the measure (i.e. an ex-ante evaluation in the sense of decision aid) or after the measure has been implemented (i.e. an ex-post evaluation in the sense of success/failure measurement) and the search for improvement possibilities.
- Accompanying the policy action.

Generally speaking the following types of evaluation can be distinguished.

Type A: Evaluation as decision aid (ex ante)

As shown in Figure 13.4, in this type of evaluation the aim is to assess and compare alternatives (e.g. A_1–A_3) according to their expected performance with respect to the indicators representing Objectives 1 and 2. The results are ranked according to the levels of utility (U_1–U_3) which are expected to be reached. Assuming to utility maximisation behaviour, the alternative which reaches the highest level will be chosen.

In this form evaluation recalls the discussion presented above – i.e. decisions in the context of SD as welfare measure. In this respect a type A evaluation seems to seek answers on the optimal allocation of resources over time – i.e. the determination of a sustainable intertemporal (social) welfare function (see e.g. Pezzey, 1997). The problems and shortcomings in this context are:

- Pervasive uncertainty about preferences and technology in the distant future – this leads to the problem of how to define equity and fairness *vis-à-vis* future generations.
- Fluctuations in population will lead to important choices – perhaps between maintaining constant population by allowing per capita utility to fall, and maintaining constant per capita utility by allowing population to fall.
- The focus on consumption together with an implicit assumption of substitutability in production ignores the special role of natural environmental resources in supporting life on the planet.

In short, the major problem in this context is the setting of a reference scenario with which alternative policy options should be compared. In other words, economic modelling has up to now not been able to supply political acting with a solution to these problems, making evaluations of the type A so dissatisfying for political actors. Still, evaluations of this type are more in demand than ever and we will try to come forward with a possible solution (see section 7.3.)

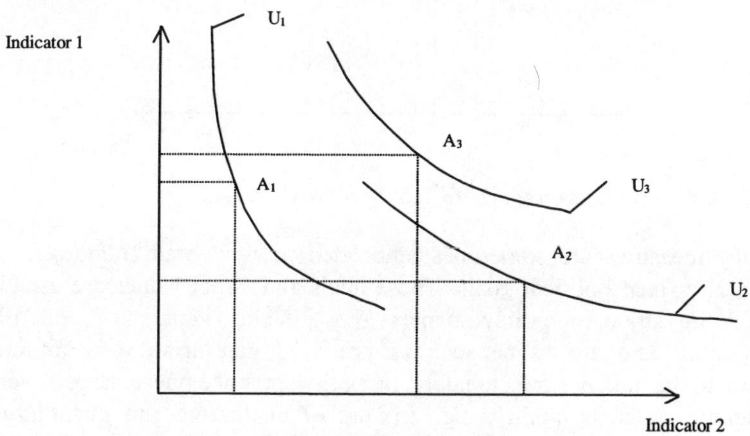

Figure 13.4 Evaluation as decision aid (ex ante)

Type B: Measurement and evaluation of results (ex post)

Case I: Evaluation *vis-à-vis* a hypothetical alternative: Assume in Figure 13.4 that A_1 is an actually existing alternative, which was set up in the past and has produced specific results over time. It is to be compared with hypothetical alternatives A_2 and A_3 by their performance along *n* criteria, which are pictured in the form of *n* indicators (in our case here *n*=2). The best hypothetical results are represented by the highest possible utility levels to be reached, U_2 and U_3 respectively. In evaluation practice such hypothetical alternatives are referred to as, e.g., best-practice scenarios, business-as-usual scenarios or basic-variant scenarios.

Case II: Evaluation with fixed political targets: Figure 13.5 shows the case of an evaluation *vis-à-vis* a set of previously fixed political targets.

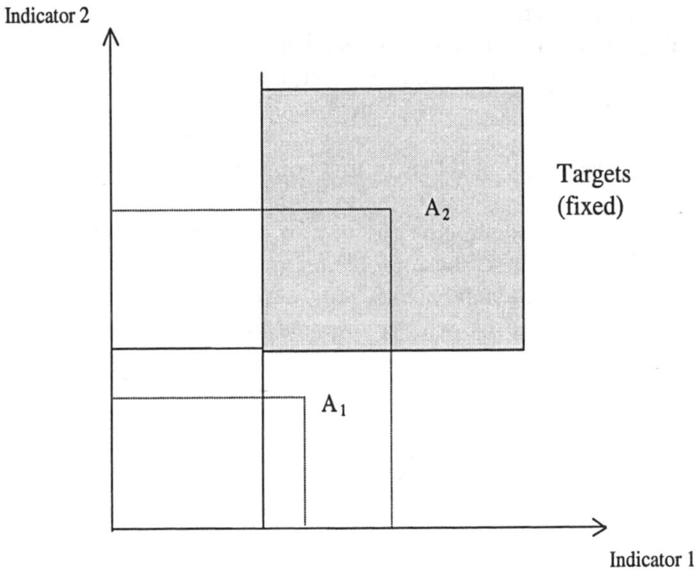

Figure 13.5 Evaluation vis-à-vis *fixed political targets*

Policy measures are sometimes embedded in an overall framework of strategically fixed political goals. These goals and target values are usually reported in strategic policy papers (e.g. White Papers of the EU Commission) and are to be seen as pre-fixed measuring rods for any measure to be taken (unfortunately in policy practice these targets vary considerably in their quality, e.g. mixture of qualitative and quantitative targets, thus posing some challenges to the evaluation method to be used). Once it becomes possible to capture the relevant data for both targets and the alternatives by indicators – as shown below – the evaluation becomes rather simple, as all that has to be done is to check whether the alternatives (A_1, A_2) are situated in- or outside the target field (in the example in Figure 13.5, A_2 is 'successful', A_1 is not). However, a further complication might occur, when an alternative is according to one criterion inside and with respect to another one outside the target zone. Then the question arises as to whether compensations between the single criteria are allowed or not or whether the evaluation method could make the trade-offs at least explicit and thus more easily manageable.

7 IS THERE ANYTHING SPECIAL ABOUT EVALUATING SUSTAINABLE DEVELOPMENT POLICIES?

As mentioned above, the necessity of evaluations in a policy context can be derived from different sources. The need for measurement of success/failure of a policy measure can be an important motivation. Equally there may simply be the need to legitimise a decision process or some action taken *vis-à-vis* the taxpayer. In some cases evaluations are even compulsory (see e.g. EU Commission, 1996; DTLR, 2001; GATT, 1994). But is it something special to evaluate policy in general or policy targeted towards sustainable development in particular? It has already been pointed out in sections 4 and 5 that there are specific characteristics in the context of decision making and evaluations focusing on sustainable development – such as uncertainty, complexity and irreversibility. Prima facie these typical properties of sustainable development actions suggest that evaluations in an environment which is highly complex, full of uncertainty and irreversible effects are necessary in order to get at least some grip on these realities. On the other hand these circumstances could suggest that it might be impossible to deduce any useful information on a scientifically sound basis at all. In the following we will therefore try to shed some light on some of these aspects – especially on the complexity issue – and try to come up with some desired qualities of methods which may be applied usefully in the evaluation of sustainable development. We will approach this issue in two ways, which explain the determination of qualities of methods able to evaluate SD aspects of policy making. On the one hand this will be lessons to be learned from systems theory and systemic intervention theory, and on the other hand it will be the basic criticism by the discipline of ecological economics of traditional economic theory and its implications for standard economic modelling.

7.1 Lessons to be Learned from Systems Theory

In an analysis of problems and specifics of policy evaluation it is helpful to look at political action from the perspective of systems theory. Policy is seen in this context as a complex, non-linear, self-referential system which calls for certain specifics in the case of interventions. (For more details on this approach an overview is provided e.g. by Willke, 1996a.) The policy process can be seen as a system in many respects – social, economic, cultural and political – where the layers of the different viewpoints often overlap and interfere with each other. Thus when adding up these systemic approaches in order to get an overview and to capture this interference, which is in many cases the real source of problems, the complexity increases and the problem becomes unreceptive to any intervention.

Basically managing SD – for example the exchange of material, energy and labour flows and the concomitant environmental problems caused by traffic congestion and waste management over time – is a multi-actor, multi-variable/criteria maximisation problem. As pictured in the different approaches above there are many decision makers and stakeholders with as many diverse interests and potential decision-making powers involved. The problems, though easily visible, are highly complex as to their causes and effects and are in many cases strongly interrelated. The time frames connected to these problems are not homogeneous, nor are their spatial contexts.

Let us therefore look into systems theory to find some explanations that might help to deal with this complexity without having to oversimplify and thus lose important information on the way.

Policy in general has to be seen (Willke, 1996a, 1996b) as a complex system which follows the logic of:

- Self-reference – this concept refers to the basic findings of Luhmann (1984), which are themselves based upon the theory of autopoiesis (for an overview see Maturana, 1982). The bottom line could be described as the capacity of systems to reproduce themselves by using the help of the elements of which they consist. This assumption causes some irritation as another important principle of systems theory – i.e. that complex systems show a tendency to open up – does not seem to hold true. It is merely assumed that systems renew themselves by an operatively closed process. But the theory states that only in their basic structure of self-guidance are systems absolutely independent from the outside and unreceptive to such influences. Of course this definition raises questions and problems in the context of intervention into complex social systems, such as public management – the ability to guide and manage these systems then becomes very limited if not impossible. We will deal with this problem in the next paragraph.
- Non-linearity – this concept reflects the fact that social systems are not 'trivial machines' as they are seen in most of the socio-economic models (based upon neo-classical economic theory). Trivial machines work on the principle of causal mechanics, where inputs and outputs are connected by clear cause–effect relations. The input–output relations in non-trivial systems, on the contrary, are based on side

effects and uncertainty and are only to be understood via the 'viewpoint' and logic of the system itself – otherwise they seem irrational, unpredictable and illogical (for a more thorough description see Foerster, 1984).

- Self-guidance – this concept refers to the capacity of a complex social or psychic system (organised as a self-referential system of standards) to guide itself. The mode of guidance is determined by an organised selectivity of expectations and the contingency of other systems and itself.

As a consequence the basic problems attached to complex systems which show these patterns are: uncertainty (in respect of their reactions as well as their internal logic) and incompatibility (with other systems), which leads to the phenomenon that objectively visible real-world problems – such as human-made environmental destruction – which do contradict attempts to explain rational, social acting can only be explained if a certain self-reference and logic of complex social systems is taken into account.

If we follow the above-mentioned findings based on systems theory, then the logical consequence will be that model building – to understand and explain problems in the context of such social systems – itself is problematic as in its own logic it acts as an 'awkward simplification' just trying to build up 'if–then' relations and simple linearity. All the models described above tried to reduce the complexity of the system, thus tapping into the 'systemic trap' all the same. But in order to manage conflicts or to solve problems in this context, it will be necessary to face this complexity and find ways to deal with it. Therefore it will be necessary to dig deeper into systems theory and combine it with intervention theory in order to find ways to overcome the trade-off between oversimplification of necessary systemic information on the one hand and the sheer oversupply of impressions and data by which political action for sustainable development can be described on the other.

If we look at measuring and evaluating policy towards SD as a problem in the context of a complex social system which is involved in guiding itself and other related systems, then we are confronted with the general problem that the need for guidance in the context of a highly developed society has increased considerably on the one hand, but the capacity to guide cannot be increased using traditional instruments (i.e. public administration or 'policy' and 'the market economy') on the other hand – thus opening up a gap of lack of guidance (see Willke, 1983). Social science is aware of this problem and one of the major focus points of intervention theory (see Willke, 1996b) tries to deal with the above-mentioned trade-off in systems theory – i.e. that the necessity of intervention seems to increase in a highly interlinked and developed society on the one hand, and the inner quality of self-reference of complex social systems makes them increasingly unreceptive to interventions on the other.

It is the above-mentioned concept of autopoiesis which is the starting point and leads to the assumption that systems are supposed to be self-referential. As a consequence this would mean that in their inner structure they are not accessible to intervention. It is understandable that such assumptions have led to a crisis of intervention theory as – if taken as an ultimate ratio – this would mean an end to any external guidance of social and psychic systems. Therefore a differentiation among the problems of complex systems seemed to be necessary in order to identify those situations where intervention is still possible and thus to open up a window of opportunity to guide systems anyway. In this respect Weaver (1996) differentiates between unorganised complexity (e.g. comparable with the molecular movement of gases) of problems, which allows for no intervention, and organised complexity, where a limited number of interdependent variables prevail. Therefore a certain estimation of patterns is possible. These problems can also be described as showing an 'ordered complexity', which is one of the characteristics of social systems as well. The central properties of problems of organised complexity are the following (Willke, 1996b):

- Non-linear linkages
- 'Inertia' of the system, indifference to the problem, multi-layers
- Existence of 'sensitive points', which enable changes
- Self-reference
- Sub-systems which are responsible for regulation.

Therefore, if social problems (e.g. public policy problems) are characterised as such, then intervention and guidance seem to be possible. As a starting point and fundamental prerequisite for success later on, the identification of these 'sensitive points' is therefore necessary.

Intervention theory, which tries to face exactly this kind of problem, states that in the case of high internal as well as external complexity of a system, context-driven guidance and control of the system has to be adopted as a next step (see Table 13.1).

If we look at a real-world context such as the design and implementation of policy measures to foster sustainable development, high internal as well as external complexity of the intervention environment seems to be a fact. Therefore it is fairly reasonable to suggest a context guidance approach as an intervention technique to be adopted.

1. For an operationalisation this would mean that as a first suggestion policy towards sustainable development should be reoriented around problems rather than institutions.
2. A second recommendation to be deduced from these findings in systems and intervention theory is the necessity to introduce feedback loops into the design of policy interventions – i.e. the continuous use of evaluation throughout the policy cycle.

Table 13.1 Characterisation of complexity

External complexity / Internal complexity	Low	High
Low	Repressive guidance/ intervention (pre-modern)	Centralised guidance (socialist)
High	Self-guidance and control (liberal)	Context guidance (modern)

Source: Willke (1996b).

7.2 Lessons to be Learned from the Limits of Traditional Economic Model Building

In the previous section we tried to shed some light on the issue of complexity of evaluations in the context of SD. This section will give some insights into an aspect which has been touched upon in the previous section but not elaborated in depth – i.e. the problem of model building and pitfalls deriving from oversimplified assumptions in this context.

As described in section 6 above, it is generally necessary to take two basic steps in any evaluation – assessment and comparison. In order to deal with real-world complexity, modelling – i.e. the simplification of real-world observations – is necessary. Traditional policy evaluation approaches (e.g. cost–benefit analysis) follow the epistemological tradition of the classic economic maximisation premise of individual behaviour, stating that rational decisions coincide with utility maximisation. Consistency is considered an important characteristic of rationality; as a consequence, the preference structure is reduced to preference and indifference relations, and both relations are considered to be of a complete transitive type. No incomparability relation is allowed (Munda, 1997).

If individual behaviours are added up, an optimising approach is adopted which is based upon the assumption that different objectives can be expressed in a common denominator by means of trade-offs (described in section 6.2 as strong commensurability), so that the loss in one objective can be evaluated against the gain in another. From a theoretical point of view, the optimising principle is elegant since it provides an unambiguous tool to evaluate alternative strategies/policies on the basis of their contributions to community welfare. From an operational point of view, the value of the optimising approach is rather limited, because the specification of a community welfare function requires complete information about all possible combinations of actions, about the relative trade-offs between all actions and about all constraints prevailing in the decision-making process. Such information is generally not available in the context of political decision making, and in any case the validity of the proposed trade-offs is likely to be contested by affected groups.

During the last two decades, more support has emerged for the view that welfare is a multidimensional concept; thus the conventional complete commensurability principle can be questioned. The inclusion of complexity and the systemic approach in respect of picturing real-world phenomena in general and SD policies in particular has already been mentioned. In an operational framework, this means that an exhaustive analysis has to take into consideration efficiency criteria, ethical criteria and ecological criteria; thus a multidimensional approach is needed.

Conventional neo-classical models which underpin evaluation methods such as cost–benefit analysis (CBA) show furthermore the following problematic assumptions:

- The Kaldor–Hicks principle: when using cost–benefit analysis the methodological assumptions follow the line that utility-based models with complete knowledge of the individual or social utility function are the rule. This leads to the consequence that complete compensation between individuals has to be possible. To give a simple example – CBA states that in the case of the use of water resources by two competing users, 'paper mill' (*P*) and 'fisher' (*F*), a compensation (practically or hypothetically) could be set up from *P* to *F* or vice versa ('willingness to pay' versus 'willingness to accept') to make up for potential losses of water quality and income decrease of the latter. From an environmental point of view this model implies that it is always possible to find an amount of money, determined by willingness to pay for environmental quality improvements or willingness to accept environmental quality deterioration that keeps utility constant. It should be noted that such models do not aim to achieve a better environmental quality, but only to incorporate the environmental impacts in the traditional price and market system. Since the objective is to keep utility constant, complete substitution between environmental quality and economic growth is always allowed and thus a weak sustainability philosophy is implied (Pearce and Atkinson, 1992, 1993). From an intragenerational point of view, the compensation model presents strong distributive impacts; the monetary value of a negative externality depends on social institutions and distributional conflicts: willingness-to-pay measures consider preferences of the higher income groups more important than those of the lower ones. If the people damaged are poor or of future generations, the cost of internalisation will be lower ('the poor sell cheap') (Martinez-Alier, 1994a, 1994b).

- From an intergenerational point of view, since future generations are not in the market, their preferences do not count; however, society as a whole may have values that deviate from aggregated individual values. Society has a much longer life expectancy than individuals; thus the value society attaches to natural resources and the environment is likely to deviate from individual values, since a simple summation of individual preferences may imply the extinction of species and ecosystems. This implies that SD policy cannot merely be based upon the aggregation of individual values and the estimation of willingness to pay at any particular point in time (Klaassen and Opschoor, 1991). Walras had already noted (quoted in Bürgenmeier, 1994) that the market cannot be used as a basis for rational collective decision making and that 'human destinies are not absolutely independent, but to some extent dependent on one another. There is a social morality which is distinct from individual morality.'

Following these observations it seems reasonable to suggest that policy evaluation methods used in the context of SD should not entirely be based upon neo-classical modelling but should allow for inter- and intra-generational justice to be included on a wider scale.

7.3 Practical/ Empirical Observations – What Other Kinds of Problems May Arise?

Having analysed different theoretical problems in dealing with policy evaluation in the context of SD more precisely, what are the problems connected with policy evaluation (see Boston, 2000; Schuh and Sedlacek, 2002)? Table 13.2 lists some of the identified problems without claiming to be comprehensive.

Table 13.2 Policy evaluation problems

Selection of adequate evaluation criteria and definition of a measure of success	• Political goals are often diverse and contradictory • Goals of political measures are weakly specified (mostly qualitative) and often incomplete • Evaluators often disagree on evaluation targets • Evaluators often disagree on success of measures or even on an improvement of the status quo.
Assessment and measurement of relevant facts	• Relevant data are often inaccessible and inadequate • A lack of relative values hinders comparisons of the following: equity, ex ante and ex post • Relevant data are often expensive to collect • Short-term time horizons of evaluation analyses cause problems of missing impacts of the measures under evaluation
Interpretation of the actual facts	• Results are often contradictory • Weights for specific criteria are hard to find – especially for qualitative data • The review of results is extremely complex in the case of clusters of measures or integrated measures
Achievement of aggregated results	• Missing standardised goals and criteria for the measures lead to incomparable judgements • It is difficult to find an aggregated index because of problems of measurement and the problem of incommensurability • Different achievement of the goals causes problems of weighting • There is a lack of generalisation of evaluation results within the legal and administrative framework

After this list of problems and insights into the nature of policy evaluation in the context of SD it will be necessary to present more details on some characteristics of evaluation methods (especially the aggregation/comparison methods). Evaluation methods are supposed to meet the following criteria:

- Credibility
- Completeness
- Participation
- Scientific soundness
- Reliability
- Objectivity.

The problem with these aspects is that they are often contradictory and not simultaneously to be found within one method (see e.g. EU Commission, 1999). Therefore we would like these specific criteria to assist in assessing the quality of evaluations:

- Ability to capture complex cause–effect relations
- Identification and involvement of all the stakeholders in the process
- Ability to deal with a large number of criteria and indicators
- Processing of qualitative as well as quantitative data, aggregation of weakly comparable and commensurable data
- Transparency of preferences and values of the different stakeholders.

7.4 Suggested Methods

Traditional evaluation methodologies (e.g. cost–benefit analysis) assume that evaluations (i.e. the comparison of alternatives according to the degree of fulfilment of goals expressed in the form of criteria) always arrive at a best possible solution, which is described in decision theory as an optimisation problem (see Simon, 1982, and section 5.2 of this chapter). The reason why such a clear judgement is possible is to be found in an implicit reduction of complexity of the problem. In a complex and strongly interrelated world such a reduction seems to be rather dangerous – especially if all the effects of a given public action, direct and indirect, positive and negative, have to be included in the evaluation. This implies that evaluating such multi-related policy programmes will always be characterised by the search for acceptable compromise solutions.

Evaluation problems of the above-mentioned type are characterised by the following properties:

- There is a high degree of incomparability of the parameters (a mix of quantitative and qualitative indicators, different time scales)

- Certain parameters could only be included in the evaluation by using rather vague replacement indicators or proxies (e.g. in the context of measuring social qualities)
- The number of stakeholders involved, as well as the number of decision makers, is large and their attitudes and values often contradictory.

An evaluation method used in such a context hence has to respect those problem properties and make a contribution to somehow overcoming them. Proponents of multi-criteria analysis (MCA) and multi-criteria decision aid (MCDA), which are based on the assumption that an evaluation on the basis of weak commensurability and weak comparability (for a definition see section 6.2) is possible (Martinez-Alier et al., 1997), have claimed to be able to do so (see e.g. Faucheux et al., 1998; Froger and Munda, 1998; Solomon, 1998). Moreover they are able to consider a large number of data, relations and objectives, so that the evaluation problem at hand can be studied in a multidimensional fashion.

These methods are widely used in private as well as public evaluation contexts nowadays. Scientific discourse about the background and design of the methods has been increasing since the 1970s (for an overview see Romero and Rehman, 1989; Despotis and Zapounidis, 1999; Munda, 1995; Vincke, 1992). In public evaluations MCA methods have been employed in a variety of fields but especially in the context of environmental policy and sustainability analysis (see Schuh et al., 2000).

A multi-criteria evaluation problem can be tackled in the following steps (according to Munda, 1995):

1. Structuring of the problem (i.e. identification of the goals and different stakeholders)
2. Constructing a picture of the 'real world' which is in conformity with the identified goals and points of view of the stakeholders (i.e. finding a set of criteria)
3. Underpinning these criteria with information and data
4. Aggregating this information by using a specific MCA method (e.g. PROMETHEE: see Brans et al., 1986; ELECTRE: see Roy, 1968).

Multi-criteria analysis – the method

Multi-criteria analysis and decision support methods are rooted in the scientific tradition of operations research. They follow the spirit of procedural rationality (in the sense of Simon, 1976, 1982[3]) and allow the analyst to take into account conflicting, multidimensional, incommensurable and uncertain effects of decisions and actions. In general an MCA presents the following features (Munda, 1995; Munda et al., 1996):

- There is no solution optimising all the criteria at the same time and therefore the decision maker has to find compromise solutions.
- The statement of preference and indifference is not enough in this approach, because when a measure is better than another one according to some criterion, it is usually worse in relation to others, so that many pairs of measures remain incomparable with respect to establishing a dominance relation.

> The principal aim in multiple criteria decision aid and analysis is not to discover a solution, but to construct or create something which is viewed as liable to help an actor taking part in a decision process either to shape, and/or to argue, and/or to transform his preferences, or to make decisions in conformity with his goals. (Roy, 1990)

At first sight a multi-criteria problem is mathematically ill defined. The consequence is that a complete axiomatisation of multi-criteria decisions is quite difficult. MCA methods try to overcome this obstacle by adding information to the analysis, thus helping to enrich the picture and producing comparability. This additional information has to be gathered from the decision maker/stakeholder in the form of preferences, weights and decision patterns. Of course it has to be admitted that this additional information is strictly subjective and therefore strict rationality of choice is not assumed. Still, by applying this method the demand for introducing explicit value statements into the evaluation will be met without leaving the premises of scientific methodologies. Another advantage of this procedure will be the visualisation of goal conflicts between different stakeholders and decision makers as well as trade-offs between different success criteria of a political programme.

Basically a discrete multi-criteria problem may be described in the following way:

$$\max\{f_1(x), f_2(x), \ldots f_j(x), \ldots f_k(x) | x \in A\},$$

where A is a finite set of n feasible actions or alternatives and $\{f_j(\cdot), j = 1, 2, \ldots k\}$ is the set of evaluation criteria considered relevant in a decision problem. In this way a decision and evaluation problem may be represented in a tabular or matrix form. Given the sets A (of alternatives) and G (of evaluation criteria) and assuming the existence of n alternatives and m criteria, it is possible to build an $n*m$ matrix P called the evaluation or impact matrix, whose typical element p_{ij} $(i = 1, 2, \ldots m;\ j = 1, 2, \ldots n)$ represents the evaluation of the jth alternative by means of the ith criterion. The impact matrix may include quantitative, qualitative or both types of information.

The ranking of the alternatives (maximising all the criteria at the same time) is then carried out by pairwise comparisons of the alternatives for each criterion. The comparison is conducted using a preference function of the decision maker. For a preference function P, alternatives a and b and criterion j,

$$P_j(a,b) = P_j\lfloor d_j(a,b)\rfloor,$$

where $d_j(a,b) = f_j(a) - f_j(b)$ gives the measured difference for a criterion j. Depending on the specific method used for solving a multi-criteria problem, these preference functions may be predefined or assumed to be known or simulated together with the decision maker. The aggregate ranking of the two alternatives is set up by summing the weighted values of the preference functions of the complete set of criteria. So the overall result is

$$\Pi(a,b) = \sum_{j=1}^{n} w_j P_j(a,b),$$

where w_j is the weight given to criterion j. The weights have to be obtained from the decision makers and they are normalised to sum to 1. If the number of alternatives is more than two, the overall ranking is achieved by aggregating the measures of pairwise comparisons. The outranking character of an alternative is measured by the 'leaving flow', the outranked character by the 'entering flow'. The complete ranking of the set of alternatives is obtained by computing the 'net flow' for each alternative – the higher the flow, the better the alternative.

According to Roy (1985), in general it is impossible to say that a decision is a good or a bad one by referring only to a mathematical model: organisational, pedagogical and cultural aspects of the whole decision process that leads to a given decision also contribute to its quality and success. As a consequence, it becomes impossible to find the validity of a procedure either on a notion of approximation or on a mathematical property of convergence. The final solution is more like a creation than a discovery. So we may conclude that the validity of a given procedure of evaluation depends on two main factors:

1. Mathematical properties that make it conform to given requirements
2. The way it is used and integrated in a decision process.

Therefore the major strength of multi-criteria methods in policy evaluations including SD aspects is that, although a high degree of complexity (as is found in real-world situations) is retained in the method, a maximum of transparency and participation in the procedure takes care of the shaping and provision of information which could be used directly as a basis of political acting.

8 SUMMARY AND OUTLOOK

The arguments presented above make it quite clear that evaluation of sustainable development has become a political necessity – the examples from the European Union (Amsterdam Treaty), the different national laws (DTLR, 2001) and legally binding multilateral agreements at the global scale (see GATT, 1994) have stressed this point.

Despite the fact that many efforts have been made to perform such evaluations, many open questions are left for further investigation, such as:

- A precise and operational definition of sustainable development and evaluation
- A definition of evaluation as a necessary element of a 'sustainable management' system
- Willingness to accept specific characteristics of sustainability – e.g. uncertainty, thresholds and high complexity.

Therefore sustainable development as a paradigm for policy making does not yield definite guidance for long-run decisions. This means that policy making is facing a knife-edge problem: on one hand objectives have to be set and the direction of development has to be chosen; on the other hand future preferences are by their very nature unknown. Hence:

- Sustainable development has to be seen as a process in the right direction, where evaluation is necessary to check and if need be to adjust the direction of the path to be followed.
- Sustainable development implies a set of constraints which defines the degrees of freedom in which direction planning and policy may move. Evaluation is therefore necessary to help in defining and adjusting these constraints.
- Sustainable development has to be seen as layers of capacity building, which may help to face those qualities described above – such as dealing with complexity and reducing uncertainty. Evaluation may help to provide feedback given this knowledge.

If we look at the role of evaluations in the framework of sustainable development, the span of possible approaches to developing and using evaluation methods appears as in Table 13.3.

Table 13.3 Approaches to developing and using evaluation methods

Purely scientific approach	Decision aid – scientifically based approach	Management by 'muddling through'
• Implies a model-oriented approach. The main emphasis is to develop evaluation models capable of complying with scientific quality criteria. • The main aim is to reduce the complexity found in the real world and to detect patterns which allow for the setting up of standard rules and scientific laws. • There is limited necessity for the decision maker to participate in the evaluation process. Science provides all the necessary models, preferences and weights.	• Although model-based, it strives to meet the requirements of the users of evaluations (decision makers, stakeholders). Therefore it aims at high transparency of the methods themselves and an intensive inclusion of interactive elements. • The main aim is to reduce complexity found in the real world. Information should not be eliminated for elegances sake, however. As the 'necessary information' to be retained is not known *a priori*, uncertainty and complexity have to be accepted. • The role of the actors within the evaluation process must be clearly defined, i.e. science only serves as evaluation assistance (provision of the method, guidance and support); the decision makers and stakeholders are the actors within the process (information on preferences, often simply as weights, achievement of compromises). • This implies that all parties involved in the measure, in the situation to be evaluated, have to participate actively in the process.	• No models are used for evaluation. • The main aim is that pre-fixed preferences and expected outcomes are verified. Thus often there is no need for transparency of the method –or it is even seen as counter-productive. • The decision maker is the driving force and actor in the evaluation process. Evaluations are seen as legitimisation of measures and preferences without intention to change them.

By looking at evaluation of sustainable development in the sense of decision aid, a paradigm shift could take place:

- Decision makers will be able to adopt different (healthier) attitudes towards problems as their features will be highlighted from many different angles and therefore a shift of preferences and weights will be easier to achieve.
- Scientists/evaluators will be forced to apply some modesty and self-criticism to their role within evaluation – their role as a neutral element and support in the process will reduce the temptation to engage too actively in the preference-building process.

Multi-criteria methods will definitely help in this respect. We have shown some of their qualities, e.g. transparency of preferences, and ability to accept uncertainty and complexity. Therefore there is a strong argument for their application in this context (see also Schuh et al., 2000; Schuh and Sedlacek, 2002).

NOTES

1 In a macro context GDP, or some variant thereof, has been used as an appropriate scalar measurement system. This view has come under heavy fire more or less from the 1970s onwards, particularly with the rise of environmental awareness in society.

2 Decisions in this context are to be seen as maximising the expected value in a decision space defined by a set of possible 'states of nature', a set of feasible acts and a set of impacts (see e.g. von Neumann and Morgenstern, 1941).

3 According to Simon, 'behaviour is procedurally rational when it is the outcome of appropriate deliberation whereas procedural rationality depends on the process that generated it. Procedural rationality characterises decisions in domains that are too complex, too full of uncertainty or too rapidly changing to permit the objectively optimal action to be discovered and implemented' (Simon, 1982, pp. 426f).

REFERENCES

Boston, J. (2000), 'The Challenge of Evaluating Systemic Change: The Case of Public Management Reform', *International Public Management Journal* (3), 23–46.

Brans, J.P., Ph. Vincke and B. Mareschal (1986), 'How to Select and How to Rank Projects: The PROMETHEE Method', *European Journal of Operational Research*, **24**, 228–38.

Bürgenmeier, B. (1994), 'The Misperception of Walras', *The American Economic Review*, **84**, 342–52.

Daly, H. (1973), 'The Steady State Economy: Toward a Political Economy of Biophysical Equilibrium and Moral Growth', in H. Daly (ed.), *Toward a Steady State Economy*, San Francisco: W.H. Freeman.

Despotis, D.K. and C. Zapounidis (eds) (1999), 'Integrating Technology and Human

Decisions', Decision Science Institute – 5th International Conference Proceedings, Athen.

DTLR (Department for Transport, Local Government and the Regions) (2001), *Multi Criteria Analysis – a Manual*, DTLR, British Government, London.

EU Commission (1996), Regulation No. 746/96, Brussels.

EU Commission (1999), 'Evaluating Socio-economic Programmes. Principal Evaluation Techniques and Tools', *MEANS Collection Volume 3*, Office for Official Publications of the European Communities, Luxembourg.

EU Commission (2001), 'A Sustainable Europe for a Better World – a European Union Strategy for Sustainable Development', Commission's Proposal for the Gothenburg European Council, EU Commission, Brussels.

Faucheux, S., G. Froger and G. Munda (1998), 'Multicriteria Decision Aid and the "Sustainability Tree" ' in G. Faucheux and M. O'Connor (eds), *Valuation for Sustainable Development – Methods and Policy Indicators*, Cheltenham, UK and Northampton, MA, USA: Edward Elgar.

Foerster, H.V. (1984), 'Principles of Self-Organisation – in a Socio-Managerial Context', in H. Ulrich and G. Probst (eds), *Self-Organisation and Management of Social Systems*, Berlin: Springer Verlag.

Forster, B.A. (1977), 'On a One State Variable Optimal Control Problem: Consumption – Pollution – Trade-Offs', in J.D. Pitchford and S.J. Turnovsky (eds), *Applications of Control Theory to Economic Analysis*, Amsterdam: North-Holland.

Froger, G. and G. Munda (1998), 'Methodology for Environmental Decision Support', in G. Faucheux and M. O'Connor (eds), *Valuation for Sustainable Development – Methods and Policy Indicators*, Cheltenham, UK and Northampton, MA, USA: Edward Elgar.

GATT (General Agreement on Tariffs and Trade) (1994), 'Preamble to the Marrakesh Agreement', Marrakesh Agreement establishing the World Trade Organisation, WTO, Geneva.

Georgescu-Roegen, N. (1971), *The Entropy Law and the Economic Process*, Cambridge, MA: Harvard University Press.

Hanley, N. and C.L. Spash (1995), *Cost Benefit Analysis and the Environment*, Aldershot, UK and Brookfield, USA: Edward Elgar.

IUCN/UNEP/WWF (1991), 'Caring for the Earth – a Strategy for Sustainable Living', UNEP, Nairobi.

Jänicke, M., P. Kunig and M. Stitzel (1999), *Umweltpolitik: Politik, Recht und Management des Umweltschutzes in Staat und Unternehmen*, Bonn: Dietz Verlag.

Klaassen, G.A.J. and J.B. Opschoor (1991), 'Economics of Sustainability or the Sustainability of Economics: Different Paradigms', *Ecological Economics*, **4**, 93–115.

Krutilla, J.V. (1967), 'Conservation Reconsidered', *American Economic Review* **47**, 777–86.

Lafferty, W.M. (ed.) (1996), *Democracy and the Environment: Problems and Prospects*, ed. by William M. Lafferty and James Meadowcroft, Cheltenham, UK and Brookfield, USA: Edward Elgar.

Luhmann, N. (1984), *Soziale Systeme – Grundriß einer allgemeinen Theorie*, Frankfurt: Suhrkamp.

Luptacik, M. and U. Schubert (1982), 'Optimal Economic Growth and the Environment', in W. Eichhart, R. Hann, K. Neumann and R.W. Shepard (eds), *Economic Theory of Natural Resources*, Würzburg: Physica, pp. 455–68.

Martinez-Alier, J. (1994a), 'Distributional Issues in Ecological Economics', paper presented at the Third International Meeting of Ecological Economics, San Jose, Costa Rica.

Martinez-Alier, J. (1994b), 'Distributional Conflicts and International Environmental Policy on Carbon Dioxide Emissions and Agricultural Biodiversity' in J.C.J.M. van den Bergh and J. van der Straaten (eds), *Towards Sustainable Development*, Washington, DC: Island Press.

Martinez-Alier, J., G. Munda and J. O'Neill (1997), 'Incommensurability of Values in Ecological Economics', in M. O'Connor and C. Spash (eds), *Valuation and the Environment – Theory, Method and Practice*, Cheltenham, UK and Lyme, USA: Edward Elgar.

Maturana, H. (1982), *Erkennen: die Organisation und Verkörperung von Wirklichkeit*, Braunschweig/Wiesbaden: Vieweg.

Munasinghe, M. (1993), 'Environmental Economics and Sustainable Development', World Bank, Washington DC.

Munda, G. (1995), *Multicriteria Analysis in a Fuzzy Environment – Theory and Applications in Ecological Economics*, Heidelberg: Physika Verlag.

Munda, G. (1997), 'Multi-criteria Evaluation as a Multidimensional Approach to Welfare Measurement' in J.C.J.M. van den Bergh and J. van der Straaten (eds), *Economy and Ecosystems in Change: Analytical and Historical Approaches*, Cheltenham, UK and Lyme, USA: Edward Elgar.

Munda, G., M. O'Connor, S. Faucheux, G. Froger and S.O. Funtowicz (1996), 'Emergent Complexity and Procedural Rationality: Post-normal Science for Sustainability', in R. Costanza, S. Olman and J. Martinez-Alier (eds), *Getting Down to Earth: Practical Applications of Ecological Economics*, International Society for Ecological Economics series, Washington, DC.

Nijkamp, P. (ed.) (1990), 'Sustainability of Urban Systems – A Cross-National Evolutionary Analysis of Urban Innovation', *Urban Europe Series*, 6, Aldershot: Gower.

Nijkamp, P. (1997), 'Environmental Security and Sustainability in Natural Resource Management: a Decision Support Framework', Research Memorandum, Vrije Universiteit Amsterdam, Amsterdam.

O'Connor, M. (1994), 'The Material/Communal Conditions of Life', *Capitalism, Nature, Socialism*, **5** (3), 105–14.

Pearce, D.W. and G.D. Atkinson (1992), 'Are National Economies Sustainable? Measuring Sustainable Development', *CSERGE Working Paper*, GEC 92–11.

Pearce, D.W. and G.D. Atkinson (1993), 'Capital Theory and the Measurement of Sustainable Development: An indicator of "weak" sustainability', *Ecological Economics*, **8**, 103–8.

Pezzey, J.C.V. (1997), 'Sustainability Constraints versus "Optimality" versus Intertemporal Concern, and Axioms versus Data', *Land Economics*, **73** (4), 448–66.

Ramsey, F. (1928), 'A Mathematical Theory of Saving', *Economic Journal*, **138**, 543–59.

Robson, C. (2000), *Small Scale Evaluation – Principles and Practice*, London: Sage.

Romero, C. and T. Rehman (1989), *Multiple Criteria Analysis for Agricultural Decisions*, New York, Elsevier.

Roy, B. (1968), 'Classement et choix en présence de points de vue multiples (La méthode ELECTRE)', *Revue française d'Informatique et de Recherche Opérationnelle*, **6** (8).

Roy, B. (1985), 'Méthodologie Multicritère d'Aide à la Decision', *Economica*, Paris.

Roy, B. (1990), 'The Outranking Approach and the Foundations of ELECTRE Methods', in B.E. Costa and A. Carlos (eds), *Readings in Multiple Criteria Decision Aid*, Berlin/Heidelberg/New York/Tokyo: Springer-Verlag.

Samuelson, P.A. and W.D. Nordhaus (1989), *Economics*, 13th edn, New York: McGraw-Hill.

Schuh, B. and S. Sedlacek (2002), 'Evaluation Nachhaltiger Stadtentwicklung – Regionale Politikfeldintegration in Wien', research report for the City Council of Vienna, University of Economics and Business Administration, Vienna.

Schuh, B., O. Schütz and F. Weiß (2000), 'Development of an Evaluation Instrument for Agricultural Policy Measures on a Regional Level with Special Consideration of Regional Sustainability', Paper presented at ESEE 2000, 3rd Biennial Conference of the European Society for Ecological Economics, Vienna, 3–6 May.

Simon, H.A. (1976), 'From Substantive to Procedural Rationality', in S.J. Latsis (ed.), *Methods and Appraisal in Economics*, Cambridge: Cambridge University Press.

Simon, H.A. (1982), *Models of Bounded Rationality*, Cambridge, MA: The MIT Press.

Solomon, L.S. (1998), 'Evaluation of Environmental Programs: Limitations and Innovative Applications', in G.J. Kaap and T.J. Kim (eds), *Environmental Program Evaluation: A Primer*, Urbana: University of Illinois Press.

Stengers, I. (ed.) (1987), *D'une Science à l'Autre: des Concepts Nomades*, Paris: Seuil.

Turner, R.K. (1993), *Sustainable Environmental Economics and Management: Principles and Practices,* London: Belhaven.

Vincke, Ph. (1992), *Multicriteria Decision Aid*, New York: Wiley and Sons.

von Neumann, J. and O. Morgenstern (1941), *Theory of Games and Economic Behaviour*, Princeton, NJ: Princeton University Press.

WCED (The World Commission on Environment and Development) (1987), *Our Common Future – the Brundtland Report*, Oxford: Oxford University Press.

Weaver, G.R. (ed.) (1996), *Culture, Communication and Conflict: Readings in Intercultural Relations*, Needham Heights, MA.: Simon & Schuster.

Willke, H. (1983), *Entzauberung des Staates – Überlegungen zu einer gesellschaftlichen Steuerungstheorie*, Athenäum, Königstein/Ts.

Willke, H. (1996a), *Systemtheorie I – Grundlagen*, Stuttgart: Lucius & Lucius.

Willke, H. (1996b), *Systemtheorie II – Interventionstheorie*, Stuttgart: Lucius & Lucius.

Index